Good God

# Good God

*The Theistic Foundations of Morality*

DAVID BAGGETT AND JERRY L. WALLS

OXFORD
UNIVERSITY PRESS

# OXFORD
UNIVERSITY PRESS

Oxford University Press, Inc., publishes works that further
Oxford University's objective of excellence
in research, scholarship, and education.

Oxford   New York
Auckland   Cape Town   Dar es Salaam   Hong Kong   Karachi
Kuala Lumpur   Madrid   Melbourne   Mexico City   Nairobi
New Delhi   Shanghai   Taipei   Toronto

With offices in
Argentina   Austria   Brazil   Chile   Czech Republic   France   Greece
Guatemala   Hungary   Italy   Japan   Poland   Portugal   Singapore
South Korea   Switzerland   Thailand   Turkey   Ukraine   Vietnam

Published by Oxford University Press, Inc.
198 Madison Avenue, New York, New York 10016

www.oup.com

Oxford is a registered trademark of Oxford University Press

Library of Congress Cataloging-in-Publication Data

Baggett, David.
Good God: the theistic foundations of morality / David Baggett and Jerry L.Walls
    p.   cm.
Includes bibliographical references and index.
ISBN 978-0-19-975181-5 (pbk.: alk. paper)—ISBN 978-0-19-975180-8 (hardback : alk. paper)
1. Religion and ethics.   2. Religious ethics. I. Walls, Jerry L.   II. Title.
BJ47.B34 2011
205—dc22      2010020028

Printed in the United States of America
on acid-free paper

*To Elton Higgs and Tom Morris*

# Contents

# Foreword

The topics of God and morality have been deeply connected
throughout the history of philosophy, and the precise nature of this
connection has been a source of lively debate for just as long. Both
concepts raise issues of perennial importance for human life and our
sense of our ultimate place in the world.

In recent years, questions about this connection have taken on
additional weight. There's been something ironically akin to an
emotional camp-meeting style revival among contemporary intellectual critics of religion who, in a torrent of immensely popular books,
have adopted the tone of an almost evangelical form of atheism, as
odd as that might sound. They write with great panache and pointed
argument against the truth and even basic reasonableness of religious belief, but the most salient feature of their recent work might
be their high-pitched rhetoric of moral outrage.

These "new atheists" in all the major bookstore chains fervently
urge their readers to adopt the view that any form of theism offering
itself in the marketplace of actual religious ideas—whether in a
temple, mosque, synagogue, or church—is false, irrational, and
morally offensive. It's especially this latter charge that seems to fuel
the entire enterprise. In their appeal to readers, their rhetoric seems
to rely on a fairly robust sense of moral good and evil, as well as right
and wrong. In fact, their arguments appear to appeal both explicitly
and implicitly to objective moral standards that, in their view, the

major theistic religions of the world flout. But honest accounts of the metaphysical status characterizing the objective morality on which they take their stand are in short supply.

To put the question as simply as possible: What would be the objective, ontological nature of a moral principle, or moral standard, in a world where mind, soul, and personhood were completely reducible to materialistic entities—whether finally spelled out in the language of matter or physical energy? It's difficult, if not just impossible, for these critics of theism to come up with an answer that seems any less "strange" than the ultimate components of the philosophical worldview they are urging us so passionately to avoid. But, notoriously, rejecting any objectively metaphysical basis for moral judgments reduces them to some form of "I don't like it" or "My peer group/cultural context/posse of fellow skeptics doesn't like it." And this takes a considerable amount of the sting out of any moral outrage that's being shown, to put it mildly.

Now, of course, the critics could argue that on any theistic metaphysical account of the objectivity of moral principles as ideas in the mind of God, or as reflections of the character of God, or as the necessary and eternal results of certain distinctively divine actions, believers, if they were honest, should find many of their own views just as morally reprehensible as the critics purport them to be. So, even if current critics don't have the metaphysical leverage for a true and objectively compelling moral critique of theistic religion as it has played out through history, they could still mount an inconsistency charge at all theists who endorse God as both morally perfect and somehow the ontologically grounding source of moral objectivity. A perfectly good being, they could argue, just would not command the slaughter of heathen, infidels, or innocents, as the various primary religious literatures sometimes represent. But this is not the strategy they need to justify their own intense righteous indignation about religion and their efforts to offer generally persuasive arguments in favor of the atheistic parsimony.

Atheists need to get as clear on the concept of God, the concept of morality, and the ontological status of the purported referents of each of these concepts, as do the theists whose views they eschew. And that's where the current book comes in and does quite a job. David Baggett and Jerry Walls present some extremely creative and clear-headed work here to untangle the cluster of issues surrounding all this. They are very well informed about the classical and current positions that have been staked out on these issues, and they are also suitably bold to take their own positions in ways that, in my view, advance the discussion considerably. The arguments and clarifications in these pages would be interesting enough in their own right, but in light of the current state of the public debate between theism and atheism, they take on even more significance. We can only hope that all parties to the dispute will take a time-out to explore these fundamental issues, read this book, and realize deeply all that is at stake in their proper understanding.

Thomas V. Morris
Wilmington, North Carolina

# Acknowledgments

It's our delight to spend some moments identifying the many folks without whose help this project could have never been accomplished. Dave's mentors Bill Stine, Herb Granger, Mike McKinsey, and Bruce Russell provided invaluable help, unstinting advice, and helpful criticisms on earlier drafts of various chapters. A dear old Wayne State friend, Sloan Lee, has been a great source of encouragement and critique for over fifteen years now, and words can't begin to express our appreciation to him; his comments on some key chapters were a great help. Other old friends from years ago at Wayne, like Steve Patterson, Ron Butzu, and Brian MacPherson, all deserve prominent mention and warm thanks as well.

Elton Higgs, now an emeritus professor of English at the University of Michigan-Dearborn and a longtime friend, deserves very special mention and thanks. Other undergraduate professors of Dave's from UM-D many years ago, Paul Hughes and Elias Baumgarten, were first instrumental at engendering his interest in these topics.

Mutual friend Mike Peterson of Asbury College was particularly helpful in enabling us to lay out the chapter on the problem of evil, for which we're deeply appreciative. Jerry's Notre Dame friends David Elliot, Alan Rhoda, and Claire Brown provided helpful criticism (David read the whole manuscript). Thanks to each of you, along with Jerry's former student Kyle Blanchette who, like Dave Elliot, read the whole manuscript for us, offering a variety of useful criticisms and suggestions. And former Notre Dame professor and now public philosopher extraordinaire, Tom Morris, deserves thanks as much as anyone, both for his encouragement and support, as well as his ground-breaking work in philosophical theology that helped shape so many of our own views, not to mention the Foreword.

Dave's longtime friends Ginger Asel and Cathy Chulis provided, appropriately enough, crucial moral support. LU friends Thom Provenzola, Ed Martin, Gary Habermas, Dave Beck, Mike Jones, Gaylen Leverett, and Mark Foreman deserve many warm thanks as well for their assistance at key junctures of the project. Thanks to LU for providing Dave with a course reduction in the spring of 2009, which helped immensely in bringing the project to conclusion. A group of students at LU deserve special mention, meeting with Dave once a week during the fall 2009 term at Barnes and Noble to go over a chapter of the book while imbibing insane quantities of caffeine, offering their takes and asking their sometimes challenging questions: Lucas DelPriore, Michael Anthony Stearns, Michael Huesser, Steven Oakley, Joshua Walker, and Mark Dickson. We're excited to anticipate the trajectory of your careers; it's been an honor working with you.

Thanks to the philosophy club at King's College and LU for spirited discussions (apologies for not mentioning all the students involved, although we must specifically mention Samuel Loncar, Steve Hudson, J. T. and Roger Turner, Maria Owen, Ryan Andrews, Albie Powers, Mike Pasquini, Wesley Grubb, and David Lahm). We received helpful insight and criticism from attendees (especially John Hare) at a 2003 Oxford Philosophy conference hosted by the SCP and BPS, the participants in the philosophy colloquium at the 2005 Oxbridge conference, the Virginia Philosophical Association meeting in Lynchburg in 2009, the 2007 and 2009 Evangelical Philosophical Society meetings in San Diego and New Orleans, respectively, and the Eastern regional meeting of the Society of Christian Philosophers at Wake Forest in 2010. James Madison's Bill Knorpp deserves many thanks for pressing us on issues relating most particularly to the first appendix. Thanks to Alvin Plantinga and Mark Murphy for access to yet-to-be-published papers read at the Notre Dame weekly philosophy colloquium. Greg Bassham, Bill Irwin, Regan Reitsma, Bill Drumin, Henry Nardone, and Kim Blessing, old friends at King's, are all warmly thanked and remembered.

Thanks to *Philosophia Christi* for permission to reprint portions of "On Whether God Can Sin," Fall 2003, and "Bruce Russell's Analogy and the Problem of Evil," Winter 2006; and to Eerdmans Publishing Company for permission to reprint a slightly modified version of "Outrageous Evil and the Hope of Healing: Our Practical Options," which first appeared in *Immersed in the Life of God*, edited by Paul L. Gavrilyuk et al. (2008).

Jerry wishes to thank the Center for Philosophy of Religion at Notre Dame, where he spent the 2009–2010 academic year as a Research Fellow, which allowed significant time to work on this book among other projects. Thanks also to Karen "Katie" Tallon for suggesting the title over lunch one day.

It has been a pleasure, as always, to work with Cynthia Read and Oxford University Press. Thanks to Ashley Polikoff, production coordinator at OUP; Dorothy Bauhoff, the copyeditor; and J. Olivia Mary, project manager at Spi Global, for their excellent work.

Finally, I (Dave) would like to thank my co-author, who is one of my dearest and oldest friends and most important mentors.

# Good God

# Introduction

In July 2009, former NFL quarterback Steve McNair, a married father of four children, was found dead, along with his twenty-year-old girlfriend Sahel "Jenny" Kazemi. The story made national news for several days when it was discovered that she had shot him and then turned the gun on herself, because she was distraught when she came to the conclusion that he was not going to marry her, contrary to what she had apparently been led to believe. As the story unfolded, it also sparked considerable debate about McNair's legacy, because he was very popular and highly admired, not only in Tennessee where he had played for most of his career and continued to live, but in the larger athletic community as well. Many came forward with tributes to McNair as a great leader and a model citizen because of community service he had done in both Tennessee and his home state of Mississippi, while others argued that the recently disclosed facts about his life disqualified him from such a lofty status.

One of McNair's more provocative critics was the controversial sportswriter Jason Whitlock, who pointedly took exception to the notion that McNair was a great leader, noting that leadership begins at home.[1] What is interesting for our purposes are the reasons that Whitlock was critical of McNair. He made it clear from the outset that he was not assuming the role of "morality police," and a few short paragraphs later reiterated that he was "not some sanctimonious moralizer." McNair's extramarital affair was not what bothered him. What did bother him, however, was that McNair showed himself to be a lousy father by spending "so much time chasing a Nashville waitress that he created the impression he lived with her." Fatherhood, he noted, is a serious responsibility that requires substantial commitment and sacrifice. Children deserve our very best and should never have to settle for anything less.

What we find both fascinating and telling here is the fact that Whitlock engages in some rather serious moral judgment of a fellow human being while denying that he is "some sanctimonious moralizer." In so doing, his analysis and critique are fairly typical reflections of the postmodern moral condition.

It has often been observed that postmodernity is characterized by fragmentation, a deep sense of incoherence resulting from the shattered visions of modernity. This is perhaps nowhere more apparent than in the moral realm, where pre-modern and modern accounts of right and wrong have largely been rejected, even while vestiges and fragments of traditional morality may still be retained and hold conviction. What is often perplexing is why those fragments remain and continue to have force. So one may easily wonder why Whitlock is so adamant about keeping the commitments of fatherhood, while he is relatively tolerant of extramarital affairs. He does insist that he did not mean to imply that he condoned McNair's affair, but again, as he makes clear, that was not his concern. To make an issue of marital faithfulness would make one a "sanctimonious moralizer," but for some reason it is still appropriate to censure parental unfaithfulness.

In 1979, thirty years before the incidents involving McNair, Yale law professor Arthur Allen Leff published an essay in the *Duke Law Journal* that probed the fragile foundations of postmodern morality. He began his essay by identifying "two contradictory impulses" that he thought were present in most people.[2] On the one hand, we want to believe that there is a complete set of transcendent propositions that direct us how to live righteously, propositions that he characterizes as "findable" because they exist objectively and independently of us. On the other hand, we want to believe that there are no such rules, that we are completely free to decide and choose for ourselves what we ought to do and be. "What we want, Heaven help us, is simultaneously to be perfectly ruled and perfectly free, that is, at the same time to discover the right and the good and to create it."[3]

It was Leff's thesis that much of what was written about law that is mysterious and confusing could only be understood in light of these contradictory impulses toward both found law and created law. Indeed, it was his sense that this tension was "particularly evident in the growing, though desperately resisted, awareness that there may be, in fact, nothing to be found—that whenever we set out to find 'the law,' we are able to locate nothing more attractive, or more final, than ourselves."[4] Of course, in traditional morality, there was something more attractive and more final than ourselves, and that ultimate reality was God himself. Leff goes on to show that coming up with a suitable moral substitute for God is no easy task. What is required is some convincing account of who, short of God, has the authority to provide normative moral evaluations and obligations. When finite, fallible beings attempt to take that role, they invariably invite "what is known in barrooms and schoolyards as 'the grand sez who'?"[5]

Leff's article concludes on a memorable, if somewhat despairing note as he acknowledges the dismal prospects if we ourselves are all we have when it comes to morality. His final lines are as follows.

> As things now stand, everything is up for grabs.
> Nevertheless:
> Napalming babies is bad.
> Starving the poor is wicked.
> Buying and selling each other is depraved.
> Those who stood up to and died resisting Hitler, Stalin, Amin, and
> Pol Pot—and General Custer too—have earned salvation.
> Those who acquiesced deserve to be damned.
> There is in the world such a thing as evil.
> [All together now:] Sez who?
> God help us.[6]

In the years since Leff wrote his article, the tension he identified has crystallized and intensified. Indeed, the tension has escalated to become an overt conflict that is at the heart of contemporary "culture wars." Consider the analysis of sociobiologist E. O. Wilson, who contends that centuries of debate have left us with just two fundamental options with respect to morality: the "transcendentalist" option and the "empiricist" option.[7] The former holds that moral principles exist outside human minds and are true independently of our experience, while the latter holds that they are the inventions of human minds, and can be explained in terms of biological and cultural evolution. The tension has escalated as more and more scientists and philosophers have not only accepted but defended the notion that morality has no ultimate source beyond us. Unlike Leff, who saw this as something of a desperate position to try to hold, these thinkers have embraced this conclusion and promoted it as a worthy rival of traditional accounts of morality.

This debate promises to remain at the forefront of cultural controversies for years to come. Wilson, himself a vocal proponent of the empiricist view, predicted in 1998 that this debate will be "the coming century's version of the struggle for men's souls." We are now well into "the coming century" and there is good reason to agree with Wilson's prediction that the conflict over the nature of morality will not only continue to be fought, but that it will be at the heart of larger conflicts as well. Wilson rightly notes that how this is settled "will depend on which world view is proved to be correct, or at least which is more widely *perceived* to be correct." Given the fact that what is ultimately at stake is which worldview is correct, the struggle can hardly be expected to be confined to the ranks of philosophers, theologians, scientists, and other academics. One of the telling signs of this is the recent popularity of the "new atheism" books that have become best sellers. A significant part of the attack on theism by these authors has been their claim that morality does not need God, and indeed that it is better off without him.

In the present volume, we engage this battle on the side of the transcendentalist view, and argue that there is much more to be "found" than ourselves so far as morality is concerned, indeed something infinitely more "attractive and final" (as Leff put it) than we. In keeping with the recognition that the debate about the nature of morality ultimately hinges on which world view is correct, our primary aim is to defend a moral argument for God's existence. We shall advance the case that moral considerations provide us with substantial reasons to believe not only in God, but a particular kind of God. This argument will dovetail with our second primary aim, which is to rebut objections to theistic ethics. In the process, we shall argue not only that morality points to God, but that morality ultimately needs God to make full rational sense.

Now let us turn to sketch what shall appear in the chapters that follow. We begin by laying out a series of interlocking and mutually supported variants of the moral argument in the first chapter, and then lay out a series of objections to theistic ethics in chapter 2. Almost all the classical objections to theistic ethics can be thought to derive from the famous Euthyphro Dilemma, and the full list of Euthyphro-inspired objections looks like this: the normativity objection, the "no reasons" objection, the abhorrent commands objection, the vacuity objection, the epistemic objection, and the autonomy objection. In subsequent chapters we attempt to answer all of these various objections, and in so doing we aim to do much more than play mere defense. By answering these objections, we thereby (actually) strengthen the moral argument(s) for God's existence. This draws together, again, our case for moral apologetics and for theistic ethics, flip sides of the same philosophical coin.

In the remaining chapters, we deploy seven distinctions that together will enable us to answer the various Euthyphro objections. Many writers have emphasized some of these distinctions, but we will consistently be applying them all, which will enable a fuller defense and stronger moral case for God's existence. This list of seven distinctions is as follows: the analysis/definition distinction, the good/right distinction, the ontology/epistemology distinction, the difficult versus impossible distinction, the equivocation/univocation distinction, the dependence versus control distinction, and the conceivability/possibility distinction. Armed with all of these distinctions, we will defuse the full set of challenges to theistic ethics, thus bolstering the moral case for God's existence.

Chapter 3 will clarify the operative conception of God that we think the moral argument points to, and chapter 4 will make clear how our view, though broadly Reformed, is distinctly Arminian. Chapter 5 explores the vital and central connection between God and goodness. Chapter 6 will delve into divine command theory, defending a version of voluntarism when it comes to moral obligations, and chapter 7 will discuss some notoriously difficult passages of scripture, like the conquest narratives, and ask whether or not they can be reconciled with a perfectly and recognizably good God. Chapter 8 covers the flip side of the moral argument: the problem of evil. Chapter 9 deals with epistemological questions that our account raises, and the last chapter extends discussion of moral apologetics and theistic ethics to issues specific to Christian theology: the afterlife, resurrection, incarnation, and the Trinity. We intentionally put off most discussion of claims of special revelation until this chapter, not because of its lesser importance, but because our analysis is intended for a wider audience than those who are comfortable with such a starting point. It's at that last stage of the argument, too, that we will focus most directly on important performative questions about the role of God's grace in enabling us to live a moral life. Again, this isn't because we are convinced that such questions are of less import than the metaphysical questions about the philosophical origins of ethics, but because this book is most especially interested in delving into those foundational matters, questions that we do think are in an important sense prior to the performative ones. If our argument works, morality should bolster confidence to say, as C. S. Lewis did, that "I believe in Christianity as I believe that the Sun has risen, not only because I see it, but because by it I see everything else."[8]

We will make use of a great many ideas from the history of moral philosophy, particularly Western moral philosophy, but we want to make clear that this is not a historical study. While we obviously hope to avoid interpretive errors, we engage these texts with the primary intent of offering a theistic vision of the shape and contours of ethics. Our goal is to bolster a moral apologetic rather than to provide original exegetical analyses of past perspectives and canonical texts, sacred or otherwise.

Finally, before embarking on our journey, a word about our writing style is in order. In light of the vital importance of the discussion for the larger culture and society, we were intentional from the start of this project to write something accessible to a broader readership than professional philosophers and theologians. If the debate over the fundamental nature of morality is indeed the form that the "struggle for men's souls" will take in the current century, then what is at stake here is far too important to be confined to the relatively narrow circles of scholars and academics. Some of the ideas can get complicated, which is unavoidable, and at times our arguments may require some effort on the part of the readers to grasp, especially those without a philosophy background. For the most part, though, we strive to write accessibly and to steer clear of philosophical jargon, or at least to relegate some of the more technical points to footnotes. If at times we have failed to conform to our plan, we hope it is the exception rather than the norm.

# I

# Moral Apologia

First...human beings, all over the earth, have this curious idea
that they ought to behave in a certain way.... Second...they do
not in fact behave in that way. These two facts are the foundation
of all clear thinking about ourselves and the universe we live in.
                                                    —C. S. Lewis[1]

Bertrand Russell gave a famous reply to the question of how he
would account for his earthly unbelief if he found out, after death,
that God actually exists: "Not enough evidence, God, not enough
evidence." If the argument in this chapter is correct, however, there
is some distinctively pointed evidence for God very close at hand, in
things that we take for granted every day.

   Arguments from design, first cause arguments, as well as
ontological arguments for God's existence tend to be the standard fare
when it comes to natural theology or apologetics. The moral
argument, by contrast, has fallen out of favor among many
intellectuals.[2] It nonetheless remains a fruitful and challenging source
of insight and topic of inquiry, and in recent years it has experienced
something of a resurgence among professional philosophers.[3]

   To refer to *the* moral argument, though convenient, is a misnomer,
because it—like the other theistic arguments—comes in many flavors.
The great philosopher Immanuel Kant provided a version of the moral
argument. John Henry Newman, Hastings Rashdall, and William
Sorley embraced variants of their own, and Henry Sidgwick

gestured in the direction of yet another, which he rejected.[4] C. S. Lewis thought a moral argument for God's existence to be persuasive, while John Mackie, another Oxford great, argued just the opposite.

Nonspecialists often have a hard time following some of the technicalities of this ongoing dialogue. The importance of the issue, though, demands that the argument(s) be given in an accessible form, and that is what we will attempt to do here. The basic ingredients of several versions of the argument can be woven together and made very clear to those lacking specialized training in philosophy or theology. Sometimes, the technicalities and jargon actually distract from the force of the argument. So, here we will give an overview that lays out the terrain and provides readers with an idea of the sort of moral argument that we will defend in more detail in later chapters. It will draw on resources from a variety of moral arguments and tie up the various strands of the discussion at the end, at which point the basic shape and texture of the argument will have emerged.

Before developing the argument, a word is in order about the role of argument in faith, or about the relationship between philosophy and religion. Faith and reason are sometimes thought to be mutually opposed, sometimes by believers and unbelievers alike, for different reasons. Believers who take this view typically see this as a way to safeguard faith.[5] If faith is beyond the realm of rational thought or scientific discourse, its legitimacy doesn't depend on meeting the rigors of the intellect. This view, called fideism, from the Latin word *fides*, which means "faith," has been held by a number of noted Christian thinkers, and although it is the minority position, it is a common stance among many believers today who have adopted the postmodern mindset that finds rational arguments to be of dubious value.[6]

Among unbelievers, the view that faith and reason are at odds typically reflects an altogether different purpose, namely, to underscore the claim that faith is utterly irrational, a claim that has received fresh impetus from the recent popular books trumpeting atheism. In many academic and intellectual circles, the prevailing view is that belief in God is neither scientifically viable nor philosophically respectable, but rather, juvenile and naïve. It's a belief worthy of the *hoi poloi*, the unenlightened among us, the ignorant mass of men. The more educated, we're told, jettison such vestiges of superstition. Religion may be comforting, a source of consolation and equanimity in troubled times, or a helpful psychological crutch for the weak. But what it is *not* is true or rationally defensible.

Along with the majority of the Christian tradition, we reject the view that faith and reason are at odds. In fact, we view philosophy as an ally, much like Francis Bacon, who thought that a little philosophy inclined a man's mind to atheism, but depth in philosophy brought men's minds to religion.[7] This is not to exaggerate what philosophical arguments can accomplish. Indeed, the last couple of centuries of philosophy have taught us that hankering after absolute certainty is usually futile. But while efforts to conclusively prove or disprove God's existence to everyone's satisfaction are sure to fail, endeavors to show religious beliefs to be rationally persuasive are still fair game, and indeed crucial.

In the spirit of Francis Bacon, C. S. Lewis believed that argument moves the battle to theistic grounds. He thought that the very act of arguing awakens our reason, and once it's awake, there's no telling the result.[8] For reason stirs the habit of attending to universal issues and withdrawing our attention from the stream of immediate sense experiences that convince us that there's nothing more to life than what meets the eye. These convictions animated Lewis to produce the popular, but justly famous version of the moral argument that appears in the opening chapters of his classic book *Mere Christianity*. We will take this argument as a starting point of our discussion.

## Intimations of Something More

Lewis began his moral argument for God by pointing to something utterly commonplace: the way we use language, especially when we quarrel. Disputants on both sides of arguments make appeal to rules or laws of decent human conduct, showing their belief in a standard of right and wrong.

Lewis favored the traditional label "law of nature" for this standard, though this moral law is something that transcends the natural order. Whereas we have no choice but to yield to a physical law like gravity where our bodies or physical nature is concerned, we do have a choice to obey or disregard the moral law in the realm of our mind and will. By "law of nature" Lewis thought we really mean a law of *human* nature, and he explained the aptness of this language by noting how we acquire knowledge of it. He thought we know it by nature and don't need to be taught it. We can just *see* the difference between right and wrong on our own, or at least we should.

Lewis was right that at least *many* moral facts seem obvious indeed. It's wrong, for example, to torture innocent children for fun, and we plainly recognize it. Although not every moral truth shines with such brightness, it's wrong to think that almost all of ethics is colored gray. Reflection yields legitimately difficult questions in ethics, yes, but a great many ethical truths remain obvious. Just as it's clearly enough wrong to put profits before people, so is it clearly enough right to accord people basic respect.

Even where people disagree on ethical matters, they often differ not so much about the ethical principles involved as about how best to apply them in practical terms. Many would, for example, lament instances of labor exploitation in China, but whereas some might think that morality thereby demands that we not contribute to China's move toward capitalism, others would say that continuing economic engagement with and encouragement of China is the best way to help alleviate such abuses. It's the relatively rare individual who feels simply no moral qualms about exploitation of the poor.

In case readers think that Lewis, in embracing objective ethics, was being self-righteous, he was quick to assure them that he didn't think that either he or anyone else always follows the moral law. To the contrary, he observed, we all fall short of it, despite our recognition of it, and we fall short of it all too often.

So this is the first part of Lewis's argument: there is an objective moral law that is binding on our actions. This is the evidence in need of explanation. The second part involves an inference, the drawing of a conclusion, on the basis of this evidence. Lewis argued that the moral law that tells us how we ought to behave gives us compelling reason to believe in God. Perhaps Lewis overstated his case in drawing such a definitive conclusion, but the evidence is still suggestive, and it is very much a live issue worth pursuing—whether the moral law gives us at least some significant reason to believe.

Lewis drew his inference after narrowing down the potential accounts of the moral law to naturalism and religion. Naturalism is the view that the physical world is all there is, and behind it is no ultimate pattern or plan or purpose. Twentieth-century British philosopher and atheist Bertrand Russell once hauntingly encapsulated this picture of reality with his famous "scaffolding of despair" litany.[9] Following George Mavrodes, let's call such a naturalistic reality a "Russellian world."[10]

A religious conception of reality, in contrast, holds that behind the physical world is something else, likely a mind of some sort. "That is to say," as Lewis put it, "it is conscious, and has purposes, and prefers one thing to another. And on this view it made the universe, partly for purposes we do not know, but partly, at any rate, in order to produce creatures like itself...to the extent of having minds."[11]

If there is something behind the universe responsible for its existence, Lewis suggests that it would have to reveal itself to us as something other than one of the facts inside the universe. Contrary to Russell's confidence that there's nothing behind the universe, Lewis insists that, because science confines its examination to the universe, it's natural that science discovers nothing beyond it. The prior question of whether there is a more ultimate explanation can still be asked, and answering it requires that we be attentive to intimations of something more. Lewis takes the moral law within us, pressing on us to behave in certain ways, as just such a clue to deeper reality. We know about this law by experiencing its pull on us from the inside, which gives us reason to think of it as a hint of something more, an intimation of something beyond the universe. In the only place to look for evidence of something transcendent, we find it.[12]

The source of this moral obligation isn't likely to be mere matter. An evolutionary account of *feelings of* or *beliefs in*, say, moral obligation is certainly possible, but how would naturalism explain obligation itself? How collections of atoms could generate and issue genuinely binding moral commands is altogether mysterious, if not absurd. Contemporary naturalistic ethicist Richard Boyd identifies goodness with a cluster of empirical properties, among them the satisfaction of mutually supportive social human needs.[13] Choices are deemed moral to the extent that they satisfy such needs. Such an account might seem to make morality objective, yet it's difficult to see how purely empirical properties could really account for binding obligation or intrinsic value. The attempt to define morality in terms of the satisfaction of our desires tries to replace theism's objective account of value and meaning with subjective satisfaction, but the exchange leaves us worse off. It remains a leap of blind faith to affirm that anything like objective obligation would emerge from such empirical properties.[14] For that matter, persons themselves, especially persons with intrinsic value and dignity, seem much less likely to emerge from valueless impersonal stuff than from the intentional hand of a personal Creator.

No, if there's something more here, Lewis suggests, it's more like a mind than a collection of atoms or set of empirical properties. The Catholic thinker John Henry Newman, a century before Lewis, had similarly argued that our conscience, particularly our feelings of guilt, lead us to conclude God exists.[15] Feelings of conscience are often directed toward fellow human beings, but sometimes our feelings of guilt or shame, which we take as evidence to suggest that we have offended someone, lack an appropriate human target. If such feelings are appropriate, they must then have a nonhuman one. Our feelings of responsibility, shame, and fear emanating from our conscience imply that "there is One to whom we are responsible, before whom we are ashamed, whose claims upon us we fear."[16]

In a similar vein, Lewis's essential argument can be summarized like this: There are objective moral facts, among them guilt for wrongdoing and duties we are obliged to obey and are responsible for neglecting, and such objective facts are better explained by a religious understanding of reality than by a Russellian world. So morality gives us some significant preliminary reason to believe in God.

As it stands, that argument, though interesting, is vulnerable to a number of criticisms, so let's turn our attention to some of the more challenging ones.

## Egoism, Sidgwick, and Kant

In the context of Lewis's rejection of cultural relativism, he makes the following claim: "Men have differed as regards what people you ought to be unselfish to—whether it was only your own family, or your fellow countrymen, or everyone. But they have always agreed that you ought not to put yourself first. Selfishness has never been admired."[17]

Interestingly, however, one ethical theory does extol behaving in a self-interested way as the very essence of morality. This theory is "ethical egoism," and it's a way to construe ethics that would undermine the moral argument.[18] If our only moral obligations, ultimately, are to ourselves, we would be hard-pressed to argue that such moral facts provide the resources to conclude that a good God exists as the likely explanation of the objectivity of moral values.

Ethical egoism contrasts with *psychological* egoism, which is the different, alleged descriptive claim that everyone, in point of fact, acts out of exclusively self-interested motivations. According to this view, everyone's deepest motivations are for the sake of benefiting themselves, although of course they might be mistaken about what course of action best does this. Recall Glaucon's story of the Ring of Gyges in Plato's *Republic* in which a ring of invisibility gives a young man the opportunity to act without conventional constraints.[19] The point of the story is to show that this egoistic motivation is common to the human condition: given the opportunity to escape unscathed from living a selfish existence, most of us would probably do it.

We will forgo providing a critique of either psychological or ethical egoism, for such arguments have been provided by others in abundance, from eighteenth-century Anglican bishop Joseph Butler's arguments against Hobbes's psychological egoism to contemporary philosopher James Rachels' argument against ethical egoism.[20] Although we're convinced by such arguments, we can't disprove egoism definitively. Just as we can't disprove that we're brains in vats or living in a Matrix world, we can't completely discredit psychological egoism or ethical egoism. But our inability to disprove it doesn't count as good evidence for it, and there are very substantial reasons against it. Even if we are not as selfless as we might like to think, and Murdoch's "fat, relentless ego" or Kant's "dear self" holds sway, the case is far from having been made that we are only selfish.

The contemporary debate between egoism and altruism is nonetheless reflective of a deeply rooted set of ethical questions germane to a moral argument for God's existence. One of the most interesting discussions of these issues comes from Henry Sidgwick, the nineteenth-century author of *The Methods of Ethics*.[21] What makes matters even more interesting was Sidgwick's own rejection of God as a solution to the problem he identified, though he recognized how God's existence could resolve it. Understanding the argument can shed light not only on the limitations of egoism, but also on the genuine insight that egoism aims to preserve.

Sidgwick identified as the greatest moral problem of his time the "dualism of the practical reason": the fact that what might serve the happiness of a given individual might conflict with what might serve the wider population. Suppose an individual, for the sake of serving the greater good, has to sacrifice his own happiness, or even his life. Would it be reasonable for him to do so? On the one hand, it seems reasonable to make the sacrifice, yet on the other hand, it seems reasonable not to sacrifice his own happiness. Sidgwick notes that among earlier moral philosophers, particularly the Greeks, belief was widespread that it was good for the individual to act sacrificially, even at great personal cost. Sidgwick recognized that such belief was partly due to a "faith deeply rooted in the moral consciousness of mankind, that there cannot be really and ultimately any conflict between the two kinds of reasonableness."[22]

Sidgwick thought that the fundamental intuitions of morality are as independently self-evident as the axioms of geometry and therefore in need of no grounding, but because of the occasional conflict between individual and corporate fulfillment, we must give up the hope of making full rational sense of morality. The fact that doing our duty may not lead to personal happiness or fulfillment, though, on his view, provides us no good reason to abandon morality. In other words, Sidgwick, like Lewis, believed that morality is objectively binding on us in a very strong sense, although in Sidgwick's case, he held this view despite the practical problem posed by the dualism of practical reason. Sidgwick leaves this problem largely unresolved, although he does acknowledge one way that the problem *could* be solved. If God served at the foundation of ethics to ensure that it's always in our best interests to be moral, that would guarantee that no conflict of the type mentioned above would arise.

Sidgwick's recognition that God's existence would resolve this problem is very close to Immanuel Kant's argument that held that the moral enterprise needs the postulate of a God who can and does ensure that happiness and virtue correspond. Morality, for Kant, as for Sidgwick, makes full rational sense only if acting morally is ultimately in our self-interest. Sidgwick saw that God might ensure this, but he didn't opt for that solution, whereas Kant did.

Sidgwick's hesitation to affirm a theistic solution was due to his belief in morality's independent self-evidence. Recall, though, that Lewis himself spoke of the clarity and self-evidence of morality. Indeed, arguably such clarity of foundational moral truths is necessary for any moral argument for God to work, for the evidence on which such argument relies has to be at least as clear as the conclusion. But whereas Lewis thought that strongly evident moral facts or truths cry out for a good explanation, Sidgwick thought that such truths eliminate the need for further explanation.

Critics of Kant's moral argument at this juncture might castigate it for the reason that it appears to be suggesting that morality pays, or even that religious ethics is altogether too mercenary, perhaps even egoistic, to qualify as a legitimate moral theory.

This criticism, though, is based on a shallow understanding of the argument. The claim is not that we should be moral to earn a reward; Kant certainly thought no such thing. He was adamant in insisting that our moral motivations could not even possibly be mercenary, or they wouldn't be distinctively *moral* at all. Rather, the claim is that, in a practical way, we have to believe that morality makes sense, that it's deeply rooted on solid foundations, and that the context we live in is thoroughly moral after all, if we are going to remain adequately committed to morality. That we must believe morality to be rational, and that morality corresponds with our ultimate self-interest, is far from saying that morality demands that we be motivated by *nothing but* self-interest. To the contrary, it's likely that self-interested motivation requires the *renunciation* of pure self-interest. It's not in our self-interest to be concerned only about our self-interest, paradoxically, just as the best way to attain happiness is to be concerned about something other than happiness.

To say that morality requires that we occasionally or often must behave for the sake of others in a spirit of genuine altruism is not to say that morality ever demands that we must behave in a way that goes against our own ultimate self-interest. In other words, a rejection of egoism doesn't imply that a healthy concern for self-interest is contrary to morality. Morality may call on us to sacrifice our own short-term interests, maybe even our lives, but in a theistic world, this isn't the same as sacrificing our own ultimate self-interest, because the sorts of benefits derived from a Russellian world don't exhaust all the benefits there are. We will argue below that the dualism of practical reason disappears in a theistic world in which morality rests on the deepest foundations possible, whereas it remains an unresolved, perhaps intractable, problem for the naturalist.


Those Odd Obligations

Closely related to Sidgwick's practical reason dilemma is what's sometimes referred to as the oddness of moral obligations. Contemporary ethicist Richard

Brandt claims that we cannot defend shirking our moral duty by claiming that discharging that duty wouldn't satisfy one's "reflective preferences." Moral duties, at least those not negated by other compelling enough reasons, are thought to confer obligations that we need to perform even if doing so is not something we want to do. This, again, is part of what Lewis was getting at in referring to morality's authority over us. Morality doesn't tell us just to do those things we already want to do. Sometimes it tells us to do what we *don't* want to do, or not to do what we *do* want to do. It's inconvenient in that way from time to time.

Sidgwick discussed how morality might not always conduce to our happiness, and isn't this just what we sometimes find so hard to take about morality? We can begin to think that it deprives us of fun or of the chance to do what will give us great happiness and enjoyment. Whenever anyone does something he genuinely thinks is wrong, isn't it likely that he's choosing to give priority to the rush and thrill of the forbidden by putting pleasure before what is right?

Plato thought that nobody would ever knowingly choose the bad, that if we make a choice to do something, it shows that we think the choice is good. Wrongdoing is only done out of ignorance, on this view. But there are other possible explanations that account for wrongdoing, including yielding to temptation, weakness of will, and corruption of character. Again, as Lewis said, we all fall short from time to time. In our present circumstances we remain imperfect. We are all quite familiar with the lure of temptation, as we are with our penchant for rationalizing our actions. A rationalization we have all been inclined to use is to question whether the action was really wrong after all. When our choices fall below the dictates of morality and we know it, one response to the resulting guilt is to acknowledge our shortcoming, but another is to lower the standard, or even to deny altogether the existence of the moral standard.

This is just when intellectual doubts about the foundations of morality can look very attractive. Morality wields authority and induces guilt, and we can begin to resent it. We start to wonder if morality is all it's cracked up to be, if it's anything more than an internalization of parental teachings, social mores, or mere convention and conditioning. Unless morality continues to be understood as resting on solid foundations, its authority comes into question, and understandably so. Why take seriously, for example, an obligation to forgo one's preferences and to do instead what one may not want to do? Do obligations really bind us even if they don't correspond with our reflective preferences?

If they do hold this authority, then moral obligations, especially in a Russellian world, can seem to be rather odd entities. So says George Mavrodes in reply to Brandt's claim that duty can exceed our reflective preferences. "This is just to bring the queer element back in," Mavrodes writes, "It is to suppose that besides the 'kind of person' I am and my particular pattern of 'cares' and interests there is something else, my duty, which may go against these and in any case properly overrides them."[23] Moral facts, obligations in particular, direct us to action in a way that no merely descriptive fact characterizing the world can do. Morality confers obligations and constraints not just on our behavior, but even on our motivations. Saving a drowning child in the hope of earning a reward, though resulting in a good consequence, is still generally thought of as less than exemplary behavior. Morality ascribes praise and blame, often independently of whether the moral agent's personal interest or advantage is satisfied, and it provides intrinsic motives to virtue without always providing obvious advantages that motivate the right behavior.

Erik J. Wielenberg tries to diminish the power of Mavrodes's argument by casting him as merely suggesting that a universe that's fundamentally unjust would be an absurd world, giving us reason to believe in a divine guarantee of perfect justice. Then Wielenberg ridicules such a view by citing Bertrand Russell's analogy of finding a crate of oranges whose top layer is all bad, and inferring on this basis that the oranges underneath must be good to redress the balance. But Wielenberg can't so easily evade the force of Mavrodes's point in his article, because the existence of binding moral obligations is harder to square with a naturalistic context than a supernaturalistic one. Elsewhere in his book, Wielenberg tries to turn the tables completely on the theists, contrasting them with grown-ups who "recognize that the fact that a given action is morally obligatory is itself an overriding reason for performing that action. A morally obligatory action is an action that one *has* to do whether one *wants* to do it or not. Rewards and punishments may provide *additional* reasons for doing what we morally ought to do, but they do not constitute the *only* reasons for doing so."[24] Wielenberg obviously wants to affirm the existence of moral realism in a strong sense here, sounding much like Lewis, but without coming to terms with just how deeply naturalism is at odds with such realism. How do such oughts exist in a world where we are causally determined to behave just as we do? How do such binding obligations come to obtain? His naturalist allies have often been the very ones most contributing to the loss of confidence in such moral realism, rendering it more than a little disingenuous for him to treat theism as the bigger culprit undermining such traditional convictions.

Now if such moral facts really exist, the glaring question that beckons to be answered is how they could ever have arisen in a naturalistic world. Moral duties impose obligations that need to be obeyed even if they don't always correspond with our cares and interests. They justify or require praise and blame for actions committed or omitted, and they require a purity of motivation. As

Lewis put it, how could bits of matter generate such authoritative demands? It's no wonder that the influential twentieth-century atheist J. L. Mackie wrote, "Moral properties constitute so odd a cluster of properties and relations that they are most unlikely to have arisen in the course of events without an all-powerful god to create them."[25] Mackie had in mind a divinely ordered naturalistic explanation rather than transcendent Platonic moral truths. His idea was that moral facts, as traditionally conceived, particularly those pertaining to obligation, exhibit features so strange that their appearance in a naturalistic world seems nothing less than miraculous. And unfortunately, miracles do not sit well in a naturalistic world! For this reason, as an atheist, Mackie himself found the notion of their existence altogether dubious.

Obviously, any such rejection of moral facts, or understanding of them as elaborate mistakes or grand delusions, would rob the moral argument for God's existence of its persuasive power. It's an argument that can only hope to sway those who have firm convictions about morality. Mackie lacked or lost such conviction, but many would disagree with him, suggesting that they can't shake their conviction that the authority of morality is undeniable. They may recognize within themselves the temptation to question the binding power of morality, especially when the pleasure prohibited or inconvenience imposed is great. They will even, on occasion, fall short and may rationalize their doing so by attempting to lower the moral standard. But few among us decide to stop respecting the moral law altogether. Even those who decide to ignore it still often believe in it, at least for a while. At least *some* moral facts seem to impose an obligation on us that applies irrespective of whether we want to obey it or not. The moral argument doesn't necessarily need many such absolute, nonnegotiable obligations, but it needs at least some. Those who think that the moral argument has such resources at its disposal would be more likely to believe that it retains great potential.

Some may attempt to blunt this force by pointing out the failures of those who hold a strong view of obligation. Simon Blackburn, for instance, contends that "people who talk much of obligation approach practical life with a certain kind of armoury, and one that may make them insensitive, cruel, inhospitable to understanding and excuses.... History shows plenty of examples where moralizing brings nothing but disaster."[26] We can concede much of this while insisting that it detracts little from the need to account for the force of genuine obligations. Even if the language of moral obligations has been abused, and even if, as is certainly true, obligations don't make up all of ethics, they remain an important piece of the moral puzzle in need of adequate explanation. Moreover, the notion of genuine obligation provides the basis for recognizing and correcting those very abuses that Blackburn identifies! Otherwise, Blackburn's complaint loses its edge completely.

Recall Sidgwick's conviction that morality doesn't need grounding because of its obviousness. His idea was that morality, despite the practical dualism problems it generates, is so obviously true that no religious or theological foundation is called for. Mackie, on the other hand, conjectured that without God it's unlikely that morality, given its odd features, is true. We consider both thinkers to be right in one way, and wrong in another. We agree with Sidgwick about the obviousness of moral truth, but disagree with him that this allows morality to dispense with the need for foundations. We agree with Mackie that moral obligations seem odd in certain respects, especially in a naturalistic world, but we disagree with the choice to give up his belief in morality as classically construed. Instead, we suggest that a firm prior conviction of moral truth provides good reason to entertain a supernatural worldview. A picture of reality in which all life is no more than a product of blind naturalistic forces and fortuitous collocations of molecules is fundamentally less adequate to underwrite morality than a personal universe created and sustained by a perfectly loving God. Traditionally conceived moral obligations, while residing comfortably in a theistic universe, are incongruous in a purely naturalistic world.

## Platonism and Existentialism

We've been suggesting that the obvious truth of morality might provide evidence for God's existence, as well as reason to think that this obvious truth depends ultimately on God. At first glance, such a claim might seem implausible, if not inconsistent. In particular, it might seem inconsistent to argue that moral truth is dependent on God if we can know it without even thinking of God. This alleged inconsistency can be dispelled if we recognize, as numerous classical thinkers have pointed out, that the *order of being* is different from the *order of knowing*. That is, the order in which we come to know things might be different from the order in which things exist, or have come to exist. Certain moral truths might be as evident to us as anything can be, but may still leave unanswered the question of where morality came from. Likewise, the foundations of morality might be at a greater distance from us in terms of immediate knowledge than morality itself.

This is a fundamental distinction, but one that is often missed, resulting in needless confusion. Recent books defending atheism have perpetuated this confusion, unfortunately, but not surprisingly. For instance, Richard Dawkins seems to ignore this distinction when he asks, "if we have independent criteria for choosing among religious moralities, why not cut out the middle man and go straight for the moral choice without the religion?"[27]

The intuition that God and morality are intimately related is a deep one that has often been recognized by noted spokesmen on both sides of the theism/atheism divide. Dostoevsky's famous line that if God doesn't exist, then everything is permitted, is one echo of this theme, as is the German philosopher Friedrich Nietzsche's confident proclamation that the "death of God" should have for one of its practical outcomes a Copernican revolution in ethics. According to this view, selfishness and pride, perhaps even ruthlessness rightly understood, should now eclipse traditionally exalted moral virtues like humility, altruism, and compassion. Upholding traditional morality after the death of God wasn't Nietzsche's concern. It was rather his agenda to effect his transvaluation of values, in an effort to infuse goodness again with strength and heroism.

Nietzsche and Mackie were atheists who saw the nonexistence of God as morally relevant, and French existentialist Jean Paul Sartre was another. For these thinkers, atheism didn't mean business as usual when it came to ethics. It meant fundamental rethinking of what ethics is all about, because they recognized the long history of a perceived connection between God and morality. They thus stand in contrast to those who think that eliminating God from the moral equation changes little or that including God adds nothing of consequence. The following passage from Sartre is worth quoting at length in this regard:

> Towards 1880, when the French professors endeavored to formulate
> a secular morality, they said something like this: God is a useless
> hypothesis, so we will do without it. However, if we are to have
> morality, a society and a law-abiding world, it is essential that certain
> values should be taken seriously; they must have an *a priori* existence
> ascribed to them. It must be considered obligatory *a priori* to be
> honest, not to lie, not to beat one's wife, to bring up children and so
> forth; so we are going to do a little work on the subject, which will
> enable us to show that these values exist all the same, inscribed in an
> intelligent heaven although, of course, there is no God. In other
> words... nothing will be changed if God does not exist; we shall
> discover the same norms of honesty, progress and humanity, and we
> shall have disposed of God as an out-of-date hypothesis which will
> die away quietly of itself. The existentialist, on the contrary, finds it
> extremely embarrassing that God does not exist, for there disappears
> with him all possibility of finding values in an intelligible heaven.
> There can no longer be any good *a priori*, since there is no infinite
> and perfect consciousness to think it. It is nowhere written that "the

good" exists, that one must be honest or must not lie, since we are now upon the plane where there are only men.[28]

This passage is interesting for several reasons, not least in its contrast of existentialism and something like Platonism, the notion that moral values exist in an intelligent heaven even though there is no God. Both of these approaches are potential ways that atheists might avoid the conclusion of the moral argument. We're inclined to think that Platonism and existentialism each captures, with some success, crucial aspects of morality, but that neither is fully adequate to account for all that morality requires.

The Platonist says there are objective moral values, every bit as transcendent and binding as Lewis believed in, but that they stand in no need of foundations. They are, rather, brute facts, perhaps like the truths of mathematics, fixed features of reality, ultimate facts about the universe of which we become aware. This view has the advantage of making sense of our abiding conviction in the truth and obviousness of morality as well as its ground in reality. It echoes Sidgwick's claim that morality is self-evident and needs no foundation, and it goes some distance in satisfying Kant's insistence that reality somehow be committed to morality. It asserts that obligations can be understood as realities that objectively exist and have binding power over us.

Mavrodes argues, we think rightly, that Plato's wordview, though not Christian, has very often been taken to be congenial to a religious understanding of the world. He continues in this vein:

The idea of the Good seems to play a metaphysical role in his thought. It is somehow fundamental to what *is* as well as to what *ought to be*, much more fundamental than are the atoms. A Platonic man, therefore, who sets himself to live in accordance with the Good aligns himself with what is deepest and most basic in existence. Or to put it another way, we might say that whatever values a Platonic world imposes on a man are values to which the Platonic world itself is committed, through and through.[29]

Mavrodes goes on to argue that this is *not* the case with a Russellian world, where values and obligations cannot be nearly so deep, having a grip only on surface phenomena. This status of moral facts in a naturalistic world heightens the seeming strangeness of morality in demanding so much while lacking sufficient grounding.

So Platonism definitely seems to hold an advantage over pure naturalism. Interestingly, it's a view of the universe shaped by, among other things, moral convictions. The explanation given for the existence of what seem to be stable and enduring moral facts is that the universe itself is a moral context. This is an intelligible view, and it's hard to refute. It's not far from the view we ourselves hold, though of course what it leaves out is the most important part of the picture, in our estimation.

Augustine, an early Christian Platonist, understandably thought it made best sense that if the highest standard of goodness is the object of the highest form of love, as it was for Plato, then the highest reality is likely to be a person. Beyond the impersonality of the Platonic Good is another problem, already alluded to by Sartre, as John Rist observes:

> Plato's account of the "Forms" (including the Good) as moral
> exemplars leaves them in metaphysical limbo. They would exist as
> essentially intelligible ideas even if there were no mind, human or
> divine, to recognize them: as objects of thought, not mere constructs
> or concepts. But, as Augustine learned, and as the Greek
> Neoplatonists had asserted, the notion of an eternal object of thought
> (and thus for Plato a cause of thought) without a ceaseless thinking
> subject is unintelligible. Intelligible Forms, never proposed as mere
> concepts, cannot be proposed as Plato originally proposed them, as
> free-floating metaphysical items.[30]

The need for Platonic forms ultimately to be grounded in a mind that recognizes them is once again keenly felt. "Free floating metaphysical items" do not have the ontological strength and stability that we think morality must have. Even if we discern these moral truths before we identify their deeper foundations, this only reminds us again that the order of knowing is distinct from the order of being.

## Freedom, Naturalism, and Moral Responsibility

Another question to raise for Platonists is this: How can they account for the freedom we need to obey the moral obligations that they affirm as part of the furniture of the universe? If we are causally determined to behave as we do, then everything that happens, including every human decision, is bound to happen just as it does. The universe itself might be a moral place, but how can human beings be morally free creatures, free either to obey or disregard the moral law? This is of course an old and difficult question, but it's not at all clear that Platonists have an adequate reply. Moral facts have no purchase unless we have moral freedom.

This problem is acute for naturalists, of course, but our point here is that Platonists who deny God's existence and who affirm causal determinism for human beings are in the same bind. Suppose you have a choice to cheat on a test or not. Morality says you shouldn't. Suppose you end up cheating. On a deterministic picture, your choice was determined, such that, at the moment you made it, the causal conditions and the physical laws at work in the world dictated that you would do exactly as you did. In those circumstances you couldn't have done otherwise. To say that you ought not to have cheated, then, is problematic, because you can't be obligated to do what's impossible to do, and in those circumstances, it was impossible that you could have done differently. Moral freedom in a determined world seems ruled out.

Marc D. Hauser takes on the charge that "biological perspectives [of morality] are inherently evil, as they create predetermined outcomes, thereby eliminating free will." He replies to this charge as follows:

> As philosophers and psychologists, such as Daniel Dennett, Steven
> Pinker, and Daniel Wegner, have argued, however, nothing about an
> evolutionary or biological perspective leads inextricably to the notion
> of a determined, fixed, or immutable set of judgments or beliefs.
> Biology doesn't work this way. Our biology, and the biology of all
> species on earth, sets up a range of possible behaviors. The range we
> observe interacts with the environment, and environments change.[31]

It's probably true that our biology isn't such that we're causally determined to behave as we do independent of our fluctuating contexts, but the important point is the more general one that, once we add both nature and nurture into the mix, a naturalistic perspective inexorably leads to complete determinism. Hauser's enlistment of Harvard psychologist Pinker to his cause seems counterproductive, incidentally, as Pinker has acknowledged, as we are about to see, that a naturalistic account of human freedom isn't adequate to sustain strong ascriptions of moral responsibility.

Pinker does, however, make some effort to defend moral responsibility on naturalist terms. In particular, he endorses the effort of those "defensive scientists" who sometimes try to deflect the charge of determinism by saying behavior is never perfectly predictable, not determined in the "mathematical sense," but only as a probability.[32] This is worse than confused. Our failure to be privy to the myriad relevant facts shaping our actions, rendering our predictions of human behavior merely epistemically probable at best, doesn't detract from how materialism in principle would almost certainly imply absolute ontological determinism of human conduct. His various conjectures of how a purely physical system might not be deterministic seem wildly implausible:

"Perhaps the brain amplifies random events at the molecular or quantum level. Perhaps brains are nonlinear dynamical systems subject to unpredictable chaos."[33] Perhaps, and perhaps the world was created five minutes ago. Mere possibility doesn't plausibility imply. Even more to the point, Pinker himself acknowledges that even if such remote possibilities obtain, we're left with nothing like free will, and no concept of responsibility.

The Platonist who wishes to affirm determinism has a few potential responses here.[34] She could say that, although the wrongdoing doesn't merit the sort of maximal blame associated with retribution, a modicum of censure is still appropriate to encourage better behavior next time. Deterrence, rehabilitation, and positive conditioning make perfect sense even in a determined world. Perhaps it might even be suggested that this is a move in the right direction toward a better world, where we strive more to understand one another's failures rather than just assign blame and exact revenge and retribution.

In response, we would suggest that trying to attain higher levels of understanding of the behaviors of others is indeed worthwhile, often noble, but the Platonist, in opting for this resolution, has subtly lowered the moral standard. No longer are moral facts binding on us the way Lewis, or Plato, thought they were, and many still do today. Morality has instead become a set of ideal guidelines rather than demands for us to abide by. There are no longer, for example, *obligations*, but mere *suggestions*. Again, we can't be obligated to do what we are either necessitated to do or precluded from doing, which is the case for all we do if we're determined. Even our decision either to use or not to use morality as our guideline is itself determined and so not free.

Here the Platonist might wish to reply by saying, in concert with many naturalists, that determinism and genuine freedom are consistent after all. When we, through reason, apprehend moral truth and choose to live according to it, we are free. Following reasons in this way may not liberate us from the causal chain, but does confer on us whatever real freedom we are capable of.

Lewis found this response unconvincing, as does the contemporary naturalistic philosopher John Searle.[35] Suppose again you're considering cheating on a test or your taxes. You apprehend, suppose, the wrongness of cheating. You ponder the choice, and make up your mind to do the right thing and not cheat. Was your choice moral, on a deterministic picture? Perhaps it was moral in the sense of corresponding to the moral truth that you shouldn't cheat, but it wasn't a morally significant decision in any deep sense. How could it be? It was a decision that, in those circumstances, *had* to be made. You were determined, causally, to do exactly as you did. Within a deterministic framework, everything that everyone does is bound to happen just as it does. To call actions we consider in accord with moral truth free moral choices does not make them so. If the determinists are right, we couldn't have done differently, ever. And if we do behave in accord with morality, it is because of physiological causes in our brain, not because of the persuasive power of abstract entities.[36]

What must be forthrightly faced here is that moral obligations require a convincing account of moral freedom and ascriptions of moral responsibility. Those unable to account for genuine moral freedom and who wish to continue speaking meaningfully of moral responsibility are likely simply to change the topic, using the same words to refer to different concepts. Take, for example, contemporary philosopher Elliot Sober's account of moral responsibility: "If an agent is morally responsible for an event (a bank robbery, say), this means (1) that the agent caused the event; and (2) that the occurrence of the event reflects on the agent's moral character." In this way, Sober says, we can distinguish moral responsibility from the mere causal responsibility that, for example, we apply to storms with no implication of moral praise or blame.[37]

Does his account of moral responsibility make sense of ascribing genuine praise or blame? We don't think so. If determinism is true, then not only are all of our actions invariably caused by prior conditions and physical laws, but so is our character. Genuine ascriptions of *moral responsibility*, if tied to our characters, would require that we are rightly regarded as sufficiently responsible for our character. If our free choices do not shape our character, we are not rightly responsible for the choices that flow from that character. Hence, we find Sober's line of thought unconvincing.

Suppose Aristotle was right that one's character is a function of what one consistently does.[38] In that case, our characters are a result of our choices, but if our choices are all determined, so would be our character. Might some people end up with a bad character, performing hurtful actions that we are inclined to call immoral? Sure. But would such persons be morally responsible for such actions and their character? Not on a deterministic picture, for genuine moral praise and blame don't fit into a picture of people who are invariably caused to do everything they do and to become whatever they become. We can continue using this language of praise and blame, and the language will continue to be taken to mean what it has meant traditionally, but we will be referring to something other than moral responsibility. When naturalists use moral language, they have to change the subject by subtly abandoning traditional moral categories, while still using words that retain their purchase from a borrowed moral vocabulary with a philosophical history that the naturalists have renounced.

Another example of the way naturalists change the topic is Richard Dawkins's chapter on the "roots of morality" in his recent book *The God Delusion*. The subtitle of the chapter is "Why are we good?" Considerations of what might lead us to behave ethically, however, do not provide an account of the foundations of ethics, nor do they answer the question of whether anything, and what in particular, is good or right and why. The result is that much of his discussion skates over superficial questions and relies on anecdotal evidence of horribly bad religious thinkers, none of which does anything to advance our understanding of the roots of morality. For the most part Dawkins avoids altogether questions of what makes morality *true*, and simply tries to provide instead a naturalistic and evolutionary account of why we occasionally manifest altruistic behaviors. Having identified such evolutionary reasons—namely, genetic kinship, reciprocation, a good reputation, and the benefits of conspicuous generosity—Dawkins acts as though he has provided insight into morality and its foundations themselves. He writes, "We can no more help ourselves feeling pity when we see a weeping unfortunate (who is unrelated and unable to reciprocate) than we can help ourselves feeling lust for a member of the opposite sex (who may be infertile or otherwise unable to reproduce). Both are misfirings, Darwinian mistakes: blessed, precious mistakes."[39] He asserts value where, on his system, no account of value has been provided. He is not entitled, on his analysis and without argument, to assert that such misfirings are *good*, only that they *are*.[40] Of course we all have the intuition that such heartfelt pity is right and good, but his naturalistic account provides no reason to take such an intuition as veridical.[41] Dawkins, too, employs moral vocabulary that retains its purchase because of a worldview that he has rejected out of hand.

American philosopher William James pointed out how the category of *regret* also doesn't fit into a naturalistic picture. In his essay "The Dilemma of Determinism," he expressed the freedom he felt to use moral conceptions about which he was confident to shape his view of the world. He wrote that, if conceptions of the world violate this moral demand, he "shall feel as free to throw it overboard, or at least to doubt it, as if it disappointed my demand for uniformity of sequence, for example...."[42] For James, as for Lewis, a potential window of insight into reality was morality, and a fixture of morality is regret over certain decisions. James wrote that

> Some regrets are pretty obstinate and hard to stifle—regrets for acts of wanton cruelty or treachery, for example, whether performed by others or by ourselves. Hardly any one can remain *entirely* optimistic after reading the confession of the murderer at Brockton the other day: how, to get rid of the wife whose continued existence bored him, he inveigled her into a desert spot, shot her four times, and then, as she lay on the ground and said to him, "You didn't do it on purpose, did you, dear?" replied, "No, I didn't do it on purpose," as he raised a

rock and smashed her skull. Such an occurrence, with the mild sentence and self-satisfaction of the prisoner, is a field for a crop of regrets, which one need not take up in detail. We feel that, although a perfect mechanical fit to the rest of the universe, it is a bad moral fit, and that something else would really have been better in its place.

But for the deterministic philosophy the murder, the sentence, and the prisoner's optimism were all necessary from eternity; and nothing else for a moment had a ghost of a chance of being put into their place.[43]

Traditional conceptions of moral freedom, moral duties, moral responsibility, genuine regret, real praise and blame are all difficult to make sense of in a naturalistic world. Those uncomfortable with watering such conceptions down have reason to take theism seriously.

Whereas Platonists firmly believe in an ultimate Good, an existentialist like Sartre denied the existence of any such Good. "There can no longer be an *a priori* Good, since there is no infinite and perfect consciousness to think it." What this means, for Sartre, is that we are radically free, not to discover morality on our own, but to forge our own values. We *invent* morality, not *discover* it. So whereas Platonists, or at least Platonists who believe in determinism, embrace objective moral values but can't account for the meaningful moral freedom that significant adherence to such values requires, Sartre endorses the strongest possible sense of moral freedom, but in the process jettisons objective moral value.

Moral freedom, contrary to Sartre's view, isn't the freedom to create and invent our own values, as if we could choose to make just anything at all valuable by happening to value it. If I valued child torture for fun, that wouldn't make it a valuable activity in any morally significant sense. Sartre simply seems to be wrong, and profoundly so, when he insists that we find no values or commands to legitimize our conduct. Sartre is assuming that, since objective moral values have God for their best explanation, unbelief in God must entail unbelief in objective moral values. If Lewis, Sidgwick, and Newman are right, however, our belief in strong moral values ought to be firm and resolute because of the obviousness of such truths in and of themselves.

There's something powerful about Sartre's heroic denial of determinism and something right about firm belief in moral freedom, but his maneuver ultimately seems unprincipled. He denies the existence of anything outside the physical world, only then to turn his back on the likely scenario to follow: a purely mechanistic picture of reality that leaves no room for genuine free will. Not only does he not endorse determinism, while giving little argument for doing so, he endorses an understanding of freedom so radical that it vitiates the possibility of any objective value system, by painting human beings as not mere discoverers of morality, but its inventors.[44]

Having relinquished objective ethics in his existentialist approach, Sartre still tried salvaging a sense of importance for our decisions, claiming that through our choices we create and invent not only our person but our very ethics of action. In our choices, we choose not just for ourselves but for others as well. We create a certain image of man in our choosing, a certain ideal. So in making choices we choose for all men.

Sartre may have been right to suggest that our choices shape who we are and that they reflect what we think an ideal human ought to be, but none of that implies that our choices determine value. He has provided simply no objective basis for our cherished moral convictions, such as the wrongness of beating one's wife or the rightness of responsible child rearing. And any sense in which our choices, construed along existentialist lines, involve a choice for all of humanity, as Sartre put it, remains more than obscure.

The Platonists try capturing strong moral truths, but have little to offer on the issue of moral freedom. Existentialists like Sartre try capturing moral freedom by assuming it as axiomatic, but they interpret it so radically that we have to discard our convictions about traditional morality. But both moral freedom, rightly understood, and stable moral truths are crucial to ethics, and no picture without both is complete. Neither the Platonists nor the existentialists discussed, in other words, seem capable of sustaining the full range of classical moral conceptions from binding obligations to real freedom to ethical responsibility.

A Cumulative Case

This treatment has drawn from various resources within the rich tradition of moral arguments for God's existence, from Newman's appeal to conscience to Lewis's argument for the objectivity of value, from Mackie's discussion of moral oddness to Kant's argument from practical rationality. A variety of conceptually distinct moral arguments are at play here, but in drawing this discussion together the way we did, it was our goal to show how they mutually reinforce one another. What the arguments hold in common may be far more important than their differences, and cumulatively they pack quite a punch, at least for those drawn to put stock in classically construed categories of moral obligation, freedom, and responsibility. Cumulative case arguments that draw from various resources in natural theology are well known and potentially highly effective; this chapter has been the narrower attempt to construct a multipronged moral argument for God's existence, recognizing the variety of moral arguments at play.

The force of the moral argument is that theism is no more outlandish or outrageous than many of our most cherished moral convictions. If we want to take seriously moral freedom, ethical obligations, and genuine responsibility, then we are hard-pressed to do so on naturalistic grounds. Such notions classically construed make little sense in a purely physical world, but they reside quite comfortably in a world sustained by a loving Creator.

There are many ways to avoid the conclusion of the moral argument, but avoiding the conclusion is not the same as averting the force of the argument. Claiming that moral conviction is nothing but expression of personal emotions, for example, would disable the moral argument from the start, even though this requires that we deny what Lewis rightly saw as the intrinsic reasonableness of moral truths. The claim that there's no getting behind ethics, that it simply comes unbidden into our lives, as Simon Blackburn says, is far from obvious, to put it mildly. In fact, it's rather unphilosophical in spirit, accepting as a brute fact what might be a crucial hint of something deeper. We have not said nearly enough to insist that those unconvinced by the moral argument are irrational, but we do suggest that those who find its evidence compelling and its conclusion reasonable are within their intellectual rights to do so. Morality, classically construed, gives those who believe in objective ethics reason to believe in God. Such an argument can play an effective part in a cumulative case argument for God's existence.

Naturalism can make good sense of why we might *feel* or *believe* that we have moral obligations, but it has a much harder time explaining moral obligations themselves, and its deterministic framework means that vital moral categories, to survive, have to be watered down and replaced. If, like E. O. Wilson[45] or Russell, we were convinced that atheism is the sober truth of the matter, then a reason for settling for substitutes of important moral categories would be that it's the best we can do. The point at issue here, though, is *whether* atheism is the truth, and we've argued that prior convictions about morality count positively in favor of theism and against naturalism.

Contra Bertrand Russell, the evidence for God's existence might have been so clear and ubiquitous that he simply overlooked it. Whereas the existentialists are right to see the importance of moral freedom, their worldview can't sustain it, not to mention the authority of moral obligations; and whereas the Platonists are right to see the authority of moral laws, they encounter severe difficulty making sense of the moral freedom we require to submit to such laws. Kant, Lewis, Mackie, Newman, Sidgwick, and Sorley all recognized the way a Mind behind the moral law can make sense of its dictates and authority and ensure its resonance with rationality—whether or not they were willing to opt for this solution. Payment of lip service to the authority and beauty of morality without finally coming to terms with the shortcomings of a naturalistic account of morality, like we find in Brandt, Wielenberg, and Blackburn, lacks philosophical credibility—no matter how many times they repeat their mantra in a loud and confident voice. More reasonable in a real sense is the recognition that Nietzsche, Mackie, and Sartre had that God's death has big moral implications, but our point is the opposite and parallel one: that God's existence potentially provides an account of just those distinctive features of morality that we are otherwise so hard-pressed to make sense of: its rationality, its need for freedom, its imposition of authoritative duties, and the like. A moral argument for God's existence can avoid the weaknesses of the thinkers we've considered while capturing their best insights by showing how profoundly resonant theism is with morality classically construed. But we've only just begun, for to make our case, we have quite a bit of work to do in remaining chapters, beginning with the most recurring and most famous objection of all, derived from the writings of Plato.

# 2

# The Euthyphro Dilemma

Consider this: Is the pious being loved by the gods because it is pious, or is it pious because it is loved by the gods?

—Plato[1]

The recent best-selling novel by Dan Brown, *The Da Vinci Code*, features the character of Leigh Teabing, who turns out to be a corrupt character but whose ideas find a strong voice:

> In terms of prophecy, we are currently in an epoch of
> enormous change. The millenium has recently passed, and
> with it has ended the two-thousand-year-long astrological
> Age of Pisces—the fish, which is also the sign of Jesus. As
> any astrological symbologist will tell you, the Piscean ideal
> believes that man must be told what to do by higher powers
> because man is incapable of thinking for himself. Hence it
> has been a time of fervent religion. Now, however, we are
> entering the Age of Aquarius—the water bearer—whose
> ideals claim that man will discover the truth and be able to
> think for himself. The ideological shift is enormous, and it is
> occurring right now.[2]

The ideological shift of which Teabing speaks and its merits or lack of them is at the heart of what this book is all about.

Ever since the Enlightenment, many leading spokesmen of Western culture have been attempting to dispense with God and religion while retaining morality. Freed from the illusion that we must be told what to do by higher powers, we are now free to discover moral truth in other ways, and to direct our own behavior with no dependence on God. The idea that God's commands dictate what is moral, a view known as the divine command theory of ethics, has been under constant fire long before the epochal ideological shift of modernity. Indeed, the most famous objection of all to this version of theistic ethics is the notorious Euthyphro Dilemma, which was first formulated centuries before the medieval theologians, let alone the Enlightenment philosophers.

The Dilemma has had extraordinary staying power that continues into the twenty-first century.[3] To cite a very recent example, in the book *Is Goodness without God Good Enough?*, contributor Louise Antony employs the Euthyphro Dilemma to critique divine command theory, and she is far from alone in thinking that the Dilemma provides a decisive case against a religious ethic.[4] References in ethics texts to the devastating effect the Dilemma has had on divine command theories are legion. In various formulations, the Dilemma anticipates just about every objection that has been subsequently raised against such ethics, so it provides a useful starting point in any analysis of the connection, if any, between God and morality. Interestingly, Antony Flew once claimed that a good test of a person's aptitude for philosophy is whether or not she can grasp the Dilemma's force and point. Before looking at Louise Antony's specific formulation of the Dilemma, let's quickly set its original context.

The Euthyphro Dilemma arises in an early dialogue of Socrates entitled, appropriately enough, *Euthyphro*. Written by his student Plato, the dialogue features Socrates questioning young Euthyphro about the true standard of morality. As a devout polytheist, Euthyphro attempts to explicate the nature and authority of morality in terms of the loves and hatreds of the gods. Since the Greek gods, by Euthyphro's own admission, could and likely did disagree about moral matters, Euthyphro is forced to say that morality is what all the gods agree on. If they all support a practice, it's an act of piety; if they all denounce a practice, it's an act of impiety.

Louise Antony writes, "Translated into contemporary terms, the question Socrates is asking is this: Are morally good actions morally good simply in virtue of God's favoring them? Or does God favor them because they are—independently of his favoring them—morally good?"[5] Note that Antony's translation involves replacing the "gods" (namely, the Greek pantheon of gods), with "God," most typically nowadays indicative of the God of classical monotheism. She also takes "piety" to mean "goodness," and she replaces the "loves" of the gods with God's "favor." Typically, God's favor is thought to be expressed in terms of commands. So, for example, God's commanding us to visit widows shows his favor of such an action.[6] Understood in this way, the first horn of the Dilemma suggests that God's commands determine the nature of goodness, and God's prohibitions determine what is bad. If God commands something, then it's good, in virtue of his commanding it (and his prohibitions determine what's bad in virtue of the prohibitions). To affirm this reply is to embrace "voluntarism" or the "pure will" theory of the good—a divine command theory of the good. The second horn of the Dilemma suggests that God's commands are what they are in virtue of God's choosing to command what is already good—this is a "nonvoluntarist" or "guided will" theory of the good. By "goodness" here we mean, unless otherwise indicated, *moral* goodness, which is one among other kinds of goodness, though a vitally important one and the focus of our current investigation.

So religious ethicists are thought to face a serious problem. Either they have to endorse voluntarism or nonvoluntarism. To embrace nonvoluntarism is to locate the authority of morality outside of God, which strikes classical theists as a huge mistake. However, to affirm divine command theory, or voluntarism, the "because God says so" approach, Antony claims, is to believe that an act's "*being good* just consists in its being chosen by God," and this entails that there's "nothing about an action in advance of its being chosen or rejected that would enable us to determine what attitude God would take toward it in some other possible world." She adds, "'Good' for the divine command theorist is *synonymous* with 'commanded by God'; we are supposed to lack any conception of what it would be for an act to be good or bad that's independent of our knowledge of what God has commanded. There is no good or bad, according to DCT [Divine Command Theory], apart from what God commands. Because that is so, there is nothing that is *inherently* good or bad, and thus nothing that *explains* God's choosing which acts to endorse and which acts to prohibit."[7] Let's take a more careful look at the problems attending each of the alternatives, starting with voluntarism.


The Vices of Voluntarism


Taking Antony's suggestive lines of argument and augmenting them a bit, we can identify half a dozen serious problems for voluntarism, practically all motivated by the Euthyphro Dilemma, and all of them recur in the philosophical literature on this topic. Although they are closely related, they remain conceptually distinct, so each one merits mention. Let's begin with the challenges, each of which will be addressed in subsequent chapters; then we'll consider some of the historical proponents of and philosophical and theological rationale for voluntarism.

First, the *normativity objection*: In the first chapter, recall, we pressed naturalists to offer a good explanation of moral authority. But a parallel question confronts theism: Why is God's command morally authoritative? Unless God's commands are plausibly thought to generate moral force, the voluntarists will be little better off than the naturalists, and their efforts to construct certain types of moral arguments for God's existence will suffer. Moreover, their account of God's moral authority must be more than an appeal to "might makes right" and a prudential fear of consequences for noncompliance. We will attempt to answer the normativity objection in our chapter on divine command theory (chapter 6).

Second, the *no reasons objection*: If God's say-so is the sole reason for the morality of an action, then there is no reason that slavery or genocide is wrong except God's command. God's commands are entirely a reflection of his own capricious choice; there are no prior reasons for them. Thus divine command theory is often thought to be afflicted with the problem of arbitrariness. And of course, if God has no reasons for his commands, then we can't anticipate what his commands will be, since they are liable to be whatever divine whim dictates, irrespective of prior reasons or the intrinsic features of the actions involved.

Third, the *abhorrent command objection*: If God's arbitrary commands dictate moral goodness, then it is conceivable that God could command us to hate him or one another, or to kill innocents indiscriminately. Atrocities committed in the name of God show this to be no merely academic matter. Abhorrent commands seem to be possible within a voluntarist system, but this means that if God were to tell us to torture babies for fun, then baby torture would be good; and if he told us not to reduce the suffering of sick children, then doing so would be bad.

Fourth, the *vacuity objection*: When we call God "good," we tend to think that such an ascription means something, that it features determinate content that at least resembles ordinary language. But if the ascription is consistent with God being horrible, his issuing of abhorrent commands and the like, then the attribution is vacuous. Goodness that's consistent with everything is meaningless, so why bother to use such language at all? Doing so implicates our use of the word "good" in a radical equivocation of its ordinary meaning. The vacuity objection is intimately connected with the "no reason" and "abhorrent command" objections, both in their origins and solutions, as we will see most clearly in chapter 7.

Fifth, the *epistemic objection*: Here there's actually a cluster of concerns, a few strands of which we will briefly mention at this point in the form of a series of rhetorical questions. If there's a conflict between, say, a divine command

and our own conscience, how do we adjudicate it? What gets primacy—the command or conscience? How is it that we can come to know that an alleged command is a genuine command of God? If our conscience helps determine which commands are genuine, does this not show a prior commitment to the authority of our conscience? Which alleged religious revelation is the right one? Without good answers to such questions, no full-fledged defense of divine command theory would be complete and no moral argument of a voluntarist could fully work, and we thus devote the penultimate chapter to epistemology (chapter 9).

Sixth, the *autonomy objection*: Many objectors to divine command ethics accuse it of detracting from our moral autonomy. Rather than carefully thinking through issues on their own, voluntarists simply consult the relevant command or allegedly sacred text to find their marching orders. (Recall Teabing's claim that man is incapable of thinking for himself.) Patrick Nowell-Smith puts the objection bluntly by claiming that such a posture is "infantile," not proper for an adult.[8] James Rachels, following Kant, echoes the concern when he stresses that moral agents must act according to precepts they can, on reflection, conscientiously approve in their own hearts, a stance that conflicts with unqualified obedience to God come what may. We will offer our solution to this objection in the last chapters (chapters 9 and 10).

## The Voices of Voluntarism

Because of such objections, the voluntarist horn of the Euthyphro Dilemma seems rife with problems, and divine command theory is widely perceived as a failed account—even in popular culture, as the earlier quote from *The Da Vinci Code* demonstrated. Divine command theory is not the only way to connect morality and God, but its historical importance and underlying rationale suggest that it's not to be handily dismissed or entirely trivialized, either. Perhaps the most important historical example of a pure will version of divine command theory in its boldest form is found in William of Ockham, whose unadulterated variant of voluntarism no doubt bolsters the worst stereotype of a religious ethicist. On Ockham's view, God's sovereign choice fills in the content of morality. Not unlike the way in which Descartes affirmed that anything would have been possible in math based on divine decree—such that had God chosen to make $2 + 2 = 5$ he could have—Ockham advances the moral analogue of such voluntarism. If God were to command, say, cruelty for cruelty's sake, or the torture of making someone watch reruns of *The Bachelor* all day long, then such acts would be rendered morally appropriate, perhaps obligatory. Ockham of course felt God never *would* issue abhorrent commands, but that he *could*. That he doesn't is one of the reasons that God is thoroughly praiseworthy. The fact that Ockham thought that God can issue such commands and, if he did, morality would follow suit, makes him a paradigmatic example of a radical voluntarist; indeed, for this reason radical voluntarism is sometimes dubbed "Ockhamism."

Ockham is not alone in embracing a pure will theory. We could readily adduce other proponents of views in this vicinity from late medieval philosophy and theology, to Reformation and Puritan theology, to British modern philosophy and contemporary analytic philosophy—though most more recent proponents of divine command theory offer more nuanced analyses than Ockham's. Surprisingly, even the philosopher Ludwig Wittgenstein seems to have endorsed a kind of voluntarism, as remarks in a letter from December 1930 that he wrote to Friedrich Waismann indicate: "Schlick says that in theological ethics there are two interpretations of the Essence of the Good. On the shallow interpretation, the Good is good, in virtue of the fact that God wills it; on the deeper interpretation, God wills the good, because it is good. On my view, the first interpretation is the deeper: that is good which God commands. For this blocks off the road to any kind of explanation, 'Why it is good'; while the second interpretation is the shallow, rationalistic one, in that it behaves 'as though' that which is good could be given some further foundation."[9]

Wittgenstein was known for the view that questions concerning the source of goodness or happiness can't be answered by appeal to the facts of the matter or how the world is. Variations on this theme run throughout his *Notebooks* (1914–1916) and *Tractatus*. Consequently, in view of his morally reductionist theology and nontraditional usage of such words as "God," he fails to qualify as a traditional proponent of divine command theory, the surface appearance to the contrary notwithstanding.

Considerably more traditional and orthodox statements favoring an ethics of divine commands can be brought forward from the writings of Augustine, Ambrose, Gregory the Great, the Pseudo-Cyprian, Isidore of Seville, Hugh of St. Victor, Anselm, and Barth, as the invaluable historical work of Janine Idziak has shown.[10] Moreover, elements (and sometimes paradigms) of divine command ethics appear in Hobbes, Locke, and such contemporary philosophers as Robert Adams, Phil Quinn, Edward Wierenga, Paul Rooney, and others.[11]

What are some of the motivations for a commitment to divine command theory, despite the challenges it faces? What is it that attracts proponents to this view? A variety of motivations can be cited, beginning with a strong desire to recognize God's status as the first and uncaused cause, and to acknowledge his supreme power.[12] Similarly, there is the appeal of analogical modes of reasoning that take legislative activity as the very paradigm of divine activity, not to mention distinctively biblical and exegetical depictions of God as our Creator and Savior who is imbued with the authority to issue binding commands. Particularly relevant here are those passages that depict seemingly immoral actions sanctioned by divine command, and the fact that medieval and other classical theologians were particularly unwilling to take liberties in interpreting them. As these various considerations show, it usually hasn't merely been a simpleminded "might makes right" mentality that has served as the basis for the appeal to divine command theory, contrary to the allegations of such historical foes of voluntarism as Ralph Cudworth.[13]

Perhaps the deepest reason why divine command theory continues to hold sway in the minds of many theists is that they have a hard time conceiving of God's commands as being irrelevant to ethics, and even less so of God himself as irrelevant to morality and its foundations. The import of the Euthyphro Dilemma, for many critics of voluntarism, is that, even if God exists, he is at most relevant to ethics in filling us in on the details, inhabiting a limited epistemic role (and perhaps a prudential one). Surely, though, they insist, he's not in any way the Author of morality. Yet, many theists typically think that God is the ultimate reason for the existence of anything that *is*, so they have a hard time buying this notion that God is irrelevant to something so important and seemingly central to the human condition as morality and ethics. To the extent that they are justified in their convictions, this point carries more than just psychological weight.

What is clear, though, are these two points: (1) If the moral argument for God's existence is to hold water, the Euthyphro Dilemma and the handful of objections it raises against theistic ethics must be answered, either by abandoning voluntarism altogether or by offering a more defensible version of divine command theory; because (2) certain variants of divine command theory, such as the Ockhamistic version as Antony depicts it, need to be rejected. The problems confronting those versions seem insuperable. What is less clear, though, is whether or not the version of voluntarism that Antony gives is the only or even best version of voluntarism and whether other, non-Ockhamistic formulations may be out there that are capable of avoiding the challenges we've seen Euthyphro inspire. We will in fact argue that a more defensible version of voluntarism is not just possible, but plausible. This will require that we offer reasonable answers to the six objections that have been raised, while doing more to spell out the tenability and attractiveness of the theory, and to these tasks we will set ourselves in later chapters. But first, let's go back and examine the second horn of the Euthyphro Dilemma—which says that God commands something because it is good—and identify some of its strengths and weaknesses.


## Guided Will Theory

Divine command theory, as Louise Antony and many others depict it, says that something is good because God commands it; it's God's command that makes it good. To avoid the various problems associated with voluntarism, some might wish to switch this around and opt for the other horn of the Dilemma: God commands something because it is good. Another way to put it is that the goodness of an action is a feature that is *independent of* and that *comes before* God's commanding it. This is the nonvoluntarist horn of the Euthyphro Dilemma—what Michael Levin calls the "guided will theory" of the good, or what Antony calls "divine independence theory."

This approach neatly avoids almost all of the major criticisms we saw directed against voluntarism. God's commands are based on what's good, so they are not without reasons, and therefore not arbitrary. Since goodness conditions God's actions, God doesn't issue abhorrent commands, and calling God good is meaningful because the standards of goodness are independent of God's commands and more than just true by definition. There's no normativity objection to answer any more, either, since God's commands aren't what constitute moral goodness, and the theory in no way capitulates to the tides of moral subjectivism.

Autonomy and epistemic objections are still possible, though. For the view says that God can still issue commands, and, if he does, this may be construed as challenging our autonomy. The alleged problem remains, for on some theories of human autonomy, it constitutes an insult to human dignity to be told what to do by God, even if he didn't decree the content of the command. We can also ask whether or not it's sufficiently clear that we can know that a purported divine command is really from God, an epistemic problem. So at first blush, it doesn't appear as if a guided will approach carries obvious advantages on those two scores, even if it does avoid the other objections quite handily—so long as God is perfectly good.

If God merely registers the conditions of the moral climate, so to speak, and then factually reports such conditions to us (perhaps via imperatives), he may be the divine moral meteorologist, but he is hardly the one responsible for the content of ethics. To think otherwise is to confuse categories; we might as well blame the weather radar for the thunderstorm that ruined our tennis match. The class of actions that God commands may overlap exactly with the category of good actions without either category being definable in terms of the other, just as creatures with kidneys and creatures with a heart overlap exactly, even though the concept of having a heart is quite distinct from the concept of having kidneys.[14] On the guided will theory, God and morality are distinct, and not just conceptually; God isn't the foundation of moral goodness, but rather at most the source of some of our moral knowledge.

This is just what's troubling to many theists, however, for it would demonstrate that God is largely irrelevant to morality. Those who are convinced that the ultimate reality is a sovereign God constrained by nothing outside himself are naturally resistant to the claim that the truth and grounding of moral goodness is entirely independent of God. Moreover, they will strenuously object to the notion that moral standards obtain that are external to God and can be used to assess God. God judges us; we don't judge him, they wish to insist. The guided will view denies that God, even if he exists, is relevant to ethics in anything more than an ancillary role of filling us in on its details and, perhaps, judging us for falling short of the standard that morality independently imposes and/or rewarding good behavior.

So in the face of all this, what's an honest theist to do? The pure will theory of the good invites a number of compelling objections, but its alternative denies that God is metaphysically relevant to morality at all, which appears tantamount to a denial of classical theism altogether.

In an effort to make the guided will view more palatable, even for theists, Richard Mouw and Michael Levin try constructing cases in its favor. Theirs are versions of divine command theory that are guided will theories; so their use of "divine command" language is different from Antony's, which equated divine command theory with voluntarism. Both Mouw and Levin wish to emphasize that God's commands must be obeyed, not because they define moral goodness, but because those commands can provide us information to which we may not otherwise be privy, and can do so in a way that doesn't impugn God's status as the ultimate reality. Let's take a look at each, beginning with Mouw.

## Defenders of a Guided Will Theory

In an early article called "The Status of God's Moral Judgments,"[15] Mouw begins by flatly stating that the *Euthyphro* provides a fatal criticism of any attempt to define morality in terms of the will of God. Mouw cashes out the Euthyphro challenge in the form of what philosopher G. E. Moore originally called the "open question argument." This argument is so called because for any purported definition of, say, the good or the moral, it is an open question whether that which satisfies the definition really is good or moral.[16] If not, the definition is simply a tautology. Here's Mouw's version that we will cash out in terms of a vacuity problem: (1) If the claim that something is moral is taken to mean, by definition, that it's commanded by God, then it doesn't make sense to say that God issues a command because it is moral. (2) However, it *does* make sense to say such a thing. (3) So, the proposed definition fails.

Notice that if "moral" means "commanded by God," then to say "God issues a command because it is moral" would be equivalent to saying, "God issues a command because it is commanded by God." The former sentence makes perfect sense in a way that the second, being circular, trivially true, and thus closed, does not. So the proposed definition of morality that appeals to God's command fails. Mouw's argument is valid, meaning the conclusion follows from the premises. If the premises are true, so is the conclusion. Let's assume the conclusion *is* true; is this a problem for the divine command theorist? Arguably not, because she could say that she isn't offering a *definition* of morality so much as an *analysis* of morality. To grasp the difference, consider a parallel case, namely, the substance we call water. It's comprised of two atoms of hydrogen and one of oxygen; that's an empirically discovered essential feature of its chemical microstructure. But long before that fact was known, people drank water and bathed and swam in it and referred to it successfully and competently, oblivious to its chemical composition. What they *meant* by "water" (by way of definition) was the clear liquid found in creeks and streams, not the chemical formulation $H_2O$—though, unknown to them, what the language of their definition referred to was a liquid with that particular molecular composition. The definition of "water" was based on its outward physical features that users of the term were familiar with; what water itself consisted of essentially, discovered later, would determine the analysis of the thing itself.

What this shows is that definition and analysis are not the same, and a divine command theorist need not merely offer a definition of morality (which may leave open its essence), but an analysis (which identifies its essence). So even if God's commands fail as a definition of moral goodness, they still might provide the true analysis of its essence. In fact, we think God's commands *do* fail as a definition of morality, thereby making it possible that those who think that morality does not depend on God can nonetheless employ the concepts of morality competently, just as people could employ the concept of water competently before the discoveries of modern chemistry. Incidentally, the water example also demonstrates another subtle point relevant here: the property of *being water* and the property of *being $H_2O$* are logically distinguishable, even if water is indeed $H_2O$ and the properties pick out the same referent—this is what enables one to *say meaningfully* that God issues a command because it's moral, even if the truth remains that morality results from God's command.

At any rate, Mouw distinguishes between the *source* of morality and *justification* of morality, and he argues that God is more properly regarded as the source of our knowledge of (certain) moral propositions than as the ultimate metaphysical basis for their truth. Using his critique of voluntarism as a springboard, he goes on to provide a guided will account. Following Wallace Matson, he is fond of the analogy of an expert math teacher on whom we can rely for correct answers. God, too, can be taken to be the perfect moral teacher whom we can trust completely. His commands may convey moral truth to us that we wouldn't otherwise be able to justify. In this way Mouw tries carving out room for taking God's commands with the utmost seriousness—a commitment echoed in the writing of Thomas à Kempis, Catherine of Siena, John of Damascus, John Knox, Catherine Booth, and even the book of Ecclesiastes, which says that the whole of our human duty can be summed up in these words: "Fear God and keep his commandments."[17]

In his more recent book on divine command ethics, Mouw seems only a little less committed to a guided will account.[18] He makes the justification/source distinction in a new way, writing "we can view God's commanding something as either a right-*making* or a right-*indicating* characteristic"—which obviously echoes the voluntarist/nonvoluntarist or pure versus guided will theory distinction. Mouw now admits that some attractive arguments in favor of a voluntarist version of divine command theory have been advanced, notably by Robert Adams—which, not coincidentally, provide more of an analysis of morality than a definition.

We will consider the seminal work of Adams in later chapters, but it will be useful to mention a criticism that Mouw launches against Adams, despite his admission of the strides that Adams has made. Mouw notes that Adams makes his theory dependent on a God of a particular nature: a God who is just, cares about human flourishing, and wants us to experience abundant life. Mouw writes that such theological concessions point in the direction of a guided will theory, for they "seem to suggest that the will of God is at least being viewed as a right-indicating factor. A morally justified action will certainly be one that promotes justice, or that contributes to human flourishing. And since we believe that God is just, or that God aims at human flourishing, we can at least take God's commands as very reliable indicators that what is being commanded does indeed satisfy the requirements for moral justification."[19]

This sort of charge recurs quite a bit in divine command literature. Louise Antony, clearly a proponent of divine independence theory, says a divine command theorist must affirm this proposition: "If God had commanded us to torture innocent children, then it would have been morally right to do so."[20] She anticipates that a divine command theorist will wish to protest that the antecedent of such a counterfactual is impossible, indeed inconceivable—that God could never condone, much less command, such a thing, that it would be incompatible with his moral nature. But if the divine command theorist protests in this way, she says, then "he reveals himself to be a partisan of [divine independence theory] after all. Only the theorist who believes that right and wrong are independent of God's commands could have any basis for thinking she or he knows in advance what God would or would not command."[21] This criticism that Antony launches against divine command theorists—that they smuggle in an element of nonvoluntarism after all—bears a striking resemblance to Mouw's critique of Adams. A great deal rides on its defensibility.

Now, in Mouw's earlier article, he stressed not just that God is a *generally reliable* moral guide, but a *perfect* one. There's a necessary relation between statements of divine disapproval and negative moral judgments, for example. Why? Because if morality is objectively true, and God is morally perfect and omniscient, then God's moral pronouncements must be entirely reliable. Interestingly enough, John Stuart Mill once made a similar claim about the potential connection between God and utilitarian hedonism:

> We not uncommonly hear the doctrine of utility inveighed against as a godless doctrine. If it be necessary to say anything at all against so mere an assumption, we may say that the question depends upon what idea we have formed of the moral character of the Deity. If it be a true belief that God desires, above all things, the happiness of his creatures, and that this was his purpose in their creation, utility is not only not a godless doctrine, but more profoundly religious than any other. If it be meant that utilitarianism does not recognize the revealed will of God as the supreme law of morals, I answer, that a utilitarian who believes in the perfect goodness and wisdom of God, necessarily believes that whatever God has thought fit to reveal on the subject of morals, must fulfill the requirements of utility in a supreme degree.[22]

Mouw's main fear in speculating about connections between God's will and any specific account of the right-making comes from his reservations about John Piper's *Desiring God*, in which Piper argues that he can be, without contradiction, a Christian hedonist.[23] Mouw's criticisms of Piper are strong, but Mouw takes from the discussion that we ought to hesitate linking obedience to God's commands to any detailed account of moral justification. However we may judge his critique of Piper, we think this further inference a spurious one.

Even if Piper's defense of Christian hedonism is mistaken, this provides no reason not to construct a more successful theory of how God can figure centrally to morality.

Although we feel the force of how Mouw's nonvoluntaristic version of divine command theory would imbue God's commands with authority, we still can't shake our suspicions that he has too quickly abandoned the effort to make room for voluntarism. Since his inferences based on Piper's hedonism seem unwarranted, and since Mouw's early analysis was uninformed by later advances in the philosophy of language, his arguments against voluntarism and for his guided view aren't persuasive. Moreover, if it turns out that he (and Antony) are wrong in presuming that the only way a voluntarist can understand divine goodness is along Ockhamist lines, then that will be another reason to withhold our assent to Mouw's position. Our primary reservation is an ironic one, because Mouw's effort, by his own account, is striving to lay out a distinctively Reformed view of divine commands. Ours is as well—though Arminian rather than Calvinist—but we submit that ours will be stronger in this respect by including an element of voluntarism, for Mouw's guided will theory seems insufficiently committed to the doctrinal view of God's self-sufficiency and moral autonomy. For if an independent morality conditions God's commands, rather than vice versa, morality seems to take on an exalted status prior to and independent of God. Mouw's guided view is simply inadequate for those theists for whom God himself is to function as the regulative center and basic metaphysical principle of reality (including the ethical aspects of reality). Ironically, Mouw's "Reformed" theistic ethic isn't Reformed enough.

Despite these reservations, though, we find a particularly telling and suggestive passage in Mouw's book that is potentially quite illuminating and hopeful. He recognizes that a guided will theory just seems inadequate when juxtaposed with an exalted view of God, and he hints at the need for some deeper synthesis of the pure and guided will theories. He writes, "But in the final analysis it does not seem quite right to treat the connection between God's willing something and that something's being morally right in too loose a manner. God is, after all, perfect righteousness in the biblical scheme of things. It is difficult to put this matter concisely—but it does seem appropriate to think that in some mysterious sense the right indicating and the right making begin to merge as soon as we pause to reflect upon divine goodness."[24] We are inclined to agree and will attempt to take this suggestive line of reasoning further, starting in the next chapter as we direct our attention to the nature of God. But first, let's give due consideration to the work of Michael Levin, another guided will theorist.

Levin tries to defend the guided will view against the charge that it calls God's omnipotence or self-sufficiency into question by making God dependent on standards of value. His strategy to rebut this charge begins by providing a criterion (or sufficient condition) for what would count as a theologically troublesome dependence relation, namely, one that involves God's being created, sustained, or changed by some substance. With this criterion in place, he then insists that this is not the way guided will theory characterizes the relation between God and morality. He writes, "The only reason for including norms among the things in the world God must transcend is a conflation of the objectivity of value with the existence of values as objects.... Objectivity is one thing, objects another; truths outnumber substances."[25] In other words, objective moral truths are not substances, and therefore to recognize them has no objectionable ontological implications.[26] Consequently, these truths in no way threaten to pose a troublesome dependence relation for God.

By way of objection, though, one might say that since God remains constrained to affirm value based on the intrinsic features of things and moral facts independent of his will, isn't he dependent on those matters after all? This includes the connections between those intrinsic features of things and true moral judgments, connections that obtain apart from him. To answer this question, Levin insists that God's independence is not violated, because that which determines that God command X is not the morality of X per se, but rather God's belief in the morality of X. "If the language of action-explanation is appropriate to God at all, God's commanding X is caused by his belief that X is to be done, not by X's obligatoriness. Inasmuch as God's commands depend on God's own judgment, God has not yet been shown to be causally dependent on anything beyond himself."[27] Levin seems to be trying to point out that God is not causally determined to behave by something external to himself here; it isn't as if the abstract truths of morality exert a causal force on God's decision to command.

Although we are inclined to agree with him in a sense, one important reason we continue to harbor doubts is that Levin's conception of what constitutes a problematic dependence relation is an extremely narrow one. God's beliefs about moral facts are what they are because of the content of those facts—facts that, on the guided-will view, exist independently of God. God believes some action is moral because it *is* moral and God is omniscient, so that action's being moral causes, in some sense, God to believe that the action is moral, which leads him to command that action, it would seem. God's action is rooted in a truth that obtains independently from him, on Levin's view, which leads us to think that this threatens God's autonomy after all.

Levin offers a further response, suggesting that, if this poses a problem, then the same is true of God's other knowledge that depends on things outside of himself. Consider his knowledge that a fire engine is painted red. God knows this because the fire engine is an object outside of himself, and its being red is what causes him to know that it is. If this is not a problem, then neither should it be a problem if God knows moral truths that obtain independently of him.

Levin then anticipates a further objection: that whereas the color of the fire engine might be seen as an indirect function of God's own will—on the view that God created the world and sustains it—the same can't be said of standards of value on the guided will theory. He insists by way of rejoinder that this objection, if sound, would preclude anything like libertarian freedom. For such freedom is not controlled by God, so his knowledge of how it is exercised depends on the choices of agents who have some measure of independence. If the objection denies any independently existing fact or autonomous expression outside the realm of God's control, then libertarian freedom is precluded.

We find this reply inadequate. Levin does not answer the challenge beyond suggesting that it carries with it an unpalatable consequence. The consequence, however, is not as hard to swallow as he thinks. As theists who believe in free will—made possible and conferred by God—we don't in fact think there's good reason to believe that such freedom compromises God's independence and sovereignty. Unlike William James, we carefully distinguish all-encompassing divine micromanagement of human choices from sovereign omnipotence.[28] A believer in meaningful free will can still see her expressions of freedom as consistent with God's sovereign control, so long as that control is not understood in the Calvinistic sense of comprehensive determinism. Without God's permissive will and sustaining grace, for example, no such freedom would be possible. For suppose that God himself bestows freedom as well as defines its limits for purposes of his own. As Alvin Plantinga writes, "God may have certain aims and goals which can be attained only with the free and uncoerced cooperation of his creatures. But even here, every free action and hence every act of rebellion against him and his precepts is totally dependent on him. Our every act of rebellion has his sustaining activity as a necessary substratum; the rebel's very existence depends from moment to moment on God's affirming activity."[29] What we wish to affirm as Christian theists is not that there's nothing outside the realm of God's control in any sense at all, but rather that there is nothing entirely independent of God in every sense. Most certainly, we want to insist, something so central as moral truth is not independent of God, the stark claims of nonvoluntarism notwithstanding.

## Is the Dilemma Intractable?

This chapter has explained the Euthyphro Dilemma, and we have seen why classical theists tend to be dissatisfied with each of its horns. To affirm that something is good because God commands it is to invite a plethora of problems, from arbitrariness to vacuity to normativity objections; but to affirm instead that God commands what is already moral makes it seem as if morality is independent of God and a standard to which God himself is accountable. Is there a way to understand morality in a way that neither makes it arbitrary nor makes God irrelevant? If the moral argument is to work, there must be. Fortunately, there is, and we hope to lay out our case in this book.

Plenty of philosophers and theologians have struggled with the Euthyphro Dilemma. Besides the pure representatives on either side of the debate, others have attempted to synthesize aspects of each horn. Murray Macbeath, for example, submits that the options presented by the Dilemma aren't exhaustive. He asks us to suppose this third possibility: God might choose actions because they maximize our happiness, which might be the reason that those commands are moral. God's reason for issuing the commands he does, however, might not be because they are moral, but because he loves us. Moreover, it is not vacuous to ascribe goodness to God despite the fact that he doesn't perform actions just because they are moral, but rather because he wants to maximize our happiness. Macbeath thereby ends up rejecting both horns of the Dilemma, arguing they are not exhaustive of the possibilities. Our own approach will bear some resemblance to Macbeath's, though we won't be so averse to cashing out our view in terms of the standard categories furnished by the Dilemma—once we make and apply certain requisite distinctions too often neglected.[30]

Others have attempted to show that the Dilemma's options aren't as mutually exclusive as they have been depicted here. Richard Swinburne, for example, echoing an aspect of the thought of Duns Scotus, distinguishes between contingent moral truths dependent for their content, existence, and authority on God's active volitions and necessary moral truths that exist independently of God and his creative activity. The distinction between necessary and contingent moral truths is a very important one, and we appreciate Swinburne's effort to effect a rapprochement between objective and subjective elements of morality. However, we are less willing than Swinburne to affirm the ontological independence of necessary moral truths, since we will argue, again, that this compromises God's sovereignty in a fashion that is both philosophically and theologically troublesome.

Seven Distinctions

By way of a quick preview of what is to come, then, allow us to say in short compass what our view will be and what the basis is for answering objections to our approach. Up until now, following Antony and others, we have discussed voluntarism largely as pertaining to the moral good—or to just "morality" per se. We now must be a little more rigorous in distinguishing between the moral good and the moral right. Issues of the moral good are axiological matters, whereas issues of moral rightness are deontic matters. Not everything that is morally good is also morally right, in the sense of being morally obligatory. Giving half of your income to the poor might be morally good, but it likely is not your moral obligation; likewise with helping out at the soup kitchen five days a week. One of the great challenges of ethics is to determine which, among many good actions, are morally obligatory. On our view, it's God's commands or will (henceforth, commands broadly construed) that best enable us to determine which actions among those that are good are also morally obligatory. God's commands determine what's morally obligatory, but not what's morally good. So our view will embrace a nonvoluntarist account of the good and a voluntarist account of the right. The challenge to our theory of the good will be to show that moral goodness is not independent of God after all, despite the fact that it's independent of God's commands; and the main task for our deontic theory of moral obligation will be to show that an appeal to the authority of divine commands doesn't fall prey to the typical problems afflicting Ockhamistic voluntarism.

We will attempt to accomplish these tasks by identifying and consistently applying seven major distinctions, which we will quickly identify here but then spend much of the rest of the book explicating in further detail at appropriate junctures. The distinctions, in no particular order, are these:

First, the *analysis/definition distinction*: This distinction arose earlier in this chapter. Ours is an analysis of moral goodness and rightness, not a semantic account of the definitions of these terms. Although semantic analyses are important, their value, in our estimation, was often overstated in twentieth-century analytic philosophy. We will assign the importance to semantics that we think it deserves, but hardly accord it exclusive pride of place in our overall approach.

Second, the *good/right distinction*: We will stop referring to "morality" in general, for the most part, and instead spend time discussing either axiological issues of moral goodness, on the one hand, or deontic issues of moral permissibility and obligation, on the other. Issues of rightness and wrongness are either matters of something being wrong not to do (obligatory) or not wrong to do (permissible); our deontic talk of "rightness" will refer to obligations unless otherwise indicated. Again, we will defend nonvoluntarism on axiological matters and voluntarism on deontic ones, especially moral obligations.

Third, the *epistemology/ontology distinction*: Ontology, or metaphysics, has to do with what the truth of the matter is; epistemology is a distinct question of how we know the truth of a matter. Recall how in the first chapter we discussed how the foundations of morality might be at a greater epistemic distance from us than the truths of morality themselves. Failure to bear this possibility (and likelihood) in mind has led to a great number of confusions.

Fourth, the *difficult versus impossible distinction*: God must be recognizably good in order for most versions of the moral argument to work, but this may be consistent with God's doing or commanding things that are hard for us to reconcile with our most inviolable moral intuitions. God's being recognizably good, however, *would not* be consistent with his doing or commanding what's simply impossible to rationally square with our most nonnegotiable moral commitments. We will attempt to provide a principled line between the merely difficult and actually impossible.

Fifth, the *equivocation versus univocation distinction*: Although God's goodness must be recognizable to be rationally believed in, the insistence that God's goodness must be exactly like human goodness is a demand for univocation; whereas accepting the idea that God's goodness is still goodness even though it's not rationally recognizable as such implicates one in equivocation. Ours will be an approach that errs toward neither of those views, but, rather, stands in the long tradition of analogical predication, according to which God's goodness, though recognizable as such, is nonetheless infinitely greater than human goodness.

Sixth, the *dependence versus control distinction*: Since we will defend moral realism—the view that there are some necessary moral truths that not even God can change—we will nonetheless argue, contra Swinburne, that such truths still depend on God in a very important sense. The conflation of dependence and control has led some mistakenly to infer that theistic ethics leads to a loss of moral objectivity.

Seventh, and lastly, the *conceivability versus possibility distinction*: That various scenarios might be conceivable—such as God's commanding us to torture children for fun—is not enough to show, so we will argue, that such a state of affairs is genuinely possible, at least if God is essentially morally perfect.

Together these distinctions, consistently applied, will provide the necessary resources to defend theistic ethics against objections and bolster the moral argument for God's existence. That last distinction, though, broaches the next topic for our investigation: What is the operative conception of God in this volume? We have said that we are Christian theists, and Reformed in our perspective, but more now needs to be said, so the next few chapters will do just that.

# 3

# Naming the Whirlwind

Why is there this almost universal moral sense? Why do we consider that "good" is a better thing than "evil"? Surely this recognition of good, so deeply rooted and so universal, is another far from negligible pointer to Reality.

—J. B. Phillips[1]

In his most recent diatribe against the God of the Bible, Richard Dawkins holds nothing back in his description of Deity—issuing a litany of moral charges made all the more striking if we imagine him reading the list in that charming accent of his: "The God of the Old Testament is arguably the most unpleasant character in all fiction: jealous and proud of it; a petty, unjust, unforgiving control-freak; a vindictive, bloodthirsty ethnic cleanser; a misogynistic, homophobic, racist, infanticidal, genocidal, filicidal, pestilential, megalomaniacal, sado-masochistic, capriciously malevolent bully."[2] Perhaps it's no surprise that Dawkins is less than impressed by the moral argument for God's existence!

We will take up some of the moral objections to the God of the Bible in a later chapter. Before we do that, however, it is important to be more explicit about our understanding of that God. We aim to do so in this chapter by laying out the general features of the God of classical theism, the God not only of Abraham, Isaac, and Jacob—but also of Anselm.

The moral argument is practically unique among the arguments from natural theology, in furnishing us warrant to infer not just that

God exists, but that a God of a particular character exists—a God who is perfectly good. The issue of what God is like, as opposed to the issue of whether he is even real, is obviously crucial in any effort to avoid the vices of voluntarism. What made Euthyphro so vulnerable to criticism in the original Socratic dialogue was his belief in quarreling, contentious, morally deficient gods. Character is key. This chapter will talk about the goodness of God, as God is classically understood, along with some of his other salient features. A later chapter will explore the metaphysical connection between God and goodness, which is a related, but different matter.

It is perhaps too often the case that philosophical discussions rest content with the minimalist question pertaining to God's bare existence, an approach that seems to committed believers in God to be existentially and epistemically thin at best. To them this is not unlike confining ethics to talk of heart-wrenching and genuinely baffling moral dilemmas while leaving those clearest acts of selfless beneficence out of the picture altogether, as if a perusal of the periphery yields more insight than an examination of the core. To understand theistic ethics, one must get beyond the mere "believe-that" locution where God is concerned and arrive at the "believe-in" locution. If God is real, then we must strive not for mere propositional knowledge or justified belief *that* God exists, but a personal acquaintance with the God who *does* exist—if such acquaintance is possible. The nature of any such relationship depends on who God is.

Now, we have begun to lay out the moral evidence for God's existence, and part of advancing those lines of argument is defending them against various Euthyphro-inspired objections. Typically such rejoinders are thought to be entirely defensive, but in this context they're more than that, because our effort to respond to objections will actually bolster the moral argument, not just for God's existence, but for a particular God's existence. We are not just defending the mere possibility of a theistic ethic, but its rational plausibility, and the effectiveness of theism to provide better explanations of moral facts than its alternatives. Answering objections to theistic ethics provides further rational warrant for the moral argument project, and if we see that a particular conception of God lends itself better to answering such objections, this will show that the moral argument, to the extent that it provides evidence for God's existence, provides evidence for that particular conception of God.

## The God of the Philosophers

We need to introduce some terminology and distinctions from the philosophy of language to facilitate our analysis, in particular the fundamental distinction between a *title* and a *name*. Some of the points we draw from this distinction are fairly subtle, but they are helpful for making our position as explicit as it needs to be.

If someone says that "God wouldn't be God unless he were all-knowing," then "God" is taken to be a title, the holder of which needs to fulfill certain criteria, such as omniscience. An atheist could affirm this, which means that using "God" as a title does not in any way commit one to his actual existence. Now take the claim that "God is omniscient." This too could be construed as another example where "God" is used as a title, but it might more naturally be spoken instead by a believer who is affirming something about God himself, a being he believes really exists. "God" is used in the latter case more as a name than as a title.

Each usage—"God" as name or title—enables us to accentuate an aspect of God's goodness traditionally understood. Taking "God" as a title, "God must be good" means that, necessarily, any being who qualifies as God must be good. Consider this analogy: Necessarily, anyone who is president of the United States is at least thirty-five years old. So the affirmation "God must be good"—like the affirmation "The president of the United States must be at least thirty-five years old"—is not about a particular being since it is consistent with there being no God at all, but rather about the requirements to satisfy the office of Deity, were any being to do so. This analysis of goodness is called "de dicto," from *dictum*, or the proposition involved, namely, *God is good*. Such a proposition is necessarily true; it can't be false, on a de dicto analysis of necessary divine goodness.

Using "God" as a name, in contrast, enables us to say something about the particular being identified as God himself. "God must be good," if "God" is a name, is saying that God himself is good, which can only be true if God actually exists. This is divine goodness construed "de re"—from *res*, meaning object; something is said of the individual who is God himself. To say that God himself is necessarily or essentially good is to affirm the moral perfection of a particular being—the being who is God.

We are going to assume that "God" is indeed a name, licensing an affirmation of his goodness understood de re; at the same time, we are going to assume that "God" also carries with it, one way or another, descriptive moral content, not unlike a title, licensing an analysis of divine goodness understood de dicto as well.[3] Now, what sort of God is likely to be the Author of morality? The late Cambridge philosopher A. C. Ewing once wrote that a being in whom the whole moral law resides could hardly fail to be perfectly good.[4] A morally deficient god or set of gods wouldn't be as good an explanation of moral facts as a morally perfect God would be. But what sort of non-Ockhamistic God is perfectly morally good, understood de re?

The God who is maximally perfect in every way, including morally, is often identified as the so-called "God of the philosophers," the God as Anselm conceived him: the possessor of the great-making properties like omnipotence, omniscience, and omnibenevolence. This "Anselmian" God is the God of classical theism, and the content of this theological view is typically thought to derive from the a priori deliverances of reason, rather than from experience or empirical considerations. God on this view is the greatest possible being who exemplifies all the great-making properties to the greatest maximal degree and to the greatest extent to which they're mutually consistent with one another; in other words, to the "greatest compossible degree."

To what extent does the moral argument point to the Anselmian God?[5] Well, there is an obvious affinity between God's perfect goodness and the Anselmian attribute of omnibenevolence, but we want to suggest that there is something else important to note here. In particular, the moral argument may give us another good reason to believe in God's necessary existence. Of course, the ontological argument and variants of the cosmological argument are widely recognized as entailing God's necessary existence, and though we think versions of such arguments are powerful, we won't pursue them here. But we would like to offer what we consider a third compelling reason to think that God exists necessarily—made all the more compelling when combined with these other pieces of natural theology. One of the key features of "moral realism" is the existence of necessary moral truths, moral truths that couldn't be otherwise, can't help but be true—truths we argued earlier that are better explained by the existence of God than by Platonism. And we contend that it certainly appears more likely that, if God is the ultimate metaphysical foundation of morality, and part of morality involves necessity, the Author must exist necessarily as well. We will lay this out in more detail later, and we realize that objections can be raised at this point. For present purposes, it suffices to suggest that, if the moral argument works, it may well offer evidence not just that God exists and is good, but that God necessarily exists and is perfectly good—stronger claims that move the operative conception of Deity into closer proximity with the God of Anselm.[6] Moreover, as already mentioned, if Anselmianism proves itself best adept at answering the objections to theistic ethics, that will bolster the case for it all the more. As we anticipate showing just this, we can at this point say, without involving ourselves in vicious circularity, that the predominant conception of God operative in our forthcoming analysis will be distinctly Anselmian.

## The God of Christianity

Our approach is Anselmian, and it is also distinctively Christian, but are these consistent? The Anselmian tradition is thought to be an a priorist tradition, a tradition built on the deliverances of reason and rationality. By contrast, the more specifically Christian points of theology derive either from explicit biblical teachings or further inferences made on the basis of such teachings and other pieces of human knowledge—so the biblical tradition is the more experiential or a posteriori. Such tenets of classical Christian teachings about God include Trinity, atonement, incarnation, and resurrection. A commitment to take the teachings of the Bible seriously, of course, invites challenges like those of Dawkins listed above—how do we make sense of the conquest narratives, the binding of Isaac, and the like? Is a synthesis possible between the a priorist tradition of Anselm and the experiential tradition of Christian scripture?

God is, on the biblical view, intimately connected with the history of the world, interacting with it and accomplishing his purposes, whereas, on the Anselmian construal, he is sometimes perceived as arid and sterile by comparison. In Tertullian we find a religious believer favoring the biblical idea and rejecting the God of the philosophers, for "What does Athens have to do with Jerusalem, or darkness with light?" he famously queried.[7] Athens for him represented the philosophical ideas of men, whereas Jerusalem represented God's revelation.

With equal vigor, proponents of the more philosophical conception of God often find the God of the Old and New Testaments to be, frankly, an embarrassment—with his bloody sacrifices and warnings of brimstone. Here is how J. L. Tomkinson, a philosopher who is squarely in the a priori camp, analyzes the problem that arises when there is a perceived conflict between the two traditions:

> The problem ... of reconciling the results of philosophical theology with the claims of some revelation must always, insofar as philosophical theology is concerned, lie with the advocates of the revelation in question. It is hardly incumbent upon the philosopher to demonstrate the compatibility of his findings with whatever may be advanced as the fruit of some revelation. This is an important methodological point. If an analysis of the received concept of God, i.e. as supreme being, leads to a conclusion which seems at odds with those of revelation, the former may claim the credentials of reason, the analysis being open to inspection by all concerned. If and insofar as the supporting reasoning seems cogent it has a claim on us logically prior to that of the interpretation of some special experience.[8]

There is a major irony in contrasting Anselmianism with a Christian conception of God, because Anselm himself was deeply Christian. To be fully

Anselmian is to allow not just the dictates of perfect being theology to function centrally, but no less so the deliverances of scripture. In this connection, Tom Morris writes that "as a Christian theologian, Anselm accepted the documents of the Bible and the traditions of the church as providing vitally important and inviolable standards for theological reflection. This is the other side of Anselm, not quite so widely appreciated in modern times."[9]

A narrowly Anselmian conception of God alone underdetermines for the devout Christian the proper content of religious belief. It may well be true that the Anselmian picture of God can't be fully derived from scriptural teachings alone, but it's equally true that important and specific content of Christian revelation is not contained in narrow Anselmianism. As long as the traditions don't conflict and aren't mutually exclusive, there is no need for the content of the one to entail the other before coming together. The differences between them might be precisely what enables the one to augment the other in important ways. Tomkinson's earlier challenge is not in the spirit of Anselmianism rightly understood, but of a distorted caricature of just the a priorist half of it. As Tom Morris points out, Anselm, like so many other medieval theologians, brought a concern for both rational cogency and biblical integrity to his theological work, and we aim to do the same. Anselmianism includes both specific and general revelation, integrating and synthesizing insights from both the experiential and a priorist traditions, offering us a philosophically and theologically powerful way to defend theistic ethics against various objections. In the rest of this chapter, we will do just that, beginning with a challenge against God's moral goodness, then a challenge against God's perfect goodness.

## A Thomistic Challenge against God's Moral Goodness

Brian Davies, a Thomistic scholar, argues in compelling fashion that Aquinas's understanding of the goodness of God is less a moral matter than a matter of God's perfection as a being who has no ontological deficiencies, and who is also the proper desire for human beings. He makes this case especially in his chapter on God's moral standing in his book *The Reality of God and the Problem of Evil*.[10] Davies wishes to argue that it isn't proper to characterize God as morally good—not because Davies thinks that God is bad or evil, but because he thinks that God's goodness is best understood in terms other than morality.

Davies is right to emphasize that goodness is more than just a moral notion. Even Robert Adams in his defense of a modified divine command theory emphasizes that goodness is much broader in scope than the merely moral.[11] To our thinking, Davies is also entirely right to insist that God is not such that he must consult an independent moral rule book before he acts and acts justly. What Davies is rejecting there is the sort of guided will theory we saw earlier, and we heartily agree with Davies that God does not consult an ontologically independent set of moral standards before acting justly, righteously, and the like.

We also readily concur with Davies's further point that we could use some real epistemic humility in supposing what it is that God can and can't morally do. We should raise such questions about what God can and can't do only with fear and trembling. John Beversluis once wrote C. S. Lewis and asked about the atrocities in the Old Testament, and in his response Lewis himself made this very point. He acknowledged "grave dangers" in calling Joshua's apparent atrocities and treacheries into moral question. And he noted that "some things which seem to us bad may be good. But we must not consult our consciences by trying to feel a thing good when it seems to us totally evil. We can only pray that if there is an invisible goodness hidden in such things, God, in his good time will enable us to see it. If we need to. For perhaps sometimes God's answer might be 'What is that to thee?'"[12]

So we can happily go along with Davies when he argues that God is God, that he is the Creator and not one of us, that he doesn't need to consult a moral rule book, and that on his reading of Aquinas, God is rationally thought to be good, in an important sense, in virtue of being the proper object of our deepest desires. However, his further claim, on these bases, that it's improper to call God either morally good or a moral agent poses quite a challenge to the Anselmian depiction of God as morally good, indeed morally perfect.

To be clear, Davies is not saying that God is evil, but that the characterization of him as morally good is somehow inappropriate, smacking of anthropomorphism. For, again, God doesn't need to consult an independent moral set of guidelines. In addition, Davies argues, the goodness of God, in the history of philosophy and theology until rather recently, has usually been less a matter of moral goodness than (1) a matter of ontological completeness and (2) God as the proper object of human desires.

Nonetheless, a few points of Davies's program strike us as less than persuasive. In responding to atheologians discussing the problem of evil, Davies wants to say that God, the Creator of all who is perfect in every respect, can't even conceivably be thought to, say, will evil for evil's sake. We can appreciate his point, along with the inherent foolishness of "judging God." Davies is entirely right in pointing out the flippant attitude with which too many people, theists and atheists alike, speak of God as beholden to a moral standard independent of him by which they feel justified to cast aspersions on the divine character for failing to live up to their expectations. (Perhaps Dawkins comes to mind!)

We might, however, suggest that a distinction is in order here. Engaging in thought experiments about what God can (and can't) do can be highly useful, even if an impeccable God indeed can't conceivably sin. The exercise is useful not just for purposes of generating conceptual clarity, but for doing solid philosophy and theology. Davies introduces a theology trump card that, in our estimation, prematurely brings to a grinding halt potentially fruitful thought experiments or explorations into implications gleaned from analyses that temporarily entertain states of affairs or divine commands contrary to fact. In our zeal to avoid "judging God," we can neglect to remember that there can be, and not uncommonly are, false notions associated with God that get packed into the word by some, and our philosophizing can help adjudicate between the resulting conflicting views about who God is.

Not every conception of God features a being in whom there's no shadow of darkness or vestige of malice—despite the legitimacy of a de dicto analysis of God's perfect goodness. But the classical monotheistic and distinctively Christian God *is* impeccable, morally perfect, perfectly loving, and the like. Davies, though casting God as neither a moral agent nor morally good, nonetheless admits that the Bible affirms that God is holy, righteous, just, faithful, merciful, and loving. Davies, though, insists that it's inappropriate to say that God is "morally good." In truth, this seems to strain credulity, and smacks of a game of semantics—this trotting out of the category of God as "perfectly complete" and castigating of the category of moral goodness, a much less obscure idea. It's true that God doesn't consult a moral rule book; and, yes, God retains prerogatives we do not have, morally speaking, and God can challenge many of our basic moral commitments. But how from such facts as these do we effect the Copernican paradigm shift to deny God's moral goodness? Much of Davies's analysis of Aquinas is consistent with the best work in theistic ethics over the last several decades, but this further denial of God's goodness is exactly where Davies is most vulnerable to criticism, in our estimation. The way he defines his terms, he's not exactly wrong, for we would admit that God is neither morally good nor a moral agent in the way that Davies casts such notions; but the sober fact is that his definition of moral goodness in particular is overly narrow and lacks sufficient motivation. So, by our lights, it betrays a failure of conversational cooperation.

Consider this sort of judgment, which we think most theists would endorse: "If God told me to torture children for fun, then that would be evidence that God isn't good." Those of us who affirm this aren't "judging God"—nor holding his divine feet to the fire or presuming that morality is independent of God or making God just like us or anything of the kind. We're making a substantive claim about a real entailment of divine love, identifying a form of behavior fundamentally at odds with what our words mean—in an effort to show that unless we retain the capacity to affirm the nontrivial truth of such a conditional, our discourse about God's love and goodness is rendered vacuous. We fall right into one of the traps of the Euthyphro Dilemma.

Davies knows this. When we asked the question, "If we thought that God was in the business of torturing people for fun, or issuing a command for us to do something irremediably awful, wouldn't we have better reason to think that God isn't good or that we missed God than that we heard him rightly?" Davies replied, "Yes, indeed."[13] Now, it's true that he then wants to go on and insist that this is contrary to fact and, given God's existence as Creator and the like, quite inconceivable. But the point is that we've got to retain the ability philosophically to say that there are some things morally beyond the pale. There are some things that God, if he's a God of love and righteousness, simply cannot do. His inability to do these things isn't because he's constrained by an external moral standard, but by his perfect nature. And there are some things that love positively constrains, thus fleshing out determinate content in affirmations of God's moral goodness. And if we can know that we can affirm such traits of God, what point is served in denying that they represent his moral goodness?

If God is the very locus of moral truth and authority, such language as applied to God functions in an importantly different respect from when it applies to us, it's true; but the new contribution by Davies here is the further inference that, owing to such distance between God and us, and to his unique status as Creator and as an ontologically complete being, God is not properly understood as morally good at all. We think that this claim is wrongly predicated on an overly narrow view of what moral goodness means.

It's far from clear that Davies's inference is warranted in any way by the category of the "completely actual"—a Thomistic notion that in truth is not nearly as transparent or pertinent as the more straightforward category of moral perfection. There are some commands and there are some states of affairs, in principle, beyond the pale, beyond which we wouldn't be reasonable or rational to call God good or perfect or trustworthy; such divine commands or states of affairs allowed by God may well represent counterfactuals, false scenarios; we think they do. Indeed, we think they represent counteressentials—impossible states of affairs. Davies and we agree on that, but nonetheless there must be some such identifiable commands or situations in order for our ascriptions of goodness and perfection to God to avoid charges of arbitrariness and vacuity.

A defense of God's goodness can go through by talking of implications of God's love, righteousness, holiness, and the like, all thoroughly biblical terms. God's goodness may be more than moral, but it's not less. What Davies substantively denies we can feel comfortable to deny as well: that God is beholden to an external morality, is just like us, and the like. But none of that seems essential to what moral goodness or moral agency requires. So at the end of the day we are left with the nagging suspicion that, having invoked this metaphysical category of perfect completeness, Davies then, through a subtle semantic maneuver, ends up denying rational ascriptions of moral goodness to God in a way that invites unnecessary misunderstanding and leaves the door open to things that should never be admitted.

## A Challenge against God's Perfect Goodness

The view that God is necessarily good implies the Christian doctrine of God's impeccability, the notion not only that God *does not* sin, but also *cannot* sin. This idea has come under fire from various quarters. Even some otherwise orthodox and traditionally minded theists have felt the perceived force of these objections and have begun rethinking their allegiance to the doctrine.[14] Rejecting the doctrine, however, carries with it a rather high philosophical cost that we should not be willing to pay, especially after we spend some time examining the arguments against impeccability. Critics of impeccability advance several arguments against it—arguments from God's power, freedom, or praiseworthiness, for example—but the paradigmatic argument we will refute is based on the notion of conceivability. Appropriately enough, we will call this argument the "conceivability argument," which can be put like this:

1. God's sinning is conceivable.
2. If God's sinning is conceivable, then God's sinning is possible.
3. If God's sinning is possible, then God is not impeccable.
4. So, God is not impeccable.

One salient example of this sort of argument comes from Nelson Pike's "Omnipotence and God's Ability to Sin."[15] Here Pike argues that since God is omnipotent he cannot be said to be essentially sinless. At first sight, Pike's argument appears to be based not in conceivability considerations so much as omnipotence considerations. But this is too hasty, as Thomas V. Morris points out: "Some criticize [Pike] for relying on too simplistic and inadequate an understanding of what the property of omnipotence involves. And it is true that he operates with a very unrefined conception. But the real problem with his argument is that he makes too quick a transition from the claim that a certain sort of states of affairs is (in some sense) conceivable to the stronger assumption that it represents a genuine, broadly logical, possibility."[16]

Premise (3) of the argument—if God's sinning is possible, then God is not impeccable—is beyond dispute, for impeccability analytically requires an inability to sin. The more controversial premises are (1) and (2)—God's sinning is conceivable, and if so then God's sinning is possible, respectively. We submit that the notion of conceivability is such that at least one of those first two premises ought to be rejected.

Premise (2), which claims that the conceivability of God's sinning leads to the possibility of God's sinning, is of course an instance of the more general claim that the possibility of something logically follows from its conceivability. That is, if we can conceive of Martians, then Martians are possible, a principle which we can generalize and dub the "conceivability principle." Now here is the issue we need to pursue in a fair bit of detail: Is the conceivability principle true? As we will see, our judgment on this has important implications for our argument.

The principle has had its notable and luminous advocates. No less than David Hume wrote the following: "It is an established maxim in metaphysics, that whatever the mind clearly conceives includes the idea of possible existence, or in other words, that nothing we imagine is absolutely impossible. We can form the idea of a golden mountain, and from there conclude that such a mountain may actually exist. We can form no idea of a mountain without a valley, and therefore regard it as impossible."[17] Descartes too seems to have accepted the principle in several passages of his own.[18] More recently, David Chalmers has advanced a version of the principle as well, generating quite a bit of attention in the process.[19]

The notion of conceivability is notoriously fuzzy. With respect to propositions, what is meant by the sort of conceivability that has at least some hope of entailing genuine possibility? Suppose we begin with a simple notion indeed, specifically, that which is conceivable by *us* (the authors). For all most people know, Goldbach's conjecture—"Every even integer greater than 2 can be written as the sum of two primes"—could be true or could be false. However, not knowing the truth value of such a proposition and conceiving of its falsehood does not necessarily make for a genuine possibility that it is false, since if it is true it is necessarily true, and if it is false it is necessarily false. Our not knowing a proposition is true does not mean we are conceiving of its falsehood, but only that it is epistemically possible for us that the proposition in question is false. Epistemic possibility does not make for the sort of conceivability we're after.[20]

Conceivability is more likely connected with what we can think of with a fair bit of clarity. The difficult question of just how much clarity is called for is of course one reason for the fuzziness of the concept of conceivability.

Conceivability on this construal is something like thinkability or imaginability. If we can think of something clearly and distinctly, we can conceive of it.

What becomes almost immediately obvious on reflection is that conceivability so understood fails to be a necessary condition for genuine possibility. For our noetic limitations preclude our ability to apprehend or imagine a wide range of propositions that are altogether true but whose complexity renders them beyond our ken. There may be many possible truths that are simply not imaginable or conceivable by us due to their complexity and our noetic limitations. The more relevant question is whether our capacity to conceive the truth of a proposition is sufficient to show the possibility of the state of affairs stipulated by that proposition. There are some consistently describable states of affairs that we cannot imagine, but are there other states of affairs we *can* imagine that *are not* consistently describable?

We are inclined to think that we can imagine with a fairly intense level of vividness the truth of certain propositions that ultimately are not consistently describable after all—and so not possible, like the falsehood of a mathematical theorem. The insistence to the contrary seems a bit question-begging to us. To say that we cannot very well be clearly imagining a proposition's truth because, as it turns out, it is not possibly true seems just to be restating the conviction that conceivability entails possibility in a different form.

If we are wrong in thinking that we can conceive of an ultimately inconsistent proposition, then it is at least still possible that conceivability entails possibility. But nothing much rides on this for present purposes, for this reason: either we can mistakenly conceive of the false truth value of Goldbach's conjecture or we cannot. If we can, then the conceivability principle is false and the conceivability argument unsound. For the conceivability principle, together with our conceiving of something necessarily false, would imply that something is possibly true when it is not.

But even if we cannot mistakenly conceive of the false truth value of Goldbach's conjecture, the interesting fact remains that intelligent people have mistakenly thought they could. Michael Hooker, for instance, wrote this: "I think that a sufficiently informed person is in a position to conceive the truth or falsity of the conjecture. I think that I, for example, can conceive of, or imagine, Goldbach's conjecture being false. Certainly I can imagine the discovery by computer of a counterexample to the conjecture, the attendant discussion of it, the subsequent revision of philosophical examples, etc."[21] Hooker himself almost immediately admits that there may be some acceptable analysis of "p is conceivable" that avoids such counterexamples to the conceivability principle. His hesitation in rejecting the principle owes to "its importance...as a philosophical bedrock....Virtually the whole history of metaphysics pivots on the principle."[22]

But the instructive point stands: it certainly seems to many intelligent thinkers that they can meaningfully conceive of the false truth value of Goldbach's conjecture. For even while they admit that they might be wrong and that they may be unable to conceive of this after all, what coaxes this admission out of them is not any intuition about conceiving, but rather the facts of the matter. In other words, it is nonnegotiably accepted that Goldbach's conjecture is true only if it is necessarily true, and if they insist that conceivability entails possibility, they must admit that they may not be able to conceive of what they thought they could conceive after all, namely, the wrong truth value of the conjecture. For if they can conceive the wrong truth value, and conceivability entails possibility, then the wrong truth value is possible, but it isn't possible, because if the conjecture is true then it's necessarily true. What this shows is that it is no easy matter, sometimes, to determine whether or not we can actually conceive of the truth of a proposition or its falsehood. Conceivability remains at present (and perhaps intrinsically is) simply too fuzzy a notion on which to base ambitious conclusions, particularly metaphysical conclusions.

To recapitulate, someone like Hooker, we are imagining, sincerely believes that he is able to conceive of the falsehood of Goldbach's conjecture. Suppose it turns out that the conjecture is true. In such a case, something has to go: either Hooker's ability to have conceived of the conjecture's falsehood, or the conceivability principle itself. They cannot both stand, since together they entail a (necessarily) false conclusion. Since the epistemic possibility obtains that there is a sense of conceivability according to which he was not actually conceiving of the wrong truth value of Goldbach's conjecture, Hooker admits that for all he knows he may well not have been conceiving of what he thought he was after all.

On such occasions it is arguable that we are unable to distinguish between a real conceiving and a pseudo-conceiving apart from an appeal to the actual realm of modalities on which these conceivings or alleged conceivings are supposed to shed light. The subjective phenomenological experiences of those persons whose conceiving is veridical remain virtually indistinguishable from the experiences of those whose conceivings are illusory. This recognition renders the conceivability principle, even if true, epistemically impotent to imbue in us much confidence in the needed claim that we are experiencing a real conceiving. So even if the principle is true, and perhaps especially if so, counterexamples to alleged conceivings abound that should radically shake our confidence in determining when we are actually experiencing a genuine conceiving on which to base an inference.

For our purposes, then, here is the central point of this discussion. We simply do not have sufficient reason to be confident both in the conceivability principle and in our ability to conceive of God's sinning, despite the initial plausibility of the argument, a finding that poses an intractable difficulty for the conceivability argument against impeccability. Recall to mind the argument:

1. God's sinning is conceivable.
2. If God's sinning is conceivable, then God's sinning is possible.
3. If God's sinning is possible, then God is not impeccable.
4. So, God is not impeccable.

Suppose it is true that the conceivability of God's sinning entails the possibility of God's sinning, possibility in the sense of broadly logical or metaphysical possibility. Now suppose someone comes along and insists that he can conceive of God's sinning. It seems easy enough. But now look at just a smattering of the profound philosophical conclusions that without much effort could be shown to leap forth: God cannot be essentially sinless; God is not impeccable; there is a possible world in which God, if he exists, sins; divine command theorists cannot consistently embrace the existence of necessary moral truths; and so forth. Unfortunately, philosophy is not that easy.

To the contrary, once (2) is affirmed, the Goldbach case should give us pause to invest much confidence in the claim that we can conceive of God's sinning. We have learned that the difference between a genuine conceiving and a pseudo-conceiving is sufficiently subtle that sometimes nothing short of an appeal to the way the world really is and can be is likely to enable us to distinguish them. Surely we can conceive of propositions being true in the vicinity of (1)—an assertion that some Cartesian demon or Humean demigod might behave morally reprehensibly. But suppose for a moment that an omnibenevolent God exists who is essentially sinless. Can we really conceive of such an entity sinning? Are we able to conceive in the requisitely clear way that an essentially sinless being can sin? Here we are inclined to echo Davies and deny that any such thing is even conceivable. Does entertaining such a confused notion of an impeccable God sinning seem worthy of an ideal cognizer? It seems unlikely. Truth be told, even a mere *de dicto* analysis of impeccability logically precludes it.[23]

The findings of the direct reference theorists like Hilary Putnam and Saul Kripke that deny the conceivability principle are enough to persuade great numbers of philosophers not to invest too much epistemic power in the fuzzy modality of conceivability. "Water is XYZ" satisfies the constraint of formal consistency or consistent describability, but is nevertheless usually thought to be necessarily false. As Brian Loar has written, "[i]t has become more or less standard at least to entertain a distinction between conceivability and possibility:

we cannot proceed unqualifiedly from conceivability to real possibility."[24] Recent work by David Chalmers has, however, resurrected some of the old faith in a new conceivability principle and bolstered the confidence of some who remain skeptical of *de re* necessity and the like.[25] Even Loar admits that deploying the standard rejection of the conceivability principle as an argument against Chalmers's impressive account is a bit too hasty. In this chapter we have delimited the scope of the discussion just to the conceivability argument against impeccability in the attempt to show that even the acceptance of the (dubious) conceivability principle does not vindicate the conceivability argument. Irrespective of the traditional construal of conceivability for which we opt, the prospects seem dim that the conceivability argument against impeccability will work. Either the conceivability principle is false, or we are left with little confidence in our ability to conceive of an Anselmian God sinning—or both.[26]

This chapter has defended an Anselmian conception of God against charges that it is unbiblical and that it wrongly predicates moral goodness and perfect moral goodness of God. In the next chapter we will further clarify aspects of God that we think are most consistent with the moral argument and then return to this connection between God and goodness, especially the nature of the necessary connection between them and their dependence relation. We hope to show that a rational affirmation of God's goodness does not require either Ockhamism or a complete divine independence theory.[27]

# 4

# A Reformed Tradition
# Not Quite Right

"Who did you pass on the road?" the King went on, holding his
hand out to the messenger for some hay.
"Nobody," said the messenger.
"Quite right," said the King; "this young lady saw him too. So of
course Nobody walks slower than you."

—Lewis Carroll[1]

Carroll's wonderful passage here is a classic case of equivocation:
using a term in the same context in more than one sense. The
importance of avoiding equivocation is a big reason that, though we
strongly wish to affirm God's sovereignty, we must reject a Calvinist
paradigm of theology. In the previous chapter we talked about God's
goodness, indeed his perfect goodness, and in the next chapter we
will discuss God's necessary goodness in more detail; in this chapter
we will talk about how important it is that God's goodness is *recognizable*. For in order for the moral argument to provide rational reason
to believe in God, God's goodness must be recognizable. Otherwise
we're using the word "good" to refer to something that isn't recognizably good, and that sort of equivocation is irrational. So the argument
we offer in this chapter is a moral and epistemic argument against
Calvinism.

This is a debate largely internal to the Christian church, and
there are plenty of committed Christians on both sides of this
particular divide. We don't want to exaggerate the importance of

the debate, but it's quite relevant to a discussion of the moral argument for God's existence. For we will argue that Calvinism and the moral argument are not a good fit at all, for several reasons, and that Arminianism provides a much better Reformed account of divine sovereignty, one aspect of which is a picture of theistic ethics at least in the vicinity of what we are attempting to construct in this book.

The Calvinism/Arminianism debate is, among other things, a battle over the right understanding of the sovereignty and love of God. Calvinists, following John Calvin, his follower Theodore Beza, and the "TULIP" of the Synod of Dort (1618–19), affirm that all human beings are born dead in sin, that God unconditionally by his will alone elects some to salvation, that Jesus died just for those elect,[2] that God's grace in those lives is irresistible, and that the elect will persevere to the end, that their salvation is entirely secure.

By way of contrast, classical Arminians, following Dutch theologian James (Jacob) Arminius (1560–1609), affirm that we are dead in our sins and unable to so much as repent of sin apart from God's grace, but that God's election is conditional, not unconditional, depending on God's foreknowledge of (divinely conferred) libertarian free choice. Jesus, they believe, died for all, and God's grace is universal in the sense that God offers a real chance for salvation to everyone, but it's resistible because people can turn down God's offer of saving grace and be damned. Arminians differ on the question of whether salvation, once attained, is forever unconditionally secure.[3]

The most overt difference between Calvinists and Arminians is the issue of God's election, whether it is unconditional or conditional. For if it's unconditional, then the question of which individual persons are ultimately saved and which are not is a matter of God's sovereign choice alone, whereas if God's election is conditional on human choice, then everyone, by God's grace, has a genuine option either to avail themselves of God's offer of salvation in Christ or not.

The most fundamental divide between these two traditions, however, as we shall see, concerns the moral nature of God, particularly how his love and goodness are understood. While differences over divine sovereignty, election, and correspondingly different accounts of human freedom are often taken to be the most basic points of dispute, in reality, the deepest conflict concerns the very character of God. And that is why this great theological dispute has so much bearing on the moral argument.

In this chapter we intend to offer a philosophical case against the Calvinistic conception of God's unconditional election. The case will provide some evidence in favor of a more classically Arminian conception, but our primary aim is to show that the Calvinistic construal is philosophically weak, first and foremost in value theory but in other aspects as well. If our argument is successful, we will thereby provide Calvinists excellent prima facie reason to go back to the Bible, where they can discover an interpretation of divine sovereignty and election that doesn't fly directly in the face of general revelation.


## Philosophy as Adjudicator

We think of our argument as unapologetically appealing to general revelation, which means that we reject the claim that philosophy can or should be ignored in the process of figuring out the answers to such questions. The Protestant principle of *sola scriptura* is sometimes today misunderstood to imply that clear thinking and good reason play no part in figuring out God's revealed truths. The primacy of the Bible in terms of its theological truth is taken to imply that exegesis, biblical interpretation, carefully isolated from any other sources of insight, ought to be able to answer any and all theological disputes that may arise.

The Bible itself is sometimes thought to teach just such skepticism about the value of philosophy. We are warned not to let anyone take us captive through hollow and deceptive philosophy, which depends on human tradition and the basic principles of this world rather than on Christ.[4] And I Corinthians 1:20 asks, "Where is the wise man? Where is the scholar? Where is the philosopher of this age? Has not God made foolish the wisdom of the world?" We saw in the last chapter that the early Christian church leader Tertullian asked, "What has Jerusalem to do with Athens, the Church with the Academy, the Christian with the heretic?"[5] Martin Luther echoed a similar sentiment: "Philosophy understands naught of divine matters. I do not say that men may not teach and learn philosophy; I approve thereof, so that it may be within reason and moderation. Let philosophy remain within her bounds, as God has appointed, and let us make use of her as of a character in a comedy; but to mix her with divinity may not be endured."[6]

Skepticism toward philosophy often reaches its fever pitch in the Calvinism/Arminianism debate, where disputants on both sides of the divide often eschew the deliverances of philosophy and insist that the question must be settled on biblical and exegetical grounds alone. Any hint of even bringing philosophical analysis into the conversation is thought to be anathema, abandoning the authority of scripture to provide reliable revelation.

Here we need to draw an important distinction. Whereas biblical authority trumps in the realm of theological norms, there are more basic philosophical processes at play that hold logical priority in the realm of basic epistemology.

For example, trust in the reliability of scripture in the first place assumes trust in the experiences of those biblical writers whose written words God genuinely inspired. Without the requisite trust in those experiences, we are left without rational conviction in the authority of the Bible. Or take the choice of the Bible as authoritative rather than, say, the Koran; this selection, to be rational, requires that we have good reasons for believing the Bible to be God's real revelation. Appeal to those considerations involves trust in reason, which involves trust in our ability to think philosophically. The Bible is to be taken as authoritative in the realm of theological truth. But before we can rationally believe such a thing, as human beings privy to general revelation and endowed with the ability to think we must weigh arguments and draw conclusions, that is, do philosophy. Proper trust in the Bible altogether involves the process of thinking rationally. It's a fundamental mistake to think otherwise.[7]

John Wesley, the founder of Methodism, said that renouncing reason is renouncing religion, that religion and reason go hand in hand, and that all irrational religion is false religion. In fact he happened to believe that a thorough acquaintance with philosophy and logic is an indispensable part of a minister's preparation.

When someone suggests that we "don't need philosophy," either in this debate or more generally, their words at best reflect a huge misunderstanding. The sentiment wrongly assumes that we are even able to understand the Bible, let alone discern that it is the ultimate revelation from God, without the capacity to think. Philosophy is, to put it most succinctly, clear thought. Perhaps it sounds pious to say that all we need is the Bible, and Protestants do in fact believe there's a sense in which it's true that Christians are to be people of one book, but it's at worst a sentiment predicated on a laughably shallow, simplistic, naïve epistemology and hermeneutic. It's just not that simple. We can't open the Bible and begin to understand it without engaging our reason, and using our critical faculties in this fashion as an interpretive tool is not to exalt the deliverances of reason above the deliverances of scripture. If, in addition to building a strong biblical and historical case against Calvinism (which we won't be doing in this book as it's outside the parameters of the project), we can also build a strong philosophical case, that's significant. Indeed, it's essential to the very process of biblical interpretation. This chapter brackets the more explicitly biblical and historical cases and offers the philosophical one, in the hopes that it can be accorded the space in the wider discussion it deserves. Philosophy can and ought to help adjudicate this intractable debate among Christians.

In laying out the philosophical case against Calvinism, we are also setting aside (with one exception) a related but distinctly different question: the philosophical defense of Arminianism. A full-fledged philosophical analysis would have to include this as part of the discussion. Most particularly, Arminianism's commitment to libertarian, contra-causal, or agent causation freedom would need defense.[8] Although we don't see the philosophical challenges facing Arminianism as anywhere near so difficult as those confronting Calvinism, we won't make that case here, holding in abeyance that discussion for another day. So without further ado, allow us to present our philosophical case.

## Compatibilism

Most Calvinists affirm that we are meaningfully free even though everything is causally determined by God. Accordingly, Calvinists who are consistent embrace *compatibilism*, the view that there is no incompatibility in affirming both total determinism and genuine freedom. On their view, all our actions, or at least all our actions that bear on issues of salvation, are specifically determined by God. However, no one is caused to act against his will. Rather, God determines our wills as well as our actions, so whatever we choose we are doing what we want, and consequently are fully responsible for it.

On our count, there are at least five major philosophical problems with Calvinistic compatibilism. First, there is the "obligation objection." To put it simply, moral duties make little sense given compatibilism. Duties tell us what we ought to do, and *ought* implies *can*. But if we are fully determined to will and to act as we do by causes outside our control, it is doubtful that there is any meaningful sense in which we can do otherwise.

An important objection to consider at this point arises within the context of Christian theology. It seems permissible to say of the human condition generally that it's at least possible in some sense for a person to avoid all sin, because Jesus constitutes an example. Clearly, though, Jesus is something of a special case. So what of Christians in general? Well, by God's regenerating grace in their lives they can indeed avoid all sin, although this doesn't actually happen in anyone until the culmination of the process of salvation. But it seems that the biblical promise in I Corinthians 10:13—that with any temptation a Christian will encounter, a way of escape is also provided—does seem to pose a problem for Calvinists. For nobody is able to do otherwise on their view (at least among the consistent Calvinists); so what sense can we make of a Christian sinning? It seems inconsistent to hold both that God determines all things, including the sins of Christians, while also always providing a way to resist temptation, thereby making it possible to resist any given sin.

But for now let's set that challenge to Calvinism aside, because instead we wish to identify a seeming problem for Arminianism instead. It involves not the regenerate, but the unregenerate, that is, non-Christians. What about them? Do they have grace sufficient to avoid all sin? If so, that's quite a strong view of what Arminians call "prevenient grace," the grace that comes before salvation, making acceptance of Christ and repentance of sin possible in the first place. If the unregenerate aren't able to avoid all sin, have we found a counterexample to "ought implies can"? For that would seem to suggest that they don't have enough grace to avoid sin for which they're culpable.

We might here stress the difference between free will and free grace, and insist that prevenient grace is only that grace by which to accept Christ as Savior, not to resist sin. Prevenient grace perhaps merely restores the freedom to receive other graces (regenerating grace, for example) by means of which one can avoid sin. Prevenient grace would not involve the possibility of avoiding all sin, therefore, except only in a secondary fashion as it ushers in the freedom (and the concomitant responsibility) of receiving that initially sanctifying grace that actually delivers from the power and dominion of sin.[9]

This response, however, seems inadequate, because unless the unregenerate are able, or at least at some point able, to resist sin, then repentance for sin makes little sense. Nor does real guilt for sin make much if any sense without freedom to refrain from sinning. So though this answer isn't without its insight, more needs to be said.[10]

Again, P implies Q, where "P" is "we ought to avoid all sin," and "Q" is "we can avoid all sin." The problem seems to be that on most versions of Christian theology it looks as if after the fall of man, P can be true while Q is false; therefore, the famous principle is false. But let's look more closely by translating the quantifications:

(P1) For any x, if x is a sin, then we ought to avoid doing x.
(Q1) For any x, if x is a sin, then we can avoid x.

If P1 is equivalent to P, and Q1 to Q, then we can examine the initial appearance about P and Q by looking at P1 and Q1. And surely, by the concept of sin, both P1 and Q1 are true. The problem with the original unanalyzed P and Q is that, to get a reading where P is true and Q false, we have to equivocate on "all," reading it in a distributed way in P ("for each individual sin x, taken on its own") and in a summation way in Q ("for the sum total of all sins added together"). And of course an argument that depends on equivocation is just a bad argument. So we don't seem here to have a workable counterexample to the "ought implies can" principle after all.[11] In a restaurant, a friend, concerned about food allergies, might ask if we can eat everything on the menu; after glancing at it, we may affirm truthfully we can, without implying we're either able or willing to break the standing Guinness record for food consumption.[12]

Many atheist philosophers who are compatibilists quietly agree that compatibilism has a hard time making sense of real duties, but they figure it's still the only game in town, and they may also believe that retaining the language of moral duties is pragmatically justified. A great many secular philosophers, though, admitting that their view entails that we can never do otherwise, suggest that we abandon the category of retribution or giving people their "just desserts." They suggest that rehabilitation or deterrence can justify punishment, but strictly speaking, retribution is inconsistent with compatibilism and perhaps best left behind, a vestige of an earlier age.

Although we consider the surrender of so important a moral category as retributive justice a strong consideration against naturalism, we appreciate their honesty in seeing the implications of compatibilism.[13] The same can't be said for Calvinists, we submit, for retribution of an extremely strong variety is essential to their theology. Not only do they believe that sinners should be held accountable in this life, they also hold that people can be justly consigned to eternal perdition for living exactly as God determined them to live. This is so void of moral sense that it is irrational to believe. So this constitutes a second criticism of Calvinism: the culpability objection.

A third troubling implication of Calvinistic compatibilism is that, on this view, God could have saved everyone without violating anyone's free will. Since Calvinists are not universalists, this means that the non-elect go to hell due to God's sovereign choice alone when they could just as easily have been reconciled to God and experienced an eternity of joy rather than an eternity of pain and sadness. If this is true, there is no intelligible sense in which God loves those who are lost, nor is there any recognizable sense in which he is good to them. This is the "bad god objection."

The fourth problem with Calvinistic compatibilism is that love relationships, by their nature and logic, are two-way relationships. God's irresistible grace, if it necessarily culminates in reconciliation and fellowship with God, seems like a divine love potion that, once administered, creates eternal infatuation in the beloved, but not genuine love. So we call this the "love objection." The logic of love requires a more substantial element of volition than what a Calvinistic compatibilist can allow.[14]

Fifth, Calvinistic compatibilists often emphasize that morally responsible actions must reflect one's character, or they aren't culpable reflections of who one is. Actions that don't reflect one's character seem objectionably random and uncaused. In reply, though, we might suggest that the Calvinists are inverting the process, putting a formed character at the start of the process rather than closer to the end where it more naturally belongs. Culpable moral development as virtue ethicists construe it—with thoughts leading to actions and then to character—is simply inconsistent with the Calvinist teaching that our actions are determined by an already existing character with which we are unavoidably saddled. This is the "virtue objection."

All five sub-objections taken together constitute a major philosophical objection to Calvinistic compatibilism, an objection that ranges over metaphysics, epistemology, and ethics.

## Euphemism

The second major objection to Calvinism is a recurring pattern of euphemism we find among Calvinist writers. When confronted with the logical problem of affirming both total determinism and moral culpability, for example, they typically try to evade the force of the problem by characterizing it as a mystery, paradox, antinomy, or "biblical tension." But dubbing a contradiction by a more pleasing locution does nothing to eliminate the problem.

Another example is that Calvinists often stress that God extends to the non-elect a genuine offer of salvation, and that they freely reject it. Again, this seems evasive and euphemistic. On Calvinist principles, it's only the elect who can actually receive salvation, so no offer of salvation to the non-elect is a genuine offer, because an offer is not genuine if there's no possibility that it can be accepted and the person offering it knows there's no possibility that it can be accepted. For Calvinists to describe such an empty offer as a genuine one is worse than euphemistic. It is deeply misleading, particularly to the uninitiated, who will typically assume that the offer really could be accepted.

In the same vein, when Calvinists are pressed on the issue of God's love for the non-elect, those whom God in his sovereign will has decided to exclude from among his chosen ones, they usually affirm that God indeed loves those unfortunate persons. His love for the non-elect, they often say, is consistent with his holiness and his justice, and with the fact that his love for the elect is a special and deeper love. God loves the non-elect, we're told, by providing for their earthly needs, their very life and breath. Giving them what they (indeed, all of us) deserve—hell—doesn't show lack of love. He's not failing to discharge any duty toward them, and their damnation will serve the purpose of accentuating God's glory and the greatness of his grace toward the elect. Calling this "love" is surely a capital case of euphemism.

A criticism of Calvinism already briefly mentioned is another example of euphemism. Christians who sin make no sense on Calvinist principles, for they can't do otherwise, yet they are said to have a "way of escape" from every temptation. But a way of escape that can't possibly be used is no real way of escape in this context. Conversational cooperation in using such words precludes doing violence to language in so flagrant a fashion. Again, contradictions don't go away by their being affirmed and euphemistically cast in more palatable terms.

This is a recurring pattern in Calvinist writers who either have no clear grasp of what is entailed by compatibilism, or who evade its implications with language that only makes sense on libertarian terms. Calvinists who engage in such euphemism when describing God's love or his genuine offer of salvation invariably seem to forget that God could save all persons with their freedom intact, as they understand freedom, but has chosen not to do so. Examples could be multiplied, but enough has been said to make clear that this poses problems for Calvinism that are not merely linguistic, but logical as well.


Radical Voluntarism

In this section, we come to one of the deepest roots of Calvinism, a root that accounts for its misguided view of divine sovereignty, as well as other problems we will note in this chapter. This root is that Calvinists assign such priority to God's will that they are voluntarists of the radical variety. Indeed, we would suggest that their view amounts to Ockhamism, the idea that whatever God says goes when it comes to morality, no matter what.

The notorious objection to such voluntarism is that it's arbitrary.[15] What if God commanded us to, say, torture children for fun? If God's will is the sole source of morality, and there are no rationally identifiable constraints, then we are never in a position to say of a particular command that God could never, by his nature, issue it. Indeed, the Calvinists think that it's not just possible that God could do something like commanding the torture of children for fun, but that, in fact, he has chosen to do something no less morally inexplicable. He has chosen that countless persons will be consigned to an eternity of utter misery as punishment for the very choices he determined them to make. This constitutes so gross a violation of our considered moral reflections that it seems rather obvious that Calvinism is in fact predicated on Ockhamism.

Now Calvinists might try to evade this charge by insisting that they deny universal possibilism and in fact affirm that there are at least some things morally ruled out. Even if a Calvinist makes this move, however, he's still implicated in an *epistemic* Ockhamism.[16] For if our noetic faculties are too skewed to trust our own moral judgments about the injustice and moral hideousness of unconditional perdition, how could we trust them on any other matter?[17] Indeed, what could be more clearly wrong than *that*? As hideous as an earthly dictator might be who chose to torture babies, his torture could at worst only be finite. By contrast, damnation involves infinite, eternal misery. For God to choose to consign persons to such a fate when he could have just as easily determined them to joy and happiness is even more morally obnoxious than the behavior of the earthly dictator. God's behavior toward the non-elect, if the Calvinists are right, strikes us as a paradigmatic example of hateful behavior, not loving behavior. Those who share our judgment will agree that this leaves Calvinists saddled with Ockhamism, which alone constitutes a powerful reason to reject Calvinism.[18]

It is worth emphasizing that Calvin and the other great Protestant Reformer Martin Luther set aside their moral sensibilities in their attempt to understand and defend the doctrine of unconditional predestination. Although each of them had the very strong moral reservations against such a view, each was willing to advocate and defend it on the ground that whatever God commands, in virtue of his commanding it, is moral. We submit that the extent to which they were willing to jettison their cherished moral convictions and insights in the process of their biblical interpretation is an example of a flawed understanding of the proper relationship between good philosophy and theology.

Calvin and Luther were, we contend, both right and wrong. They saw a crucial connection between God and ethics, but they embraced a biblical interpretation that profoundly distorts the nature of this connection. Consider these words from Calvin: "It therefore seems to them that men have reason to expostulate with God if they are predestined to eternal death solely by his decision, apart from their own merit. If thoughts of this sort ever occur to pious men, they will be sufficiently armed to break their force even by the one consideration that it is very wicked merely to investigate the causes of God's will. For his will is, and rightly ought to be, the cause of all things that are."[19] What Calvin is saying is clear: God's will, whatever that happens to be, determines what's morally right. This view is indistinguishable from pure voluntarism. For Calvin, God is the foundation of ethics, all right, though a few lines later he denies that he advocates "the fiction of 'absolute might' or a 'lawless god' who is a law unto himself." These remarks do not easily cohere with his earlier one, however.

Luther also endorsed unconditional predestination while recognizing the moral challenge it poses, writing that

> Doubtless it gives the greatest possible offence to common sense or
> natural reason, that God, Who is proclaimed as being full of mercy
> and goodness, and so on, should of His own mere will abandon,
> harden, and damn men, as though He delighted in the sins and great

eternal torments of such poor wretches. It seems an iniquitous, cruel, intolerable thought to think of God; and it is this that has been a stumbling block to so many great men down the ages. And who would not stumble at it? I have stumbled at it myself more than once, down to the deepest pit of despair, so that I wished I had never been made a man.[20]

Yet despite his visceral intuitive resistance to the doctrine of unconditional pre-destination, Luther maintained that there's no injustice in the way God metes out salvation and damnation. To those who thought otherwise, he replied, echoing Calvin, that "God is He for Whose will no cause or ground may be laid down as its rule and standard," for "nothing is on a level with it or above it, but it is itself the rule for all things." He went on to insist that "what God wills is not right because He ought, or was bound, so to will; on the contrary, what takes place must be right, because He so wills it."[21]

Both Calvin and Luther wished to say that God's will trumps. This was a crucial mistake because philosophically it's indefensible. For if God's command renders something obligatory, and there's nothing higher than God's will, then there's nothing in principle preventing God from commanding the torture of children for fun. His command would render such behavior not just morally permissible, but morally obligatory! If the Calvinists counter that God never would command such a thing, they are implicating themselves in an inconsis-tency, for they have already accorded primacy to God's will over his character. That maneuver of gesturing toward God's character, right as it is, is not avail-able to them any more; their appeal to God's nature stands at odds with classical Calvinism's exclusive focus on God's will. Radical voluntarism can't be reined in. Unconditional reprobation, or even single predestination with the non-elect invariably bound for hell even if they aren't strictly predestined for it, already constitutes an example of something we are unable to square with anything remotely recognizable as goodness and love.

Either divine command theory has to go, or, at a minimum, moral con-straints on God must exist. The constraints might well be internal to his nature, but Calvinists can't appeal to such constraints with so radical a commitment to voluntarism as we see in Calvin, Luther, and in the logic required for squaring the implications of classical Calvinism with our moral intuitions.

## The Terrible Tenet

By the "terrible tenet" we refer to the maximally tragic plight of the unconditional reprobate. A clear implication of either high five-point Calvinism or even four-point Calvinism[22] (or really just an affirmation of unconditional election) is that there are some for whom there is no hope, nor was there ever any hope. Before they were ever born, if Calvinism is true, God by his sovereign decree alone, unconditioned by any foreknowledge of these people and their free choices, abandoned them in the sinful condition into which they were to be born. Either Jesus did not die for them, or, even if he did, there's no chance they can respond to God's offer of salvation in Christ. Hell is the invariable home of the non-elect, ultimately because of God's choice alone. This is hard teaching indeed.

Some might respond by saying that the Bible just includes hard realities, and we must allow scripture to judge us, not vice versa, which is true. The Bible can and indeed does challenge our sense of right and wrong and the philosophies of men. The priority that philosophers assign to our ability to reason is of course another large reason that many Christians are skeptical about philosophy. Not only does the Bible itself warn against being led astray by bad philosophy, this has been a recurring problem in modern theology when theologians elevate human reason above scriptural authority, often distorting or denying the riches of classic orthodox faith. They cavalierly excise those parts of scripture that are too challenging, or they mistakenly think that scripture has to be interpreted in ways that conform to reason as defined by modern man or secular systems of thought.

While we reject this approach, we want to insist that unless care is taken when avoiding these mistakes, we risk throwing the baby out with the bathwater. Assume counterfactually for a moment that the Bible told us to do some hideous thing like yank out the claws of cats for our amusement. We would be well within our epistemic and moral rights to assume, if the Bible really taught such a thing, that it wouldn't be a book to believe. Faith and reason, rightly understood, must be harmonious. At a minimum, for example, scripture must be understood in a way that's consistent and coherent, not just internally, but also with what we know outside of scripture.

This is the large grain of truth in John Locke's recognition that, though the Bible is entirely reliable, reason can help us understand it rightly. This doesn't mean that its contents have to be knowable a priori, but its teachings can't so fundamentally grate against our rational or moral deliverances that our belief is rendered simply irrational or immoral. That's the path of dogmatism and fideism, and that's where a simplistic hermeneutic that excludes the relevance of philosophical considerations can land us. So we have a balancing act on our hands here: On the one hand, we wish to avoid the path of watered-down modern theology, while on the other, we must avoid the path of simple fideism.

We submit that at this juncture what might help us achieve the needed balance is a useful distinction, between what might be *hard* for us to understand on the one hand, versus what seems exceedingly irrational if not *impossible* (rationally, if not psychologically) to believe on the other. The earlier example of a command to torture kids for fun would be one that would be exceedingly irrational, if not impossible, for us to believe came from God. In contrast, an example of something hard, but not impossible to understand, are the Old Testament conquest narratives. We will take these up in a later chapter, along with a considerably more extensive discussion of the hard/impossible distinction, but for now we will simply say that it is at least possible to make moral sense of these, difficult as it may be. This distinction between what's *hard* to understand on the one hand, and what we will just call *impossible* to understand or rationally believe on the other, can help us avoid the extremes of both fideism and theological liberalism. What merely *exceeds* our reason may be hard to understand, like the Trinity, but it's still perfectly rational to believe in it; what fundamentally *violates* our reason or nonnegotiable moral intuitions, in contrast, is beyond the pale and so irrational to believe.[23]

For a telling instance of this, consider how confusion over this distinction recently led both John Beversluis[24] and Antony Flew[25] to accuse C. S. Lewis, in his later years, of opting for Ockhamism over moral realism. Their mistake was generated by how they construed the fact that Lewis came to believe that the death of his wife, tragic though it was, didn't constitute an intractable instance of the problem of evil. They erroneously equated this with the conviction that, for Lewis, nothing in principle could ever count as an intractable instance of the problem of evil, something Lewis never said or implied. That his wife's death didn't count as such an instance was just the first half of Lewis's point; the second half is that in principle some such instance can indeed be conceived. In fact, the salient example that he would tend to identify here is extreme Calvinism, which would render the problem of evil truly intractable by, as Lewis put it, sneaking a bad god in through the back door.[26]

Lewis's point here is one we have already noted: it is not just hard to reconcile unconditional reprobation with a morally perfect God, but simply impossible. Whatever the Bible teaches about God's sovereignty (and the project of this book strongly endorses God's sovereignty where morality is concerned), surely we are rational, if we are capable of loving God with all of our minds, to insist that it does not entail a tenet so terrible as this.[27]

If the Bible did indeed teach such a doctrine, wouldn't it be more rational to believe that it's not morally reliable? Fundamental to our conviction that scripture is reliable is the trust that God, as perfectly good, would not deceive us. If God is not recognizably good, however, we are not warranted in this trust. And again, if unconditional election is true, God is not recognizably good, and the problem of evil is intractable. So Calvinism has devastating consequences for our very ability rationally to trust the teaching of scripture as a reliable revelation. Once more, we have seen that Calvinism leaves us with insuperable philosophical difficulties, both ethical and epistemological.

In the face of this reality, commitment to the truth of biblical revelation gives us powerful reason to reject Calvinist theology. Calvinists should bear in mind that their interpretation of the Bible is just that: an interpretation. It should give Calvinists serious pause that the majority of Christians throughout the world and down the ages do not interpret scripture as teaching unconditional election and the terrible tenet, and indeed the doctrine did not comport with the general tenor of Christian thought prior to Augustine.[28] Moreover, the fact that there are viable interpretative options from which to choose that violate no sound principles of exegesis, whereas their interpretation flies so violently in the face of some of our clearest and deepest moral intuitions, gives Calvinists overwhelming reasons to find a better biblical interpretation.[29]

## A Semantic Phenomenon

Finally, Calvinists consistently insist on defining sovereignty as all-encompassing divine determinism; anything less than his micromanagerial and meticulous providence is unworthy of the greatness of his sovereign power. Usually without calling Arminians heretics, most Calvinists nonetheless think that any view of divine sovereignty that's less controlling than this is a woefully inadequate substitute. Anything less really is tantamount to a denial of sovereignty; univocality where "sovereignty" is concerned is paramount for them.

Interestingly, and most tellingly, although they're adamant about avoiding equivocation on that word, they insist that the terrible tenet isn't so terrible, and that what appears to be a lack of love for the non-elect is really love after all. It's not the same resplendent love as God has for the elect, of course, but it's still real love, we're told. So what they are suggesting is that we can, in all good conscience and intellectual integrity, characterize God's unconditional choice of some for eternal misery and reprobation as loving behavior, and this despite the fact that he could have saved them without in any way violating their freedom. Calvinists are entitled to their own moral sense, but this behavior that they attribute to God seems about as paradigmatic of *unloving* behavior as anything imaginable, as we have argued already.

The conjunction of these two semantic decisions, though—the nonnegotiable insistence on univocality when defining sovereignty as all-encompassing divine determinism and the willingness to engage in the most extreme sort of equivocation on the nature and implications of love—strains credulity to the breaking point. They insist that they can't possibly budge on their definition of sovereignty, despite the fact that their semantic obstinacy on that matter results in a plethora of intractable philosophical objections, but where love is concerned, they're willing to countenance the most radical sort of equivocation. Neither decision seems adequately principled, either biblically or philosophically. For if sovereignty can be interpreted in a way that, though comprehensive, doesn't entail the terrible tenet, is rooted in solid exegesis, and can avoid the sort of equivocation on love that Calvinism entails, then that, we argue, is the rational way to go. Philosophy will have played a key role in adjudicating this debate and declared Calvinism (in a key aspect of its soteriology) dead in the water. Loving God with all of one's mind demands a more credible theology than Calvinism can offer.[30]

In September 2006 Pope Benedict XVI delivered a remarkable lecture at the University of Regensburg entitled "Faith, Reason, and the University: Memories and Reflections."[31] The address stirred the ire of many Muslims, evoking demands for apology and no small amount of violence from sectors of the Islamic community, which was regrettable if not unsurprising. Unfortunately, the ink spilled on that needless controversy distracted from the central themes of that remarkable speech on the relationship between faith and reason, an understanding that resonates deeply with what we have been arguing in this chapter.

In the speech, the Pope discussed the emergence of voluntarism in the late Middle Ages—after the later Augustine's predestinationist ideas were largely set aside for centuries—that gave rise to the image of a capricious God not even bound to truth and goodness. Implicated were not just certain segments of Islamic thought, but sectors of Christianity as well, where "God's transcendence and otherness are so exalted that our reason, our sense of the true and good, are no longer an authentic mirror of God...." Contrasted with such Ockhamism is a historical Christian faith that insisted that between God and our created reason there exists an analogy in which "unlikeness remains infinitely greater than likeness, yet not to the point of abolishing analogy and its language." Benedict laments the efforts at de-hellenizing Christianity by so accentuating God's transcendence that he becomes unrecognizable: "God does not become more divine when we push him away from us in a sheer, impenetrable voluntarism; rather, the truly divine God is the God who has revealed himself as *logos* and, as *logos*, has acted and continues to act lovingly on our behalf."

If God exists, he's not just one more item in the inventory of reality, but the key to understanding the whole. Heraclitus, a philosopher born in 533 B.C. in Ephesus, a Greek colonial city in Asia Minor, argued that wisdom consists in understanding the hidden harmony of the *logos*, an intelligent, impersonal law that guides all change. This philosophical view was part of the intellectual milieu in which the writer of the New Testament book of John composed the fourth Gospel that starts like this: "In the beginning was the Word (*logos*), and the Word was with God, and the Word was God." Jesus, it was claimed, is this divine *logos* to whom John referred, except not an impersonal force, but a Person, God the Son, who animates the world, holds it together with his power, and makes sense of all reality. Using rationality and logic and our best philosophical tools and moral insights isn't contrary to God's plan for Christians. It's all part of our God-given nature and his general revelation to us, by which we can determine in the first place that the Bible is God's special revelation to us and by which we can best interpret it in a way that accords with God's morally perfect and recognizably good nature.

There are aspects of God that *transcend* our reason to be sure, but God doesn't call us to believe anything *opposed* to reason. This distinction is one that some popular postmodern Christian writers often fail to grasp, and they thereby tend to make a virtue of incoherence. Donald Miller, for instance, in the chapter on worship in his best-selling *Blue Like Jazz*,[32] writes that he *wants* God to contradict reason and not to make sense to him, because he wants a God of mystery and transcendence. "Not making sense" is the obvious ambiguity here, so we would reply: "*Exceed* our reason, sure, but not *go against it altogether*. For example, we don't want nor could we in good conscience worship a God who commands the torture of innocents for fun, nor one who both can and cannot lie." Such a God would contradict our reason and not make sense, but he would hardly be worthy of worship. Countenancing incoherence little safeguards God's ineffability.

By contrast, moral apologist C. S. Lewis is known for insisting on the need to avoid equivocation about God's goodness, echoing John Stuart Mill's diatribe against equivocation about morality. Lewis didn't insist on univocality the way Mill did, though, but rather he likened legitimate discrepancies between our vision of the good and God's to that between a perfect circle and a child's first attempt to draw a wheel. God's goodness exceeds ours, but it's still ultimately recognizable, perhaps with difficulty in some cases, as real goodness nonetheless. Lewis thus stood in the Thomistic tradition of analogical predication of which the Pope was speaking. God's good can't be our evil. Lewis was a moral realist, who believed morality is objectively true and rationally accessible, at least to a significant degree. We may not always see what God's goodness entails, but we can be confident of some things it precludes.

If morality is to count positively in favor of God's existence, as Kant thought, rather than negatively against it, as Hume did, God's character must be recognizably good. That a believer like C. S. Lewis believed in the power of moral arguments in favor of God's existence demonstrates his lifelong fidelity to the idea that God, though transcendent, remains meaningfully good—not safe, but recognizably loving all the same. Ockhamists and Calvinists forfeit the resources with which to build any such moral apologetic, by abandoning the axiomatic moral convictions on which such inferences are based.

So the problems with Calvinism stack up: Compatibilism, Euphemism, Radical voluntarism, the Terrible tenet, and a Semantic issue, which form the acrostic CERTS—only these are bound to leave a bad taste in your mouth.[33]

# 5

# God and Goodness

Nothing...will be called good except in so far as it has a certain likeness of the divine goodness.

—Aquinas[1]

Thus far we have discussed the goodness, perfect goodness, recognizable goodness, and even the necessary goodness of God. Now, however, we come to what is perhaps the ultimate question of all when it comes to God and morality: the connection between God and the Good itself. To address this question adequately, we must say more about God's necessary goodness in order to answer a common refrain among skeptics toward theistic ethics. Recall how they note that voluntarists often qualify their theory by insisting that only the commands of a *perfectly good* God would count as morally authoritative. When voluntarists make this move, the critic charges, they betray their theory as an example of divine independence theory after all. They have admitted, so the argument goes, that they are committed to moral standards independent of God, standards by which we can rightly and reasonably call God good. We disagree, and this chapter will explain why.

We have taken pains to defend the goodness of God, and will continue to do so, but we have also argued that, in our estimation, there's a close connection between God and goodness, a dependence relation of some sort. In a sense, the challenge we have to answer is a variation on the Euthyphro Dilemma: If goodness depends on God, then isn't the characterization of God as good circular, vacuous, arbitrary, and all the rest? In this chapter and the next we will deny that this is so. Although goodness is not a function of God's commands, nonetheless we will argue that goodness is not in fact independent of God. There is another option beyond an Ockhamistic voluntarist account of the Good and a divine independence theory. Goodness can ultimately depend on God even if it does not depend on God's *commands*.

## Theism and the Real World

As we have seen, skeptics of theistic ethics have a notable forebear in Socrates. Paradoxically, perhaps, his skepticism played a role in leading Plato to posit the existence of the Ideas or Forms, unchanging, eternal Truths. This has come to be known as the aforementioned "Platonic realism," which affirms the existence of both necessary truths and necessarily existing entities. Examples of the former from the realm of mathematics would include that $2 + 2 = 4$ and from the realm of morals that torturing innocent children for the fun of it is bad. Among necessarily existing entities would be such members of the Platonic pantheon as numbers, propositions, essences, and properties.

Platonic realism affirms the necessary existence of these invariant truths and entities. Anything susceptible to change or malleability is associated with the world of mere images and shadows. The "real world"—in contrast with the world of mortgages and car payments that college seniors envision—features realities not at all capable of change or fluctuation. A second and related feature of such realism is the mind-independence of these truths. Plato's quest for objectivity was a reaction against the fickle nature of the Greek gods. Truth for him was not rooted in divine whim, but instead was thought to be completely stable and ontologically independent.[2]

Realist thinkers like Nicholas Wolterstorff and Richard Swinburne, among contemporaries, affirm the ontological independence of Platonic truths. This is a view that has held great sway in much of Western philosophy, and continues to do so today. There is, of course, an important reason and intuitive force behind such realist assumptions. The Platonic entities posited by the realists are said to exist necessarily, and Platonic truths said to obtain necessarily. Such truths are the same in all possible worlds, and could not be different from what they are. It is an easy leap from such features of these necessary realities to think of them as ontologically independent of anything else. Our physical life is dependent on oxygen, without which we would die. Dependence in such a case introduces the possibility of our physical life coming to an end. Since the necessary truths simply cannot be snuffed out in any analogous fashion, they are naturally thought of as existing independently, beyond anyone's control.

Not all theists have been so easily reconciled with the central claims of realism, however. For pushing the realist line can be seen as a challenge to some of the tenets of classical theism. Specifically, the ontological independence of necessarily existing entities—their *aseity*—and the invariance of necessary truths seem to run counter to an affirmation of God's absolute sovereignty and the way he is thought to superintend all of reality. If God cannot alter the contents of such truths, and something exists apart from God, then God is limited in his power and authority, so the argument goes.

Both theists and atheists are aware of such tensions. J. L. Mackie, for instance, insisted that once someone affirms unchangeable moral principles, there is no further need for God to sustain morality. For such truths can stand on their own as an independent basis for ethics. Similarly, Ralph Cudworth suggested that affirming necessary truths goes counter to theism, since an affirmation of theism would require a denial that anything else is necessarily true.[3]

Cudworth's worry is not without precedent in the history of Western philosophy. A radical affirmation of God's power and sovereignty has most often been taken to imply that God's prerogatives are without constraint or limit of any kind. Descartes, for instance, seems to be an example of a philosopher and theist who believes that even mathematical and logical truths are contingent (or at least not necessarily necessary) due to God's ability to alter their contents. This obviously accounts for why Descartes is often cast as a "universal possibilist"—someone who believes that anything at all is possible if only God wills it. Descartes wrote that God laid down the mathematical truths that we call eternal, just as a king lays down laws in his kingdom, and that they depend on him completely. He added that it is

> useless to inquire how God could from all eternity bring it about that it should be untrue that twice four is eight...for I admit that that cannot be understood by us. Yet since on the other hand I correctly understand that nothing in any category of causation can exist which does not depend upon God, and that it would have been easy for him so to appoint that we human beings should not understand how these very things could be otherwise than they are, it would be irrational to doubt concerning that which we correctly understand, because of that which we do not understand and perceive no need to understand.[4]

That last argument is suggestive. Descartes is quite the obstinate Anselmian, putting more stock in his understanding of God's total sovereignty and *aseity* than in what follows from our failure to understand certain implications of universal possibilism—and even our suspicions that some things are impossible. Descartes attributes his inability to understand to God-imposed limits on human rationality. For Descartes, in order for the eternal truths to be genuinely dependent on God, they must be within his control; God must have the ability to alter their contents.

The examples Descartes uses are from mathematics, but the same procedure could apply to ethics, as Ockham seems to have done by affirming that morality is totally dependent on the will of God. He advanced this claim by drawing a radical distinction between any given act and its moral characteristics, and contending that it is possible to separate those characteristics from the act. Thus, even an act like hating God could have its evil characteristics separated from it and become a good act if God willed it: "God is able to cause all that pertains to X as such without anything else which is not identical with X per se. But the act of hating God, as far as the sheer being in it is concerned, is not the same thing as the wickedness and evilness of the act. Therefore, God can cause whatever pertains to the act per se of hating or rejecting God, without causing any wickedness or evilness in the act."[5]

Such an approach would preclude unalterable moral axioms and necessary moral truth, which quickly leads to some troublesome implications, to put it mildly. To feel the force of the problem, take the example of slaughtering an innocent child: a plausible candidate for a necessarily bad action. Yet if God's sovereign volitions dictate the content of morality, then how could such moral badness be nonnegotiable? For God's command could ostensibly contravene and override the bad moral characteristics and make it the epitome of a noble action.

With this background, we can see more clearly the issues at stake in the Euthyphro Dilemma. It is common to think that if morality depends on God, then God could have decreed anything whatsoever and it would have been moral. Dependence is thought to entail control. So on the one hand, such a radically voluntaristic view like Ockham's is starkly at odds with realism or, historically, natural law. If morality, on the other hand, rests on objective, necessary truths that not even God can change, then voluntarism is taken to be false, for morality would be independent of God. What is a thoroughgoing theist to do? Affirm realism and deny that God's sovereignty encompasses the realm of necessity, or affirm voluntarism and deny that there are any necessary (moral) truths? Neither option is very palatable, and if those options were the only ones, the theistic ethicist would indeed be rational to change his view. Fortunately, there is a third option, and it is an option that we embrace.

The third alternative, though, is hardly a philosophical novelty. It has a venerable history in the tradition of Christian thought that has taken a number of notable forms, including the following: Augustine's "divine ideas tradition"; Leibniz's effort to root mathematical truth in God's noetic activity; Aquinas's insistence that anything, that in any way is, is from God; Berkeley's radical idealism; Descartes' view of constant creation; and even Jonathan Edwards's misguided attempt at temporal parts theory—all of these were efforts motivated by the theological conviction that God is at the root of all that is. It's essentially the view that his creative power is what sustains reality and that absolutely everything apart from him is dependent on him. The impulse and theological rationale behind such maneuvers, if not always their specific formulations, is one with which we entirely sympathize and wish to retain.

Following Tom Morris, we call the solution to our puzzle here—this third option between realism and voluntarism—*theistic activism*. According to this view, a divine intellectual activity is responsible for the framework of reality. "A theistic activist," writes Morris, "will hold God creatively responsible for the entire modal economy, for what is possible as well as what is necessary and what is impossible. The whole Platonic realm is thus seen as deriving from God."[6] The trick in effecting this rapprochement between realism and classical theism is to affirm the necessary existence and invariable nature of the Platonic realm while denying its *aseity,* or absolute independence, an attribute of God alone. This approach maintains the dependence on God of all that exists, while also enabling us to reject universal possibilism. It is worth understanding how such notions developed over the last several decades among professional philosophers, so let's take a few moments to review this.

A Narrative of Necessity

Although philosophers from Aquinas to Hegel to Leibniz discussed necessity, the recent discussion of the topic in relation to God was largely generated by the work of Alvin Plantinga, particularly his landmark volume *The Nature of Necessity*. We shall begin, however, by looking at another of his works in which he especially argues against the universal possibilism of Descartes. Examining Descartes' arguments, Plantinga shows that the debate over universal possibilism boils down to a conflict over intuitions. Specifically, the conflict is between the intuition that (1) some propositions are impossible, and the intuition that (2) if God is genuinely sovereign, then everything is possible.

When the tension is stated this baldly, most are inclined to reject (2), for if literally everything is possible, then we lose the very ability to engage in meaningful religious discourse. If God's features are not at least somewhat accessible to our understanding, then our language about him fails to communicate. Unqualified voluntarism may appear at first glance to exalt God and his mystery, but where it actually leads is to blatant contradiction and a cognitively vacuous notion of the divine. By contrast, a rejection of universal possibilism is an affirmation that some propositions are true necessarily, and others impossible, and it would seem that every theistic ethicist ought to realize that they are functioning under this constraint.

Some thinkers have held, however, that an affirmation of necessity is inconsistent with full-fledged theism, as we have seen. They perceive these unchangeable necessary truths to be in competition with God, to be constraints on him, and consequently threats to his sovereignty. However, if we draw a distinction between control and dependence, and rationally deny Descartes' assumption that dependence always requires control, then we can claim, with plausibility, that necessary truths do not pose a threat to Anselmian theism after all. This seems to be the direction Plantinga is moving in his rejection of the Cartesian intuition that if God is genuinely sovereign then everything is possible. Closer to the end of *Does God Have a Nature?*, Plantinga speculates about the possibility that the necessary truths might depend on God in a sense other than control, a possibility that could well suggest that exploring the realm of abstract objects (necessarily existing entities and necessary truths) is tantamount to exploring the very nature of God. Plantinga ends the piece by posing a number of questions: "Can we ever say of a pair of necessary propositions A and B that A makes B true or A is the explanation of the truth of B? Could we say, perhaps, that [necessarily $7 + 5 = 12$] is *grounded in* [it's part of God's nature to believe that $7 + 5 = 12$]? If so, what are the relevant senses of 'explains', 'makes true' and 'grounded in'? These are good questions, and good topics for further study. If we can study them affirmatively, then perhaps we can point to an important dependence of abstract objects upon God, even though necessary truths about these objects are not within his control."[7]

Plantinga himself took up such questions two years later in a presidential address to the American Philosophical Association entitled "How to Be an Anti-Realist," offering a way to affirm such a non-control dependence relation. In an effort to mediate the realism/anti-realism dispute, Plantinga first distinguishes between existential and creative anti-realism. To be an *existential* anti-realist with respect to other minds, for instance, is to deny their actual existence. By contrast, *creative* anti-realism, deriving its inspiration to Kant, posits that things in the world owe their fundamental structure and perhaps their very existence to the noetic activity of minds. The creative anti-realists Plantinga then takes as representatives of one side of the dispute are those like Richard

Rorty who want to claim that truth itself amounts to nothing more than prov-
ability, or verifiability, or perhaps warranted assertibility. In other words, truth
is a status we bestow by our use of language, not a function of the way things
are independently of us and our beliefs. Plantinga demonstrates how Putnam
too makes a similar claim that truth is just verifiability.[8] "On Putnam's view,
therefore, whether dinosaurs once roamed the earth depends upon us and our
linguistic practices."[9]

After arguing against Rorty's and Putnam's versions of anti-realism,
Plantinga tries to capture the central impulse of anti-realism in his own account.
That central impulse is that truths cannot be totally independent of minds or
persons. As Plantinga puts it,

> Truths are the sort of things persons know; and the idea that there are
> or could be truths quite beyond the best methods of apprehension
> seems peculiar and *outre* and somehow outrageous. What would
> account for such truths? How would they get there? Where would they
> come from? How could the things that are in fact true or false—propo-
> sitions, let's say—exist in serene and majestic independence of
> persons and their means of apprehension? How could there be
> propositions no one has ever so much as grasped or thought of? It can
> seem just crazy to suppose that propositions could exist independent
> of minds or persons or judging beings. That there should just *be* these
> truths, independent of persons and their noetic activities can, in
> certain moods and from certain perspectives, seem wildly counterintu-
> itive. How could there be truths, or for that matter, falsehoods, if there
> weren't any person to think or believe or judge them?[10]

Platonism goes counter to this anti-realist impulse of which Plantinga speaks.
Note that Plantinga is not rejecting the objectivity associated with realism, only
the mind-independence. Here are his own words on the matter:

> So what we really have here is a sort of antinomy. On the one hand
> there is a deep impulse towards anti-realism; there can't really be
> truths independent of noetic activity. On the other hand, there is the
> disquieting fact that anti-realism, at least of the sorts we have been
> considering, seems incoherent and otherwise objectionable. We have
> here a paradox seeking resolution, a thesis and antithesis seeking
> synthesis. And what is by my lights the correct synthesis, was
> suggested long before Hegel. This synthesis was suggested by
> Augustine, endorsed by most of the theistic tradition, and given
> succinct statement by Thomas Aquinas:

Even if there were no human intellects, there could be truths because of their relation to the divine intellect. But if, *per impossible*, there were no intellects at all, but things continued to exist, then there would be no such reality as truth. The thesis, then, is that truth cannot be independent of noetic activity on the part of persons. The antithesis is that it must be independent of *our* noetic activity. And the synthesis is that truth is independent of our intellectual activity but not of God's.[11]

Plantinga's suggestion is interesting, for what he is attempting to provide here is a way to make sense of how such propositions can depend on God without their truth being subject to his control. What he therefore attempts to provide is what he had been pointing toward in *Does God Have a Nature?*: namely, a nontrivial dependence relation of even necessary propositions on God other than one of control. Plantinga is not suggesting that a necessarily true proposition is true just because God *believes* it. Instead, he suggests that such a proposition exists in the first place because God *conceives* it. Propositions, on his view, are best thought of as thoughts of God. Rather than compromising the necessary existence of propositions, Plantinga's view accounts for it, for God is a necessary being who has essentially the property of thinking just the thoughts he does. These thoughts, then, are conceived by God in every possible world and hence exist necessarily. So God believes a proposition because it is true, but the proposition exists because God thinks it. In this way Plantinga argues that the best way to capture the central insight of anti-realism[12] is by being a theist.[13]

Applying this analysis to ethics, consider the proposition that it is bad to torture sentient creatures for the fun of it. Such a proposition is plausibly taken as necessarily true. On Plantinga's creative anti-realist view, God believes such a proposition because it is true, rather than its being true because God believes it. Consistent with Plantinga's rejection of universal possibilism, not even God could alter the truth value of the proposition. To this extent, Plantinga seems to embrace the guided will horn of the Euthyphro Dilemma. His version of the guided will view is not, however, a pure divine independence theory as Antony depicted it, for the proposition expressing such a truth exists due to God's thinking it, which he always has and always will. So the proposition expressing such a necessary truth depends on God, even though God does not and cannot alter its contents. Of course God has not the slightest intention to alter it, for there's perfect resonance between his nature and will. From this perspective, Plantinga affirms a substantive dependence relation of necessary truths on the creative activity of God, carefully distinguishing such dependence from the issue of control. It is important to emphasize that Plantinga recognizes this maneuver is in the spirit of Augustine's divine ideas tradition as well as an important strand of Thomistic thought. As such it is generally consonant with some powerful historical elements of the Christian tradition, elements that provide abundant resources to answer Euthyphro objections.

In a more recent work, Plantinga suggests that what we can learn from Christian scripture and by faith gives us a clearer view of the world. Now we see, for example, "what is most important about all the furniture of heaven and earth—namely, that it has been created by God. We can even come to see, if we reflect, what is most important about numbers, propositions, properties, states of affairs, and possible worlds: namely, that they really are divine thoughts or concepts."[14] Plantinga calls such a view *theistic conceptualism*. He adds that though such a view is controversial, it is certainly the majority opinion in the tradition of those theists who have thought about it. On such a view, propositions are divine thoughts, properties divine concepts, and sets divine collections. For a theistic activist, a careful distinction between questions of dependence and control allows an answer to the Euthyphro Dilemma that can serve as an important component of any thoroughly theistic metaphysic with a strong commitment to moral realism.

Applying a theistic activist model to value theory, Tom Morris writes:

Distinguishing carefully between issues of dependence and control is itself of some significant philosophical interest. For consider as an example the famous Euthyphro problem concerning morality. Is whatever is right right because God wills it, or does God will whatever is right because it is right? It has been thought by many philosophers that if morality is dependent on God, it follows that God could have made it right to torture innocent people for pleasure merely by willing it. This is the extreme position of theistic voluntarism, for which William of Ockham is notorious. On the other hand, if morality rests on objective, necessary truths such as that it is wrong to torture innocent people for pleasure—truths outside God's control—then it is widely held that this entails that morality is independent of God. On the view of theistic activism, moral truths can be objective, unalterable, and necessary, and yet still dependent on God. Thus, activism offers us a new perspective on the Euthyphro dilemma for morality. And this should come as no surprise, since theistic activism can be understood, in part, as resulting from an attempt to deal with what can be considered a parallel and more general Euthyphro-style dilemma for modality: Is it merely the case that God affirms the necessary truths because of the way in which they are true, or are they necessarily true because of the way he affirms them?[15]


## God is the Good

We have been speaking of the dependence of moral goodness on God, in accord with the classical theistic view that everything apart from God depends on God. But when it comes to the ultimate Good, we are inclined to say more than that it depends on God. In some important sense we wish to argue that God *just is* the ultimate Good. This view, too, has a venerable history within Christianity. Thomists, Anselmians, theistic Platonists, and theistic activists, including such contemporary analytic philosophers as Alvin Plantinga and Robert Adams, all concur that on a Christian understanding of reality, God and the ultimate Good are ontologically inseparable. We have been discussing Anselmianism and theistic activism; now we will all too quickly discuss a few other currents of Christian thought that connect God and the good. These are obviously deep waters, and no one chapter or book can begin to do justice to it; it's as if we're showing you a sprawling metropolis over the course of a week. The best we can do is hit some of its highlights. Let's start with an all-too-brief word about Thomism, without any pretense that we're doing it justice. (Doing so would take us too far afield in light of our present goals.)

Norman Kretzmann and Eleonore Stump contend that the central thesis of Aquinas's meta-ethics is that the terms "being" and "goodness" are the same in reference, differing only in sense. A thing is perfect of its kind to the extent to which it is fully realized or developed; the extent to which the potentialities definitive of its kind—its specifying potentialities—have been actualized. In acting, a thing aims at being. "The actualization of a thing's specifying potentialities to at least some extent is, on the one hand, its existence as such a thing; it is in this sense that the thing is said to have being. But, on the other hand, the actualization of a thing's specifying potentialities is, to the extent of the actualization, that thing's being whole, complete, free from defect—the state all things naturally aim at; it is in this sense that the thing is said to have goodness."[16] Being and goodness, then, co-refer, picking out the same referent under two different names and descriptions, echoing Davies's point from an earlier chapter.

Since Aquinas took God to be essentially and uniquely "being itself," it is God alone who is essentially goodness itself. This allows us to make ready sense of the relationship between God and the standard by which he prescribes or judges. For the goodness for the sake of which and in accordance with which God wills whatever he wills regarding human morality is identical with his nature. Yet since it is God's very nature and no arbitrary decision of his that thus constitutes the standard of morality, only things consonant with God's nature could be morally good. "The theological interpretation of the central thesis of Aquinas's ethical theory thus provides the basis for an objective religious morality."[17] Note again the intimate connection between God and goodness and an instance of a guided-will theory of morality that is neither Ockhamism nor divine independence theory.

We are inclined to think that the ultimate ontological inseparableness of God and the Good is something of an axiomatic Anselmian intuition; a vision apprehended, not just the deliverance of a discursive argument. That so many solid theists through the centuries have gravitated toward such a view bolsters this impression. If God is the ultimate Good, such that necessary moral truths are reflective of an aspect of God, then indeed Plantinga is right that to apprehend such truths is to catch a glimpse of God himself. Moreover, if such dependence or even identity obtains or is even possible, then the Euthyphro Dilemma is effectively defused and the moral argument for God's existence accordingly gains strength.

To see another plausible account of the view that God is the Good, let's review this aspect of Robert Adams's *Finite and Infinite Goods*. Borrowing some themes from Plato, Adams insists that it is natural for a theist to take God as best filling the role played by the Beautiful in *Symposium* or the Good in the *Republic*. Adams takes intimations of an ultimate Good or ultimate paradigm of Beauty as veridical, akin to beatific visions of God among theists. It is in view of the similarity of these perceptions that he thinks it only natural that a theist would take God himself to be what we apprehend in those moments. In a later chapter we will take up important epistemic issues concerning this apprehension of God's goodness, but for now it's important to notice that it's because God has the recognizably good character he does that it's rational to see him as the entity who satisfies our description of the ultimate Good.

On Adams's view, the infinite and transcendent Good, understood as God himself, is central and foundational to the right moral theory. He notes that Platonic theories of the good, which resonate with this notion, are often neglected, while Kantian, Aristotelian, and utilitarian approaches in ethics flourish. Although his own theory is a theistic Platonic account, he emphasizes that it is more theistic than Platonic. For while he tries to think through the whole area of ethics from a theistic point of view, he does not agree with everything in Plato, key points of resonance notwithstanding. Adams does not view badness or evil as a commensurate contrast with the Good. Badness, though real, is not so deeply rooted in reality as the Good. Satan on a Christian view is not the ontological grounding of evil in anything like the same way that God is of the Good. Satan is instead a mere created entity dependent for his existence on the sustaining activity of God. Badness tends to be cast as a privation or perversion of the Good, on a Christian understanding, not its equal and opposite paradigm.

While an equation of God and Goodness has obvious appeal, it also runs into a difficulty that has considerable intuitive force, namely, that it seems implausible to suggest that God could be identical to some abstract object or property like Goodness. Adams addresses this challenge by first noting a recurring debate among Plato scholars as to whether the Forms are best understood as archetypes, properties, or universals on the one hand, or standards, paradigms, or exemplars on the other. Among these options, Adams thinks it makes best sense to think of God functioning as the *exemplar* of Goodness. Thus understood, we can make better sense of God constituting Goodness, in the sense of being its exemplar, perfect standard, ultimate paradigm, and final source. The tension between person and universal, or substance and property, is thus avoided.[18] Some philosophers have argued, moreover, that Plato's Forms themselves might best be understood as particulars rather than universals, and so we might suggest, following them on this point, that a person like God might function more paradigmatically as the ultimate Good than would some abstract principle or impersonal truth.

In identifying God with the ultimate Good, Adams does not want to claim that the role filled by the Good captures every meaning of the word "good." For the word "good" is used in everyday conversation in many different ways, including instrumental, emotivist, and colloquial, not all of which are particularly related to the ultimate intrinsic Good. Adams is most interested in talking about the Goodness signified by uses of the word "good" or "goodness" in contexts when such words refer to something like *excellence*.[19]

The role of our desires, on Adams's view, is to fix the reference of our value terminology to a property or object that has its own nature independent of our desires. He writes that if there is indeed a single best candidate for the role of the Good itself, or the property of goodness, there may certainly be some things that do not agree with it, and therefore fail to be good, though virtually all of us think they are good. But a property that belonged mainly to things that almost all of us have always thought were bad, he insists, would certainly not be filling the role picked out by our talk of goodness.

For Adams, whatever best fills the role of Goodness is an object of admiration, desire, and recognition, at least commonly and to some degree. He insists that if we do not place some trust in our own recognition of the good, we will lose our grip not only on the concept of good, but even our cognitive contact with the Good itself. The claim that he is advancing, however, is more subtle than the notion that the Good is always the object of our *eros*. The thesis in this vicinity that seems to Adams the most clearly correct is that to the extent that anything is good, in the sense of "excellent," it is good for us to love it, admire it, and want to be related to it, whether we do in fact or not. Adams believes that "x is excellent" implies not only that it is good to value x, but also that this goodness of valuing x is grounded in the excellence of x and independent of ulterior values that may be served by the valuing.

As a theist, Adams understandably thinks that it is most plausible to take God as best filling this role, and heartily commends other theists to do the same. On this basis Adams then makes the claim, roughly following Plato, that the property of goodness consists in the relation of resemblance to the ultimate Good, so that finite goods are themselves good to whatever extent they measure up to the ultimate standard. We completely concur with Adams that these moves are quite natural for any committed theist, perhaps especially any theist of the Anselmian variety. Adams doesn't say merely that the Good depends on God, but that God is the Good. He endorses an identity relation, according to which the Good isn't merely a property of God, but God himself, which helps avoid some of the classical objections to simplicity.[20]

Thinking about some of the distinctive features of Plato's form of the Good gives us all the more reason to think that God best satisfies such a description. The Good for Plato was no garden-variety form, but the one that had ontological primacy over all the others, the ultimate standard for all evaluations of the good. It is likened to the sun and is said to be the source of all that exists. Self-predication is also less a problem for the form of the Good than it is for other Platonic forms, as the Good is plausibly thought of as good in and of itself, indeed the Supreme Good, just as God is thought of by classical theists. Moreover, Platonists naturally think of the ultimate intrinsic Good, like theists think of God himself, as the ultimate source of all the best and truest happiness of which we are capable. The affinities between the Platonic conception of the Good and God himself are so pervasive and striking at so many levels that it is hard to exaggerate.

## Taking Divine Necessity Seriously

Before moving on, we wish to point out and apply a few of the interesting implications of this connection between God and goodness in moral apologetics. We will begin by contrasting two arguments, both of which initially seem to assume the falsity of Anselmianism. As we shall see, however, only one does so in an objectionable way, since the other is meant, or at least is able to be construed, along more epistemic lines than metaphysical ones. Then we will identify an upshot from the discussion that will help explain why certain arguments that suggest that atheism leads to moral nihilism may well lack persuasive force. The reason is connected with the presupposition and methodology of one of the arguments earlier subjected to criticism.

Let's start with an argument that C. Stephen Layman rejects that looks like this:

1. If God does not exist, then there are no objective moral truths.
2. At least some moral truths are objective.
3. So, God exists.[21]

By "objective moral truths" the first premise means moral truths that do not depend on human belief. Layman rejects this argument because of misgivings over this premise. If Platonism, for example, were true, which he thinks is a plausible enough theory, (1) would be false. Platonism, if true, would show that (1) is false by stipulating a scenario in which the antecedent (God does not exist) is true and the consequent (there are no objective moral truths) false. For Platonism would suggest that there are necessary moral truths, truths that obtain in all possible worlds—even worlds in which God does not exist.

At first glance, Layman seems to be assuming the contingency of God and falsehood of Anselmianism. The only way that there could be "atheistic worlds" (worlds at which God does not exist) is for God's existence to be contingent. If God were necessary, the Platonic counterexample would not be available. No world with objective morality but without God would be possible because no world without God would be possible. What the counterexample needs, to go through, is the genuine metaphysical possibility of an atheistic world, and its mere epistemic possibility is not nearly enough. Michael Martin's critique of Paul Copan's objections to atheistic objective morality seems to fall prey to this very mistake of assuming otherwise.[22]

Even if one were to assume the necessity of God, however, an atheist (who is not a naturalist) could still argue for the (at least possible) truth of the Platonic counterexample. For affirming God's "necessity" is ambiguous between affirming his necessity de dicto and his necessity de re. The de dicto reading is that

4. Necessarily, a qualification for being God is necessity,

which could be a true proposition even if God does not exist. The necessity of God would be a condition for satisfying the office of Deity, but the office would be empty. Nonetheless, the atheist is affirming an important sense in which necessity is attached with God, although it would be analogous to "Santa lives at the North Pole." The de re reading of God's necessity, in contrast, would be this:

5. God necessarily exists,

which predicates of God the necessary or essential property of existence. Those uncomfortable with treating existence as a predicate could instead say that God exists in this and all possible worlds and avoid the appearance of predicating of God the property of existence. God's de re necessity would entail the falsity of the Platonic counterexample.

The committed Platonist (or other nontheistic moral realists) would consider himself justified to reject the first premise, whereas one might expect that the believer in God's necessary existence would be inclined to accept that premise. Interestingly, though, Layman himself is a classical theist, not a Platonist (at least not an atheistic one). He's not likely to believe that God is contingent, so why does he reject (1) by putting such stock in Platonism? Perhaps for this reason: his rejection of it is not because he is convinced it's false, but because he thinks it lacks justification, or wide enough support, or sufficient obviousness. It still may be (nontrivially) true, but it may be thought to be a bad premise in an argument designed to convince the unpersuaded. If someone is skeptical of the dependence of morality on God, or of evidence that morality provides for God, she will likely be at least as skeptical of God's necessity. So Layman may have simply recognized, in light of the epistemic possibility of the falsehood of and the somewhat principled resistance to (1), that the more epistemically humble path was to look elsewhere for a better moral argument for God's existence, which he in fact does, an argument we consider later in the book.

We wish to compare and, more importantly, contrast Layman with John Milliken. In a recent article in *Philosophia Christi*, Milliken tried to answer Michael Martin by arguing "not that morality *must* depend upon God, but that it *may.* This avoids the thrust of Martin's objection, for I can admit that there could still be morality without God," Milliken writes.[23] A world without God as Milliken envisions it includes "beings like ourselves [who] would still place demands upon one another even if there were no God."[24] Note how what Milliken envisions is a world just like ours, holding everything equal, but without God. We see what he is trying to do here, but if God exists necessarily, which is among the implications of Anselmian theology, a world with no God in it but with creatures just like us is a metaphysical impossibility. Milliken makes note of this, but suggests that there is wisdom in keeping this metaphysical issue distinct from the purely meta-ethical one of whether the existence of morality is compatible with the nonexistence of God.

Although exploring counterpossibles can be instructive, we are inclined to think that the metaphysical issue is the most relevant consideration of all to the meta-ethical question, and we're applying it unapologetically. Had Milliken pointed out the metaphysics/epistemology distinction, like we did in assessing Layman's argument, perhaps he could have salvaged his point, but casting it the way he did makes it vulnerable to criticism. Bringing to bear the metaphysical point on the meta-ethical discussion provides, by the way, a better answer to Martin than Milliken's distinction between "must" and "may." That distinction of Milliken's seems unhelpful in this context, for it is unclear what sense of possibility he's using. He doesn't mean metaphysical impossibility, presumably, since he himself is inclined to think that an Anselmian God exists. If it's just epistemic possibility, that's too weak and uninformative a concept on which to make a substantive meta-ethical point. A better answer to Martin's claim that realism challenges theistic ethics, especially in light of the narrative of necessity chronicled in this chapter, would have been that the Anselmian can make better sense of necessary truths than Martin can; such truths are thoughts God thinks in this and all possible worlds, as Plantinga argues in "How to Be an Anti-Realist."[25] So we disagree with Milliken that we can so casually affirm moral truths in an atheistic world, at least without a more principled rejection of Anselmianism. And this naturally leads to the main upshot that we wish to emphasize to finish this chapter.

Entitled to Tenacity

We would like to point out one prominent implication of our discussion. Recall the argument rejected by Layman that had for its first premise that "If God does not exist, then there are no objective moral truths." Since we are inclined to persist in our belief that a world in which there's no Anselmian God is in fact something of a world about which nothing with much confidence can be said, in a real sense we think that the first premise would be right; if God doesn't exist, there are no objective moral facts, because such a world would feature nothing at all—because no such world exists or even possibly could exist. Nonetheless, we agree with Layman that this premise is not a good starting point in moral apologetics. Why is this?

Because most typically when a conditional says "If God doesn't exist, then objective moral facts don't exist," its speaker means to convey approximately this, echoing Milliken: "Hold everything equal, assume the world just as it is, but exclude from the picture God's existence; in such a world, moral facts don't exist." To be conceivable, this scenario has to assume less than an Anselmian

God, but go ahead and try to do it for a moment. Exercise your imagination if you're a theist, and assume for argument's sake that God doesn't exist, that the atheists are right. We still have relationships, though, and what seems like love and intersubjective moral agreement. Moreover, we have instrumental reasons to live ethically and perhaps strong convictions about the objective nature of morality and the various "satisfactions of morality" that we all feel when we do the right thing. Add it all together, and a quite complex picture results. If we assume for a moment that a world at that level of sophistication is possible without God's existence, without God's having created it and upholding it, then it seems to us, frankly, that atheists would be well within their epistemic rights to retain some obstinacy on the matter of secular ethics. This is true even if the moral argument is a powerful argument that offers positive evidence in favor of theism. Secularists who attempt to build nontheistic ethical theories would still face their challenges, challenges that may well prove intractable, but encountering challenges would not make them irrational for not immediately giving up. Every worldview has its hard questions to answer. And in truth, our secular counterparts would have quite a bit of fodder to work with to build such an ethic. We are inclined to think that their efforts would still ultimately fail, but what we are taking seriously here is that if God doesn't exist, then Anselmian theists are radically wrong.[26] Our own effort at making sense of morality would have failed, and our fundamental picture of reality would be completely mistaken. And in that contingency, we would concede philosophical defeat on this issue.

But we are convinced that God *does* exist, and also that the most rational position to hold is that God exists and exists necessarily. And an important part of our case for this view of God is that it makes such great sense of morality in terms of its salient features like objective good and bad, right and wrong, rights and duties, moral freedoms and responsibilities, necessary truths and deep regrets, guilt and fulfillment, and the like. If God exists, then that would provide evidence of such moral facts; and such moral facts give evidence that God exists. If the connection between God and morality is as intimate and organic as we would argue that it is, this is exactly what one should expect.

Again, however, we retain the vital recognition that, if we are wrong and God does not exist, then we are radically and profoundly wrong. God's existence altogether alters our picture of reality, and we cannot overstate the significance of this fact. Anselmian theists are right and atheists radically wrong, or atheists are right and such theists are radically wrong. It's an obvious point, but it's worth saying: the way the world is makes a great deal of difference. Either a theistic world or an atheistic world is the actual world; speculations about the features of the nonactual world need to exhibit a great deal of epistemic humility—on both sides of the philosophical aisle.

Since we are not comfortable pontificating about the features of an atheistic world that we think we have excellent rational reason to consider not just counterfactual, but an intrinsically and intractably impossible world, we would not be inclined to couch a moral argument for God's existence in terms of what such a world would be like. In this sense we agree with Layman that the first premise isn't a good starting point. We can, however, shift gears a bit and couch the argument in abductive terms, an inference to the best explanation, arguing that theism explains commonly accepted features of morality better than atheism does. This approach, while still requiring epistemic humility, nonetheless has the clear advantage of not requiring confident proclamations about features of an atheistic world. In one sense, this is more charitable to our atheistic friends, since we are admitting that we are radically wrong if their basic worldview is right, and, in such a contingency, that we may well be wrong about morality itself in ever so many ways. On the other hand, though, our approach shows some tough-mindedness with our secular dialogue partners because we are not willing to grant them the plausibility or possibility of moral Platonism, at least not without a stronger argument than that it is epistemically possible or vaguely conceivable.[27] We are also less willing than Milliken to "hold everything equal" and assume for argument's sake that God does not exist, which we think would put theists at a huge strategic disadvantage. We don't resist just to win an argument, however, but because we take seriously what is genuinely possible or impossible on the picture of God that we think is most rational. And this view of God rules out treating the biggest counterpossible of all like a garden-variety counterfactual where God is so easily excisable from the metaphysical equation.

Since the more typical attempt by theistic ethicists is to argue, as William Lane Craig does, that atheism leads to moral nihilism or something in its proximity, perhaps we can understand why such arguments tend to be so little persuasive, at least for principled and thoughtful atheists who recognize all the resources at their disposal to avoid nihilism.[28] If they have rationality, intersubjective moral agreement, the satisfactions of morality, and lifelong loving relationships and social networks to build on, they're far from irrational to resist, at least for a while, an argument like Craig's that secular ethics lacks the resources to prevent a slide into moral nihilism. Even if Craig's argument ultimately works, there's a reason that it lacks the persuasive power that many theists think it has. We are not suggesting that the argument is ultimately unsound, and it does well have its place. Our alternative suggestion, however, is predicated on a reminder to our atheistic friends that the world as they conceive it is one that we consider to be fictional, no less than they think that about a theistic world. We are intentionally attempting to take seriously the implications that one and only one of these two competing worldviews is the true picture.

We consider something about Craig's approach to be ironic. When Layman assumes that if for all we know God may not exist then we need to allow room for the metaphysical possibility of atheism, Craig rightly points out that all that follows is that we should admit the epistemic possibility that God does not exist. And when critics ask Craig to entertain a scenario where God issues an utterly evil command, Craig appropriately discounts the value of such a thought experiment by reminding us that it represents a counteressential and utterly impossible scenario on his view of a perfectly good God. But when theorists attempt to construct secular ethics based on features of the actual world—features that on Craig's view and ours are impossible without God's existence—he plays along and implicitly grants them this permission to use these materials to build their system. There's value in doing so to show the challenges that such efforts still face to answer various objections. However, there should be more explicit recognition of the point that, if God is Anselmian, this world, with its present features, is an impossible one without God. By playing along, Craig (if he's right) is letting atheists construct their moral system on features of a world that can only exist if God exists, and some of these features are remarkable enough to imbue in the atheists, appropriately enough, quite a bit of confidence. That it's an epistemic possibility that God doesn't exist may be true, but as Craig well knows, not much follows from that. By not making this point explicit at this key juncture of the argument, Craig's diatribe against secular ethics fails to carry nearly as much weight, in our estimation, as his defense of theistic ethics. And, unfortunately, he also implicitly bolsters the conviction of secular ethicists that there's nothing suspect about their methodology, which, we argue, is potentially question begging.

# 6

# Divine Command Theory

Our bearing towards God must be characterized by reverence, love, and fear—reverence for Him as a holy lawgiver, love for His beneficent rule, and fear of Him as a just judge.

—Immanuel Kant[1]

A humorous example of theistic ethics comes from *The Simpsons*, where divine command theory is given a voice in the character of Homer Simpson's incessantly cheerful, inordinately religious, winsomely sanctimonious neighbor Ned Flanders. Gerald J. Erion and Joseph Zeccardi explain:

> In Springfield, Ned Flanders exemplifies one way (if not the only way) of understanding the influence of religion upon ethics. Ned seems to be what philosophers call a divine command theorist, since he thinks that morality is a simple function of God's divine command; to him, "morally right" means simply "commanded by God" and "morally wrong" means simply "forbidden by God." Consequently, Ned consults with Reverend Lovejoy or prays directly to God himself to resolve the moral dilemmas he faces. For instance, he asks the Reverend's permission to play "capture the flag" with Rod and Todd on the Sabbath in "King of the Hill"; Lovejoy responds, "Oh, just play the damn game, Ned." Ned also makes a special telephone call to the model train room

in Reverend Lovejoy's basement as he [Ned] tries to decide whether to baptize his new foster children, Bart, Lisa, and Maggie, in "Home Sweet Home-Diddily-Dum-Doodily." (This call prompts Lovejoy to ask, "Ned, have you thought about one of the other major religions? They're all pretty much the same.") And when a hurricane destroys his family's home but leaves the rest of Springfield unscathed in "Hurricane Neddy," Ned tries to procure an explanation from God by confessing, "I've done everything the Bible says; even the stuff that contradicts the other stuff!" Thus, Ned apparently believes he can find solutions to his moral problems not by thinking for himself, but by consulting the appropriate divine command. His faith is as blind as it is complete, and he floats through his life on a moral cruise-control, with his ethical dilemmas effectively resolved.[2]

But this isn't entirely a laughing matter. Just this week, as we write this chapter, Iran's Supreme Leader, a Muslim cleric, warned the citizens in Tehran and elsewhere in the country to put a stop to their protests over alleged corruption and voting irregularities in the recent election of President Ahmadinejad and that, if their protests didn't stop, there would be a steep price to pay. By placing his imprimatur on the "official" government gloss on the election, his seems likely to be only the latest example of the way in which religion can be used to disguise and perpetrate injustices. Divine command theory stands as one of the biggest culprits in the minds of those who issue such criticisms of religion as undermining real morality.

So far in this volume we have argued that Ockhamistic voluntarism is too crude an expression of theistic ethics and does indeed fall prey to a number of intractable criticisms and should therefore be left behind. At the same time, however, we have argued that taking the features of morality seriously gives us excellent reason to think that it's God who best explains it. This, however, requires that we spell out a theistic ethic that avoids Ockhamism. One of the things this entails is that a defensible view of religious morality requires that God's goodness be recognizable and without blemish or darkness. We have stood in the tradition of Thomists, Anselmians, and theistic activists who argue that God himself is good and, indeed, the ultimate Good. We both predicate goodness of God and identify God with the Good, and we have sketched some of the ways in which this has been done by philosophers and theologians through the centuries. This has helped demonstrate some of the powerful resources at our disposal as Christian theists to defend such a view with some real rigor.

Our axiological theory (of moral goodness) is distinctly nonvoluntarist, but our deontic theory (of moral obligation) is not.[3] Moral obligations are the clearest example of what is morally right, or wrong not to do. Something can be morally good without being obligatory; moral duties, in contrast, are not voluntary, but required. They are authoritative, prescriptively binding, indications of what we morally ought to do. They are the sort of thing that we are morally blameworthy if we fail to do. In this chapter we will defend a version of divine command theory—not of moral goodness (axiology), but of moral rightness (deontic matters)—in our continuing effort to bolster the moral argument.[4]

## The Range of Ethics and the Semantic Turn

First, let's see how this discussion fits into the larger framework of ethical theory. Ethics is typically divided into three categories: applied ethics, normative ethics, and meta-ethics. *Applied ethics* is much like it sounds. It deals with real-life ethical questions like euthanasia, abortion, torture, and area-specific ethical questions such as those found in medical ethics, business ethics, environmental ethics, and the like.

*Normative ethics* is usually said to concern the nature of right and wrong, issues of moral obligation, permission, and supererogation, which involves actions that go above and beyond the call of duty. An example of a supererogatory action would be giving half of one's income to charity; it's praiseworthy if we do it, but we're not blameworthy if we refrain from doing it. Robert Adams, in his recent book on moral virtue, speaks of "substantive ethics" rather than normative ethics in order to include not just theories of moral obligation, be they Platonic, Kantian, or consequential, but also accounts of the kind of people we ought to be, such as virtue theories like those we find in Aristotle.[5] This chapter will spell out and defend a version of divine command theory of moral rightness, so the chapter will heavily focus on normative ethical matters, but there's a reason that the chapter is sandwiched between others on axiology and epistemology. A defensible version of divine command theory raises a wide array of questions, some of which we have anticipated and answered in advance, and others that we will take up in subsequent chapters.

Finally, *meta-ethics* is the most theoretical aspect of ethics of all. It asks fundamental prior questions about ethics like these: Are there any objective moral facts? What is the relationship between morality and rationality? What do terms like "right" and "bad" mean? How do we know the content of moral truth, assuming there is any? Some philosophers, like Phil Quinn, practically equate meta-ethics with issues of moral semantics. We instead think of meta-ethics more broadly as encompassing issues of metaphysics, semantics, epistemology, and the connection between morality and rationality, all of which we will touch on in subsequent chapters.

In twentieth-century analytic philosophy, however, Quinn was not alone in thinking of meta-ethics primarily or exclusively in terms of the meanings of moral terms. Moreover, quite a number of these philosophers also began to take this meta-ethical concern as the most important of all philosophical questions pertaining to ethics. The result was a "semantic turn" in philosophy generally and in ethics particularly, in part fueled by the work of Wittgenstein and the logical positivists. The guiding theme of much of the philosophical work generated by these thinkers was that defining moral terms exhausts the essence of ethical inquiry—a conviction that guided more than just those philosophers who reduced morality to emotivism.[6]

An examination of the logic of moral language in fact yields considerable insight into the way it is used. Consider, for instance, our language about obligation, such as this example: one morally ought to perform some action to help disenfranchised persons. Such language is not merely descriptive, but prescriptive and evaluative, involving the adoption of a particular kind of attitude toward the action so characterized. To call something obligatory is to prescribe the action for ourselves and to affirm that one should be committed to it when appropriate circumstances arise. It is also to prescribe it for others, and it suggests other insights as well, none of which we deny.

Nonetheless, one of the guiding motifs of this book is that this emphasis on semantic issues, though indeed interesting and illuminating, is nevertheless far from the last word on or the deepest inquiry into the subject. The meaning of "right" is one thing; the essence or nature of rightness is quite another; and likewise with other pieces of moral terminology. Now, these definitions and essences are related, but the relation is certainly not a simple identity, as we noted in the last chapter and will see even more clearly in this chapter.

The work of more recent philosophers led to a more nuanced understanding of these matters and a move away from an overly narrow focus on semantics. Until those developments, though, even Adams, who would later use these advances from the philosophy of language to revise his own work, gravitated toward a heavily semantic analysis of moral rightness. We will call this earlier body of work by Adams the "early Adams" material, to distinguish it from his later work that incorporated new insights in the philosophy of language. Before examining the seminal work on divine command theory by Adams, though, it's appropriate to examine another dimension of the historical study of the way that obligation language has been used, because doing so raises some issues directly germane to our project.

## Alasdair MacIntyre: the Limits of Historical Analysis and His Thomistic Shift

Moral obligations by no means constitute the whole structure of morality. Indeed, we will argue that they might more properly be thought of as a small closet right inside the front door of a sprawling castle, leaving the further reaches and loftiest peaks of morality in entirely different areas. Some philosophers, in fact, think that a focus on obligations largely can be eliminated altogether. By shifting the focus away from what we ought to do and instead asking questions about what sort of people we should be, they put the focus on virtues more than duties. Aristotle, for example, placed little focus on moral obligations, but a tremendous focus on the virtues. We ourselves will discuss the virtues in a later chapter, and we too will come down on the side of saying there's an important sense in which they are in fact more important than duties. However, it's our contention at the same time that moral obligations, at least at this stage of our moral development, constitute a vitally important and, indeed, essential aspect of ethics, and that no ethical theory at this stage of the game could hope to be complete without an adequate account of them. And to the extent that an approach to ethics seems incapable of sustaining a good enough account of moral obligations, such a deficiency counts as evidence against that approach.

One of the most brilliant ethicists of the twentieth century was Alasdair MacIntyre, and what he has to say about moral obligations is quite suggestive.[7] We will note an interesting transition in his thought, stretching from his earlier *A Short History of Ethics* to his later work that, though departing from some of his earlier analysis, was in certain ways anticipated by the earlier work. Early on, MacIntyre, the consummate philosophical historian, basically tells a tale according to which we shouldn't be surprised that moral language about obligations today lacks force and coherence. For such language has been severed from its original foundations and now its remaining fragments persist without sufficient social foundation. The original foundation for the notion of obligations, he argues, was a rigid hierarchical social structure in ancient Greece, where individuals within the community had clearly defined roles and social expectations within the *polis*. What naturally developed were obligations imposed by society to perform well in those specific roles. With the breakdown of such social hierarchy, obligations were less tied to social relations and came to be seen more and more as obligations *simpliciter*. At this point they were abstractions more than specific societal duties associated with one's lot in life, culminating, centuries later, in a focus on "doing one's duty for duty's sake alone." This in time led more and more commentators to raise questions about the propriety of taking as authoritative such alleged abstractions.

What often today contributes to the skepticism toward moral obligations is what we saw in the first chapter: on occasion it appears as if doing one's moral duty can conflict with one's self-interest. On such occasions it's potentially quite rational to wonder if the moral duties are real or not, whether they are a sober fact, or merely a useful fiction or a social construct. Morality inherently carries a strong sense of authority, perhaps the sort of authority that trumps all other reasons; yet if we're wrong about that, then on occasion it would certainly be preferable to know that and avoid an unnecessary sacrifice of self-interest. Unless the presumed authority of morality is real, why continue to be committed to it, especially when doing so is painful or costly? MacIntyre thinks that part of the story of why morality is not taken with adequate seriousness by some is that it has been implausibly assumed that morality can retain its force apart from the sort of social system that invests it with significance.

MacIntyre himself came to see the limitations of his early analysis, most particularly in its failure to reckon seriously enough with the metaphysical questions that the existence of moral facts invites. We can see the feet of the genetic fallacy at the door, for example; how the language of moral obligation originally came about does not settle the question of the metaphysical status, essential nature, or real authority of moral obligations themselves. We can also ask this: Even if the notion of obligation made great sense in an ancient Greek civilization in which it was tied to clearly defined social roles, was it actually *true* that real obligations obtained in that situation? That the language cohered with the way the society understood itself along hierarchical lines is arguably neither necessary nor sufficient to show that real obligations obtained. If the obligations did obtain, the idea that they obtained merely or mainly because of the way that society functioned strains credulity. MacIntyre may well be right to see an important social dimension of moral obligations, something we will see again when we return to Robert Adams's work later in this chapter, but acknowledging that point is a far cry from admitting that the sum and essence of moral obligations is exhausted by a close look at ancient Greece. MacIntyre's analysis can also make a great deal of sense of why the notion of obligation may have been widely felt and perceived in that historical scenario as authoritative and why, in contrast, moral obligations today seem to have lost some of their force in the popular imagination. But what we should do about this—and how we should best process that insight—is another matter altogether. The historical facts themselves do not begin to settle that question.

MacIntyre's historical analysis is characteristically rife with insight, but what strikes us and others as dubious is the way, in his early work, that he tries to process this insight when it comes to the connection between God and ethics. After arguing on historical grounds that there was an original social dimension to moral obligation, and noting the loss of moral authority that's resulted from a breakdown of a rigid social hierarchy, he seems to reject any effort in the history of ethics to use theism in a positive way to formulate moral theory. In *A Short History of Ethics*, he consistently portrays theistic ethicists as either radical voluntarists or philosophers assiduously endeavoring to use the God hypothesis as a stop gap measure. In particular, he thinks it is misguided to use theism to repair the breakdown that he attributes to the loss of the original hierarchical context where moral obligation language emerged. We think this unfairly and uncharitably trivializes the intelligent and, in our estimation, indispensable appeals to theism to make full sense of the normative force of morality, moral obligations in particular.

We are inclined to agree with the general thrust of MacIntyre's analysis that there is an important social dimension to moral obligations, indeed one that cannot be eliminated, but we strongly resist his further and spurious (early) inference that this somehow reveals theistic ethics to be superfluous in solving the challenges assailing ethical theorists. Again, the coherence of moral obligation language and societal expectations in ancient Greece is not enough to show why real obligations obtained there. The normative force needed to explain the authority of moral obligations needs an account, even in ancient Greece! Rather than appealing to the way things were back then as an answer to the normative question of where the authority of morality resides, it just pushes the question back a step. More theory is necessary; this is one of the reasons that historical analyses like MacIntyre's earlier work, however insightful, remain limited and necessarily so. Historical inquiry into how obligation talk arose is one thing; ontological questions of whether obligations exist and what their ultimate essence might be is another matter altogether.

As far as historical analyses go, incidentally, another aspect of the story that can serve as an important supplement to that of MacIntyre comes from Elizabeth Anscombe, one of Wittgenstein's famed students. In an important article written several decades ago, she gives a powerful, historically informed semantic consideration that can be construed as good evidence that we should look beyond history and semantics into questions of the ultimate foundations of morality. In "Modern Moral Philosophy," she makes a case that to understand the way the moral language-game is played we have to see the way it developed out of a specifically theistic context in the Western world.[8] In this context, oughtness and rightness and other moral concepts were tied to the commands of God. Lacking such undergirding assumptions, our moral terminology lacks not only important historical foundations, but also persuasive rational warrant, and retains force only insofar as it illegitimately borrows against that history. So "ought" language still may be thought to retain much of its authority, even in the minds of secularists who typically fail to recognize that this happens in part because of the lingering effect of theistic assumptions from earlier generations. In his desire to construct a coherent and structured historical narrative, MacIntyre seems at certain junctures in his analysis too cavalier in domesticating theism. Indeed, he tends to treat God as one more garden-variety item in the inventory of reality and a failed explanatory construct to fix a theoretical problem rather than the Ultimate Reality who, if he actually exists, bears profoundly on everything.

Our aim is not to enter the fray of a historical dispute about the origins of moral language about obligations, especially because we don't invest such investigation with the authority to settle the ultimate philosophical questions that such language raises. We're instead directing our attention to those questions themselves, but only after registering a few of our reasons for disagreeing with any claim, explicit or implicit, that historical analysis alone can settle the philosophical questions that morality raises. In later chapters we will take up epistemic and rationality matters in greater detail. The main question that we are taking up in this chapter is where moral obligations come from and what accounts for their normative force and binding authority. One option is to deny that morality has this authority, in which case there's nothing to explain. We tried making clear in the opening chapter the reasons we don't consider that to be a reasonable option; we consider it more intellectually honest to admit that there is moral truth, including binding moral obligations, and then ask what best explains them. So the normative question looms: What makes moral obligations authoritative? We have made it clear where we think the answers do not reside: Platonism, social hierarchy alone, naturalism, and so on; now we will lay out where we think they do.

Before we do, however, we would be remiss not to mention the important and huge shift in MacIntyre's own thought after his earlier work, a shift in a direction with which we are very sympathetic. And the transition was perhaps not so surprising after all, because, by MacIntyre's own admission, imbedded within *Short History* was an inadequately formulated and uneasy allegiance to strands of Aristotelianism. He admits that in his haste to criticize aspects of Aristotle's ethics, like its ties to his context and its exclusion of women and slaves from possibilities of virtue, he hadn't realized how the later Aristotelian tradition had itself largely purged itself of such "inessential and objectionable" elements. "Aristotle's ethics, in its central account of the virtues, of goods as the ends of human practices, of the human good as that end to which all other goods are ordered, and of the rules of justice required for a community of ordered practices, captures essential features not only of human practice within Greek city-states but of human practice as such."[9]

The version of Aristotelianism to which MacIntyre would eventually be most drawn was Thomism, which is ironic in certain respects in light of his consistently negative earlier depictions of theistic efforts to inform morality. But in light of his strong teleological focus, and of the fact that most of his earlier ire directed against theistic moralists was aimed at the voluntarist camp, it's perhaps not altogether surprising after all. His openness to a theistic ethic is still tempered, however, by his insistence that capturing the ultimate truth of the matter always remains a provisional and tentative enterprise; the best we can do is choose the tradition we think best fits us, or that we feel chooses us. Although we respect his epistemic humility here, his assignment of primacy to the role of one's moral narrative is, in our estimation, a bit overstated; but it's still remarkable that the chapter on Aquinas in *Whose Justice? Which Rationality?* and the closing chapter of *Intractable Disputes* offer so many of his views on what God does for ethics.[10] The first book says we need a (roughly) Thomistic doctrine of grace; the second says that without a theistic doctrine of creation, human rights is an absurd notion.

MacIntyre's more recent openness to theistic morality even reveals a modicum of openness to voluntarism (or at least a consideration of what such openness would require), as a fascinating article of his, written twenty years after the original publication of his *Short History*, illustrates. In "Which God Ought We to Obey and Why?"[11] MacIntyre describes the sort of possible variants of voluntarism that could in principle work, and the key component he identifies is a view of God as fundamentally just. Otherwise the theological voluntarism will both fall prey to intractable arbitrariness objections and create in its adherents a profound disconnect between feelings and will, a divided mind in which obedience to divine commands combines with a justified judgment that in some respects it is bad to do what God commands. Virgil's representation of Jupiter (in sending Mercury to convey his command to Aeneas to leave Dido and to sail to Italy) in the *Aeneid* is an example of such a deficient god. MacIntyre criticizes the early Adams for failing to incorporate enough aspects of justice into his divine command ethic, rendering it ultimately as vulnerable to arbitrariness as Ockam's, and Adams himself would later admit that MacIntyre on this score was right, leading to a revision of his theory in his later work. To Adams's important work we now turn.

## The Early Adams

A big contributor to the resurgence of divine command theory in the last few decades is Robert Adams, whose 1973 groundbreaking article "A Modified Divine Command Theory of Ethical Wrongness" drew great attention.

Subsequent work by such philosophers as Quinn, Idziak, Wierenga, and others have produced more and more precise formulations of the theory, innovative efforts to answer various objections, and a recovery of historical defenses of such a view. In terms of formulation, defense, and historical recovery, divine command theory has definitely registered its comeback among contemporary philosophers. It was Adams, though, who got the ball rolling, and his is an important example of both the importance of the role of semantics as well as its limitations that we mentioned earlier. The evolution of his own thought after writing that first essay, later penning its sequel "Divine Command Metaethics Modified Again," and a whole book on theistic ethics after that, serves as a microcosm of developments in the philosophical scholarship on divine commands. Sketched below is the story of this transitional development in Adams's thought.

Adams confines his initial version of divine command theory ("DCT") to matters of ethical wrongness, not to ethical terms in general, although he thinks he can extend it to ethical obligatoriness and permittedness. Quinn's 1978 book on divine command theory did in fact extend with logical rigor a theistic analysis across the range of deontic concepts. Adams qualifies his own theory as a "modified" theory of DCT because he renounces certain claims that are commonly made in such theories. He characterizes the *un*modified DCT of ethical wrongness as the theory that ethical wrongness *consists in* being contrary to God's commands, or the claim that the word "wrong" in ethical contexts *means* "contrary to God's commands." It affirms the logical equivalence of the following propositions:

1. It is wrong (for A) to do X, and
2. It is contrary to God's commands (for A) to do X.

Though these are affirmed to be logically equivalent expressions, this theory also affirms that (2) is conceptually prior to (1), so that (2) explains the meaning of (1), not vice versa. So, as Adams characterizes the unmodified theory, it does capture the asymmetry that a definition or analysis of meaning must feature, but it remains a straightforward definist analysis of (ethically) "wrong," a semantic analysis of DCT.

Adams rejects this approach, thinking it immediately susceptible to an intractable objection: such an analysis of meaning could not be right because not all people who use the term "wrong" *mean by* the term what this theory claims that they do. An empirical investigation into the way people actually use this language reveals that not everyone ties moral talk to divine commands. Adams, for instance, thinks no atheist would use "wrong" in this sense— though an atheist, without contradicting himself, could affirm this semantic analysis of DCT, but then insist that, since God does not exist, any such moral affirmation is in error. The atheist would be an "error theorist," in other words, or could affirm the "Karamazov hypothesis" that, since there is no God, every-thing is permitted (nothing is wrong). But Adams's point is well-taken: not everyone uses "wrong" to mean contrariety to God's commands, not even all theists. This leads Adams to think that he needs to restrict the scope of such language usage. A restriction of scope to an analysis of "wrong" in Judeo-Christian religious ethical discourse, then, is the first step toward Adams's modified theory. The second step toward his own theory comes about as a result of his answer to arbitrariness concerns afflicting the unmodified theory. On Adams's view, "It is contrary to God's commands to do X" implies "It is wrong to do X" only if certain conditions are assumed, namely, only if God has the character of loving his human creatures. In the contingency in which God issues a patently unloving command, like commanding cruelty for its own sake, Adams thinks his concept of ethical wrongness, rooted as it is in the com-mands of a God presumed to be loving, would just fail.

The rationale for this view will give us clearer insight into why Adams accords such importance to how people use moral language. In a semantic or definist analysis of DCT, the important question is how words are used. What sort of factors contribute to the development of such language usage thus becomes a most relevant consideration. In the experience of many individuals, the framework of their religious life has conditioned and colored their ethical conceptions and terminology. If so, it is easy to see why the concept of God's will or commands plays a central function in their lives, or in what Wittgenstein might call their distinctively religious "form of life" involving a vast web of beliefs, practices, and customs. In the language of such people, moral terms like "right," "wrong," and "obligatory" will often most naturally become tied to God's will. In the unthinkable situation envisioned in which God radically departs from moral expectations, the believer's moral terminology would break down. So Adams arrives at his modified view by confining DCT to an analysis of language among those in the Judeo-Christian tradition and by presupposing that God is loving. If the latter assumption turns out to be false, what follows is the loss of ability to say any actions are right or wrong. Presumably such believers would then need to rethink their moral language.

Given this logical possibility, his theory, though definist, is not rigidly so. For if it *were*, there could be no logically possible space in which the believer's moral language could break down this way. In terms of emotional and voli-tional attitudes and in terms of meaning, the expressions "It is wrong" and "It is contrary to God's commands" are, on Adams's view, virtually but not entirely identical, the slight differences normally being of no practical importance. The slight differences in associated attitudes and conversational implications between moral and theological predicates allow logical space for the arbitrariness counterexample and the resultant breakdown of moral language among believers. Recognizing this, however, is not, on Adams's view, inconsistent with the claim that part of what believers normally mean in saying "X is wrong" is that "X is contrary to God's will or commands."

Adams's initial view here raises a number of questions and has large implications for such matters as the possibility of ethical discussion between believers and nonbelievers and vacuity objections to DCT. Six years after that first article, Adams published another that began to mark a major shift in his thought. Almost as a precursor to this impending transition, Adams's first essay ends with him grappling with difficult questions concerning the relevance of semantics to ontology. He rhetorically asks what the relation is between philosophical analyses and philosophical theories about the natures of things, on the one hand, and the meanings of terms in ordinary discourse on the other. He admits that he remains somewhat befuddled on the issue, attributing his confusion to a lack of philosophical development into the nature of meaning.

Then he read an important set of papers by such philosophers as Donnellan, Kripke, and Putnam, whose work provided some of the answers for which he was searching. These developments enabled him to modify his theory again and to effect a definitive move away from just semantics to include both semantics and ontology. Their work makes an impressive case for the view that there are necessary truths that are neither analytic nor knowable a priori. Adams was convinced by their work, and he came to think that the truth of ethical wrongness is of this sort. He uses an example of individual identity to demonstrate that if such an identity holds, it holds necessarily given the transitivity of identity, even though such an identity cannot be established except by empirical investigation. If the identity actually holds, then a world in which they are distinct is still epistemically possible (in that we can imagine such a world for all we know), but it lacks broadly logical or metaphysical possibility. A world in which an entity is not itself is not a genuine possibility.

This is similar to Putnam's example of water, which we adduced in an earlier chapter. The essential nature of water is that it is comprised of two atoms of hydrogen and one of oxygen—and if we tire of the water example, just pick some other natural kind like a molecule of gold, with the essential property of an atomic number of 79, and run the same thought experiment. If such an analysis of the molecular composition of water is true, then it is a necessary truth but not knowable a priori. We can't figure out the makeup of water from our armchairs; it takes empirical research. Coming across a liquid just like water in various respects—transparent, suitable for drinking, tasteless—we can intelligibly ask if it is water, and test whether it is water by a laboratory analysis. If the composition of the liquid turns out to be, say, XYZ instead of $H_2O$, then we are entitled to deny it is water. The warrant for our denial is not an analytic truth, though, for it is dependent on whether what we have been referring to all along is in fact $H_2O$. That is an empirical question. What *is* analytically true is that if all of what we have been referring to as water has been of a single nature, then water is liquid that is of the same nature as *that*. Though it is an empirical truth that water is $H_2O$, Putnam argues that it is metaphysically necessary.[12]

Exploiting such insights, Adams changes his mind on the question of whether every competent user of "wrong" in its ethical sense must know what the nature of wrongness is. In this way, in his latest theory, he is able to jettison that aspect of his old theory according to which language has to be relativized to different linguistic communities. Words can be used to signify a property by people who do not know what the nature of the property is. To bolster such a point, Adams cites Plato's notion that there could be something that every soul pursues, doing everything for its sake, divining that it is something, but unable to say exactly what it is.

Competent users of the word "wrong" need to know such things as these: it refers to a property of actions, attitudes, and so on, and that people are generally opposed to actions and attitudes considered wrong, and that people count such wrongness as a reason for opposing such actions and attitudes. Adams thinks competent language usage here also requires opinions about what sorts of actions have this property and perhaps some fairly settled dispositions as to what will count as reasons for and against regarding an action as wrong. Though such knowledge and dispositions are necessary and perhaps jointly sufficient for competence in the use of a word, they are not sufficient to determine what wrongness is in its very essence. As Adams puts it, "What it can tell us about the nature of wrongness, I think, is that wrongness will be the property of actions (if there is one) that best fills the role assigned to wrongness by the concept."[13]

What this underscores is a real shift in Adams from semantics to ontology. Our language picks out the relevant concept to refer to as wrongness. By "wrong" we come to refer to actions and attitudes possessing the aforementioned features of which competent speakers of the term must be aware. However, just as water would still have existed even if no human being had named it, the same is true of wrongness. So though our semantics enable insight into what competent users of a term must know, it is inadequate for providing an analysis of the nature of the concept picked out by the use of the word. By the term "water" we contingently began rigidly designating a certain liquid as water based on its visible features, but water itself in its essential makeup *just is* $H_2O$. That state of affairs, since it obtains in the actual world, is metaphysically necessary. Likewise, by the term "wrong" we contingently began rigidly designating certain actions and attitudes as possessing features of disapprobation, but wrongness itself in its essential makeup is not captured by those criteria for competent usage. Adams, of course, thinks that what makes something wrong is that it is *contrary to the commands of a loving God*. This is the property that makes something essentially wrong, that best fills the role designated by the concept of wrongness. This fact, if Adams is right, is metaphysically necessary if true in the actual world.

Recall that in his earlier theory Adams was grappling for something beyond mere semantics, which suggests that, even then, he was sensing the need for further developments in the philosophy of language, particularly as it pertains to meaning. When these became available, he was immediately able to modify his theory in such a way that, first, we need not index ethical conceptions to linguistic communities and, second, clarified the shift from semantics to ontology, giving us more of what we want in a DCT. In other words, he made a major shift from mere claims about language to more substantial claims about the essential nature of what our moral language signifies.

## Finite and Infinite Goods

After another twenty years passed, Adams published the culmination of his three decades of thinking about DCT in the powerful book *Finite and Infinite Goods*, a very important contribution to the literature on theistic ethics. Adams begins the book by assigning priority to the good over the right; in the previous chapter we briefly looked at what he said about God and goodness, and now let's take a look at what he says about God and the right.

Since Adams's theory of the right presupposes his theory of the good, a few of his points about the moral good bear reiteration. The ultimate good on Adams's view includes not just the moral, but also intellectual and aesthetic excellences. The sublime, the beautiful, the intrinsically excellent, all represent the ultimate Good that Adams thinks is a role best fulfilled by God himself. This is a compelling vision indeed, one steeped in medieval thought, and one that, if accurate, would ensure that Truth, Goodness, and Beauty all ultimately cohere. This is in diametric contrast with the tendency of postmodern thought to see a deep tension between the true, the good, and the beautiful, a tension that ultimately leads to their fragmentation. Such fragmentation makes settling for a beautiful lie, a useful fiction, or the painful truth the best we can do; a sobering picture indeed—but not an accurate depiction of reality as Adams sees it.

Adams does not so much try to say exactly what the nature of the good or beautiful is, beyond saying that any instance of it resembles or images God, its ultimate source and exemplar, in some sufficiently relevant sense. Saying more than this has to appeal to things that we think are good or beautiful. This makes it difficult to say what the good is, but it leaves open the possibility that Godlikeness may still explain what sort of property it is.[14] Adams takes as veridical those intimations of a transcendent Good that we experience at certain moments of our lives, mere glimpses though they be. The ultimate Good is transcendent in that it vastly surpasses all other good things and all of our conceptions of it. The same is true of beautiful things that give us a sense of being dimly aware of something too wonderful to be contained or carried either by our experience or by the physical or conceptual objects we perceive. And yet there is something in these beautiful things that draws us in and inchoately promises us fulfillment, not mere fleeting satisfaction, if we could but bathe in its source. Adams thinks this suggests that the ultimate Good is always higher than the human realm, not unlike how Platonism would have it, but certainly in a way that is consonant with certain religious conceptions. Finite goods, on his view, derive their value by relevantly imaging this ultimate Good who is God himself.

With this powerful picture of the good in place, he turns to examine the nature of the right. His theory of the right covers what it is not wrong to do and what it is wrong not to do, that is, ethical permission and ethical obligation, respectively. Based on the semantic features of obligation, Adams argues that there is an important social dimension to moral obligations and that DCT best captures it. Before we explain how, it bears emphasis that Adams is in agreement with MacIntyre in seeing a vital connection between moral obligation and particular social relationships. This illustrates a most important lesson: MacIntyre's historical analysis, contrary to MacIntyre's own early deployment of it, is not at all inconsistent with a thoroughgoing theistic ethic.

Adams argues that the facts of obligation are constituted by broadly social requirements. Agreeing with John Stuart Mill, Adams thinks that it is a truth of meaning that obligation concepts are tied to social context. In laying out his analysis of the nature of the right, Adams makes the same assumptions about semantics and metaphysics that he did when analyzing the nature of the good. Once we understand the concept of obligation, we ought to ask what, if anything, best fills the role. So, what can be learned from the semantics of obligation? What must be true on broadly semantical grounds of anything that is to count as moral requirement or moral obligation?

Adams notes that we should care about complying with it, first of all. It needs, moreover, to be something that one can be motivated to comply with on good grounds that can be publicly inculcated. Given this public dimension, part of taking moral obligations seriously is to acknowledge that it is appropriate for someone to feel guilty for doing something wrong and for others to blame them in cases where there are not sufficient excuses. The social dimension of guilt is also apparent from the fact that it is connected with harm and with alienation from other people. The way we learn guilt originally is typically from a strained relationship when we were probably too young to understand rules. Adams attempts to give a richer account of deontology than just "duty for duty's sake," by saying that valuing one's social bonds gives reasons to do what is required by one's community. Not every community-conferred obligation is moral, but Adams delineates a personal conception of obligation in which we can see social facts as constituting obligations independently of our moral evaluation of those facts.[15]

Human social requirements can get us closer to the better reasons for complying on which moral obligation insists. Morally good reasons will arise only from a social bond that is truly good. One's attitude toward community is important. For one is willing to comply, not as a means of satisfying a desire to belong, but as an expression of one's sense that one already does belong. Reasons for complying are also affected by our evaluation of the personal characteristics of those who make up the community and our assessment of how the demands serve the community.

The fact remains, however, that human social requirements fail to cover the whole territory of moral obligation and can, moreover, conflict with each other without a clear way for such conflicts to be adjudicated. In light of this reality, Adams introduces a theistic adaptation of social requirement theory. In so doing he presupposes his earlier theistic conception of the ontological inseparability of God and the ultimate intrinsic good on which all lesser, finite, and mixed goods are based. Adams claims that a theory of the good for which God is the constitutive standard of excellence need not presuppose moral obligation, but his theory of moral obligation does presuppose his theory of the good. Only a God who is supremely excellent in being, in commanding, and more generally in relating to us, is one whose commands can plausibly be regarded as constituting moral obligation.

Adams argues that besides the reason-giving force of such a DCT, it also satisfies the demand for objectivity by grounding morality in God's eternally supreme excellence. Moreover, DCT meets our expectation that a sound theory of the nature of right and wrong will yield a large measure of agreement with our pre-theoretical beliefs about these matters, particularly by allowing our preexisting moral beliefs to function as a constraint on our beliefs about what God commands. Furthermore, by offering a convincing account of the nature of obligation, DCT easily satisfies the principle that genuine facts of moral obligation should play an essential part in our coming to recognize actions as right and wrong. Finally, DCT provides distinctively rich resources for making sense not only of how guilt involves an offense against a person, but also how forgiveness is possible. For the God of Christian theism, for example, is the Supreme Person who is offended by our moral failure, as well as the one who has provided a way to take our guilt away and restore our broken relationships.

We consider Adams's case to be a powerful one, and his analysis of moral obligations both persuasive and a useful corrective to other analyses that leave out important aspects of ethics, as we are about to discuss.[16] Note that on a view like his, the meta-ethical answer to the question of whether objective moral facts exist is an emphatic yes; indeed, he thinks, and we concur, that there are necessary moral truths. In terms of metaphysics, God is the ultimate Good and God's commands constitute genuine moral obligations, which have a normative force that goes far beyond the merely prudential or rational.

## A Way Out for the Naturalist

William Lane Craig is an intelligent contemporary proponent of divine command theory. In his debate on the topic of ethics with Paul Kurtz, he argues for a version of divine command theory of moral obligations, and we concur with almost all of what he says there, although in an earlier chapter we expressed a few reservations about some of his bold criticisms of atheistic ethics. We pressed the distinction between ontological implications of atheism on the one hand and, on the other, the epistemic point that a world as complex as the actual world, if it's an atheistic one, would ground quite a bit of rational tenacity for naturalists. Even if Craig's argument works, though, we have reason to believe it won't likely be highly persuasive to the committed atheist or as powerful as the positive case for theistic ethics.

Now we wish to highlight another aspect of his case with which we have a slight qualm. He writes, in the spirit of Adams, that "On the theistic view, God's moral nature is expressed toward us in the form of divine commands that constitute our moral duties. Far from being arbitrary, these commands flow necessarily from his moral nature."[17] What remains a bit unclear to us is the sense in which Craig is referring to necessity here. At a minimum he means that God necessarily does not issue commands inconsistent with his essential goodness, a claim with which we wholeheartedly concur. But his language does not rule out a more ambitious reading instead: All of God's commands are a necessary result of God's nature. And in a later portion of the published version of the debate, Craig replies to a criticism by Walter Sinnott-Armstrong by writing about how his (Craig's) version of DCT is designed to evade the problems generated by the Euthyphro Dilemma. Craig writes, "The arbitrariness horn of the dilemma, which concerns Sinnott-Armstrong, is avoided by rejecting voluntarism in favor of God's commands' being necessary expressions of his nature."[18]

Such language gives credence to the latter interpretation: that God's moral perfection necessarily entails all and only the commands that God in fact issues. In making this move, Craig no doubt aims to avoid the voluntarist label. While this is certainly a legitimate concern, if this is indeed his objective, we think his effort is misguided for three reasons. First, to say that God's commands render something obligatory is to embrace voluntarism. It strikes us as equivocal to suggest otherwise. Second, there's a huge morally relevant difference between the voluntarism embraced by Adams, Craig, or this book, on the one hand, and Ockhamistic voluntarism on the other. It is important to highlight the distinction between our version of voluntarism and the radical version that cannot avoid arbitrariness. Craig's choice to avoid the term tends to conflate views that are clearly distinct. Third, we think there are compelling theological reasons to make room in our ethical theory for divine prerogatives when it comes to his commands. If an Anselmian God is free in the libertarian sense and sovereign in the classically Arminian sense, there's excellent reason to think that some of his commands are optional or could have been different. God has latitude, and on occasion chooses from various alternatives. All of the alternatives are consistent with his nature, of course, but the idea that he's locked in and must issue just those commands that he does paints an objectionably constrained view of God's freedom. It strains credulity, for example, to insist that God's command for us to give 10 percent of our income could not have been that we give 11 percent instead—despite the resulting complexities for the mathematically challenged. We are very open to the truth of a great many obligations being necessary truth, but we remain unconvinced that they must all sport this modal status. Craig's suggestion seems possible, but not plausible, and represents an unnecessary effort to avoid the stigma attached to voluntarism; any careful reader can see already that Craig is far from an Ockhamist.

Murphy offers a different critique of Craig's analysis, claiming that if "moral obligation is just about universal, objective, other-directed rules of conduct with which we have exceptionally strong reasons to comply, then we have not seen any reason to suppose that a theistic grounding is called for. But if moral obligation is not adequately set apart in terms of these features, then

DIVINE COMMAND THEORY   121

there is space for Craig to reassert his position."[19] The basis for Murphy's contention here is that moral value can be grounded in prudential value—value associated with what is good for us as human beings—and can, as such, satisfy those four requirements of morality. With Craig, however, we harbor serious doubts about the effectiveness of Murphy's case here, especially his inference from "X has prudential value" to "X is something that morally ought to be done." Craig puts it well when he writes, "There seems to be an enormous gap in Murphy's argument at this point. How does it follow from Homo sapiens' reflective and objectivizing intelligence that what is conducive to human flourishing is morally good?"[20] Even more, we can ask, how does it follow that it is a matter of moral *obligation*?

We wish to conclude our discussion of moral obligations with another point of Murphy's with which we take issue as well. He notes that Adams has given some clear reasons to think that moral obligations do contain more than those four characteristics mentioned earlier (universal, objective, etc.). Murphy writes: "Adams's clearest argument for the ineliminably social character of obligation appeals to conceptual connections between moral obligations and guilt and between guilt and demands made in social relationships."[21] We have seen this already, and we agree that this is a rationally compelling piece of evidence to suggest the social nature of moral obligations. Murphy argues that this aspect of moral obligations in particular is one that the naturalist will have a considerably harder time making sense of. But then he adds this: "I do not think that the defender of a wholly nontheistic ethical view should be greatly bothered by this sort of argument. Suppose that we simply jettison the notion of moral obligation—what's wrong with that?"[22] The nontheistic ethicist can still, after all, talk about morally good and bad states of affairs, what's reasonable and unreasonable to do, and other sorts of obligations—legal, cultural, and social. "If the nontheistic moral philosopher is denied the concept of the morally obligatory, he or she may well claim that it is a piece of conceptual baggage that ethics is better off without."[23]

Our response to this is straightforward. Paying that price is just much too steep for anyone who takes morality seriously. Frankly, there are better reasons to believe in moral obligations than to believe in naturalism. If one of them has to go, we are inclined to think that the rational course of action is to abandon naturalism instead.[24] If our goal is the pursuit of truth rather than winning an argument, then what good reason is there to deny what seems undeniable: that there are authoritative moral obligations? If one's worldview does not adequately explain the nature of that authority, so much the worse for that worldview. If an alternate account can and does explain it, then that counts as positive evidence in favor of that worldview.

To be clear, the question isn't whether the consequences of losing obligation in morality are too awful to be endured. The question is whether it is true or not that there are moral obligations. If not, it doesn't matter how terrible the consequences are. In *The Abolition of Man*, C. S. Lewis says that if truth turns out to be terrible, the man standing in the *Tao* will not then switch sides.[25] *Letters to Malcolm* features the scene where he says that even if—*per impossibile*—God was "a losing cause," one would not turn quisling. He says that one should be like the good men in Norse mythology: "The trolls and giants win, but let us die on the right side, with Father Odin."[26] The truth is the "right side," wherever it leads. A worldview-driven denial of what seem obvious, namely, moral duties, does not show fidelity to the sober truth. If moral duty does not exist, we are hardly obligated to pretend it does. But if there is good reason to think that moral duties really exist, we should own up to it, even if it requires a fundamental change in our worldview.

Finally, there's a paradox when it comes to our obligation to obey God's commands, a paradox that resides at the heart of divine command theory and beliefs about God's authority over rational agents, and an issue Murphy considers at length in his book on divine authority.[27] Although many would consider it to be obvious that, if the God of classical theism exists and issues commands, then his commands ought to be obeyed, others reject this.[28] Even apart from their reservations over divine command theory, such critics insist that God, even if he exists, is irrelevant to morality except in prudential ways. Many, in fact, take this to be the import of the Euthyphro Dilemma. We have argued and will continue to argue, to the contrary, that God by his nature deserves our trust, allegiance, and obedience, and that included among reasons to obey God's commands are not only prudential and practical ones, but prescriptive ones as well.

As we conclude this chapter, let us consider the reasons we normally ascribe authority to someone. Sometimes it is a simple matter of power. A person who has the legal power to enforce his will, for instance, has a certain kind of authority. Another source of authority is knowledge and information. We recognize as authorities those persons who have sufficient mastery of a field or discipline that they can command respect for what they know and understand. A third source of authority is moral integrity and character, the sort of authority that appeals to our conscience and demands respect in a deeper sense than the authority that comes from mere power, or even knowledge. Indeed, a person who has mere power or legal authority but who lacks moral integrity lacks the authority to command our respect, even if he has the power to enforce his will on us.

Now then, God has supreme power, knowledge, and goodness, and all of these underwrite his moral authority. He created us and this world and stamped us with his image, and has the power to hold us fully accountable for our actions. Since he has perfect knowledge of us, he understands perfectly what is good for us and our flourishing. Moreover, since he is perfectly good he desires our well-being and does everything short of overriding our freedom to promote it. In view of his nature as a perfect being, there are no good grounds for doubting his authority. There can be no blindsidedness, no bias, no imperfect understanding, no possibility of misuse of power, or having obtained it wrongly. If all rational withholdings are blocked, we ought to accept God as an authority. And part of what is involved in that is accepting his commands, unless we have good reason to do otherwise; but again, with a perfect being, there can't possibly be good reasons to do otherwise. In short, we think the issue of authority is a matter of power, knowledge, and character, all of which add up to *moral* authority.[29]

# 7

# Abhorrent Commands

Shall not the Judge of all the earth do what is just?

—Genesis 18:25

In his autobiography, John Stuart Mill characterized his father like this: "His aversion to religion, in the sense usually attached to the term, was of the same kind with that of Lucretius: he regarded it with the feelings due not to a mere mental delusion, but to a great moral evil. He looked upon it as the greatest enemy of morality: first, by setting up factitious excellencies—belief in creeds, devotional feelings, and ceremonies, not connected with the good of human kind—and causing these to be accepted as substitutes for genuine virtue: but above all, by radically vitiating the standard of morals; making it consist in doing the will of a being, on whom it lavishes indeed all the phrases of adulation, but whom in sober truth it depicts as eminently hateful."[1]

In our effort to defend theistic ethics against such criticisms, thus bolstering moral apologetics, we have spelled out and considered implications of a nonvoluntarist account of the good and a divine command theory of moral obligation. We have tried to explain how the voluntarism we embrace avoids Ockhamism and answers normativity questions. But now a cluster of concerns rear their head that we must address: the "no reasons," "abhorrent commands," and "vacuity" objections to voluntarism. Commentators often call the first two objections "arbitrariness" problems, and such arbitrariness concerns are merely the flip side of the vacuity objection. So this chapter will attempt to answer these various objections, and in the process to shed more light on how our view informs a range of issues that such criticisms raise.[2]

## The Achilles' Heel of Arbitrariness

In a sense, all three of these criticisms—*no reasons, vacuity,* and *abhorrent commands*—fall under the general penumbra of arbitrariness concerns and capture aspects of the same problem, though they remain conceptually distinct. Again, the *no reasons objection* says that God's commands are not rooted in anything but divine caprice, and our obedience is nothing but deference to a powerful authority; the *vacuity objection* says that if God defines morality, then calling God good or his actions right lacks determinate content; and the problem of *abhorrent commands* raises the terrifying prospect of God issuing the command of something irremediably awful, thereby rendering it moral. What is our answer to these objections?

The *no reasons objection:* This objection has two distinct but related forms. One says that God has no reasons for the commands he issues; this raises the specter of divine caprice. The other says that, as a result, we have nothing to base our moral decisions on except God's commands; we can call this the "blind obedience" aspect of the objection. God may have commanded us to feed the hungry, but he could have told us to ignore them; his decisions aren't based on reasons, but divine caprice. If they *were* based on reasons, we're told, then it's those reasons, not God's commands, that would serve as the heart of morality. But since he doesn't issue commands based on reasons, all we have is an arbitrary morality, something that could have been very different from what it is, and our duty reduces to obedience to arbitrary commands.

How do we respond to this objection? To begin with, we affirm that God indeed has reasons for the commands he issues, but we reject the notion that this leads to a divorce between God and ethics. If "God is good" is true both as a predication and identity, a typical reason that God issues the commands he does is that the actions he commands are good. Recall that the goodness of an action, on Adams's account, comes from its relevant resemblance of God's nature. An action such as loving one's neighbor, then, is good in virtue of resembling God's own loving and relational character. We agree with Craig and Adams that all of God's commands are deeply resonant with his character, and that divine command theory must be built on the foundation of God's loving nature.

Discerning or apprehending that an action is a morally good one gives us reasons to perform it. But such reasons don't count as a moral obligation unless the reasons are strong enough. Without adequate reasons, we may rightly choose not to perform the action. It might still be good to perform it, but we're morally permitted to refrain; not every opportunity to do good introduces a new obligation. The command of a perfectly good God who created us in his image, for the purpose of communion with him and with one another, qualifies as the kind of reason sufficient to generate an obligation. If the action in question is good but not divinely commanded, it would still be morally permissible to perform it, perhaps even morally laudable, but not morally obligatory.

In light of the social dimension of moral obligations, what would make an action obligatory without such a divine command? We could say, "It's just obvious the action is morally obligatory," but that's an epistemic point, not an ontological explanation, and, even if it's true, it's consistent with a wide variety of moral theories, divine command theory among them. Our contention has been that divine command theory provides a stronger account of where moral obligations come from than accounts provided by naturalists, who may well recognize the reality and power of moral obligations just as clearly as anyone but who, nevertheless, struggle to provide an adequate explanation for them.

So if God's commands are rooted in his goodness and his sovereign choice is based on his love and wisdom, then his commands don't lack good reasons, nor does our obedience. Divine command theory does not make God capricious, nor us blindly servile, contra the blind obedience charge. And since God himself, on our view, is the Good, then the reasons for God's commands rooted in goodness don't drive any sort of wedge between God and morality.

Since not every good action is obligatory, it is important for a moral theory to provide a way to distinguish between actions that are good but not obligatory and those that are obligatory. Utilitarianism often has a notoriously hard time doing this, but divine command theory does not. However, since there is a genuine distinction between the good and the right, then it would seem that God must have more reasons than an action's goodness to command it and render it obligatory. This, we suggest, is where his wisdom and love come in, but also an element of divine prerogative, which we have already mentioned and will discuss further in a moment. To get a sense of the constraints of God's love and wisdom, consider earthly parents. They may on occasion deem a punishment necessary for their child, but as to what exactly the punishment is, they typically have latitude on the matter. Perhaps several alternatives would be equally effective, whereas others would be clearly incommensurate with the wrongdoing or even deleterious to the child. This is where their sensitivity and discernment come in. God, of course, is subject to none of our struggles to figure out his course of action, but surely it's plausible to think that at least on occasion he has at his disposal more than one alternative consistent with his perfection. The person who would deny this bears the burden of proof and owes us some good reason to think this is not so.

Recall our resistance to Craig's suggestion that every command is necessary. Some of God's commands are likely necessary, perhaps most, but the idea that each and every divine command has to be issued and couldn't have been different seems implausible to us. In an effort to avoid the worst forms of arbitrariness objections, it's understandable that Craig wants to suggest that all of God's commands are necessary. But again, we think this needlessly overstates the case by failing to distinguish between what's negotiable and nonnegotiable in ethics. When it comes to necessary moral truths, Craig is completely right, but not all moral obligations are plausibly thought to be necessary truths, such that they could not possibly be different. It's possible, but not likely, and the evidence doesn't point in that direction. It's true that God wouldn't change his command for us to worship him, but what principled reason is there to insist that all the dietary laws of the Old Testament had to be exactly as they were? Choice of one over the other seems to fall within God's legitimate range of freedom and authority. For another example, Robert Adams suggests that certain practices of euthanasia might be possible instances where divine latitude obtains.

We could also accentuate a different sort of example, from among the so-called "imperfect duties," which we have a general obligation to fulfill, like feeding the poor. Such a duty allows for exceptions and can be satisfied in various ways. It doesn't, for example, require that we give to the poor every chance we get. Kant distinguished such duties from "perfect duties," which admit of no exceptions and prescribe a specific action. A robust theistic ethic like ours recognizes God's authority to issue commands to particular people at specific times, rendering what might be a mere imperfect duty into a strong concrete prescription for someone. The locus of authority for morality, on our view, is not an impersonal law but a personal God, who can speak and direct us to action in a way that bears resemblance and functions analogically to a vocational calling specific to individuals. What this means, though, is that two people walking down the street who come across a homeless person might have different duties toward such a person. God's prerogatives to speak and guide in a personal way means that not every obligation he imposes applies equally to everyone in a similar set of circumstances, contra Kant, as we saw in the previous chapter. It might also suggest that, depending on the particular commands God has issued, what appears to be the fulfillment of a duty might actually be supererogatory, and what appears on another occasion to be supererogatory might be the fulfillment of an obligation.

The apostle Paul spoke of his "heavenly calling" to which he was obedient, a calling that God obviously didn't intend for everyone. Yet there was nothing objectionably arbitrary about God's choice to call Paul in this manner, as it was designed, ultimately, to serve as a blessing for all, to spread the message of God's salvation beyond the confines of Judaism, just as God had planned all along.[3] The idea that God provides specific, concrete callings and commands makes moral sense of the New Testament text that says that anyone "who knows the right thing to do and fails to do it, commits sin."[4] If the verse means that we need to do every moral deed we possibly can, the obligation would be onerous and would preclude not only the category of supererogation, but any measure of freedom in the moral life. A more sensible reading, both exegetically and philosophically, is that he who is genuinely led to do a particular good deed sins if he refrains from doing it. This serves as a reminder of the richly personal and relational component of our voluntarist analysis, an aspect easily overlooked in the haste most show to recklessly distance themselves from bad forms of voluntarism. The analogy between morality and vocation here also bears relevance to dimensions of divine hiddenness, as Paul Moser argues in his powerful book *The Elusive God*, an issue that we will discuss at greater length in a later chapter.[5]

So we wish to preserve room for an element of divine prerogative in our DCT, but hardly to suggest that it's within God's character to abrogate morality altogether. That is out of the question, as we're about to see. It may well be, nonetheless, within God's prerogative to confer on us duties by commands he didn't have to issue, but the pool of alternatives from which he chooses are all consistent with his perfect and loving character.

The *vacuity objection*: This objection also comes in a few different but related forms. If God is the source of morality, then saying "God is moral" is alleged to express a trivial truth, to be tautologous, and not substantively and informatively true. When we say "God is good," that is supposed to mean something determinate, but if goodness is a function of divine say-so or even a function of God's character *whatever that may be*, then the ascription seems to lack the determinate content we think it has.

Let's address this point first. If God is the ultimate Good, how can he also be called good meaningfully? We've touched on this before, but, again, the concepts of godness and goodness are distinct, even if their referents are one and the same. We learn our concepts of goodness from the bottom up, but this leaves open the possibility that ontology functions top down and that God himself is the ultimate Good. What we refer to by goodness, having learned the concept and having come into a clearer and clearer understanding of it, could well be, most ultimately, God himself. And we've argued that this is the case.

We will have more to say about this when we discuss epistemology in a later chapter.

For now let's move closer to the second variant and real heart of the vacuity objection. *Why* do some suggest that divine command theory results in the loss of the content of moral language? Because, so the objector says, God has ultimate authority to do what he wants, to issue the commands he chooses, and he could command us to do things utterly at variance with morality as we understand it. God could radically alter the contents of morality and make right wrong and good bad. On this sort of analysis, the truth of "God is good" is consistent with God being, to all appearances, bad, even irremediably bad.

Although it should be obvious that Ockhamistic voluntarism is vulnerable to such criticisms, it should be equally obvious that our view of voluntarism is not. The divine prerogatives we affirm are in no way like the notion that God could completely turn morality on its head and render good evil, or vice versa. In fact, we have argued, to the contrary, that our foundational convictions about what is good and bad and how such words are used must be taken with the utmost seriousness—and that doing so contributes to the evidential case for theistic ethics. Rational belief in God's goodness demands it. Ours is not an Ockhamistic or fideistic affirmation of divine goodness no matter what, but a theory that says God's goodness is most plausibly thought to be perfect, without defect, and recognizable. God is not just good, but the ultimate Good, and this is exactly why we retain confidence, even with some fear and trembling, in identifying some things as morally beyond the pale, commands and states of affairs that a perfect God would not issue or allow, respectively. The challenge of handling problematic commands will be the topic for the remainder of this chapter, and this is related to the challenge of handling problematic states of affairs, the classic problem of evil, a topic that we will take up in chapter 8.

These vacuity objectors entertain a certain kind of scenario, one in which God, for example, tells us to torture children for fun. They then ask us to consider the implications of divine command theory. God has issued the command, rendering the action commanded obligatory. At that point "Child torture for fun is morally obligatory" would be true, and the recognizably determinate content of moral language would have disappeared. Their basic point is a semantic one—namely, that any theory that results in such obviously vacuous moral language is a failed theory. Divine command theory, as a result, is bankrupt. Notice the way such objectors reason: they ask us to envision a scenario in which such a proposition would be true, then they basically say that this results in something absurd and unacceptable—arbitrary or vacuous moral language.

And this is exactly why the vacuity objection, at least in this form, is the flip side of the *abhorrent command objection*. For this objection, too, asks us to think about what divine command theory implies. If God were to issue a morally abhorrent command, he would render the action, no matter how seemingly bad, morally obligatory. So this objection also imagines that it's at least possible that God could issue some morally abhorrent command. And then it rightly says that those premises together yield the possibility that something so hideous as child torture for fun could become morally obligatory. But rather than assuming that state of affairs as possible for purposes of argument and making a semantic point, the abhorrent command objector simply stops and says, morally speaking, that something has obviously gone awry. Any theory that entails the possibility of the morality of child torture is a failed theory. The abhorrent command objection is less a semantic point than an ontological one; rather than just bristling over the bastardization of moral language, it instead insists that morality itself just can't feature such nonsense. But what's more important to notice than the differences between the vacuity and abhorrent command objectors is what they hold in common: the assumption that, say, it's possible that God could issue the command that we torture children for fun.

The badness and wrongness of child torture for fun sports the requisite credentials to qualify as about the best candidate for a necessary moral truth that we can imagine. This is what makes the common appeal to such an example no surprise. If divine command theory abrogates such a moral commitment, there's excellent reason to reject divine command theory. Some versions of divine command theory, we have seen, do fall prey to this criticism. Ours does not. For if child torture for fun is necessarily and irremediably bad, as it surely seems to be, our account is not only that God never *will* command it, but that he *can't*. The moral truth in question would be a reflection of his very nature, upheld by his faithfulness to it in this and all possible circumstances. It's potentially a veridical window of insight into an aspect of his own holy and loving character. To issue a command at variance with it would be to deny himself, which God simply can't do.

This point needs strong emphasis. When we say that God can't issue a command like child torture for fun, some wish to resist, saying God *could*, but of course he never *would*. We agree he never would, but reject the idea that he could, and we insist unequivocally that unless God can't issue such a command, divine command theory would fail. For consider this argument:

1. Divine command theory is true.
2. God could (though he never would) command us to torture children for fun.
3. So, child torture for fun could become morally obligatory.

The argument is a valid one. But the conclusion is unacceptable, and we assert so unapologetically. If readers insist on further reasons for our confident claim, we submit that they are confused, for what could we possibly appeal to as more morally obvious than the falsehood of that conclusion? In order for an argument to get off the ground, there has to be an axiomatic starting point. The falsehood of the conclusion qualifies as a good one. So we consider ourselves eminently justified to treat it as such.

So far so good, but at this point there's a parting of the ways. Critics of divine command theory take Ockhamism as paradigmatic and assume that DCT is the culprit. DCT basically entails that anything and everything, morally speaking, is possible, and thus entails a rejection of necessary moral truths. It makes morality a matter of divine caprice. So, understandably, critics reject Ockhamism, but, mistakenly, they reject divine command theory generally. Our version of divine command theory, in contrast, is not at all susceptible to such criticisms, and in fact it gives us excellent reason to reject *the other premise*. That is, we reject the claim that it's possible that God could issue a genuinely morally abhorrent command. His essential goodness precludes it. At this point our solution should come as no surprise, since it's been a recurring motif of our whole approach. Our confidence is rooted in classical Christian convictions about God's impeccability and essential goodness discussed and defended in earlier chapters.

Some would respond to our solution by saying that God can do anything, and they insist that it's wrong to say otherwise. God is sovereign, all-powerful, and without constraint; he can do all things. To which our response is this: If God could, in fact, do just anything at all, then he could, say, sin, and God can't sin. Or he could commit suicide, or lie, or deny himself, or make twice two five, or both exist and not exist in the same sense at the same time. The Bible itself makes clear that God can't do everything. He can't be tempted to sin, for example, we're told, or deny himself. Does this mean he's not omnipotent? Not at all; it just means that we need a more sophisticated analysis of omnipotence than an affirmation of it so simpleminded that we end up spouting contradictions and incoherence. God can do everything that's consistent with his perfect nature. Sinning is not. This doesn't show that God is "limited," but rather that his perfection is without limitation. The ability to do some things, such as lie, is a weakness, not a strength. It's not that he isn't free to sin; rather, he's entirely free from any vulnerability to sin. It has no hold on him and does not constitute a temptation for him. He is essentially good, morally perfect, without defect or darkness. This means not only that he would never issue a command that would break any inviolable or necessary moral truth, but that he could not. There is no possible world in which he does. The very status of those invariant truths is rooted in his perfect and unchanging nature. So the abhorrent command objection simply fails to stick to our version of voluntarism.

One more word is in order at this point before proceeding to the next section. Walter Sinnott-Armstrong criticizes William Lane Craig's divine command theory by writing this: "If God commanded us to rape, that command would not create a moral requirement to rape. Of course, Craig says that God never would or could command us to rape. However, it is not clear how Craig knows this or how an all-powerful God could be limited in this way. After all, God is supposed to have commanded Abraham to murder his son, or, at least, try to murder him. Moreover, even if God in fact never would or could command us to rape, the divine command theory still implies the counterfactual that, if God did command us to rape, then we would have a moral obligation to rape. That is absurd."[6]

Sinnott-Armstrong raises a few issues here, from an epistemic question, to the binding of Isaac, to his last point about counterfactuals. We will take up the first two questions later, but for now notice his claim that, even if God can't issue a command to rape, it's still true that *if* God commanded rape then rape would be morally obligatory, according to DCT. We consider this claim remarkably confused. On standard accounts of counterfactuals like this, the necessary falsehood of the antecedent—God commands rape—would render the conditional at most trivially true. It would be on a nonsensical par with "If $2 + 2 = 5$, then rape would be morally obligatory." We are reminded of our earlier concern about the unwarranted certainty among thinkers who presume to pontificate about features of an impossible world. We can only guess that it's the ubiquity of such cavalier pronouncements that imbues Sinnott-Armstrong with the courage to confidently proclaim what sounds like simple nonsense here. Craig puts his own reservations about Sinnott-Armstrong's (and Antony's) claim like this: "Even if we...reject the usual semantics and allow that some counterfactuals with impossible antecedents may be nonvacuously true or false, how are we to assess the truth of a statement like this? It is like wondering whether, if there were a round square, its area would equal the square of one of its sides. And what would it matter how one answered, since what is imagined is logically incoherent? I do not see that the divine command theorist is committed to the nonvacuous truth of the counterfactual in question nor that anything of significance hangs on his thinking it to be nonvacuously true rather than false."[7]

Belief in God's goodness rules out some commands and also renders impossible some scenarios occasionally but mistakenly entertained as possible. But which ones? To this we now turn.

## Drawing the Line

Since God is God, and we're not, and his ways are as far above ours as the heavens are above the earth, it would make sense that on occasion we might encounter some real difficulty understanding the wisdom of his ways. His goodness must be recognizable for our ascriptions of goodness to him to remain meaningful, but there could still arise occasions when it isn't easy to see the goodness of what he commands. In fact, it would seem that some of God's commands might in a real sense involve something that is morally bad. We are all familiar with circumstances where the only available moral choices are in some way bad. Suppose we come across a bully who can only be stopped by a physical altercation. Either we allow an innocent victim to be bullied or we resort to violence to put it to an end. Or suppose a nation must either confront an aggressive and belligerent neighbor or watch them invade and subjugate a pacifistic society. Even if what we seek is good, namely justice, our actions will result in certain bad states of affairs, such as the loss of life and other ravages of war. Yet even in such cases, our moral obligation might be clear. And this means that doing something in some sense bad might be morally obligatory. So this disinclines us from a straightforward affirmation that everything God commands is something he commands because of its goodness, even if we want to say something like that as a good first approximation.

But this leaves us with the challenge of identifying what in principle could be commanded by God and what couldn't. We cannot categorically say that if an action is (in some sense) bad, then God can't command it. Just as the goodness of an action doesn't necessarily entail its obligatoriness, the badness of an action doesn't necessarily entail its wrongness. Axiology and deontology, though intimately related, remain distinct arenas of moral theory. How bad, though, could an action be and still be commanded by God? It's crucial to our theory that we begin by drawing the line that we first discussed in chapter 4: the line between what may be *hard* for us to understand and what is simply *impossible* to square with our most nonnegotiable moral insights. It's highly intuitive that such a line exists. A divine command for us to visit the fatherless and widows in their affliction would clearly be easy to understand and appreciate, not hard in the least, so clearly on one side of the line. A command to rape and pillage hapless peasants in a rural village of Africa would be on the other side of the line. We would be more rational to believe that we have missed God on that one than that God has commanded such atrocities. But what about the biblical prohibition of homosexual behavior, or what about the practice of euthanasia, or certain abortion cases? As soon as we insist that God's goodness must be sufficiently recognizable, critics naturally wish to ask about cases "in the middle," where moral intuitions vary.

We aren't insensitive to this concern, but we think it can be answered. So where do we draw the line, as it were, a line that God can't cross and still rationally be said to be perfectly good? Surely he can issue commands that are hard for us to understand, but there must be some things that would be impossible for us to make sense of morally, inconsistent with our nonnegotiable moral commitments. By appeal to moral commitments here, we don't mean moral beliefs that we hold merely strongly, but convictions of the deepest ingression that are truly nonnegotiable, and unable to be relinquished—not just psychologically, but rationally, at least without perverting morality itself.

In general, what God can't do is anything in diametric opposition, irremediable tension, or patent conflict with our most nonnegotiable moral commitments. God can't, for instance, issue a command for us to torture children; but he may well be acting in accord with moral perfection when he, say, allows death to take place in a fallen world. But identifying such examples on either side of the line still leaves unanswered where the line is, and providing that answer in a noncircular way is indeed difficult to do. It's also entirely likely that the line is impossible to draw with utter precision; philosophers from Aristotle to Kant have recognized that a certain vagueness in ethics is unavoidable (without such vagueness entailing anything like moral anti-realism).

In drawing a line, we are not simply attempting a first-order analysis of the nature of wrongness or badness here, but rather something more general. We are attempting to suggest a working criterion for identifying an action that is wholly beyond the pale, not just something contingently wrong or something in some sense bad but still potentially justified, but rather something irremediably bad, unable in principle to be reconciled with morality. Such a bad divine command or state of affairs would be rationally inconsistent with an impeccable God. But again, as intuitive as the existence of such a line is, saying where it is and what the necessary and sufficient conditions are for crossing it is notoriously challenging.

To get our bearings, suppose that God told us to torture children for fun. What larger story could we tell to make sense of the resulting suffering? What feature of God's goodness would lead to a command like this? What proposition, consistent with an impeccable God, is thought possibly true that would entail such a command? Needless to say, we seem hard-pressed to provide any such thing. The best explanation of our inability to do so is that there is none, and thus that this is something impossible, in the broadly logical sense, and not merely difficult, to reconcile with an impeccable God.

In contrast, take the biblical prohibition of homosexuality. What proposition, consistent with divine impeccability, would entail such a prohibition? Perhaps something like this: God created people male and female and intended them for heterosexual relationships, not same-sex ones. In fact, this isn't just a remotely possible claim, but clear biblical teaching. Our present point isn't that such a claim is true and that homosexuality is wrong, but rather that it is significant that we can imagine a possible story consistent with the conjunction of divine perfection and this sort of prohibition, unlike the command to engage in child torture.

So here is what we propose: when confronted with a candidate for appraisal, some alleged or hypothetical command by God or state of affairs allowed by God, we should ask if we can identify a possibly true proposition, consistent with God's moral perfection rationally construed, that would potentially entail such a command or state of affairs. If we can identify such a proposition, then the command or state of affairs in question can be said to be reconcilable with our nonnegotiable moral commitments; if we can't, then it isn't reconcilable. This was the very basis for our earlier rejection of Calvinism, but it's a procedure that can't be applied to throw out biblical proscriptions of homosexuality.

Although there's an element of circularity here, we contend that it's not a vicious one, for we can't help but appeal to our most basic moral intuitions or apprehensions when trying to identify the line between what's merely hard and what's actually impossible to make moral sense of in terms of potential divine commands.

Readers familiar with contemporary philosophy of religion might recognize that our proposed algorithm bears a hint of resemblance to Alvin Plantinga's free will defense against the logical version of the problem of evil. Ours is an attempt to show that the line is significant between what's hard and what's impossible to square with nonnegotiable moral intuitions. Some divine commands would be hard to make sense of but still rational to believe and obey, while other putative commands are beyond the pale and can't rationally be accepted. This carves out the needed space for our critique of Calvinism without implicating us in a slippery slope by sanctioning a rejection of any biblical interpretation that happens to challenge just any preexisting moral preference.

## The Conquest Narratives and the Binding of Isaac

At this point in our analysis, we must discuss the inevitable question that arises at this juncture. As Christian theists, we take biblical teachings seriously. But the Old Testament contains divine commands to wipe out Canaanites in a fashion that includes killing innocent children. God tells the Jews to kill entire populations, leaving no one behind. Ask most thoughtful traditional theists about this, and you will most likely be met with grimacing visages and furrowed brows. These passages are difficult, and no matter what we might say about them, we won't dispel the mystery of them. Here's a painful and paradigmatic example: "When the Lord your God brings you into the land you are entering to possess and drives out before you many nations—the Hittites, Girgashites, Amorites, Canaanites, Perizzites, Hivites, and Jebusites, seven nations larger and stronger than you—and when the Lord your God has delivered them over to you and you have defeated them, then you must destroy them utterly. Make no treaty with them, and show them no mercy."[8]

We have argued that God doesn't and can't issue irremediably evil commands, yet Yahweh, we're told, issued commands to destroy certain nations, killing men, women, and children. So either (1) Yahweh isn't God, (2) we're wrong about God's inability to issue irremediably evil commands, (3) these biblical stories aren't literally true, or (4) such commands aren't irremediably evil. Our whole theory is predicated on Yahweh being God, so (1) is not an option for us. Nor is (2).

It's of course possible to opt for (3) and to deny that the biblical stories in question are a true account of either God's intentions, or what actually happened. Robert Adams has made just this move with another problematic Old Testament story: the binding of Isaac. We read that God tells Abraham to offer his own son Isaac as a sacrifice. Adams denies that this happened. He supposes this command to be utterly irreconcilable with nonnegotiable moral intuitions, impossible and not just hard to make sense of. In an effort to bolster his case theologically, he writes, "I agree in fact with Jeremiah that the true God never commanded any such thing—never even thought of doing so, as Jeremiah put it." He refers here to Jeremiah 7:31: "They have built the high place of Topheth...to burn their sons and their daughters in the fire; which I did not command, nor did it come into my mind." Adams roots his voluntarism in the commands of a loving God, and thus argues that the scriptures must be creatively and sensitively interpreted. Comparing scripture with scripture, he decides to confer primacy on the passage from Jeremiah, from which he derives a general prohibition against child sacrifice admitting of no counterexamples, which precludes a literal interpretation of such narratives.

More recently, several philosophers have begun constructing similar arguments either that the Christian God isn't moral or that the biblical narrative can't be interpreted as literally true when it says that God issued such commands. And it's instructive to note that their logic deeply resembles our own when it came to Calvinism. When a particular interpretation stands too much at odds with nonnegotiable moral intuitions, the interpretation has to go, or a high view of biblical authority has to go, or we must deny God's goodness. Of course, it should not be assumed that a literal interpretation is the only one that is true to a high view of the authority of scripture. Taking scripture seriously requires thoughtful, sensitive interpretation, and it may well be that the troublesome text itself gives us significant clues that it should not be read literally. If so, it does not represent a high view of scripture to insist on a literal reading nonetheless.

At any rate, we respect the force of the dilemma when an interpretation of scripture clashes with our moral judgments; and as mentioned, we resonate with its logic if the instances in question are indeed examples of divine commands that are impossible to square with nonnegotiable moral insights and commitments. However, we want to explore the difficult option of affirming (4) and suggest that it may not be impossible to square these commands with our deepest moral intuitions. That it is difficult, we readily admit, but perhaps the conquest narratives don't represent that sort of intractable violation of morality after all, despite their awfulness.

It is our judgment that critics who reject this option outright have been too hasty in doing so, or have overstated their case. For instance, Randal Rauser advances a rather ambitious thesis when he blames all manner of modern violence on the conquest narratives, and waxes eloquently about the "sorry spectacle of attempting to convince ourselves and others of that which everybody knows cannot be true." Unlike Wesley Morriston, who pushes defenders of the historicity of the conquests for the set of morally sufficient reasons for the conquests (which is admittedly difficult to generate), Rauser more ambitiously claims that the conquest narratives are logically incompatible with a perfectly loving God. This is a claim that has the virtue of being falsifiable, and the vice of being false.[9]

The first step to show this is to apply the aforementioned algorithm for determining where the conquest narratives and binding of Isaac stand relative to the line we drew earlier. If we can make a good case that the conquest narratives are at least possibly reconcilable with divine impeccability, that will be enough to answer Rauser's claim about logical impossibility. So, can we identify a proposition or set of propositions consistent with God's essential goodness that would lead to his issuing such commands? It's difficult, to be sure, but it's nothing like the challenge of defending unconditional reprobation. For suppose that God knew that unless he were to command the Israelites to wipe out their enemies, they themselves would be wiped out. And suppose further, as the Bible teaches, that Israel was God's chosen vessel to provide a way of salvation to the world—including those very people wiped out in those genocidal attacks. That we're told the Canaanites were evil and were to be annihilated does not tell us their eternal fate. Biblical teaching is clear that we are all profoundly sinful and deserving of death, including the Jews who did the killing.[10] It was God's grace, not their goodness, that spared them from God's wrath. Is it not consistent with a perfectly good God that he would want what is in the ultimate best interest of every person, even if that were to include, if necessary, some warfare along the way?[11] If he knew that his people chosen to offer that salvation would be wiped out without his commanding the conquests, then it would seem that he could issue such commands without violating his perfect goodness. Could he have done it differently? We have no idea what to say to this, but we have argued that he retains prerogatives on how to go about accomplishing his purposes. This gives us prima facie reason to consider the conquest narratives logically consistent with God's perfect goodness—in a way that unconditional reprobation is not.[12]

More needs to be said, though, because of the well-worn distinction between a *defense* and a *theodicy*. A defense has the relatively modest aim of offering a possible reason why God allows evil, thereby showing that God's existence is at least logically consistent with evil, whereas a theodicy has the more ambitious goal of identifying plausible reasons, if not his actual reason for doing so. So far we have provided something of a defense of the conquest narratives, by suggesting that there might be some unique mitigating circumstances that made the otherwise inscrutable commands morally consistent with God's perfect goodness. The commands surely involve doing something that is bad in a very real sense; we're not denying that killing people, even guilty people and certainly innocent ones, is a bad thing in significant ways. But again, not everything bad is morally prohibited. Taking a child's life is bad, undoubtedly, yet in certain lamentable circumstances it might be morally permissible, from an abortion to save the life of a mother to collateral damage in a just war. God is the author of life, and it's his prerogative to take it away, and presumably his prerogative to use human agency to do so, so long as he has morally sufficient reasons.

Although we don't pretend to know all the reasons behind God's commands in the conquest narratives, we wish at least to gesture in the direction of a theodicy. The demand that we be able to construct an exhaustive list of reasons strikes us as only reasonable if we're entitled to expect a full theodicy here, and we're not yet convinced of that. A more epistemically humble question to ask is this: What reason do we have to insist that it wasn't God's moral prerogative to use these means at this juncture of salvation history?

Again, the annihilation of the Canaanites does not necessarily entail their damnation, despite the sinful condition of their culture. For a culture can be corrupt while some within the culture have yet to make a final determination to resist God's grace. So it is entirely possible that the conquest narratives are consistent with God's doing all he can to save the Canaanites and to do what's best for them in the long term. We are simply not told that there was no hope for them in the afterlife, and so we are at liberty to refrain from assuming they are without hope. Perhaps some in that culture had made their final determination against God, but the passages do not say that each and every one did. We feel free to reject the idea that none of the Canaanites, even the children, are without hope—even in light of the communal nature of sin and responsibility.

We admit that if we were required to read these passages as holding that all the Canaanites, including the children, were all immediately relegated to hell, that reading would entail a depiction of God's character well nigh impossible to square with our best moral intuitions. A loving God would plausibly do more to offer his grace and salvation to the Canaanites, even if posthumously. The text doesn't force the harsher reading on us, and various textual clues point against it—from reminders of Israel's own sinfulness to the redemption of some among the Canaanites. A loving God would do no less than all in his power to bring about their eternal salvation, short of violating their free will. Moreover, according to Christian thought, the deaths of those Canaanites were partially instrumental in making possible the coming of Jesus through the preserved remnant of Israel. God, we contend, would give even those Canaanites a full and free opportunity to repent of their sins and be saved through Christ. Such an account of what God's perfect goodness entails regarding the Canaanites makes possible the attempted moral reconciliation of God's perfect goodness with the conquest narratives. It's still challenging to effect such reconciliation, but, we contend, not impossible for an Anselmian theist.

If God does all he can, short of violating the free will of people, to draw them to himself and confer on them a full, free, fair chance at salvation, then the conquest narratives aren't just possibly reconcilable with our moral intuitions, but plausibly so. And there's every reason to think an Anselmian God would indeed reach out with that kind of universal offer of salvation. If the very Author of life and paradigm of Goodness chose in his providence and wisdom to tell the Israelites to engage in warfare with foes for whom God does all he can to confer eternal salvation, it is far from clear that the loss of those lives represents the sort of irredeemable evil that some take it to be. We remain unconvinced, not to mention mindful of the need for profound epistemic humility in these matters.[13] The class of divine actions morally precluded by Anselmianism is broader than unconditional damnation, but it's not been effectively shown that the conquest narratives are among those actions.

Again, we want to reiterate that we are not insisting that the conquest narratives are intended to be read as straightforward literal accounts. Indeed, there may be some telling textual clues that they should not be read in this way.[14] Our purpose has been to argue that even on the most difficult case, the assumption that they are to taken as straightforward literal accounts, it is not impossible to square these stories with our deepest moral intuitions, difficult though it surely is.

The Ultimate Moral Resource

In concluding this chapter, we want to suggest that the ultimate theological resource and revelation from God, for the Christian, that helps reconcile the wars of extermination and expressions of God's wrath in the Old Testament and New with our moral intuitions is the redemptive life, death, and resurrection of Jesus. We read the Old Testament as a precursor to the New, involving the selection and purification of a particular people through whom God would send his provision of salvation that would be available to all. We see Jesus as mercifully satisfying God's demand for perfect obedience. Jesus offered himself as a sacrifice and defeated the power of sin and evil so that we might be forgiven our own debts and offered eternal life.

The binding of Isaac takes on new significance in this light. In Genesis 22:1–9, God tests Abraham by commanding him to sacrifice his only son, Isaac, through whom God had promised to bless his progeny. God speaks to Abraham, commanding him to sacrifice his beloved son as a whole burnt offering, and Abraham sets out to comply. At the climax of the story, Abraham binds Isaac on the altar and takes a knife to kill him, but the voice of an angel stops him by declaring that Abraham's obedience was enough. As instructed, Abraham then finds and sacrifices a ram instead. Kierkegaard is famous for taking the passage as paradigmatic of the "teleological suspension of the ethical," according to which obedience to God trumps morality itself.[15] He no doubt has pushed many readers to personalize the narrative of the binding of Isaac and ask themselves what they would personally do if they thought God commanded something like this. But of course the story thus construed has been shorn of nearly all its unique theological and historical significance. The quest to derive universal principles from a story like this is at cross-purposes with the particularistic, gradualist, and narrative-driven character of many portions of scripture, particularly in the Old Testament. One who wishes to read them with a genuine openness to their wisdom and revelatory nature would be well advised not to so recklessly and spuriously traverse the hermeneutical gap.

Genesis clearly states that God was testing Abraham, so that the reader knows in advance that it is not really the will of God for Abraham to do this.[16] Abraham, of course, does not know it, and so the point of the test is to see the extent of Abraham's obedience. For the reader, the dramatic tension is not the content of the command, but whether Abraham will fully trust God, and what God will do to stop it. Including Abraham's story in the history of revelation was a much more powerful way to show that God does not, in fact, want child sacrifice than just to say so.

Christian readers, however, have always seen in this story a profound fore-shadowing of another scenario in which the Father actually allowed his Son to be sacrificed. Rather than being spared by a ram caught in the thickets, the Son was himself the lamb of God who died to take away the sin of the world.[17] And he went to his death not as a helpless child, but as a perfect man who willingly offered his full obedience to his Father in a fallen world bent on killing him. While the story of Jesus is even more surprising than the story of Isaac, perhaps in another sense it is not. Is the face of Jesus surprising when omnibenevolence takes human form?

It is worth emphasizing here that the book of Hebrews, which reflects at length on the sacrifice of Christ, describes him as one "who for the sake of the joy that was set before him endured the cross, disregarding its shame, and has taken his seat at the right hand of the throne of God."[18] The sacrifice of Christ was not a sacrifice into oblivion, but a sacrifice with the prospect of resurrection and exaltation as its final outcome. In view of this, perhaps it is not surprising that the author of Hebrews explains that Abraham obeyed God when called to sacrifice Isaac because he reasoned that God can raise the dead, and must have been planning to do so if he were to fulfill his promises through Isaac, as he had promised.[19] God's ultimate ability to rectify things as shown in the resurrection provides ways to square even difficult commands with his perfect love and goodness that are simply out of reach if death is the last word.

# 8

# The Problem of Evil

Is [God] willing to prevent evil, but not able? Then is he impotent.
Is he able, but not willing? Then is he malevolent.
Is he both able and willing? Whence then is evil?
Is he neither able nor willing? Then why call him God?

—David Hume[1]

In the film *Hannah and Her Sisters* is a scene where Mickey, the character played by Woody Allen, announces to his Jewish parents that he no longer believes in God. When they react in horror, he appeals to the problem of evil, asking how God can allow things like the Nazis. His mother, who has fled to the bathroom, calls out to her husband to explain how this can happen, to which he replies: "How the hell do I know why there were Nazis? I don't know how the can opener works." This comment, as we shall see, represents an interesting line of thought in recent literature on the problem of evil, a line that has both its notable advocates as well as critics.

The problem of evil has long been the chief weapon in the arsenal of those who reject belief in God. It represents the main counterpoint to the traditional arguments for God's existence, especially a God who is perfectly good. The classic expression of this is Hume's *Dialogues Concerning Natural Religion*, where the author concedes that the argument from design has a certain force, and gives us reason to believe the minimal claim that something remotely like a human mind is responsible for the created order. However, the problem of evil poses an insurmountable obstacle for any who wish to draw a stronger conclusion than this. In particular, we have no reason to believe that the creator is good. Rather, the most reasonable thing to infer from the evidence of the created order is that the creator is amoral.[2]

Now whereas the problem of evil stands as a counterpoint to the other traditional theistic arguments, it stands most directly opposed to the moral argument. Indeed, the argument from evil goes head to head with the moral argument in such a fashion that both cannot survive the showdown. Either the problem of evil completely undermines belief in a perfectly good God, as Hume argued, or the moral argument decisively undercuts the argument from evil.

In recent literature, of course, the logical version of the problem of evil has received the most attention. It is widely agreed that this version of the problem has been effectively answered by Alvin Plantinga and others. Even more recently, however, proponents of the argument from evil have recast it as an evidential or probabilistic argument. In particular, they have targeted the Anselmian view of God, the view we have defended, arguing that evil renders belief in such a God irrational at best. Bruce Russell, for example, one of the leading contemporary atheological proponents of the problem of evil, early on argued that God could do a lot more to reduce suffering. In particular, he contended that God could intervene at least one more time to reduce suffering without entailing ubiquitous ad hoc interventions and resultant massive irregularities in the operation of the physical laws. So God, if he exists, should have intervened more than he has, and if so he is hardly the Perfect Being that Anselmians claim he is.

In this chapter we will subject Russell's arguments to scrutiny to illustrate that the sort of probabilistic arguments he represents do not undermine our moral argument. Of course, we can hardly engage the whole spectrum of theodicy literature, nor can we ignore the challenge posed by evil. Our purpose here is to respond to one forceful challenge that has considerable currency in the contemporary debate to show how the theodicy debate bears on our larger project. In our second appendix, we extend our discussion of the problem of evil.

Before we get to Russell's more recent arguments, a bit of background is in order. Peter van Inwagen responded to Russell in his "Atlantis" example in which he showed that, to preserve the lawlike regularity of the world, there must come a point at which God will refrain from saving a fawn from fire, for example, even though performing this act of mercy would not significantly decrease the lawlike regularity. Here is van Inwagen's scenario: Atlantis is sinking and Russell is in charge of allowing refugees onboard the escape ship. He can let in between none and 1,000, it's up to him. But with each person he lets onboard, the chances of safe arrival for the ship decrease. If he allows just one refugee onboard, the two of them will have a 99.9 percent chance of a safe arrival; if he leaves behind just one, there is a 99.9 percent chance that the ship will sink. Although it's clear that it wouldn't be morally acceptable for Russell to take none, one, or a mere handful of refugees aboard, he will nonetheless "close the hatch in the face of someone whose admission would not significantly decrease the ship's chances of reaching the mainland safely."[3] And van Inwagen conjectures that God may be in a similar situation with regard to eliminating evil from the world.

## Russell's Latest Argument

In a recent paper, Russell wishes to exploit a point he thinks van Inwagen's illustration concedes: namely, that a good being would not allow "much more evil than is needed to bring about some greater good or to prevent something equally bad or worse."[4] Similarly, no good captain of a rescue ship would save only ten out of a thousand when saving many more would be possible without greatly reducing the likelihood of a successful operation. Russell gives an abductive argument designed to show that there *is* much more horrible suffering than is needed, a premise that he then uses to argue that believers, in the face of such excessive suffering, are not rationally entitled to believe in the perfect being of Anselmian theology. He is even adamant, unlike William Rowe, that unpersuaded theists are irrational.[5]

The claim that this world contains far more evils than a theist can accommodate is a highly ambitious one that begs to be scrutinized. The stakes are high enough, and the claim is important enough, to warrant careful examination of its basis and justification. Russell's abductive argument for the factual premise of his argument from evil goes something like this:

1. It seems, on reflection, that there is much more horrible suffering of the innocent than is needed to bring about counterbalancing goods, or to prevent significant evils.
2. The best explanation of why it seems that way is that it *is* that way.[6]
3. If that is the best explanation, then we are justified in believing that there is much more suffering of the innocent than is needed to bring about counterbalancing good, or to prevent significant evils.
4. Therefore, we are justified in believing that there is much more suffering of the innocent than is needed to bring about counterbalancing good, or to prevent significant evils.

Now here is the argument in which he uses that factual judgment, conjoined with an ethical premise that Russell takes to be analytic:

5. If God exists, then there would *not be* much more suffering of the innocent than is needed to bring about counterbalancing good, or to prevent significant evils.[7] (ethical premise)
6. But *there is* much more suffering of the innocent than is needed to bring about counterbalancing good, or to prevent significant evils. (factual premise)
7. Therefore, God does not exist.

Confronted with a variety of heinous evils in our world, enough to turn our stomachs and make us weep, we are unable to see any morally sufficient reason for all of them. Russell admits that our inability to see something usually gives us reason to believe it is not there only if we are justified in believing that if it were there we would see it. But he denies that this is always the case. For presumably we are justified in believing we are not in a Matrix world, even though we do not have reason to believe that if we were in the Matrix we would see it, that is, would realize we were in it. We are justified despite this counterfactual inability, he argues, because a real world better explains our experiences than the Matrix hypothesis. Other things being equal, simpler and ontologically abstemious explanations trump more complex ones.

Russell thinks we can be justified in believing that there is no point to so much terrible suffering even though we don't have reason to believe that we would see the point if there were one. The simplest hypothesis to explain why we see no sufficient moral reason to justify the existence of so much terrible suffering is that there *is* no such reason, rather than that there is one but it is beyond our ken. Atheism is the more parsimonious, less obscurantist explanation, and so we are justified in believing that there is gratuitous suffering that is analytically inconsistent with an Anselmian God. Obviously, then, Russell thinks there are two options here for accounting for the millions of instances of seemingly needless suffering we can observe in the world: (a) God exists but does not prevent them for reasons beyond our ken (this is the view of the "cognitive limitation" defenders of theism like Wykstra, not to mention Mickey's father in the scene from *Hannah and Her Sisters*), or (b) God does not exist. The rational answer, he argues, is (b).

## Russell's Analogy

For the unconvinced, Russell offers a further analogy to answer the claim that we lack the epistemic resources to be justified in believing that there is such excessive suffering. Indeed, it is his conviction that his analogy undermines any such appeals to our epistemic limitations. He came up with it several years ago, and it figures centrally in his more recent paper as well. Let us call it, appropriately enough, "Russell's analogy."

For brevity's sake, let us quote Russell's earlier and more succinct formulation of the argument: "Is the view that there is a God who, for reasons beyond our ken, allows the suffering which appears pointless to us any different epistemically from the view that there is a God who created the universe 100 years ago and, for reasons beyond our ken, has deceived us into thinking it is older? It does not seem to be.... If it is not reasonable to believe that God deceived us, for some reason beyond our ken, when he created the universe, it is not reasonable to believe that there is some reason beyond our ken which, if God exists, would justify him in allowing all the suffering we see."[8]

Russell elaborates on the analogy further in a later essay, writing that, for all the credulous "infant-earther" knows, God may have had reason to deceive us about the age of the earth.[9] Perhaps God wants us to think that the world is older because he wants us to believe that natural disasters, wars, slavery, and other horrible tragedies have transpired hundreds of years ago. God also may want us to have some idea of how they, or their consequences, can be overcome by examples of what we think are actual cases where they have been overcome. For instance, we can learn valuable lessons from our beliefs about the Civil War. But it is better for us to have this information without, rather than with, the actual suffering entailed by that war. Of course Russell thinks this leads to an absurd conclusion, and that is just his point. Just as we should not be moved by such considerations to doubt whether the earth really is over 100 years old, likewise we should not doubt that there really is gratuitous evil.

On this basis, Russell opts for a view that William Rowe would call "unfriendly atheism": barring substantial evidence in favor of God's existence, theists are not rationally entitled to believe in God because this is positively irrational in the face of the problem of evil. Part of Russell's broader case is that the arguments for God's existence all fail, so there isn't substantial positive evidence for God's existence, and that therefore, in light of the negative evidence of the problem of evil, theists are irrational. Because the best explanation of apparently pointless suffering is the actual existence of pointless suffering, we are required, Russell argues, to believe that God does not exist.

Russell asks his opponents to subject his analogical argument to scrutiny, so we will oblige. It is clear that he believes the analogy to be a good one. The logic of the credulous "infant-earther" and that of the tenacious theist strikes Russell as the same. He describes the cases as similar and parallel. No analogy is perfect, of course, but he seems to think that enough overlap obtains to make the argument predicated on the analogy work, and that no relevant disanalogies undercut the argument in any significant way.

One virtue of the analogy is that it gives an instructive reflection of the way that many atheists view tenacious theism. Tenacious theists who point to potential goods beyond our ken and our inability to judge whether there is gratuitous evil are thought to be in the same epistemic boat as "infant-earthers" who doubt whether the earth is really over 100 years old because of the logical possibility that God could be deceiving us about it. As Russell sees it, the faith of tenacious theists is just as misguided, predicated on a remote logical possibility involving mysterious causal connections, needless ontology, obscurantist theology, and too little confidence in our epistemic capacities. To say that we are not epistemically qualified to be justified in believing that there is gratuitous evil, Russell writes, deprives us of the capacity to insist that we are rational and justified in the belief that the earth is more than 100 years old.

This remarkable claim, if true, would be a devastating critique of theism, or at least of those "cognitive limitation" theistic defenders (like Wykstra) who deny the factual premise. When we bear in mind that Russell takes the moral premise to be analytic, this puts theists in quite the pickle. Things are quite different, however, if we can identify some relevant disanalogies between the beliefs of the "infant-earthers" and the tenacious theists, and likewise between rational "old-earthism" and the belief that gratuitous evil clearly occurs.

Notice that Russell's analogical argument features two sets of comparisons. First, he likens the "infant-earther" with the tenacious theist. Second, he likens the commonsensical evidentialist who rightly considers himself justified to believe the earth is over 100 years old with the rational atheist convinced by the problem of evil and unimpressed with the mere logical possibilities the theist provides for why God allows apparently pointless suffering. Of course the analogy features two sets of contrasts as well: the "infant-earther" versus the commonsensical evidentialist; and the tenacious theist versus the rational atheist.

The question is whether the tenacious theist really is on the same epistemic footing as the "infant-earther." To begin with, we can note the difference in the hypotheses under consideration. The tenacious theist is refusing to rule out belief in God on the basis of the problem of evil, whereas the "infant-earther" is skeptical that the earth is over 100 years old. So the tenacious theist is stubborn over a metaphysical view, while the infant-earther is skeptical about a widely accepted scientific view about the physical world. This might be seen as a distinction without a difference, but it is instructive insofar as it reminds us that the problem of evil pertains to a philosophical matter. It is a question not of physics, but metaphysics. The assertion that determining whether God exists is analogous to determining whether or not the earth is over 100 years old is enough to strain the credulity of most who hear it.

The age of the earth is an empirical matter. Unless we are fixated on Cartesian certainty, we will naturally feel confident in the findings of science here, and rightly so. Russell attributes this rational confidence and epistemic justification to the ability of abduction to get around riddles of induction and the inaccessibility of certainty. Abduction always involves one explanation among others, none without its critics. At any rate, the best available evidence we have to answer the question about the earth's age comes from an examination of the world and natural inferences made on that basis. We have no particular reason to be skeptical about such findings and deliverances, nor to think that the question—either by its nature or because of our own limitations—is beyond our epistemic reach. So we have no principled reason to be seriously open to logical possibilities at variance with the best scientific account. There is absolutely no positive evidence that the earth is only 100 years old.

Can the same be said about tenacious theism and the challenge of the problem of evil? It is doubtful, unless we assume that the sorts of possibilities that theistic defenders identify to help explain suffering are on an epistemic par with the logical possibility that God is deceiving us about the age of the earth. Surely, though, theists are not rationally compelled to believe that. They rather tend to think of such possibilities as real and living plausibilities, and rationally so unless their case for theism truly has as little going for it as "infant-earthism."[10] If we have free will, it is not just possible, but likely, that its misuse and abuse can produce a great deal of tragic suffering. If a stable natural order is required for the sake of providing a context in which we can grow morally and spiritually, it is not surprising that such a context will produce pain and suffering.[11] These are not merely remote logical possibilities, and this points up a vitally important relevant disanalogy between the "infant-earth" example and the problem of evil discussion.

Another telling disanalogy is that the "infant-earth" example requires wholesale and systematic deception. Russell rightly notes that deception is not always wrong, but the scenario as Russell depicts it makes it seem that it would indeed be *quite* wrong (not that Russell intended that). It would raise profound questions about God's goodness if he were to accord such little importance to truth and show us such little respect by deceiving us in such a fashion.[12] Russell's suggestion, recall, is that a believer in an "infant-earth" might propose the possibility that God deceived us about the age of the earth because he wanted us to learn the lessons of history without all the suffering actually taking place. But systematic deception about the past would clearly not be the only way to teach lessons about the horrors of wars and slavery. We learn from hypothetical situations and fictional stories the various results of going down certain paths. Some might not take such teaching to heart, true enough, but neither do people always learn the lessons of history, even if it would never occur to them to question the accuracy of their history books.

It is hardly fair to say that tenacious theists are positively *deceived* if God chooses not to reveal his reasons for permitting particular horrendous evils to them. Even if they appeal to our having certain cognitive and epistemic limitations that leave some aspects of how to resolve the problem of evil mysterious, at most they inhabit a position of less-than-full disclosure, not systematic and wholesale deception. Sure enough, sometimes refraining to divulge information is morally tantamount to lying, just as allowing to die on occasion is just as bad as killing. More argument is needed, though, to show that the conceptual and moral distinction here between deception and nondisclosure is not relevant. Such a distinction and its potential to undermine Russell's analogy can hardly be ignored, for if the earth is just 100 years old, contrary to all sorts of counterevidence, we're radically and systematically deceived.

Russell's response to this critique is that, whether it's deception or nondisclosure, God must have morally sufficient reasons for doing either one. We agree, but our point here is that morally sufficient reasons for nondisclosure are usually considerably easier to generate than an adequate justification for pervasive deception. So we contend that this point effectively undermines his analogy that compares nondisclosure with patent deception.

What about the Ethical Premise?

Even if Russell's analogy fails, his factual premise may still survive. Suppose we were to grant that this premise holds, despite any remaining misgivings about it. His argument now features the factual premise, an ethical premise he takes as analytic, and the conclusion—that God does not exist—follows deductively! Is theistic tenacity indeed irrational? Is this a slam dunk case against theism? Is Russell right to think that atheism is the dictate of rationality in the face of the problem of evil?

Not quite. For there is another alternative besides atheism and the cognitive limitation defense of theism. Rather than questioning the factual premise, let us suppose that we question the moral premise, which Russell takes to be analytically true. This premise, again, asserts that if God exists, there would not be much more excessive suffering of innocents than is needed to bring about counterbalancing good or prevent significant evil. What's irreconcilable with God, Russell asserts, is anything more than a modicum of gratuitous suffering.

We hear of horrible cases of child killings and are inclined to agree with the factual premise that the world would have been better without such needless and excessive sufferings. But the question still remains whether the moral premise is true that says God, if he exists, would prevent such sufferings, or at least many more than he does. If such sufferings are not needed, it seems intuitive at first to say that a perfectly good God would indeed prevent them, or at least many more of them than he currently does.[13]

Notice that any perceived justification of God is here cashed out in terms of positive consequences produced (or negative ones avoided) by the suffering, consequences not otherwise achievable (or avoidable). Michael Peterson would instead suggest a less consequentialist analysis of the justification for allowing suffering.[14] It is not the case, he argues, that each instance of cruel evil is required to produce some further good. Rather, a world in which there is, say, meaningful freedom is a world that must contain the *possibility* of such instances of suffering. Once free will is conferred, its use and misuse may produce horrible and needless suffering.[15]

The late Cambridge philosopher A. C. Ewing similarly recognized how the appeal to human free will warrants saying that moral evil, at any rate, is not directly caused by God but is due to the abuse of free will that need not have occurred and for which man, not God, is to be blamed. "We should note that if the indeterminist view is adopted it will not come under the heading of a solution which makes evil a necessary condition of certain goods, since it is not necessary that free will should be abused if it exists. But it would make the *possibility* of evil a necessary condition of certain goods...."[16] Take freedom out, and remove moral evil, but also remove all the goods organically connected to freedom, indeed, human persons themselves.

Russell cites the tragic case of Ariana, a girl thrown to the floor for not eating properly and then killed by her parents pouring water into the unconscious child's mouth until she drowned.[17] Ariana was malnourished, dehydrated, and had lost more than half her blood on the day of her death. Such hideous evil tears at our hearts, and no right-thinking theist should insist that Ariana's suffering was necessary. It was tragic and pointless, and the world would have been better off without it.

But God's conferral of meaningful freedom on those parents meant that they could abuse it horribly, and they did. Indeed, doesn't the extent of our horror presuppose that they were more than what a naturalist like Russell has to say they were—complicated organic machines whose behavior fit perfectly into the inexorable working order of a physical universe? The theist can declare such an event as utterly tragic, a choice of willful resistance against God's call to love, a morally culpable decision crying out for ultimate justice. Arguably the

very force of Russell's example here derives from intuitions and strong commitment to moral realism at variance with the implications of his worldview—
or at least better explained, we've argued, by theism. His atheological argument
from evil predicated on a desiccated ontology is hardly the penetrating explanation that Russell exalts it to be.

Much of this world's suffering is far from necessary, but its possibility is
necessary in a world of freedom. We can say the same about the possibility of
sufferings in a world featuring a stable natural order. Such a world will likely
feature more, maybe many more, sufferings than are strictly necessary to produce relevant goods or avoid comparable things that are bad. But can we claim
to know necessarily or analytically, or can we even claim to be justified to
believe, that an Anselmian God would not create such a world? No, we contend, Anselmianism does not entail the impossibility of such a world, nor is
there, to our knowledge, a necessary moral truth that precludes it.

This analysis seems to suggest that Russell's ethical premise, far from
being analytically true, is false, and so his argument unsound and confidence
in it misplaced. The sufferings themselves are most assuredly *not* needed to
produce goods not otherwise achievable or to avoid comparable evils. Only
the *possibility* of such sufferings is needed, which is quite different. If this
criticism of Russell works, it shows that atheists need to retreat yet more in
this discussion. Not only has the logical argument from evil died a painful
death, Russell's "one more time" claim has fallen to van Inwagen's Atlantis
scenario. Now it would seem that the theist is capable of sustaining the case
that far more sufferings are reconcilable with an Anselmian God than just
those required to avoid evils just as bad or worse, or those required to secure
sufficiently worthwhile goods that otherwise would be impossible. The atheological argument from evil is at least on the road to dying the death of a thousand qualifications.

Russell now admits, and claims it to be consistent with his approach all
along, that some suffering might be necessary that isn't offset by avoiding
worse evils or generating greater or equal goods—if indeed, say, we're meaningfully free. But to make his case that there are far more sufferings than are
morally justified, he needs an argument that a good God would not create the
actual world.[18] Can Russell sustain the case that it would have been better for
God not to create at all than to create this world? It is doubtful, and we see no
reason why theists are not rationally entitled to tenacity until someone does.
His case would require more than showing that there are many instances of
excessive sufferings, which seems true, but that there are more and worse of
those than there are countervailing or parallel goods overall. And the case of
whether there are depends on the evidence for Anselmian theology. To the

extent that independent reasons exist for such theology, we have more grounds for doubting Russell's insistence that we're rationally constrained to give up theistic belief. If Russell's response is that this expands the discussion to include more than the problem of evil, he's right, and we contend that the discussion must be sufficiently contextualized in this way to avoid being more than an empty and artificial intellectual exercise.

It is plausible to think that there would be a great number of occasions during which God would not intervene to stop people from exercising their wills in terrible ways if he went to the trouble of creating a world featuring such freedom. By parity of reasoning, the case is similar with a world of stable natural laws, assuming that God saw its creation as valuable enough to effect in the first place. Assuming that God sees value in creating a world of meaningful freedom and stable order, it is doubtful that he would intervene often to thwart people's evil expressions of freedom or disrupt the natural order unless the overall balance between goods and evils in the world began to tip in the direction toward evils.

## Some Russellian Responses

Russell, who's quite tenacious himself, can respond to these points. He has insisted that his formulation of the argument from evil is theoretically neutral regarding consequentialism and can be read in a way amenable to deontologists. He would ask us to construe counterbalancing goods broadly enough to include deontological considerations. Moreover, he can deploy his argument not only in terms of the actual gratuitous suffering that exists, but against the broader possibility of such sufferings by strengthening (as he has) the moral premise to read as follows:

> 5*. If God exists, then he would *not allow* much more suffering of the innocent than *the allowing of which* is needed to bring about counterbalancing good, or to prevent significant evils.[19]

It also might be suggested that our critique of Russell is an elaborate rejection of the factual premise after all. Because of such values as free will and a stable natural order, isn't this chapter arguing that there are no gratuitous evils after all, for they are sufficiently counterbalanced by those valuable goods? This would be a misreading, perhaps owing to a distinction that has yet to be made. Russell infers from sufferings that fail to satisfy his counterbalancing criterion that such gratuitous sufferings (at least in excess) are ultimately unjustifiable, that God has no morally sufficient reason to allow them, or even their possibility. These notions are all packed into his moral premise that asserts no good God would allow such evil. We reject, however, the inference from gratuitous suffering to ultimately unjustifiable suffering. Consequently, we accept that a good God wouldn't allow suffering for which there aren't morally sufficient reasons, but we reject the notion that Russell's problematic gratuitous sufferings are simply to be equated with ultimately unjustifiable sufferings.

The distinction between gratuitous suffering and ultimately unjustified suffering may rest on how much value we place on certain intrinsic goods. Russell concedes the potential intrinsic value of free will, but still doesn't, we contend, genuinely leave open enough room for the intrinsic good of God's allowing the actual world to "play out." If Russell can't accommodate this actual world, his concession to the potential value of free will amounts to very little. He insists that, even if God went to the trouble of creating a world with free will and stable natural laws, he would not allow a world like this one, even though creating a world with traits like physical laws and meaningful free will introduces the possibility of great suffering. This is, needless to say, a highly ambitious claim, and one we find unpersuasive. Although in principle reason does rule out some things for a good God—unconditional reprobation, a command to torture children for fun, and certain qualitative and quantitative evils—the claim that this world belongs in that category is far from obvious, to put it mildly.[20]

At any rate, even if we concede Russell's factual premise (though perhaps not the analogy he uses to promote it), our real point of departure from him is the moral premise. For we don't deny that there are all sorts of regrettable sufferings that the world would be better off without, but our claim is that the world as it is has not been shown to be a world an Anselmian God would not create.

## The Good Parent Analogy

This explicitly shifts our disagreement to a different analogy of Russell's from the one we've been considering. His "good parent" analogy is meant to bolster his moral premise—the premise that says that if God exists, then there would *not be* much more suffering of the innocent than is needed to bring about counterbalancing good, or to prevent significant evils. In a nutshell the analogy goes like this: it isn't wrong for a good parent to intervene to prevent her son from hitting his infant brother with a hammer. In fact, it's wrong *not* to intervene in such a case, because there is no sufficient counterbalancing good that would justify nonintervention. The parallel question is: Why doesn't God, if he exists, intervene?

Here's how Russell puts it in a yet more recent article:

A good parent would prevent his teenage son from hitting his infant brother with a hammer even if it meant that he would have to interfere with his son's freedom of action (though even this would not interfere with the son's freedom of will since the father's intervention would not alter his son's will). Freedom of action is an intrinsic good, but it is not the only intrinsic good, and suffering is an intrinsic evil. So God, if he exists, would, like a good parent with the requisite knowledge and power, intervene in some actual cases to prevent people from exercising their free wills.[21]

Despite the fact that Russell puts great stock in this analogy, it suffers from serious limitations, a few of which we will mention. First, consider the important disanalogies between God and human parents. Earthly parents bandage bruised knees and wipe bloody noses. God doesn't. Or if he does, he does it indirectly through the hands of people, like parents, who have the special and blessed privilege to raise children in this world. Of course, earthly parents often intervene to prevent harm to their children, but God does not intervene every time earthly parents do or would. God's goals, though analogous to those of earthly parents, are not precisely the same. God has quite a broader perspective than earthly parents. Part of this broader perspective is that God has means of rectifying evils in the long run that earthly parents cannot, and this requires them to intervene in cases when God may not be required to. Moreover, parents may put a stop to something they consider harmful to their children that could well turn out to be beneficial; presumably, God knows things that earthly parents don't and never makes these sorts of misjudgments. Of course, not every harm turns out to be beneficial to one's earthly existence, that's true; we have accentuated this point throughout this chapter. But the suggestion that God is under the obligation to prevent such harms is quite an ambitious claim, reflecting, in our estimation, more certainty than is warranted. God's doing so would preclude the possibility of a huge swath of meaningful human choice in this world. Besides, even earthly parents sometimes allow their kids to make mistakes from which they may or may not ultimately benefit, but the importance of according them the necessary space to become responsible for their own choices requires such a step. Why doesn't Russell emphasize this aspect of the analogy between God and parents rather than just those instances of intervention?[22]

The second major problem we see with the analogy is that, if God did in fact intervene anywhere near the extent to which Russell suggests he should, God's interventions couldn't help but become objectionably ubiquitous. Recall the distinctive version of Russell's argument: that there is far more suffering in this world than is necessary. This means that a great amount of suffering would need to be eliminated on his view. In fact, the suggestion of his good parent analogy would be this: every time one child is going to harm another, God is supposed to intervene and put a stop to it. An earthly parent would, yes, at least a good earthly parent, but God himself? If God did do this, it would mean a world in which children never hit each other. In fact, earthly parents would be liberated from the job of helping to prevent such things. For if they didn't stop it, God would! Indeed, if a parent didn't feed his child, God would; if a parent pushed his child out a high window, God would catch him. It takes very little effort to see that the practical result of this Russellian demand is that God's interventions in this world would be ubiquitous (even if far less than universal), which would also have the effect of radically undermining the standard expectations of "good parents" on which the whole analogy rests. Since God may well and plausibly does have excellent reasons to retain elements of divine hiddenness, he would have compelling reasons not to intervene in the world so obviously.

Before the problem of evil can get off the ground, moreover, the atheologian needs a robust moral theory to sustain a principled commitment to the moral premise. Naturalists who are relativists, subjectivists, or nihilists are obviously in no position to believe such a premise.[23] No, an effective case requires a sturdy commitment to moral objectivity and realism, and Russell asserts that he can affirm such ethics in a way that's consistent with his atheistic worldview. But the driving theme of this entire volume has been that theism better accounts for a moral commitment of that kind than either naturalism or Platonism. And most thoughtful theists, on reflection, simply don't feel the force of Russell's argument. Or perhaps more accurately, they do feel its force, but they're not persuaded that it rationally requires that they abandon their convictions. Nor is it obvious to us. We're more inclined to think that taking seriously categories of injustice and tragic suffering, not to mention our obligation to reduce such evils in the world, provides evidence for God after all.

Lastly, Russell insists that a good God would intervene at least sometimes to prevent people from exercising their free will. By "sometimes," how often? If God were to intervene like this, isn't it likely that he would do so under the radar, so to speak, at least most of the time? Occasional stories of miraculous deliverances or interventions are told that usually fall on deaf ears among atheists, so evidence for just what Russell asks for might be available but ignored. And if God's interventions are usually more covert, Russell has no good reason to think that God hasn't done just this on occasion, but in a way that doesn't undercut our confidence that the world operates according to causal laws and that genuine human agency exists. Believers in God's occasional interventions in this world do believe that God, in his wisdom, might occasionally intervene and, say, thwart an evildoer's plans. But short of ubiquitous intervention that puts a stop to such plans nearly all the time, Russell can continue insisting that God allows too much evil in the world. But such assertions do not constitute a good argument.

So we find this analogy of Russell's to be patently weak, too, and to offer little reason for the sort of confidence in it that Russell needs to make his case. It does not provide nearly the decisive support for the moral premise as Russell thinks it does. It's not enough to appeal to "obviousness" when it comes to a claim so ambitious as the assertion, in essence, that God wouldn't allow the actual world to obtain. And the appeal is no less to "obviousness" or "intuition" just because it's dressed up in the attire of abduction. In debates about the resurrection of Jesus, skeptics sometimes point to the possibility of a bundling of naturalistic explanations of various phenomena, like alleged appearances, the transformation of Paul, and so on. But such attempts suffer the defect of mounting improbabilities, because they would all have to operate at the same time, and there's no compelling reason to think that such unlikelihoods cohere in such a way. But the theist who wishes to mount a cumulative case for theodicy does not suffer this disadvantage, because a good God's existence is entirely compatible with and makes great sense of the simultaneous operation of a variety of explanations, ranging from elements of divine hiddenness, human cognitive limitations, the efficacy of causal laws, the intrinsic value of free will, and the like. So Russell's insistence that atheism "better explains" the sufferings of this world is a claim that remains susceptible to strong criticism, and likely is a thinly veiled effort to hide the fact that Russell just takes something as obvious that in fact is far from it.

The kind of world we live in is one in which gratuitous evil is possible. But its actuality per se is not nearly strong enough to carry the day for the evidential argument from evil. If Russell could show that the world on balance contains more gratuitous suffering without any parallel goods, pleasures, joys, opportunities, and meanings, then that might be interesting for the nontheist. It is a case that is yet to be made.

It is important to reiterate the significance of this conclusion to our overall project. In the previous chapter we examined difficulties posed by commands of God that are admittedly hard to understand, and we argued that there are plausible strategies for turning those challenges aside. Here, we have examined some contemporary versions of the problem of evil, a classic challenge to God's goodness that poses difficulties equally if not more formidable to understand. As we noted at the beginning of this chapter, the relationship between the problem of evil and the moral argument is nothing less than a mutually frontal assault. It is our contention that the moral argument can withstand the best shots the problem of evil can deliver, and that its survival must inevitably weaken and finally defeat the stiff challenge mounted by the problem of evil.

# 9

# Knowing God's Will

Jim said it made him all over trembly and feverish to be so close to freedom. Well, I can tell you it made me all over trembly and feverish, too, to hear him, because I begun to get it through my head that he was most free—and who was to blame for it? Why, me. I couldn't get that out of my conscience, no how nor no way.... It hadn't ever come home to me, before, what this thing was that I was doing. But now it did; and it stayed with me, and scorched me more and more. I tried to make out to myself that I warn't to blame, because I didn't run Jim off from his rightful owner; but it warn't no use, conscience up and say, every time: "But you knowed he was running for his freedom, and you could a paddled ashore and told somebody." That was so—I couldn't get around that, no way. That was where it pinched. Conscience says to me: "What had poor Miss Watson done to you, that you could see her nigger go off right under your eyes and never say one single word? What did that poor old woman do to you, that you could treat her so mean?..." I got to feeling so mean and so miserable I most wished I was dead.
                                        —Huckleberry Finn[1]

In Mark Twain's classic *Huckleberry Finn*, Huck's conscience bothers him horribly that he's helping his friend Jim escape from slavery into freedom. It's a powerful piece of literature because it depicts a conflict between what Huck's conscience is telling him and what nearly every reader thinks is the moral course of action. Conscience, after all, is supposed to confirm if not reveal the contents of morality, not obfuscate it or stand in conflict with it. Huck's situation is a no-win scenario, as a result; either he ignores his conscience and helps his friend, or he obeys his conscience and betrays him.

How do we know what's right? If God is the Good and his commands constitute moral obligations, at some point we must ask how it is that we come to know his will. Presumably his will is prior to his commands; in fact, this is why some moral theorists, like Phil Quinn and Mark Murphy, have argued for advantages to a divine will theory over a divine command theory, a distinction that won't further detain us here. How we come to know God's will or commands, though, is an important epistemic challenge we must address, the last of the six objections to divine command theory that we mentioned in chapter 2. Doing so will provide us the opportunity to discuss several related issues: comparisons and contrasts between divine command theory and natural law, connections as we conceive them between morality and rationality, and distinctively epistemic reasons to take the moral argument seriously. But we begin with the last of the important set of distinctions that, we argued, collectively answer the Euthyphro Dilemma, namely, the distinction between the order of being and the order of knowing.

## The Order of Being versus the Order of Knowing

A child might learn his multiplication tables from an older sibling or a teacher, but that sibling or teacher is hardly the ultimate ground or explanation for why the multiplication table holds true. The source from which we gain knowledge is one matter; what made the subject matter true and knowable is quite another. The former is an epistemological issue; the latter is a metaphysical or ontological issue. The medievals recognized this, and distinguished between the order of knowing and the order of being, and this is a crucial distinction to bear in mind when it comes to ethics. We may learn that stealing is wrong from reading an ethicist, but the wrongness of stealing has its springs in different sources entirely. Thus atheists make a good point when they stress that the fact that some moral truths may have been learned from Christian teachings doesn't go to show that religion must necessarily be the ultimate cause or ground of those truths. This is true, although if we're right, it wouldn't be surprising that some important moral truths would have been revealed to us by God that we may not have otherwise come up with on our own.

We have been arguing that God is the ontological source of morality, its ultimate foundation, in virtue of his character and the commands or will that flow out of that character. The scope and shape of our theory have been decidedly metaphysical rather than epistemological. We have held in abeyance and intentionally deferred most epistemic questions until now for a strategic reason, namely, that it isn't, strictly speaking, central to our theory. As we see it, one could be a theistic ethicist and subscribe to any of a wide variety of mechanisms by which God reveals his will to us. The basic argument that we have been advancing doesn't delimit such epistemic options just to one or two possibilities. In this way epistemology functions more at the periphery than the center of our approach. Nonetheless, at some point we need to deal with this question, so we intend to do so here in the penultimate chapter of the book.

Drawing the distinction between being and knowing is a well-worn path for those who answer the challenge against theistic ethics that emphasizes that even atheists and secularists can know what is right or good apart from any explicit reference to God. Paul Copan, for example, reminds such critics of the being/knowing distinction and then drives home the further point that the critic is also saddled with the burden of providing a plausible story of his own about what makes such knowledge possible. Robert Adams makes much of the being/knowing distinction in his classic work on divine command theory as well, then uses William Alston's epistemological framework to lay out a workable moral epistemology. Alasdair MacIntyre pushes a similar distinction in his classic "Which God Ought We to Obey and Why?"[2] John Milliken, too, in an effort to answer vacuity objections like those of Kai Nielsen that would seem to require standards of goodness independent of God, takes advantage of the difference between ontology and epistemology. Here is how Milliken deploys the distinction:

> While it is correct to think that a substantive description of God as good requires our having an independent conception of goodness, this independence can be of two kinds. Let me illustrate them with an example: Imagine a language called Twing someone makes up and sets down in an official manuscript. Suppose Tim learns Twing indirectly from some friends who speak it. Suppose further that one day he stumbles upon the official manuscript, reads it, and exclaims, "This thing is written in perfect Twing!" Tim is here making what is for him a substantive statement. He has an independent concept of perfect Twing that applies in this case. Contrast this case with Tim finding some other manuscript (perhaps a translation of Homer) composed of Twing accompanied by the same exclamation. In the first case, Tim's evaluation of the manuscript depends upon a merely *epistemically* independent conception of perfect Twing. In

fact, his conception is *ontologically* dependent, for his conception of perfect Twing traces back to the very source he now evaluates. In the second case, Tim's conception of perfect Twing is both epistemically and ontologically independent of the manuscript he is evaluating. Returning to the case at hand with this distinction in mind, it is clear that, in order to make a substantive ascription of goodness to God, our conception of it need only be epistemically independent and not ontologically so. In other words, it is only necessary that we learn what is good from instances other than God. It would be a real and important discovery for us that what we antecedently understood as the good is exemplified in God, even if He is ultimately its source. This objection therefore fails as an argument for the autonomy of ethics.[3]

In fact, God may well have strategic reasons to structure human experience so that we learn about morality "bottom up," as it were. Early on in life our concerns tend to be predominantly if not exclusively egoistic, then gradually the scope of our concerns expands to include family, then friends. Ultimately, the scope of our moral concerns can encompass the whole of humanity, people we have never met or future generations, animals, or even the environment. What started out as good, understood to be what was good *for us*, can eventually broaden to include what's good for others and what is good not just instrumentally or extrinsically, but intrinsically as well. There's nothing in our moral epistemology functioning in such a manner that precludes the possibility that, ultimately, what we come to discover to be the ultimate source of morality is God himself, whom we perhaps earlier had come to think of as good. Explanations have to stop somewhere; so there's nothing in principle, from that perspective, that makes God as the ultimate stopping point any more problematic than any other.

If the argument of this book holds water, then it wouldn't be the least surprising that God had, by whatever means he chose, conferred on or imbued in human beings clear apprehensions of foundational moral truths that a reflective person would consider to be nonnegotiable. Again, if a moral argument for God's existence is to work, it requires moral premises that are taken to be at least as secure epistemically speaking as the conclusions are about God's existence. Rather than this showing the autonomy of ethics or superfluity of theistic ethics, this is a basic prerequisite for any workable piece of moral apologetics. That some (mistakenly) infer on the basis of the utter clarity of moral intuitions that no further explanation for their truth is required, natural or supernatural, indicates that their belief that the content of morality, at least when it comes to its main contours, is not up for grabs. Thus the United Nations can often agree on basic principles of justice and human dignity, and, in *The Abolition of Man*, C. S. Lewis was able to talk at length, and historically document, what he called "the Tao": moral principles that can be found the world over and throughout history in a wide array of religious and philosophical systems. But that state of affairs, we have emphasized, is potentially consistent with a variety of moral theories, including a theistic ethic. In fact, before this chapter is done, we will argue, in an epistemic variant of the moral argument, that theism, specifically Anselmian theism, is what best explains this epistemic reality.

Natural Law Theory

Although we have spent much of our time discussing divine command theory, another important theistic ethic is natural law theory, and we need to spend at least some time discussing it in this chapter because of its relevance to the epistemic questions that theistic ethics raise. Natural law theory is a rich tradition of theistic ethics, and one with which we feel considerable resonance. Some of the historical tensions between natural law and divine command theorists are legend, but we wish primarily to emphasize instead those aspects in which these two traditions are able to dovetail with and importantly augment one another. We agree with Mar and Hanink that "the best expression of divine command morality and the best expression of natural law ethics…form a structural unity."[4] When we remember that (paradigmatic natural law theorist) Thomas Aquinas himself counted obedience to divine commands as the highest virtue, the hope of a successful rapprochement between divine command and natural law ethics seems eminently reasonable.

Natural law can have a number of different meanings, from Stoical analyses to Aristotelian, Hobbesian, Thomistic, and contemporary nontheistic ones, so we need to do a little work of disambiguation to make it clear how we will be employing the notion. The parts of natural law theory to which we are drawn and that resonate with the analysis we have provided include the following: that it roots morality in God; God gives the natural law, expressing it throughout creation and in human nature; and the natural law, ultimately, is a reflection of his providential purposes and his own nature. The good is prior to the right for a natural law theorist like Aquinas, although we prefer moving from the good to the right via divine commands (rather than a "nondefective" inference from the good to the right). Moreover, natural law theory is epistemologically significant, for the natural laws provide those principles of practical rationality by which our actions are reasonable or unreasonable. Rational beings like us are able to grasp our share in the eternal law and freely act on it. Natural laws are both prescriptively binding on us as well as universally knowable by nature. Aquinas takes it that there is a core of practical knowledge that all human beings have, even if the implications of that knowledge can require some work to figure out and even if strong emotions or bad dispositions can sometimes thwart that knowledge. Natural laws direct us toward the good, which provides us reasons to act, since the good is what brings to perfection the natures that we have been given.

Natural law has a long and rich history in Christian thought, and it can serve well as the basis for something like "general revelation," to which we have appealed throughout this book. At least thoroughgoing theistic natural law theists tend to believe that God has manifested his moral law by writing it into our nature as human beings and in other aspects of his ordered creation as well. Despite our fallen condition, it remains profoundly true on the Anselmian view that human beings have been created by God, in his image, and for his purposes. Before the Mosaic law was given, sin (though perhaps not transgression) was possible, not only among the Israelites, but also in those nations that did not have access to the Jewish law even after it was given. As Arthur Holmes puts it, "The biblical direction is rather that the creation bears witness to the moral law, that creational indicators point to good ends God intended in making us as he did, and that God's law is the law of creation."[5] Among such revelation is the biblical recognition of universal spheres of human action such as those delineated in the second half of the Decalogue and the divine appointment of some universal types of social institutions, such as those embodying the husband-wife relationship, economic relationships, and the political order. Sensitive and discerning attention paid to God's purposes behind such institutions, tempered by considerations of love and justice, can reveal important aspects of God's will. In fact, Alasdair MacIntyre argues that natural moral indicators about justice might well tell us which God we ought to obey.[6]

Along the same lines, Robert Adams's social analysis of moral obligations emphasizes the relational aspects of divine commands.[7] Similarly, John Hare highlights God's "call" rather than "commands" to illustrate how God created us with an emotional and affective nature so that we "feel the pull" of God's call toward our highest good. God's moral law fits that nature well, spelling out what love requires of us and directing us to follow as co-lovers with God.[8] These approaches, along with the fact that God does not provide every moral answer to us in a clear-cut way, "undercut the Kantian objection that divine commands would violate an individual's autonomy, for our relationship to God should be one of mutual love and respect, one that blossoms into deep and lasting friendship, rather than a dictatorial power relationship."[9] Advancing this point in an epistemic direction, Holmes adds that "if the law of God is attested by essential structures of human nature, by our common needs and spheres of action, then these factors are likely to influence the ethical thinking and moral decisions even of those who do not acknowledge the Creator. If God's laws are indeed beneficial, then people are somewhat likely to recognize it, whether or not they recognize the lawgiver."[10]

The epistemic power of natural law makes sense of conscience and moral intuitions, while providing a better alternative to saying that these are the main or only way in which we acquire moral knowledge. The power of conscience and moral intuitions is obvious; sometimes their deliverances are as nonnegotiable as anything can be. But on less clear matters these can also mislead us. Conscience, for example, can become seared, weak, or, as we saw in the fictional portrayal of Huckleberry Finn, unreliable because of a particular sort of cultural or subcultural conditioning. According too much importance to conscience and intuitions can also smack of privileging some special sort of moral faculty, which strikes most contemporary thinkers as epistemically indulgent. Some moral intuitions are indeed beyond negotiation, and we haven't hesitated to appeal to them in our own analysis, but at most these play one role, albeit a crucial one, among many others in a full-fledged moral epistemology.

The point to grasp is that theistic ethicists have a broad array of resources at their disposal to construct a workable moral epistemology: natural law, conscience, moral intuitions, general revelation.[11] In fact, we are also able to tap into the sorts of resources that naturalists and Platonic realists appeal to, ranging from the ways in which our minds are structured, distinctive features of consciousness, how we use and acquire language, our natural tendencies toward socialization, and the constitutive rules of institutions. Ours is a more expansive way of construing epistemology, encompassing the whole plethora of possibilities for how we might come to know the contents of morality, including resources that are not so readily at the disposal of naturalists, such as special revelation. Atheists can of course appropriate, say, biblical teachings like the Golden Rule, primacy of justice, or responsibility to feed the poor, but as Anselmian theists we have distinctive reasons to take such teachings as morally authoritative.

Carving out room for an element of voluntarism makes such special revelation, and even more personally directed divine commands or calls, a living possibility. Given the profundity of God's wisdom, our fallen states, and our cognitive limitations, we should retain, in addition to firm and nonnegotiable moral commitments, enough epistemic humility to admit that our efforts to discern moral truth are subject to correction and errors. C. S. Lewis once wrote,

"Five senses; an incurably abstract intellect; a haphazardly selective memory; a set of preconceptions and assumptions so numerous that I can never examine more than a minority of them—never become even conscious of them all. How much of total reality can such an apparatus let through?"[12] Our rational trust in God's goodness enables trust in his provision of moral knowledge and the wisdom we need to conduct our lives and societies, but our very real cognitive limitations should remind us all to retain a tremendous amount of epistemic humility, a virtue sometimes sadly lacking in all of us.

It bears emphasis once more that natural theology, as we are deploying it, assigns ultimate emphasis neither to human nature nor even to the whole created order, but rather to God himself. On John Wesley's view, the moral law, flowing from the fountain of God's love and goodness, will, if followed, make for our well-being and happiness. Wesley saw that it was adapted to the nature of things as God created them. But if the standard of morality depends on the nature and relations of things, then it must depend on God, because those things themselves, with all their relations, are the works of God's hands.[13] Moreover, since no account of human flourishing is complete that doesn't include communion with God, man's *summum bonum* is impossible apart from reconciliation and fellowship with God. Along with other classical theologians, Wesley recognized that the final end of human beings is union with God, an experience in which we shall become co-lovers with God and enter into the love that exists between the three persons of the Trinity.[14]

Natural law makes morality rationally compelling and authoritative, but not everyone agrees that morality possesses such rational warrant, so to this issue we now turn.

Morality and Rationality

The connection between morality and rationality is a fertile topic of discussion, and we're going to limit our comments to a few of the implications of our analysis to this important question. Is morality always rational? Might on occasion morality demand one thing and rationality another? How should an Anselmian answer such questions? The question is important because if there's a wedge between morality and rationality, occasions where our overriding reasons to act would lead us to do immoral things, then this would radically weaken the rational force of morality, thereby weakening the moral argument for God's existence. On the other hand, if theism provides a better account of the rational force of morality, then this would bolster the moral argument by offering a distinctively epistemic variant of it.

It should be obvious on the basis of our natural law commitments alone that morality is something that we think it is indeed rational to do. Rationality of course can mean different things, from means-ends analyses to egoistic analyses to theistic accounts. Perhaps not surprisingly, ours tends to be a thoroughgoing theistic account.[15] In fact, to our thinking, there's a vitally important parallel between morality and rationality. C. S. Lewis recognized this in his book *Miracles*; the third and fifth chapters parallel one another. The third chapter pertains to the limitations of naturalism in accounting for rationality, whereas the fifth chapter argues by parity of reasoning for a similar limitation besetting naturalism in accounting for morality. We are inclined to concur that the challenges confronting naturalists are similar in cases of both morality and rationality. Victor Reppert and Alvin Plantinga have more recently highlighted some of the challenges confronting naturalists in making sense of rationality, and we would like to quickly tip our hat in the direction of their arguments.[16]

In the first chapter, we identified some of the challenges that naturalists encounter in their attempt to account for moral freedom, without which morality is rendered irrelevant. The challenge they face in accounting for rationality bears a resemblance. Rationality at a minimum requires sensitivity to evidence, reasons, and argument. If, however, we are causally determined to behave as we do, and that includes our thoughts and the conclusions we come to on the basis of reflection, then those conclusions aren't ultimately a function of reasons and evidence but rather of the physiological operations of our brains in accord with the causal laws of the world. Taking seriously evidence and reasons requires an understanding of reality in which evidence and argument are more than misleading phenomena that have bubbled to the surface of our consciousness. A theistic understanding of reality, while perhaps not the only worldview that carries this advantage (idealism would be another), is still, we are inclined to think, the best one. We don't intend to delve further into such arguments from reason, because for present purposes it would take us too far afield, but it's important to emphasize that a strong focus on reasons and evidence is more obviously at home in a deeply relational and personal universe as theism depicts it than a mechanistic naturalistic one, as the atheist conceives ultimate reality.

The central question of why we should be moral, of why morality provides us a reason to act, is inextricably tied to the question of the ontological status and prescriptive force of morality. If morality is largely illusory or a matter of subjective preference, then it would seem likely indeed that there could be many occasions when doing the "moral thing" would be irrational. Since many people, theists and atheists alike, rather believe that morality, especially all-things-considered moral obligations, always provide the strongest rational reason to act, then those people would have reason not to think that morality is just a matter of satisfying subjective personal preferences.

In striking contrast, ethicist Bruce Russell attempts to defend a version of moral skepticism, arguing that moral requirements don't always provide overriding reasons to act. He asks us to consider this scenario:

> A young woman has her heart set on getting into medical school. If she gets in, through hard work and dedication she will graduate and become a good physician. However, even after much study she has been unable to score high enough on the MCATs to be admitted to any medical school. She finds herself with an opportunity to cheat that will ensure her an MCAT score that is high enough to gain admittance to some medical school and so to eventually fulfill her lifelong dream. Her patients will not be harmed by being treated by an incompetent physician because she will not be an incompetent physician once she receives the necessary training. At most the only person who will be harmed is the person denied admittance to medical school because this young woman will take one of the available places and so leave one less slot to be filled. Assume that this person will only be slightly harmed and that somehow the young woman knows all this. It would be wrong for this young woman to cheat to get into medical school, but why isn't it true that if she does not care about cheating, then what she has most reason to do is to cheat if she knows she can get away with it?[17]

And he provides a second example as well:

> Suppose your son has robbed a rich man of his jewels, the police are after him, and he asks you to help him escape to Brazil. You know you can arrange things so that neither of you will get caught. You also know that if he is caught he will be sent to prison and his life will be ruined, but if he escapes, he will have a good life in Brazil. It would be wrong of you to help him escape, but why isn't it true that what you have most reason to do is to help your son escape justice?

On the basis of these scenarios, Russell thinks that he has shown that moral requirements don't always provide overriding reasons to act. By "moral requirements" we take it that he means more than merely prima facie moral duties that might be overridden by other considerations or supererogatory actions that there might be moral reasons to do but not any actual obligation to do. Russell's argument, we presume, is that ultima facie (or all-things-considered) moral duties do not always provide overriding reasons to act. This is a serious challenge, because if it holds, it would radically undermine the rational authority of morality. Quite contrary to the way rationality and morality dovetail perfectly in natural law theory, Russell's story would shake our confidence in the prescriptive force of morality, thereby undermining the moral argument for God's existence. Does his argument work? We are not inclined to think so, for a number of reasons.

To begin with, take the student who is considering cheating on her MCATs. Built into the thought experiment are a number of controversial features. This isn't a criticism yet, just an observation. For example, we are to assume that the damage done to the student excluded on the basis of the cheater's subterfuge will be mild. We are to assume that the student who cheats her way into medical school has what it takes to become a good doctor. We are to assume that somehow the cheater knows in advance the consequences of her actions and the efficacy of her plans. None of this is true to real life, of course. Now, admittedly, thought experiments do this all the time, and they are nonetheless useful for eliciting intuitions on certain matters. But in a case like this, where Russell wants, on the basis of this example and another, to infer that the rational basis of morality is compromised, the distance between his hypothetical assumptions and real situations where none of these hypothetical features are in place becomes relevant. For he's assuming as a genuine possibility a scenario that is remotely conceivable at best. Qualified to this degree, his thought experiment is seriously compromised in terms of what we can successfully glean from it.

But let's set those concerns aside, though they are considerable and significant. Even more troubling is Russell's completely consequentialist analysis of the whole matter. The cheater figures, "Well, I'm going to benefit a great deal, and this other person I'm replacing is only going to be hurt a little, so this means it's rational for me to cheat." This demonstrates an impoverished understanding of what rationality involves. Aren't the relevant moral considerations here, including deontological ones like the intrinsic wrongness of cheating under at least most circumstances, relevant to the deliverances of reason and rationality? Rationality expunged of the relevance of morality is a thin, myopic, and emaciated notion indeed.

Now, there's a sense in which we can agree entirely with Russell. If he wants to water down the concept of rationality in this case just to whatever is in the perceived this-worldly interests of the cheating student who, Russell says, "doesn't care about the cheating," a student who obviously has a major character flaw, then we might agree that there's a sense in which it's rational for this student to cheat. Her salient "reasons for action," on Russell's construal, pertain in this case just to the satisfaction of her own personal subjective and self-interested desires. It would seem pretty clear, the way Russell has thus stacked the deck, that morality isn't going to function to provide her compelling reasons to act. But what are we entitled to infer on the basis of the fact that a person who doesn't care about cheating doesn't find moral considerations against cheating relevant to her actions? This is a far cry from any compelling reason to think that morality lacks rational authority. To the extent that we confine discussion to what the student has personal subjective reason to do from inside her truncated egoistic perspective, we could grant Russell's point without in the least losing confidence that genuine moral duties give us overriding (objective) reason to act.

The prior disagreement we have with Russell concerns the propriety of his reducing "reasons for action" to the subjective preferences of morally jaded persons. His thought experiment had to be so qualified to make his argument go through that it left little on which to base any substantive inference. It certainly isn't enough to warrant Russell's ambitious conclusion that ultima facie moral duties don't always provide overriding reasons to act.

Or take Russell's second thought experiment. The father somehow, again, "knows" that his son's life will be ruined by going to jail. This leaves us needing to know considerably more. Is the son's life going to be ruined because he simply has to face the consequences of his actions? Plenty of parents would say that the loving thing to do in such a case is to allow the son to face the music and pay the penalty for his wrongdoing. A father's duty is not just to help his sons out of jams when he gets the opportunity (recall this point when we discussed Russell's good parent analogy in the previous chapter). If, rather, the father somehow knows that the son, after being sent to prison, will experience excruciating burns in the jail cell the week he arrives, or will get a sentence wildly disproportionate with the nature of his crime, then justice would not demand that he be punished in that way. Justice and morality itself, then, wouldn't confer on the father an ultima facie duty to refrain from helping his son. But in that case the thought experiment wouldn't help Russell's case at all. Of course, we don't have such crystal balls to know the future, but if the father did have such privileged epistemic status, the father's duty to refrain from helping his son would constitute a prima facie duty at most, and it would thus be able to overridden.

So we see little reason here to think that Russell has shown that genuine moral duties don't provide overriding reasons to act. For those who think of moral reasons as providing one kind of reason to do things, one kind of reason among others, and not necessarily a binding or authoritative sort of reason, our moral obligations may not be the most rational thing to do, on their view. We can without objection concede their point if we're talking about certain relatively trivial moral matters. Let's suppose we have every reason to think that blowing the whistle on a colleague would threaten our own job, and suppose further that the nature of the colleague's wrongdoing doesn't attain to so great a level that we deem the loss of our own job as worth it. We might suggest that, though we have some moral reason to blow the whistle, it may not be the most rational thing to do. But that would also be in part because we think that, as a moral agent with morally legitimate concerns about self-interest, we truly don't have a genuine moral obligation to blow the whistle, or at most a prima facie one. It wouldn't be wrong to blow the whistle; thus, doing so would be morally permissible, perhaps even praiseworthy, but it wouldn't be obligatory. If something is a genuine, binding moral duty, in contrast, then it plausibly carries with it the best reasons to act.

Holding such a view doesn't make it true, of course, and there remain thinkers who would argue that it's in fact false. But for a first go at a reply, we would suggest that there are good reasons to take seriously the sort of story we're telling: that there are prescriptively binding moral obligations that we are responsible to discharge and our failure to do so renders us morally blameworthy; and that such duties are rationally authoritative as well. This is commonsensical; it's highly intuitive; it accords with biblical teachings about the moral duties we are obliged to fulfill; it accords with the way moral language tends to be used; and it's a great candidate for a deliverance of natural law. There are ample reasons to take such a possibility with the utmost seriousness; it's at least not obviously wrong, and the rational authority of morality should not be lightly discarded. That it can be doubted isn't by itself good enough reason to doubt it; and that it's so often thought to be a matter of common sense and a clear deliverance of reason gives us excellent reason to demand better evidence against it than what Russell provides before forfeiting it.

Rationality obviously includes far more than merely moral considerations, but just as obviously it is typically understood to allow certain moral obligations and principles pride of place and even occasional primacy in our decision-making. Of all the various reasons to act, moral obligations are distinctively thought to provide compelling and overriding reasons. Those whose worldview can't sustain this case hold a defective worldview. If morality is real, then when someone has a real and binding moral obligation, even if discharging the duty isn't perceived to be in one's own interests, or in line with one's desires, or a function of one's preferences, it's still the rational thing to do. Moral authority in such situations would still apply, which requires a strong view concerning both the existence and prescriptive strength of moral responsibilities.

## The Relevance of Worldview

Earlier we saw, in "Religion and the Queerness of Morality," philosopher George Mavrodes emphasize just this prescriptive power of moral obligations. He especially wished to characterize moral obligations as an odd fit for a (Bertrand) "Russellian" world in which the ultimate constituent realities are atoms and molecules. He did this not because he thought, as Kant did, that obligations were necessarily the only or most important thing to morality; nonetheless, Mavrodes intentionally confined his attention to obligations in an effort to demonstrate that their existence would be potentially illuminating in various ways. In particular, it would not always pay to discharge our duties in a Russellian world. That is, fulfilling our moral obligations in an atheistic world (assuming there are moral obligations in an atheistic world) would at least on occasion likely result in a net loss for the moral agent. In fact, this would be true in an appreciable number of cases, as Mavrodes observes. In certain cases of truth telling or repaying a debt or keeping a promise, and perhaps even more clearly in those rarer cases where the performance of a duty risks death or injury, one must sacrifice Russellian goods to do the moral thing. So if one is an atheist in a Russellian world, then he's faced with a choice: Either affirm that morality and rationality sometimes dictate different things and then either infer that we should do the moral, irrational thing anyway, or do the rational thing and ignore the dictates of morality.

Notice how sharp is the contrast here between the theist who believes in ultima facie prescriptively binding moral obligations and the skeptic who rejects the existence of such duties or their rational authority. The theist affirms that there are such duties, which are in our ultimate self-interest because loving God and doing right are always in our ultimate self-interest. So it's always rational to do such duties and acknowledge their authoritative force. The skeptic denies this, saying instead that morality seems to lack rational authority or perhaps authority altogether, for sometimes it's just too costly. Now, both thinkers could be said to be thinking in a way that's rational in at least one sense. Each is thinking through the implications of their worldview in a way that is not obviously unreasonable or irrational.

What this shows, then, is that the meta-ethical question about morality and rationality is inextricably tied to ultimate questions of ontology and metaphysics. The right ultimate view of reality is plausibly the one that will be most likely to produce the right analysis of the relationship between morality and rationality. Both the atheist and the theist are predicating their approach on a fundamental axiom: that the world makes sense. It wouldn't make sense if the world required us to do what isn't in our ultimate self-interest. We think this was Kant's insight when he suggested that the moral enterprise needs, in a deep and radical way, the postulate of a God who can, and will, make happiness correspond to virtue. Morality fails to make sense when that correspondence fails. It's the atheistic world in particular, however, that introduces the failure of this correspondence. Reality itself must be committed to morality in some deep way for morality to make sense. Morality really must be a very deep feature and fixture of reality in order for its demands to retain their authoritative force. In an atheistic world there just doesn't seem likely to be the sort of ontological foundation to morality that renders it always rational to both believe in and do what's morally binding. The picture is very different for a theistic world of a certain sort.

Among the rather interesting implications of this little discussion is the following. The atheist probably conceives of good in terms of things like happiness, self-realization, pleasure, esteem, contentment, knowledge, or something of that ilk. We shouldn't exclude from the list the so-called "satisfactions of morality," the feelings of fulfillment that come from behaving morally, which can be among the most deeply gratifying feelings of which human beings are capable, including atheists. At any rate, their view of the good is explicable somehow in such terms. Now let's suppose the atheist is confronted with a stark choice between what he believes would be a morally obligatory thing to do if morality indeed exists authoritatively, on the one hand, and something good and prudential, on his construal, on the other. Presumably many atheists would do the "moral" thing in a number of cases, even if it meant a sacrifice of some measure of prudence, be it pleasure or what not. But the costlier the fulfillment of the duty and the more good that would have to be sacrificed, the less rational doing the "moral" thing would appear to be for the atheist. Ultimately, the pendulum is going to swing, and the rational course of action will likely be deemed the choice of the goods otherwise lost over that of the duty.

Now consider the Anselmian's analysis. On this worldview, there are indeed occasions when we may be called to discharge a moral duty that will result in the sacrifice of some good, as we've discussed in previous chapters. But though the action one might be called to do is bad, it will never be irremediably evil. For example, the taking of life is always in some sense bad, but it may be justified, perhaps even obligatory, as in a just war, in which case it isn't evil in the way that the gratuitous and unjustified taking of life is. Nor is the student's refraining from cheating on her MCATs, on our view, an irremediably bad thing, but rather just a necessary sacrifice that the theist can trust God, in his providence, to redeem. In fact, it's a good thing! Due to the divergent implications between theism and atheism, therefore, there is a huge parting of the ways between these two worldviews and their proponents on the meta-ethical question of the connection between morality and rationality.

## Layman's Argument

In an earlier chapter we discussed a moral argument that C. Stephen Layman rejected, and we promised to come back to the one he accepted, and we do so now. It's an epistemic moral argument that pertains exactly to this issue of the rational authority of morality. Layman prefaces his argument by rightly suggesting that any such argument, moral or otherwise, must be part of a cumulative case for theism; the question is not whether it by itself is enough to demonstrate God's existence, but whether it can contribute positively to an overall case. In a nutshell, he begins his argument by accepting what Bruce Russell rejects: The Overriding Reason Thesis (ORT), which says "the overriding (or strongest) reasons always favor doing what is morally required."[18] Layman, like us, thinks the evidence for this thesis is strong and deeply intuitive and it shouldn't be rejected quickly. For the falsehood of ORT greatly undermines the rational authority of morality.

Although Layman thinks ORT is true and deeply important, he denies that it is a necessary truth. For he asks us to consider a possible world in which a powerful evil demon rules who torments the virtuous while granting eternal bliss to the wicked. ORT in such a world would not be true. Fair enough, but, echoing an earlier motif, we would suggest that Layman's sanguine entertainment of such a possibility lacks justification. Although the scenario he depicts is in some important sense conceivable, it's not at all clear that it constitutes a genuine possibility as he suggests, and in fact if an Anselmian God exists, it isn't possible. So, assuming it as a genuine possibility begs the question by tacitly assuming the falsity of Anselmianism. We are not doing just the same thing in reverse by presupposing Anselmianism; we're suggesting that since Anselmianism and the genuine possibility of Layman's evil demon world can't both obtain, evidence is called for before embracing one or the other. Merely positing possibilities doesn't make them actual, a point that would benefit Russell to remember as well. At any rate, Layman accepts ORT, as do we, and then continues to build his argument from there.

Layman introduces the Conditional Thesis (CT), which says that "if there is no God and no life after death, then the ORT is not true."[19] His argument for CT involves a case not unlike those of Russell's, where a person has strong reasons to steal but not enough moral justification. The choice to steal, taking into account this-worldly goods alone, would be extremely prudent, but nevertheless morally impermissible. So the person has "overriding reason to steal assuming that there is no God and no life after death."[20] Layman hammers out his intuition on the case by identifying this principle: "If considerations of prudence [what Russell calls agent-centered reasons] and morality conflict, and if the prudential considerations are momentous while the results of behaving immorally are relatively minor, then prudence overrides morality."[21]

Now, it might appear that CT casts doubt on ORT, and it undoubtedly does from the atheist's point of view. This appears to be Russell's modus operandi as he thinks about morality from an atheistic perspective. But Layman adds that "it is hardly fair simply to assume that atheism is true, when an argument for theism is being offered. And surely we ought to be reluctant to jettison ORT."[22] Instead, he would encourage readers to remain open to the possibility of both ORT and CT being true. And if they are both true, what follows is this: Either God exists or there is life after death in which virtue is rewarded. Note that this leaves open the possibility of something like karma instead of a theistic universe, so an atheist could consistently accept both ORT and CT, but Layman's response to this approach is instructive:

> Given that reincarnation and karma hold in the absence of any deity, the universe is governed not only by physical laws (such as the law of gravity) but by impersonal moral laws. These moral laws must be quite complex, for they have to regulate the connection between each soul's moral record in one life and that soul's total circumstances in the next life, including which body it has, its environment, and the degree of happiness (or misery) it experiences. Thus, these impersonal moral laws must somehow take into account every act, every intention, and every choice of every moral agent and ensure that the agent receives nothing less than his or her just desserts in the next life. Now, the degree of complexity involved here is obviously very high, and it serves a moral end, namely, justice. But a highly complex structure that promotes justice can hardly be accepted as a brute fact. Such a moral order cries out for explanation in terms of an intelligent cause. And if the moral order is on a scale far surpassing what can be attributed to human intelligence, an appeal to divine intelligence is justified. Hence, the moral order postulated by nontheistic reincarnation paradoxically provides evidence for the existence of a personal God.[23]

We will spend more time discussing the afterlife in the next chapter, but first we need to briefly discuss the problem of divine hiddenness.

## Divine Hiddenness

A recurring epistemic challenge to theism is the question of divine hiddenness. God, we have argued, has revealed himself, but there is also a hiddenness that must be acknowledged. He's not peeling back the heavens and showing himself to us in that way. Pascal offered reasons for God's hiddenness, such as God's desire to woo our hearts and not merely overwhelm our minds with light, thus coercing our belief. We first broached this subject in chapter 3 when we distinguished the "believe-that" and "believe-in" locutions.

We submit that, ironically, there may be something merciful about God's hiddenness. According to most Christian theologians, the reason that the angels who rebelled against God are beyond redemption is that their rebellion was done with maximum light and revelation at their disposal. Theirs wasn't a half-hearted rejection or rebellion, but a clear-eyed, open rebellion in the full light of God's goodness and love. That sort of definitive rejection is something from which there may be no turning back. God, in his mercy, perhaps knows that many of us who initially resist his overtures of love will, in time, come around. So his hiding himself from us to some extent might be a way in which he gives us more time and opportunity to feel the force of our sin and failures and the power of his love and grace.

Paul Moser in his recent work on divine hiddenness has offered a fresh and bold approach to this classical question of divine hiddenness, emphasizing that our religious epistemology has to take it seriously.[24] God both reveals and hides himself, and Moser argues, consistent with Christian theology, that the reason for this is that God's purposes aren't just to generate propositional knowledge of his existence, but a more deeply personal sort of knowledge. God is a loving Father who, in his filial love, speaks to us all but in different ways and at different times, in an effort to invite us into a loving personal relationship with himself. Much of what Moser has to say comports nicely with the focus of the next chapter, where we broach the issue of relational ethics.

Moser argues that a relational God of love is not content merely to provide discursive evidence of his existence in order to elicit cognitive assent or function as the conclusion of an argument; rather, God desires to be known for nothing less than this robust end: fellowship and morally perfect love between him and human beings. Moser thus suggests that evidence for God cannot be mere spectator evidence, but something both more authoritative and volitional than that. God, on Moser's view, hides from those who do not desire a relationship or life-changing knowledge of him. God conceals himself from those who do not recognize the existential implications of belief in God, whereas he does reveal himself to those who recognize and desire to live with the implications of knowing God. Moser writes that "God would restrain divine manifestations, at least for a time, to at least some humans in order to enhance satisfaction of God's own diverse perfectly authoritative and loving purposes regarding humans."[25]

A theistic conception of reality fundamentally alters everything. For if God is the ultimate reality, our quest for wisdom is a quest for him, a personal being, not just principles or platitudes. And if the context in which we find ourselves involves God drawing us into loving relationship with him, then a logic of relations more than a logic of propositions reigns. As C. S. Lewis put it, "If human life is in fact ordered by a beneficent being whose knowledge of our real needs and of the way in which they can be satisfied infinitely exceeds our own, we must expect a priori that His operations will often appear to us far from beneficent and far from wise, and that it will be our highest prudence to give Him our confidence in spite of this."[26]

Philosophers tend to discuss propositional knowledge before other kinds of knowledge, like competence knowledge or personal acquaintance.[27] But the biblical picture of knowledge, ultimately, carries with it considerably more than propositional significance alone. Surely there's much of that, but even more fundamentally there's knowledge of people and ultimately of God himself. The Old Testament was clear in its denunciations of pagan religions that tied religious practice to sexual ones like temple prostitution. Ironically, then, knowledge of God is expressed biblically in the same terms as marital intercourse. Knowing God and his knowing us is as personal and intimate as it gets. The reason that holiness is not optional for those who would commune with God is that that kind of intimacy with a perfect being requires increasing purity and perfection within us, which only God can generate. And as we grow in that relationship, according to the biblical worldview, our eyes are increasingly made open to apprehend more of him and his goodness.

# 10

# Ethics and Eternity

Imagine there's no heaven
It's easy if you try
No hell below us
Above us only sky
Imagine all the people living for today....

—John Lennon[1]

Blaise Pascal, the great French mathematician and philosopher, thought it was remarkable that intellectuals would draw up their theories without consideration of whether or not there's an afterlife. For him this question made a huge difference not only in how we should understand morality, but indeed our entire lives. He once wrote that "the immortality of the soul is something of such vital importance to us, affecting us so deeply, that one must have lost all feeling not to care about knowing the facts of the matter. All our actions and thoughts must follow such different paths, according to whether there is hope of eternal blessings or not, that the only possible way of acting with sense and judgment is to decide our course of action in the light of this point, which ought to be our ultimate objective."[2]

Immanuel Kant, too, believed that the question of the afterlife is relevant to ethics, for a few different reasons. The demands from morality require a process that is never fully completed in this life; moreover, not all the virtuous in this life are happy, so belief in an afterlife is necessary if we are to rationally believe that there's ultimate correspondence between happiness and virtue. Kant called the possibility of the general union of happiness and virtue "the highest good."

Most typically, however, whenever a discussion of morality broaches the question of the afterlife, it's assumed that the purpose of doing so is to offer a prudential reason to live morally. Threats of hell, especially, can be used as the ultimate trump card to answer the question of why we ought to live morally. The reason that zealous religious proponents often give for why we ought to be moral is that we had better live morally or else! Critics rightly see this not-so-veiled threat as a potential instance of an elaborate appeal to force: We need to live morally and obey God or else we will be relegated to hell. Obeying God and morality promises heaven. Such a paradigm is not only a deficient account of the reason to be moral, it's probably downright deleterious to proper moral motivation. Although we agree and would echo such a sentiment, we remain convinced that there's considerably more here that needs to be said. Criticisms predicated on bad theology shouldn't set the terms of this discussion.

The crux of the matter, as we see it, is not merely whether there is an afterlife, but what sort of afterlife there is, if there is one. And this question is obviously closely connected with whether or not God exists and what God's character is if God is real. The moral argument of this book has been that God does indeed exist, and that God is good, indeed perfectly good and the Good itself. So in this chapter we set out to round out our analysis of theistic ethics by discussing a cluster of related questions that we have yet to discuss in enough detail, all of which pertain to this issue of the afterlife. These include Kant's concerns about morality and happiness, the question of virtue, and such distinctive Christian teachings as the Trinity, incarnation, atonement, resurrection, and heaven and hell.

## Virtue

It's hard to overestimate the importance of virtue to moral theory, because what virtue theory provides is a shift in focus away from merely *what we do* to the very important question of *who we are*. Earlier in the book, we admitted that moral obligations, as important as they are, constitute perhaps the vestibule of a sprawling mansion, and that the farther reaches of morality leave rights and duties far behind. Broaching the topic of virtue affords us entrance into a huge and ornate interior hall of that mansion. Virtue pertains to what we do when nobody is watching, learning to love things in the right way and to the right degree, and an increasing resonance between our lower and higher order desires.[3] Christian theology, ultimately, is less concerned with our actions and more concerned with our being, the state of our moral and spiritual well-being. God, according to classical Christian orthodoxy, is not merely interested in guiding our paths, but transforming our souls and characters. So an emphasis on virtue theory can be profoundly congruent with Christian thought; indeed, it can function as an overarching aspect of moral theory under which rules, proper considerations of self-interest, rights and duties, and divine commands can all find their proper niche.[4]

Kant thought that the only action possessing moral worth is one motivated by respect for the moral law: doing something one ought to do and doing it for that reason alone. Although we think moral obligations are important, and we have spent considerable time discussing them, we demur from Kant on this point. Instead, we would argue that someone who has the sort of character that naturally leads her to do the right and good or virtuous thing shows the greater moral development than the person doing the right thing merely out of duty. This is not to disparage the value of the right action performed by a person in a situation where doing the right thing is extremely difficult, and in tension with strong opposing inclinations, but surely morality has more to say than merely "do your duty." In fact, we are inclined to think that, ultimately, rights and duties will come to be seen as an ancient relic, the mark of an early stage in our moral and spiritual pilgrimage. George Mavrodes captures this insight when he writes

> I come more and more to think that morality, while a fact, is a twisted and distorted fact. Or perhaps better, that it is a barely recognizable version of another fact, a version adapted to a twisted and distorted world. It is something like, I suppose, the way in which the pine that grows at timberline, wind blasted and twisted against the rock, is a version of the tall and symmetrical tree that grows lower on the slopes. I think it may be that the related notions of sacrifice and gift represent (or come close to representing) the fact, that is, the pattern of life, whose distorted version we know here as morality. Imagine a situation, an "economy" if you will, in which no one ever buys or trades for or seizes any good thing. But whatever good he enjoys it is either one which he himself has created or else one which he received as a free and unconditional gift. And as soon as he has tasted it and seen that it is good he stands ready to give it away in his turn as soon as the opportunity arises. In such a place, if one were to speak either of his rights or his duties, his remarks might be met with puzzled laughter as his hearers struggled to recall an ancient world in which these terms referred to something important.[5]

He goes on to note that even in this life, we may see glimmers of this in contexts ranging from family life to battlefield situations, where people move beyond mere morality, and display extraordinary love and sacrifice. Although these may be exceptional instances in our fallen world, he suggests that they may point to a future day when redemption is complete, all things are made new, and the language and concepts of morality are obsolete.

Virtue theory at least inches us closer to these deeper facts to which Mavrodes points. Our actions put us on a trajectory of character; the more we perform right (or wrong) actions, the more they become a part of who we are, and the more difficult it becomes to deviate from such a course. This is a key insight of virtue theory, and a part of any full-fledged moral theory. As a result, discussing morality without an adequate focus on virtue leads to a deficient analysis, for morality involves considerably more than merely performing the right actions. Indeed, performing the right actions itself requires that due consideration is paid to more than actions, such as the ability to put ourselves into the shoes of others, empathizing with and anticipating their needs, cultivating the right sorts of sentiments, capacities, moral sensibilities, and dispositions to behave virtuously in a variety of circumstances and in the face of strong temptations to do otherwise.

Philosophers sometimes debate whether or not God has duties. For reasons we've been discussing, we're inclined to think it's a bit of a misnomer to characterize God as having duties. Because he is morally perfect, he couldn't fail to fulfill any duties he might have.[6] Moreover, to the extent that God is constrained at all, it's by what's internal to his character. Tom Morris has it right when, after denying that God has duties, says that God, since he's morally perfect, acts in a way "functionally isomorphic" with a being who perfectly fulfills all his duties.[7] But it doesn't add anything essential to say God has duties, and saying that he does actually conveys a mistaken impression. It adds nothing to say that Jesus was doing his duty when he went to the cross; but saying that he did it out of his inestimable love, setting aside his rights in the process, speaks volumes.[8] What matters in God's case is that his character is, and ever has been, entirely impeccable, perfect. It's his character and virtue that matter, not his "duties." God's virtue far exceeds what would look like the discharging of duties anyway; his love and perfect goodness go well beyond merely the perfect fulfillment of duty. We saw this in an earlier chapter when we lamented the way in which Calvinists defend what we consider a deficient conception of God by couching the discussion merely in terms of what God's duties are and aren't, leaving the far more important issue of recognizable divine love largely out of the discussion.

In the previous chapter we saw that part of the epistemic story the Christian theist can tell about morality involves God's issuing commands consistent with our nature, the way he has made us. God can be trusted to tell us to do what it is in our interest to do and what, down deep, we already want to do. C. S. Lewis used the example of sexual fidelity as one of those creational indicators discussed in the previous chapter. When we listen to just about any secular musician sing about love, we hear him or her extol the beauty of exclusive love and undying commitment to and with that one special person; there's nothing romantic or heroic in a song about promiscuity. When we're commanded to be faithful to our spouse, we're being told to do something that in our heart of hearts we already most want to do. God's rules, which may on occasion be hard to understand, can still, we may trust, be what is best for us in light of the nature with which he's imbued us. Even a guided-will moral theorist would acknowledge as much. Contra Sartre, we think the evidence suggests that, before we were made, God had a preexisting pattern for our design in his mind, and that pattern was fashioned after his image and for his purposes. When it comes to a consideration of the virtues, this is important because, at least as the Aristotelian tradition understands matters, a big part of what determines virtuous traits of character is the kind of beings we are. Aristotle held a profoundly teleological conception of all aspects of reality, not just human beings. This commitment to a teleological understanding of reality held sway in Western philosophy for a very long time; around the time of the Enlightenment this notion began to lose its hold on the popular imagination. But what's vital to recognize is that Aristotle's conception of human teleology profoundly resonates with the Christian conception that God created and designed us for specific purposes and ends in mind, the most important of which is fellowship with God himself, and secondarily peaceful and loving fellowship with one another. This is what made even possible the grand Thomistic effort at synthesizing Christian and Aristotelian insights. Who and what we are and ought to be shapes the relevant list of virtues that in this life we should increasingly manifest as stable traits of character.

Earlier we offered a critique of Alasdair MacIntyre's historical analysis, at least in his *Short History of Ethics*, as an example of overreaching. What makes ironic MacIntyre's skepticism of the relevance of a theistic framework to a workable ethic is that he personally came later to believe that a Thomistic framework of virtue theory is the best available way to capture that social aspect of moral theory that began to fragment from ancient Greece onward. Recall his conviction that this fragmentation and decline of a social hierarchical understanding of accepted social roles led to a loss of much of the power of moral language to carry with it what had formerly been supposed to be its normative force, including its capacity to undergird thick ethical concepts like shame and honor. It's interesting and instructive indeed that in his later work he would embrace the idea that a rich Thomistic structure could help remedy this deficiency.

In agreement with the later MacIntyre, we think that a full-fledged theistic ethic captures the necessary social dimension of ethical theory. We have even defended what we consider a necessary element of voluntarism to which the early MacIntyre expressed nothing but vociferous opposition, though in the process he failed to distinguish between Ockamistic and nonOckamistic variants of voluntarism. His later work is more balanced in this regard, and his developing conviction that a theistic framework can help provide the sort of teleological framework necessary for ethics strikes us as entirely sound. Indeed, MacIntyre points to this lost teleological framework as the reason for the emergence of utilitarianism in the form that it has taken. This happened first because confidence in the Aristotelian/theistic vision of a distinctively human end or purpose was shaken, only to be replaced by the goal of mere happiness, understood as a psychological state. This attempt to explicate the goal of ethics as mere happiness, particularly by the utilitarians, inevitably became vulnerable to numerous criticisms. The notion of a human telos is a much richer notion than mere happiness, since it includes both that for the sake of which actions are performed but also that "by appeal to which we can understand which types of actions should be performed and why."[9]

Oliver O'Donovan has attempted to spell out a distinctively Christian teleology in his brilliant book *Resurrection and Moral Order*.[10] O'Donovan's argument is that the resurrection of Jesus, and all that it represents, helps provide the sufficiently rich picture of human teleology that moral theory requires.[11] The resurrection is the central Christian doctrine relevant to understanding morality, for it was the definitive divine act that marked the power of God at work redeeming the world to himself. It revealed both human sin and human potential, and it ushered in a new order, making available the same power that raised Jesus from the dead to be at work within us, transforming us into his likeness, as God originally intended, and revealing what can be our own hope that death is not the last word. The apostles proclaimed the resurrection of mankind in Christ and the renewal of all creation with him, issuing in a call for us to respond to a world order restored in Christ.[12] The meaning of human morality can only be understood by this restoration of the created order and its full disclosure as manifested in the resurrection.[13]

In our own way, we wish to echo this case in the following and final sections of this chapter and book in which we hope to tie together loose ends and round out our overall analysis. We can't help at this juncture in the argument to delve into some distinctively Christian theology, but since it would be a bit odd that a book emphasizing the possibility and importance of divine existence and revelation would spend all its time dwelling on general revelation alone, we do this bit of apologetics unapologetically. We are of the firm conviction that Christian theology provides the best way to extend our analysis of morality—one important reason, though hardly the only one, to think that such theology is true.[14]

## Relational Ethics

We have offered versions of the moral argument, and have attempted to answer objections, and in the process have done more than play defense; we have, to the extent we have succeeded, strengthened the case for moral apologetics. We have argued that the Anselmian God exists and best explains the moral commitments we all should have. Christianity thus argues for a powerfully personal understanding of reality, and this necessarily results in a shift when understanding ethics away from a list of rules and toward a relationship with other persons, and ultimately, God himself. This makes sense of why virtue would ultimately take primacy over moral lists and rules (as important as some rules are), since virtues are traits of persons, and we have argued that a personal God resides at the foundation of ethics.

This means that the moral argument does not just involve abstract reasoning and explicitly discursive inference. It includes those, most certainly, but it also speaks and tugs more inwardly, more implicitly, more gently, wooing both the heart and the mind. As C. S. Lewis observed, morality speaks to us not so much from the outside in as from the inside out. If God is the source and root of morality—in any fashion close to the way that we have depicted it here—then the tug of morality within us is less like a cold deliverance of reason, and more like a warm and personal invitation to come and partake, to drink from a brook whose water quenches our thirst in the most deeply satisfying way we can imagine. The voice of morality is the call of God to return to our only true and ultimate source of happiness. It's not an overactive superego or a societally imposed joy-killing curfew, but an intimation of the eternal, a personal overture to run *with* rather than *against* the grain of the universe. It's a confirmation of our suspicions that love and relationship have not just happened to bubble up to the top of the evolutionary chain, reflecting nothing, but rather that they penetrate to the very foundation of all that is real. Reason and relationship, rationality and relationality, go hand in hand, and they weren't merely the culmination of the elaborate process that enabled us to reflect about it all and inquire into the meaning of life; no, they were what began it all and imbued the process with meaning right from the start.

And now it's time to move from that ornate hall of virtue in the castle of morality into one of its spires. For morality, on a Christian understanding, is not just about forgiveness and alleviation of guilt, nor is it mainly about growth in virtue culminating in perfection, as important as these processes are. Ultimately, it's about something even more important, to which the moral perfection serves as but a necessary prelude. Although it's true that virtue theory is consistent with Christian ethics, we would contend that, ultimately, a true understanding of the human condition and telos reveals even more: that ethics must be understood relationally. It's not a matter of following the rules; it's not ultimately even a matter of finding forgiveness and being transformed into a state of moral perfection. It's about relationship with the God whose triune nature enabled him to be a God of perfect love before any human beings were created. As much as human nature might provide clues to the content of morality, this is why, at the end of the day, we are inclined to say that it's God's nature and image, in whose ours was created, that ultimately reveal the most veridical picture of moral reality. The Trinity is the ultimate reality, if Christianity is true, a God whose nature is reciprocal self-giving love. The bedrock of reality is this personal God with whom we are invited to be in relationship.

Virtue itself is relational. Experience reveals that we grow to become like those with whom we fraternize. Relationship with God is what makes us more like him; intimacy with Christ makes us fully human. By hiding his words in our heart we become better able to resist sin; by yielding to his will we walk uprightly; by allowing the power of the Holy Spirit to animate us, we find deliverance from the bondage to sin. Virtue, to our thinking, is not just a set of dispositional qualities; it's a function of ongoing relationship. Intimacy with God is what engenders holiness of heart. Trust in his faithfulness and goodness manifests itself in a holy life. Morality, ultimately, for the Christian, is all about relationship, first and foremost with God, and then secondarily with others. All the law and the prophets, Jesus assured us, hang on these two commandments: To love God with all of our hearts, souls, and minds, and our neighbor as ourselves.[15] This is the positive function of the Old Testament law. It was never meant to be a way to secure a relationship with God. Jesus came along and didn't focus on dietary, Sabbath, or circumcision laws; in fact, he committed technical violations of Sabbath and dietary laws. Jesus discerned the spirit of the law, rather than getting caught up in its letter, and he taught that it's love of God and neighbor that the law was all about. He saw that the Mosaic law was to be understood in terms of the Abrahamic covenant from centuries before, a covenant that promised God's universal offer of salvation to all the nations. Indeed, legalistic readings that do not recognize the priority of personal relationship with the God behind the law miss the whole point.

Far from a mindless fideist, Abraham became the father of true biblical faith. For we're told that, having been promised that his descendants would come through Isaac, Abraham believed God would do it, even if that required raising Isaac from the dead. This, we're told by Paul in the New Testament, is what paved the way for the Abrahamic covenant in which God promised to spread his salvation to all the world. Faith in God to fulfill his promises is the basis of the sort of faith in God's power and goodness by which any of us becomes liberated from a life of sin. We don't achieve holiness by our own efforts, but rather by trusting God to accomplish the task within us, transforming our hearts and lives into the likeness of Christ by resources that far exceed any that we have on our own.[16]

Most importantly of all, morality is not only about transformation, but ultimately about creation, according to the New Testament model. God doesn't merely offer us forgiveness of our sins and a perfection of our character, as profound as those are, but rather he effects a creative act by which his very life comes into our own and makes us into new creatures altogether, able to participate in God's redemption of creation through the work of Christ. But the process of being changed into very different creatures from what we are can be painful, and there are times when we may wish God would stop all the painful surgery.

Perhaps this indulgence of Christian lingo and foray into New Testament theology may strike some readers as unconventional stuff, and it *is*, admittedly, especially if it's true. But this is what classical Christianity teaches and what G. K. Chesterton called the wild truth of orthodoxy, and it's important that we dwell on these teachings long enough to disabuse readers of common misimpressions about what the connection between God, morality, and the meaning of life is all about. Even many Christians fail to grasp the significance of the points we're about to make, which leads to all sorts of mistaken theologies and practices, including a warped conception of Christian morality and lives filled with needless tension and guilt. In fact, as we will see, there is a human penchant for misconstruing the relationship between God and the good life that manifests, in different ways, in both believers and unbelievers. We will uncover what the common mistake is, and by correcting it by appeal to biblical teaching on the matter, we can highlight a more truly Christian understanding of the significance of morality.

## Biblical Faith and Real Freedom

When medieval Christians appropriated Aristotle's ethics into their own, one of the more distinctively theological virtues added to the list of Aristotle's virtues was faith. In the first chapter, we argued against the construal of faith as essentially fideistic or symptomatic of epistemic disadvantage. Having done that, we now need to discuss what biblical faith actually is, because it's central to an understanding of Christian ethics. Faith is confidence in God's goodness and faithfulness, and this is not inconsistent with evidence; such biblical trust in God's power and provision is not an irrational commitment. To the contrary, it is a decision rooted in excellent reasons to believe in God's trustworthiness and covenantal fidelity. Faith biblically understood is an intellectual virtue, a mean between credulity and unprincipled skepticism.[17] To the extent that we have argued that God is loving by nature and perfectly good, and recognizably so, we have offered reasons to believe that God is indeed completely trustworthy. Rather than eliminating the need for biblical faith, such an argument clears the way for it.

Faith thus connects to our discussion in an important way. Again, if it's biblical faith we're discussing, the profound confidence in God's power and goodness that such faith represents stands in contrast with the radically limited nature of human resources to live a good life. Atheists often understand the moral argument to imply that atheists can't be "moral," and usually defenders of the moral argument have to spend considerable time disabusing them of the notion that this is the primary bone of contention or topic of discussion. Plenty of atheists live lives that are morally exemplary in numerous ways. But now that we're looking at this issue, an important point bears emphasis. All human beings, even the best among them, are, if Christian theology is true, radically sinful. We *all* fall short, time and again, as Lewis emphasized in the first chapter, and it's exactly such failures that drive us to recognize our need for help and grace. Perhaps it's natural for atheists to think of themselves as not all that bad, morally speaking. After all, theirs is a rosier picture of the human moral condition, in one sense. Comparing themselves to other people on purely human terms, they probably measure up pretty well. Similarly, they tend to retain quite a bit of optimism when it comes to man's prospects for moral reformation on the basis of human resources. It's not surprising that one like Kai Nielsen points out that atheists often live altruistically, find meaning in life, and express considerable compassion.

The Christian picture is at once both more pessimistic and optimistic than the naturalistic alternative. We are, all of us, on our view, deeply affected by sin. From our actions to our motives and attitudes, we are corrupt and, if so, we need more than reformation. We need radical transformation. The message of Christianity isn't for us to try to be really good. Rather, the message is to entrust ourselves into God's hands to do what we can't do on our own. Our moral strivings for perfection, or sometimes mere decency, invariably fall far short, until we are exasperated at our prospects for success. Powerfully aware of the depth of our corruption, not merely a partially deformed character but a radically sinful nature, we ask God to do what we can't. The work of salvation involves a creative act of God, one of complete moral transformation, delivering us from our sinful natures and enabling us to experience the very life of Christ within. If Christianity is true, we are worse than we think, all of us, yet able to become far better than we think, too, through the power of faith in Christ. We can be made perfect, and at a deeper level, we can be made holy, reflecting God's own character.

This process of salvation involves our going from slaves to sons. The way to become free is to become a slave to God. Attempts to assert ourselves and our own will, instead of God's, result not in freedom, but in bondage. There's obviously something paradoxical here, but the biblical inversion of the picture just sets right what the secular mind has gotten completely upside down. There is, it would seem, deep within the human race, a profound penchant for enslaving ourselves. The apostle Paul argued that his fellow Jews did it by priding themselves in the law that God had given them, preferring to interpret it as a badge of honor that separated them from the Gentiles. Others do it by thinking that salvation is something that they can earn by living morally. Even Christian believers end up in bondage to sin once more when they forget that the process of salvation is by grace through faith from beginning to end and instead conjoin their faith with legalistic attempts to showcase their piety and appease God in the process. All of these mistakes involve absolutizations of the self and perversions of the truth that God himself is the one true good and that relationship with him is the only means by which we can truly become morally perfect. Tapping into the meager set of human resources alone will never do the job. We are entirely at God's mercy to imbue our lives with true moral power.

In a clear clash of incommensurable paradigms, the biblical picture of salvation entirely turns on its head secular concepts of autonomy that presuppose that freedom is something to which we're entitled or something with which we're born. No, what biblical revelation teaches is that freedom instead is a gift. If we have it, it's because God himself has endowed us with it. In our sinful and corrupt states, it is not a natural condition. God gives us enough freedom to make our choices culpable, but all of us go wrong and do so quite a lot, resulting in poignant feelings of moral failure. Those feelings, we submit, aren't illusory or imaginary; they are, at least sometimes, absolutely correct. They enable us to sense our shortcomings and to know that we need help. But a biblical portrait of reality reminds us that guilt is secondary; it's not our worst problem. The deeper problem is alienation from God, of which the guilt is but a symptom. In our alienation, moreover, we are increasingly bound and shackled by sin. Our very efforts to insist on our independence and sovereignty reveal how deeply held in bondage to sin we are. When we use what autonomy we have to assert a self-referential existence, we lose more and more of our freedom. Hell is, ultimately, a place where all freedom has finally been relinquished, resulting in a state of utter and irremediable perversion, a most horrific prospect if there ever was one. We may not agree entirely with William James that the hell to be endured hereafter, of which theology tells, is no worse than the hell we make for ourselves in this world by habitually fashioning our characters in the wrong way, but he's certainly on to something.[18] Both John Wesley and C. S. Lewis also emphasized the continuity between our character in this life and the afterlife.[19]

Heaven, in contrast, is a place for slaves—slaves to Christ and to others. For in such slavery, paradoxically, comes the freedom, the real freedom, for which we were designed. Rather than asserting our own will, we submit to God's will, and then discover that doing so provides the deepest fulfillment of which we're capable: We can spend eternity bathing in perfect Beauty and Goodness and Truth, wrapped in arms of love. Those who insist on finding their own fulfillment end up losing it; those who give up the quest for their own fulfillment find it.

## Moral Motivation, Self-Interest, and Sacrifice

The previous chapter's discussion of morality and rationality covered *reasons* to be moral. What about *motives* to be moral? Descartes expressed the view that since in this life there are often more rewards for vices than for virtues, few would prefer what is right to what is useful if they neither feared God nor hoped for an afterlife. His idea is that religious conviction can bolster one's moral commitments, which again raises in the minds of some the concern that this is an inherently flawed kind of moral motivation. Often under the dutiful influence of Kant, moral philosophers typically bristle at the suggestion that the motivation for morality is one of earning a reward or avoiding a punishment. Divine retribution or reward seems unable to constitute a legitimate form of moral motivation, yet it is suggested that it's just this condition that often resides at the heart of religious ethics. Rather than feeding the poor or housing the homeless out of genuine concern for their welfare, the ultimate motivation would instead be sheer self-interest, precisely the kind of mercenary motivation of which Socrates, long before Kant, was so critical in the *Euthyphro*.

The power of God to effect his purposes might constitute a motive for someone to conform, but as moral motives go, this one can easily be twisted out of shape. As Alasdair MacIntyre puts it, "If I am liable to be sent to hell for not doing what God commands, I am thereby provided with a corrupting, because totally self-interested, motive for pursuing the good. When self-interest is made as central as this, other motives are likely to dwindle in importance and a religious morality becomes self-defeating, at least insofar as it was originally designed to condemn pure self-interest."[20]

This type of objection has the most force when we see the sufferings of hell as an externally imposed punishment, bearing no necessary relation to the nature of the moral action involved. The objection loses much of its momentum, though, when the anguish of hell is a function of a life of evil marked by an increasing rejection of light and steadfast refusal of God's overtures of love. This point too is vulnerable to a Kantian-styled objection that criticizes moral motivation to avoid evil simply to avoid the anguish that is typically a natural consequence of such actions and attitudes in a moral world. To the Kantian we concede some ground on this point; heaven and hell do, at some level, appeal to self-interest. However, not all self-interest is selfish, and proper self-interest is a legitimate part of genuine moral motivation.[21] This is particularly the case when the self-interested motivation takes for its normative form the *renunciation* of self-absorption and self-indulgence. Further, an action that is in one's self-interest may have been sufficiently motivated by something other than self-interest, thereby qualifying as something truly praiseworthy.

Kant himself insisted that practical rationality demands the postulate of a God who will ensure, ultimately, that the virtuous are the happy. George Mavrodes writes that "what we have in Kant is the recognition that there cannot be, in any 'reasonable' way, a moral demand upon me, unless reality itself is committed to morality in some deep way."[22] Theistic ethics provide an account of how reality itself is thus committed, thereby providing a liberation from a Stoic commitment to morality without the psychologically vital confidence that reality itself is ultimately concerned about the best interests of moral persons.

Lest this defensive maneuver designed to salvage the connection between God and morality, against Kant's objection, make us lose sight of an important point, remember that the criticism of theological ethics at this point is its "vice" of solving a heretofore intractable moral dilemma. Recall Sidgwick's "dualism of the practical reason" from the first chapter. The dilemma resides in attempting to reconcile morality as concurrently requiring sacrifice of self-interest and protection of self-interest. What we have are some steps in the direction of accounting for a meaningful, coherent, and consistent way to retain both of these moral intuitions in a way that truly does justice to both. This isn't an ad hoc measure to make theism relevant; it's an attempt to show, once more, the way a theistic worldview makes better sense of commitments that we already have. Heaven and hell can offer substantive motivation to live morally, and perhaps even to endure sacrifice of personal interest or even persecution. Since it is often agreed that the proper contents of ethics are not what is up for grabs so much as any sufficiently motivating factors to do what's moral, the doctrines of heaven and hell may well provide some hard and needed motivation to live the kind of moral life that makes best sense when understood within a larger context than this life alone.[23]

Religious conviction can, should, and often does contribute to a healthy sense of moral motivation. Religious conviction gone awry can, we all know, contribute to a modern-day pharisaic, negative, unloving attitude and lifestyle; but equally undeniable is that religious conviction has often contributed to a heightened concern for the welfare of suffering people, a passion for upholding the dignity of human life, and a commitment to serve others selflessly and sacrificially. The New Testament teaches that all the laws and prophets of the Old Testament can be captured in the Golden Rule: doing to others as we would have them do to us; as well as bearing the burdens of one another, and loving God with all our being and our neighbors as ourselves—adherence to which includes a big role for moral imagination. When any of us, in the name of Christ, expresses our religious convictions in a manner at variance with these foundational truths, our action simply does not represent Christianity, except in name only, according to the normative standards of biblical teaching.

In truth, great numbers of religiously motivated believers demonstrate a profound capacity for altruism by perceiving human relationships as reflective of the divine. Think of St. Francis of Assisi, for instance, who entirely took to heart biblical injunctions about pleading the cause of the poor and oppressed, visiting the fatherless and widows in their affliction, and living worthy of the Christian vocation to which he was called. His love for God translated into an insatiable love for people, and most especially a commitment to, and love for, the poor. For he said he loved the poor not because they were poor but because Jesus is in them, taking literally the scriptural teaching that when we do something for the least of those among us, we do it for God. He found among the poor and those afflicted with leprosy whom he served, as Tony Campolo once put it, an almost sacramental infusion of the person of Christ, waiting to be loved and cared for. Recall seeing Mother Teresa pouring out her energies in a lifetime of selfless service for the poor and marginalized. Or consider again Francis, exchanging his clothes with those of filthy beggars or kissing his lepers, or Francis Xavier or St. John of God, who are said to have cleansed the sores and ulcers of their patients with their tongues, such benevolence as to make us, in the words of William James, both admire and shudder at the same time.

Even if an unbeliever retains faith in a moral universe, there remains a qualitative difference between the Christian and the secular moralist. As William James puts it in *The Varieties of Religious Experience,*

> Morality pure and simple accepts the law of the whole which it finds reigning, so far as to acknowledge and obey it, but it may obey it with the heaviest and coldest heart, and never cease to feel it as a yoke. But for religion, in its strong fully developed manifestations, the service of the highest is never felt as a yoke. Dull submission is left far behind, and a mood of welcome, which may fill any place on the scale between cheerful serenity and enthusiastic gladness, has taken its place.... It makes a tremendous emotional and practical difference to one whether one accepts the universe in the drab way of stoic resignation to necessity, or with the passionate happiness of Christian saints. The difference is as great as that between passivity and activity, and that between the defensive and the aggressive mood....If religion is to mean anything definite for us, it seems to me that we ought to take it as meaning this added dimension of emotion, this enthusiastic temper of espousal, in regions where morality strictly so called can at best but bow its head and acquiesce. It ought to mean nothing short of this new reach of freedom for us, with the struggle over, the keynote of the universe sounding in our ears, and everlasting possession spread before our eyes....This sort of happiness in the absolute and everlasting is what we find nowhere but in religion.[24]

The contrast that James notes here between the Christian and Stoic is a powerful one that can serve to correct a mistake recently made by some ethicists. Donald Hubin, for instance, argues that if one believes that God will ultimately effect perfect justice, then obeying God can never result in a sacrifice of one's interests. Since compensation comes in the eschaton, according to classical Christian theists, benefits for obedience will always ultimately outweigh the costs. For this reason, he denies the claim that religious conviction makes sense of self-sacrificial behavior; to the contrary, religious conviction would render truly self-sacrificial behavior for the theist impossible. Unless there's a net personal cost for the moral agent, there is no real self-sacrifice. If God punishes evil and wrong and vindicates righteousness, "acts of morally laudable, altruistic, *genuine* self-sacrifice are not consistent with the thesis of theism."[25]

William Lane Craig has written in response that "persons who endure the hardships [Hubin] mentions do make tremendous, genuine self-sacrifices, even if these sacrifices do not involve permanent net losses by the individuals involved, and if Hubin denies that they are genuine, then he is using 'genuine' in an idiosyncratic way, so that his claim that theism is incompatible with morally laudable acts of genuine self-sacrifice is evacuated of significance."[26] To illustrate Craig's point, just imagine that someone, out of love for another, was willing to endure years of excruciating pain. Even if the person were later compensated with far more years of great pleasure, that's no evidence to suggest that a sacrifice wasn't made in the first place.

Hubin's criticism trivializes the sufferings of this life in a way that sounds more like what Stoics do than Christians. It's true that Christians believe that the sufferings of the present age pale into insignificance in light of the eternal glory to come, but that is not to deny that the present pain and sacrifices are real. Christians do not deny the sufferings in this world, even while suggesting that they are not ultimate; indeed, Christianity takes suffering with dreadful seriousness. How we handle the suffering and anguish that we invariably experience in life is one of the most important factors in our relationship with God and spiritual growth. Somehow pain and suffering are down at the center of things, as Nicholas Wolterstorff puts it, adding that we serve a God of suffering love whose tears are the meaning of history.[27] The Bible is simply replete with instructions about how to handle suffering, grieve deeply but with hope, trust God through pain, and allow God to redeem it. Christian thought reminds us that our response to pain involves a choice, that our pain pales in comparison to the glory to come, that God promises to be with us through it and not put on us more than we can bear, and to let pain enable us more fully to identify with the sufferings of Christ—who endured pain beyond anything we can imagine out of his love for us.

Nor do Christians devalue the goods of this world, even though we believe that they derive their goodness from God. Ours is not a Platonic quest to escape this world and its attendant evils, nor is our corporal existence taken to be an inherently bad state of affairs from which we will one day be liberated. Part of the significance of the incarnation, atonement, and resurrection of Christ is that this world and our bodies are among what the sacrifice of Jesus, in an act of true cosmic significance, redeemed. Heaven will not be inhabited by disembodied souls, but by people with resurrected and glorified bodies. Christians aren't Stoics, despite the fact that we can glean many nuggets of wisdom from them.[28]

In his classic *Sources of the Self*, Charles Taylor highlights some of the crucial contrasts between Christian and Stoic thought:

> The specificity of this Judaeo-Christian affirmation of life has often
> been lost from view. In particular, the contrast with ancient pagan
> philosophy tends to be forgotten. Christianity, particularly in its more
> ascetic variants, appears a continuation of Stoicism by other means,
> or (as Nietzsche sometimes says) a prolongation of Platonism. But

for all the strong resemblances to Stoicism—for instance, in its universalism, its notion of providence, its exalting self-abnegation—there is a great gulf. In fact, the meaning of self-abnegation is radically different. The Stoic sage is willing to give up some "preferred" thing, e.g., health, freedom, or life, because he sees it genuinely as without value since only the whole order of events which, as it happens, includes its negation or loss, is of value. The Christian martyr, in giving up health, freedom, or life, doesn't declare them to be of no value. On the contrary, the act would lose its sense if they were not of great value. To say that greater love hath no man that this, that a man give up his life for his friends, implies that life is a great good. The sentence would lose its point in reference to someone who renounced life from a sense of detachment; it presupposes he's *giving up* something.[29]

The Christian martyr gives up his life in order to follow God, the ultimate Good. The willingness of Jesus to go to the cross involved a sacrifice, even if he did it with his eye on the glory to come as the savior and redeemer of the world. Socrates tried to convince his friends that his death was great gain, whereas Jesus endured agony and anguish in the Garden of Gethsemane. It's true, and important, that on a biblical worldview a life of holiness through faith in Christ is always in one's ultimate self-interest, but at the same time it's a life that may well involve the genuine sacrifice of some goods of great value. Ultimately, though, God will indeed redeem our sufferings and sacrifices as we trust him, and manifest a new order in which good doesn't need to be sacrificed for good.

The fact that the ultimate Good is an infinite one has profound and far-reaching consequences that radically challenge secular morality premised on the assumption that the goods available are finite, if not painfully limited. The best we can hope for is to parcel out many of these goods in the most equitable fashion practical. In striking contrast, Christians hold that the ultimate Good is an infinite Good that is equally available to all; it's not a finite pie that needs to be cut up and shared or meted out in some sort of consequentialist compromise. There's enough goodness for everyone to be fully satiated—indeed, infinitely more than enough.

## The Death of Death and Hope of Heaven

The life, death, and resurrection of Jesus mark the coming of God's kingdom. When we give a cup of cold water to the thirsty, effect justice for the oppressed, or hold a cool compress to the brow of a suffering AIDS victim, even now the kingdom of God breaks through and manifests in this world. The kingdom of God isn't just later in heaven; Jesus said it was at hand. The Holy Spirit, for example, is an eschatological reality, a mark of the kingdom, and he beckons to each of us. Ours is far from a reductionist analysis of reality predicated on the idea that what happens around us is somehow less important than it seems. No, it's *more* important than we can imagine. William James once said that the knights of Ockham's Razor, partisans of parsimony (metaphysical thinness), feared superstition, whereas he feared desiccation, and we agree. This life is neither a dream nor an ephemeral happenstance; it is all too real. Moral demands on us aren't a figment of our imaginations or subjective preferences; they are as objective as can be. This is a world in which our choices shape our characters and our destinies.

We have argued for a thoroughgoing personalist and relational ethic, a theocentric vision of moral reality that invites us not merely to honor a moral code or impersonal law, or even to strive for a life of virtue, but to enter into a relationship with the One who is Goodness itself, or perhaps we should say, Goodness Himself. God, and only God, on our view, is the source of our truest happiness and the fulfillment of our deepest longings. In the Old Testament, there wasn't much of an emphasis on the afterlife, and C. S. Lewis conjectures as to the reason why. God wanted us first to hunger for righteousness and holiness, apart from any potentially distracting considerations about eternity. Then, and only then, as icing on the cake, God would reveal that the enjoyment of the Good could be one's eternal preoccupation.

Time and again, at the heart of the Christian message is a suggestive paradox echoing its refrain in different keys: To enjoy eternity, begin by seeking something other than eternity. By losing one's life, one gains it. By confessing and repenting of one's sin, one is forgiven. By dying to self, one comes alive in Christ. By pouring one's life into another, one can be filled. By acknowledging our weaknesses, God's strength is perfected in us. By renouncing a self-referential life, we can do the most self-interested thing of all.

The Mosaic law didn't make sin possible; it merely amplified the sin that was already there. Rather than doing away with the law, Jesus embodied it to the full, manifesting its true spirit, yet ended up dying not for his sins but for ours. Only he was ever able to fulfill it perfectly, and only through his sacrifice are we now able, through Christ, to satisfy the law. We are invited to die with Christ so that we might be raised with him. Then the power that raised Jesus from the dead can be at work within us, enabling us to live as we were meant to live in fellowship with God and one another. We can't do it on our own; all our righteousness is as filthy rags, as Isaiah famously put it.[30] Our hope is in

Christ, and we are both saved and entirely transformed by God's grace through faith alone. Rightly understood, morality is not about following rules, or even growth in character. It's about a relationship; only trust in God's goodness and power enable us to achieve true holiness. Immorality and unholiness just *are* unbelief, and holiness just *is* trust in God and his perfect provision.

The apostle Paul at one point forges an interesting connection between God's sovereignty and goodness. In his epistle to the Galatians, he makes it clear that a narrow and confident focus on the Mosaic law is of a piece with old pagan idolatry, which assumed that God wants gifts from us to earn his favor. This sort of theology is antithetical to Christian thought, which suggests instead that this would rob God of his sovereignty. For God would, at some level, be acting on the basis of what he needs. God does not need anything from us. He is wholly self-sufficient. In a sense, God doesn't even want our obedience. He wants *us*, for if he has us, our obedience will follow. For our faith in his goodness and love will invariably issue in a presentation of our bodies as a living sacrifice to him. There's not so much as even a tension between faith and works, according to Paul; biblical faith looks like holiness, and sin is unbelief, lack of trust in God's goodness and power. This illustrates, among other things, the relevance of the right moral theory to how we actually live our lives; it also shows the wisdom in the biblical idea that, ultimately, all sin has its root in a faulty conception of God.

That God needs nothing from us is crucial to his goodness. Since he doesn't need anything, he is free to be perfectly good. Otherwise there would always be a part of him driven by his need. The pagans believed in such needy deities, and Paul says they didn't give thanks to them. Why? It can be plausibly argued that they weren't grateful because they didn't think of the gods as good, for such gods, driven by their own needs, were as mercenary as those described by Euthyphro.[31] The Anselmian God is not. He doesn't need us, but he does love and want us, and he invites us to participate in his redemption of this world and to enjoy him forever as his children liberated from the bondage of sin.

The event of Christ's coming, death, and resurrection marked his victory over what Paul characterizes in personal terms as the elemental forces of this world. Be they economic, political, or psychological forces, Christ's victory showed that they aren't what is primary in this world. Those who think that nothing matters so much as the right political order or economic system, or those who think that there's no deliverance for them from psychological hang-ups or behavioral addictions, needlessly subject themselves in bondage to what is less than ultimate. If Christianity is true, the power of God that raised Jesus from the dead is at work in this world and is available to each person, to deliver them from what holds them in bondage and set them free as children of God to fulfill the mission for which God created them. Christian salvation is inextricably tied to God's purposive creation; God doesn't merely wish to save us from sin and enable us to achieve intimacy with him and one another, he wants to empower us for a meaningful life in this world. A Christian vision thus connects meaning and purpose with the life of holiness that comes only by faith in Christ. In him we are offered a life that's truly meaningful, that satisfies our deepest longings, that gives us what our best selves most strongly yearn for already. In Christ are the life and freedom for which we were made. This is a Christian understanding of morality richly understood, a meaningful and purposive life free from bondage, a loving life of intimacy with God and others. It's a compelling vision indeed, and one, we have argued, worthy of our most serious consideration.

Contrary to Lennon's haunting lyrics, we believe and have argued that God's reality offers us not just the hope of heaven and liberation from a self-imposed and sin-induced hell, both now and later, but the deepest satisfactions of which we're capable. Such trust in God's goodness shouldn't inspire any killing, but it is worth dying for, and it is certainly worth living for.

# Conclusion

In this book, we constructed our case for a moral apologetic first by weaving together several versions of the moral argument that collectively pack quite a punch, then by strengthening the case further by fleshing out plausible details of a theistic ethic. By integrating insights from two bodies of literature—moral apologia and theistic ethics—we sought to show the mutual relevance of advances in each discussion. In the process we drew several distinctions in an effort to show that various Euthyphro-inspired objections to theistic ethics failed to undermine a moral apologetic.

The distinctions we drew and applied in our articulation and defense of theistic ethics can be individually found peppering the literature, but our aim was to bring them all to bear simultaneously in order to consolidate the insights they afford. Although conceptually distinct, their cumulative force carries considerable weight for the project of defending a robust theistic ethic and philosophically powerful understanding of the foundations of morality. The distinctions encompass issues of scope, semantics, modality, morality, epistemology, meta-ethics, and ontology. Table 1 reiterates the full set of distinctions.

Drawing on these distinctions, we have seen that there is no need to assume that competent users of moral language must presuppose that moral terminology gets defined by appeal to God. Nonetheless, we have argued that God still functions as the foundation of morality, and we illustrated this possibility with the

TABLE 1  Seven Distinctions

| Scope | Semantic | Modal | Moral | Epistemic | Meta-Ethical | Ontological |
|-------|----------|-------|-------|-----------|--------------|-------------|
| Definition/ Analysis | Univocation/ Equivocation | Conceivability/ Possibility | Good/Right | Difficulty/ Impossibility | Knowing/ Being | Dependence/ Control |

famous example of how people used to know that water was the wet stuff in lakes and streams without knowing its essential nature (scope distinction). As for the essential nature of morality, the question is ambiguous between the good and the right, so, having made this distinction, we tied the former to God's nature and the latter to his commands (moral distinction). Such voluntarism naturally raises questions like, "What if God were to command child torture?" But we have seen that moral states of affairs that we can conceive, or think we may be able to conceive, may not actually be possible, because they are incompatible with God's essential nature of moral impeccability (modal distinction). Some have argued that inferences to such a God's existence are undermined by the fact that plenty of people from an array of worldviews are able to grasp moral facts clearly. We have argued to the contrary, however, that such nearly universal moral insight doesn't at all detract from the possibility that God is the ontological ground of morality, because the way of knowing goes in one direction, while the way of being goes in another (meta-ethical distinction). Similarly, the necessity of certain moral facts and their resulting inability to be changed doesn't rule out their dependence on God, because we can and must distinguish between dependence and control and between necessity and aseity (ontological distinction). This still makes some divine commands difficult to square with inviolable moral intuitions, but not impossible, while others are flat impossible (epistemic distinction). Thus we could argue against a Calvinist paradigm for constituting an outright violation of ineliminable moral intuitions, even while making the case that Old Testament conquest narratives, as difficult as they are to reconcile with morality, are not impossible after all. This is closely related to why God's love and goodness must be understood analogically, rather than univocally or equivocally (semantic distinction). Although God's ways are above ours, we haven't been called to believe anything irrational.

Quite the opposite. By answering normativity, epistemic, autonomy, and various arbitrariness objections to theistic ethics, we didn't play mere defense, but attempted also to bolster the moral argument(s) for God's existence and, just as important, for his perfect, necessary, and recognizable love and goodness. What emerged from our articulation and defense was a vision of ultimate reality that substantively informs our understanding of natural law, the problem of evil, conquest narratives, and the moral relevance of the Trinity, incarnation, resurrection, and afterlife. What we set out to do in this book was nothing more and nothing less than contribute to the resurgence of moral apologetics, because we are convinced that moral arguments for God's existence are powerful and persuasive, but too often neglected in natural theology. In so doing, we have also joined what E. O. Wilson has described as the "battle for men's souls" in the current century. The battle over the ultimate nature and foundations of morality is indeed finally a battle over which worldview is correct, and the numerous practical implications that are involved.

At the end of our introduction, we quoted C. S. Lewis: "I believe in Christianity as I believe the Sun has risen, not only because I see it, but because by it I see everything else."[1] Without harboring any illusions that the moral argument for God's existence settles the matter or does all the necessary apologetic work, we have argued throughout this book that morality serves to point us to a transcendent source and, ultimately, to God himself. Keeping with the sun analogy, we have argued that the failure to discern this truth is tantamount to mistaking the flickering images inside Plato's famous cave with the sun itself.

Recently a major poll among professional and aspiring philosophers asked a series of questions about morality, metaphysics, and the like, and among the results were these: the preponderance of contemporary philosophers are skeptical about God's existence while, at the same time, retaining quite a bit of confidence in objective morality.[2] We have argued that confidence in morality should serve to point us in the direction of God, and yet we understand some of the reasons for the results of this poll. In fact, we think we can explain them quite well, in a way altogether consistent with the force and thrust of our argument.

Confidence in morality—its reality, objectivity, prescriptive force, authority—is a prerequisite for a workable moral argument for God's existence. Since morality is the evidence adduced by the argument, the evidence must be at least as strong as the conclusion, if the argument is to possess rational force. We tend to be partial to the thesis that the evidence for objective, authoritative morality is about as strong as it can be, perhaps even more readily apparent than the evidence for the existence of God himself. But if so, this shows that someone can be rational to believe in objective morality, even while finding dubious the notion that God exists. Rather than ruling out what we have argued for, this is what we should expect if indeed the evidence for morality itself is strong enough to sustain an argument for God's existence.

Recall the way in which epistemology works bottom up. What's at the bottom for present purposes are firm moral convictions—torturing babies is wrong, exploiting the poor is unjust, and so on—convictions that theists and atheists readily agree on, and rightly so. Perhaps some might suggest that we should refrain from endorsing such atheistic affirmations, since we believe and have argued that God is the author of morality. But this is to confuse the way in which epistemology works with the way ontology works. Even if we're right and God serves as the metaphysical foundation of ethics, it doesn't follow that atheists aren't able to apprehend and affirm the authority of morality.

Nietzsche is an example of someone who grasped far reaching implications that follow from rejecting God's existence. There's something refreshingly bold and honest about the way he saw among such implications a radical revision of traditional values and the loss of the necessary foundations for morality classically construed. But ultimately, we find Nietzsche's mistake to be far more insidious than the mistake of an atheist who retains his convictions about objective moralilty and its binding authority. For Nietzsche, in rejecting classical morality—eschewing the need to help the poor, reach out to the marginalized, promote justice, and such—was losing his very humanity. Even if his approach was laudable from a strictly logical standpoint, representing a bold willingness to follow the implications of his atheism, it was, from another perspective, less honest and more tragic than the atheist who remains a moral realist.

The atheist or naturalist, on our view, who retains moral objectivity may well be underestimating the evidential force of morality for a transcendent source, but her mistake is not affirming morality itself. She's at her best in doing so. Our intent is not to undermine such a commitment, but to affirm and celebrate it, for we are convinced that imbedded within just that commitment are the seeds of the moral argument. We retain great hope for such thinkers to see this for themselves because, in our estimation, unlike the emulators of Nietzsche, they have yet to deny their humanity and harden their hearts to the evidence that morality provides.

In a sense, the two sorts of atheists—the moral objectivist and the Nietzschian—broadly represent the two sorts of opponents with whom we have been engaging in dialogue within this book. The naturalistic moral objectivist represents the moderns engaged in the so-called Enlightenment project to make sense of morality without God, seeking alternate foundations. Nietzsche and followers of his ilk represent the growing postmodern skepticism toward objective morality—skepticism that invariably deadens their ears to hear the moral argument for God's existence. Although we think there's something bold and honest about the postmoderns and their moral skepticism, not to mention certain important insights, ultimately we think theirs is the bigger mistake. They have lost both God and morality, and they remind us of these words from William James: "If your heart does not want a world of moral reality, your head will assuredly never make you believe in one."[3]

Nietzsche was, as Ian S. Markham with some rhetorical hyperbole puts it, the "last real atheist."[4] Whereas Nietzsche understood the transcendent nature of classical morality and the implications of atheism, contemporary atheists who think God can be painlessly eliminated from our ontology and yet remain sentimental about moral discourse fail to take Nietzsche seriously enough.[5] Ontologically speaking, God's nonexistence has huge implications, and the cavalier and sanguine dismissal of God as morally irrelevant bespeaks a particularly poignant sort of blind spot. As Gary Shapiro puts it, the "smug non-believers ridicule [Nietzsche's madman's] quest; they see theism as a quaint, discarded superstition. The madman replies: God is not simply a fictional personage who can be ignored; human culture, in murdering or sacrificing its central organizing principle, now faces the consequences. The smug atheists of the marketplace...don't see that God's murder effectively eliminates any analogous principle of meaning...."[6]

At the same time, however, there seems something profoundly right about not giving morality up. Epistemically, we're all trying to figure out the truth about our world, and the obviousness of morality should give one pause to give it too quickly. Earlier in the book we critiqued Calvinism for various reasons, among them that such theology is well nigh impossible to square with a recognizably loving God. Yet we know and are personally acquainted with quite a number of professing Calvinists who would readily affirm their belief that God loves everyone. Although we continue to insist that Calvinism poses an intractable problem for such a belief, we don't lament their belief that God loves everyone, just as we refuse to lament the moral realism of atheists—even though we see a sort of irrationality at play in both circumstances. In each case, we affirm such convictions and encourage their adherents to continue cultivating them, for we are convinced that it is those very convictions that can point them to a more coherent view of reality, one that makes better sense of them, one in which those beliefs fit comfortably rather than awkwardly.

If this world is indeed an atheistic world, note again all the materials at the disposal of the atheist to construct a workable ethical system: relationships, the satisfactions of morality, love, intersubjective moral agreement—and the list goes on and on. It's altogether understandable why someone who is convinced that this is an atheistic world might well initially think that God is unnecessary and superfluous when it comes to justifying morality. With all these other resources at their disposal, why is God needed? When the deliverances of morality are so crystal clear for all to see, theists and atheists alike, why bring in the useless hypothesis of God?

We have already emphasized that, in fact, we think these various pieces of evidence make best sense in a theistic world and, if an Anselmian God exists, such evidence wouldn't even be around, for nothing at all would be around. But here in the conclusion, we wish to extend our analysis in a slightly different direction. In particular, we want to argue that, while it may be possible to domesticate such evidence and and treat it as harmless to the atheistic world view, such evidence can and ought to serve to point us to a deeper vision of reality than naturalism can provide. To make our case, we're going to enlist again the assistance of a few insights of C. S. Lewis.

Consider Lewis's doctrine of *transposition*, which he first detailed in a sermon at Mansfield College, Oxford, on Whit Sunday and later published in 1949 along with other addresses. The essence of this doctrine lies in the suggestion that higher truths are embedded in lower ones.[7] He offers several analogies for us to understand his meaning. If a language with twenty-two vowel sounds is translated into a language that has only five, each vowel in the lower must be able to represent more than one value. Or in a piano version of an orchestral score, the same piano notes that represent flutes in one part may represent violins in another. Transposition can only happen if the lower medium is understood in light of the higher. If the higher medium is not known, then all we are left with is the lower. But if Lewis is right, the lower can only be truly understood in terms of the higher, and without it there is no sense of transposition.[8] Someone who has heard the piano version of the orchestra piece and not the original will only hear the piano version being played. Lewis compares the reaction of a naturalist told of a higher world to a person told of solid objects who is only familiar with two dimensions.

> You keep on telling me of this other world and its unimaginable
> shapes which you call solid. But isn't it very suspicious that all the
> shapes which you offer me as images or reflections of the solid ones
> turn out on inspection to be simply the old two-dimensional shapes
> of my own world as I have always known it? Is it not obvious that
> your vaunted other world, so far from being the archetype, is a dream
> which borrows all its elements from this one?[9]

Here the skeptic can rationally draw the conclusion that what is said to be transposed, what is said to be the spiritual, is just the material. What we view of heaven and of God is merely our imaginations running wild with what they have available from our own world. The problem arises from the fact that we must use images and concepts taken from this world to represent the world that is to come, or, in the Platonic sense, we have to use the shadows and the imperfect to describe the perfect.

Lewis returns to these themes in *The Silver Chair*, where he depicts skepticism of the notion that higher truths are embedded in lower ones. Jill and Eustace have been trapped underground in a land of people who have lived their entire lives there and have never seen the sky. They have gone down there to rescue Prince Rillian, but the witch puts them under a spell. She begins to convince them that the world above does not really exist, but is merely an exaggeration of the underworld. When Jill and Eustace describe the reality of the sky and the sun, the witch replies,

> "Hangeth from what, my lord?" asked the Witch; and then, while
> they were all still thinking how to answer her, she added, with
> another of her soft, silver laughs: "You see? When you try to think
> out clearly what this sun must be, you cannot tell me. You can only
> tell me it is like the lamp. Your sun is a dream; and there is nothing
> in that dream that was not copied from the lamp. The lamp is the real
> thing; the sun is but a tale, a children's story."[10]

She also uses this logic against Jill and Eustace when they try to describe Aslan, claiming that Aslan is like a cat, but a much bigger cat that was produced by their imaginations. "And look how you can put nothing into your make-believe world without copying it from the real world, this world of mine, which is the only real world."[11]

Puddleglum, the companion of Jill and Eustace, responds to the Queen's logic by admitting that she may indeed be right—that what they were saying was made up and that the outside world they are trying to explain may truly just be an exaggeration of the underworld. But if so, the "imagined" world seems a great deal more important and real than the underworld. He states that it would be quite odd that the imaginary play world is so much richer and fuller than the underworld.

> That's why I am going to stand by the play-world. I'm on Aslan's side
> even if there is no Aslan to lead it. I'm going to live like a Narnian
> even if there is no Narnia...we're leaving your court at once and
> setting out in the dark to spend our lives looking for the Overland.
> Not that our lives will be very long, I should think; but that's a small
> loss if the world's as dull a place as you say.[12]

Lewis thought that it was only natural that skeptics about supernaturalism, those who only knew the lower, would not be able to discern the higher. The skeptic's conclusion in every case of transposition is going to be that the spiritual is taken from the natural, that it is nothing more than a mirage or an imaginary extension of it.

The brutal man never can by analysis find anything but lust in love; the flatlander never can find anything but flat shapes in a picture; physiology never can find anything in thought except twitchings of grey matter. It is no good browbeating the critic who approaches a transposition from below. On the evidence available to him his conclusion is the only one possible.[13]

Lewis gives another example to explain how someone who only knows or believes in the lower can struggle to understand the higher. They see only the facts and perceive none of the meaning. Dogs, according to Lewis, do not understand pointing. You point to some food on the floor and the dog will first look at your finger and even sniff it. To the dog, your finger is only your finger and nothing more. It does not understand the relationship between the finger and the food on the floor because its world is "all fact and no meaning."[14]

In concert with naturalists who are moral realists, we largely concur on the moral facts, but have argued that such facts bespeak a truer meaning, one we can come to see by taking our moral commitments seriously and discerning their odd fit with naturalism. To do so is to allow them to point to something more ultimate and revelatory of reality, much as the sun is more ultimate than the shadows.

It may be penultimate, but since there is nothing desiccated or deflationary about morality, it lifts our gaze upward, not downward. In the introduction, we cited an essay by law professor Arthur Leff in which he analyzed a contradictory impulse in our desire to believe both that there is a set of transcendent "findable" moral principles that tell us how to live, and also that we are completely free to decide what is right and wrong. We want to be both "perfectly ruled and perfectly free." He noted a "desperately resisted" awareness, however, that at the end of the day, we will "locate nothing more attractive, or more final, than ourselves." This of course agrees with E. O. Wilson's contention that in the "battle for men's souls" in this century, empiricism rather than transcendentalism will prevail.

It has been our contention, in contrast, that the reality and authority of morality derives from a source higher and richer, more "attractive and final" than anything we can generate or muster as finite human beings. Those with eyes to see can indeed find that there is a law to be discovered, not manufactured—found, not created—but a law not of oppression, repression, or suppression, but of liberation. And the ineffable beauty of the infinite and transcendent Author of this law—of whom we catch compelling if inchoate images when we see justice effected or mercy freely conferred—fills us with confidence that by tasting and seeing the Source we will find our deepest satisfaction and truest liberation, perfectly ruled, yet perfectly free.

# Appendix A:

## Answering the Extended Arbitrariness Objection to Divine Command Theory

A deontic version of divine command theory (henceforth "DCT") holds that

1. If God commands X, then X is morally obligatory, and morally obligatory because God commands it.[1]

A standard objection to divine command theory offers an instance of (1) featuring for X something that is morally reprehensible, like this:

2. If God commands rape, then rape is morally obligatory, an unpalatable enough implication to refute DCT.

A reply usually thought effective to such an objection claims this:

3. God can't issue irremediably evil commands.

God's goodness, moral and otherwise, and his perfection are thought to preclude such a possibility. The claim is not merely that God *wouldn't* issue such commands, but that he *couldn't*. For if God could issue such a command, even if he never would, DCT would entail that rape could become morally obligatory, even if it never would, and we would still have a defeater for DCT. So God can't command rape, child torture, and so on, at least if DCT is to avoid intractable problems.

### A NEW ARBITRARINESS OBJECTION

Louise Antony and Walter Sinnott-Armstrong have launched a fresh accusation against DCT, even if God's nature precludes commanding anything so morally heinous. Sinnott-Armstrong puts it this way: "Even if God in fact never would or could command us to rape, the divine command theory still implies the counterfactual that, if God did command us to rape, then we would have a moral obligation to rape."[2] And Antony puts it similarly: "If DCT is correct, then the following counterfactual is true: If God had commanded us to torture innocent children, then it would have been morally right to do so."[3] Their critique concedes for purposes of argument that God can't issue such irremediably awful commands, but they still insist that, if God did, then DCT would entail that such evils would be morally sanctioned, and, hence, so much the worse for DCT.

What should we say in reply to such an argument—an argument that we can dub an "extended arbitrariness objection" to DCT (or some might prefer to call it an extended reprehensible command objection)? The issue comes down to the truth value of the counterfactual, indeed counteressential, "if God had commanded rape, then rape would be morally right," and what DCT says the truth value should be. If the conditional is false and DCT says it's true, then DCT is defeated.

On standard semantics, conditionals with impossible antecedents are usually said to be trivially true.[4] Antony thinks this is regrettable, and claims instead to be going with ordinary intuitions, which don't treat all such counteressentials as trivially true.[5] She's presuming by her own admission the viability of some system of relevance or paraconsistent logic for counterfactuals. She doesn't, however, fill in any details about what this nonstandard semantics would look like. Her motivation here, though, is clear, for if the problematic conditional were merely trivially true according to DCT, her critique of DCT would be powerless. So her and Sinnott-Armstrong's critique of DCT is predicated on nonstandard semantics for counterfactuals—but more than that, a semantics that will result in the problematic conditional being false and DCT entailing instead that it is true.

So to make their case a bit, how might we go about turbocharging available accounts of the semantics of counterfactuals that quantify over possible worlds by incorporating impossible worlds?[6] Perhaps like this: a counterfactual R, that is, a sentence of the form <If A were true, then B would be true>, is true in a world W if and only if in the closest possible world or impossible world W* to W, B is also true; otherwise R is false in W. The truth of a given counterpossible conditional will, on such an account, be determined by the truth of the antecedent and consequent of the conditional at the impossible world closest to the actual world. This would then leave it an open question which of the following impossible worlds is closer to the actual world: one in which God commands rape and rape is obligatory, and one in which God commands rape and rape is not obligatory.[7]

Antony frankly admits that she's employing an intuitive approach; her gesture in the direction of relevance or paraconsistent logics seems designed to carve out space for such intuitions. But of course waving the wand of some generic nonstandard semantics doesn't guarantee her the results that she's after. If, however, she wants to conduct the discussion at the level of intuitions, let's indulge her request. When Antony considers a proposition like, "If God had commanded child torture, then child torture would be right," she understandably balks. Presumably she does so because she's convinced, as many of us are, that child torture is wrong and necessarily so and that nothing could change that. Let's set aside concerns of ethical anti-realists and assume the necessary wrongness of child torture. Antony's claim, it would seem, amounts to the suggestion that such moral realism stands at odds with divine command theory. It seems that her main reason for thinking that, in the closest impossible world in which God commands child torture, child torture would still be wrong is because of the epistemic status of such a moral truth. Child torture is just obviously wrong and nothing could alter that fact. If divine command theory asserts otherwise, even in some remote counteressential sense, so much the worse for DCT. If we were to confine the ways in which morality could depend on God to DCT, the defeat of DCT would show more generally the irrelevance of God to ethics, at least ontologically.

There are two main objections that we would like to raise against Antony's (and Sinnott-Armstrong's) argument. One consideration is what Mark Murphy calls an explanandum-driven consideration, and the other an explanans-driven consideration.[8] An explanandum-focused consideration is the attempt to provide some explanation as to how some feature of moral judgments or morality is possible or actual or necessary. In this connection, the supreme confidence we have in the wrongness of child torture, for example, even on the assumption that our confidence tracks a necessary truth, provides no reason at all to conclude that God is irrelevant to ethics. An explanans-driven consideration is rooted instead in what theists bring to the table, such as the conviction that God is the ultimate explainer of all that exists and obtains. On this basis, we will argue that the classical theist has little to be concerned about when it comes to Antony's argument, for there is little reason to think that she will get the truth values she wants for the relevant counterfactuals if we assume the existence of an Anselmian God. We will first flesh out the explanandum-focused argument, then turn to the explanans-driven argument.

## EXPLANANDUM-DRIVEN CONSIDERATIONS

The explanandum-driven consideration begins with recognition of the obviously wrong nature of certain actions like rape. Their reprehensible moral status is the likely reason that Antony and Sinnott-Armstrong think that DCT is on the wrong track, because nothing and nobody could alter that. The sort of argument they are constructing, then, seems to be rather bottom-up, and it likely looks something like this:

4. We can be entirely confident in proclaiming the wrongness of rape, but
5. If DCT is true, it would shake such confidence, so
6. DCT is false.

Certainly some versions of DCT would shake our confidence in such moral proclamation. An Ockhamistic version of DCT, for example, as popularly depicted, would allow for rape to become morally permissible or even obligatory. But even a divine command theory that assumes that God neither would nor could command rape is vulnerable, Antony and Sinnott-Armstrong contend, presumably because of a clear-cut enough intuition that DCT, counteressentially, would, if God commanded it, make rape right, and that, since rape could not possibly become right, DCT is thus mistaken.

Does, however, a commitment to DCT require that one's confidence in the wrongness of rape be shaken? One reason that Antony suggests that it does is because such confidence signals a departure from DCT and a move toward what she dubs a "divine independence theory" of morality. This sort of charge often echoes in the literature on theological voluntarism. If we have supreme confidence in the categorical wrongness of some action, then such confidence stands in irremediable tension with one's commitment to DCT, so say such critics.

What seems fairly obvious on reflection, however, is that this is a mistake. It's an illegitimate effort to infer an ambitious ontological conclusion on the basis of a spurious argument with an epistemic premise. Our supreme and unshakable confidence in the wrongness of rape simply doesn't answer the metaphysical question about the foundations of morality. It remains entirely possible that God functions at the foundation of ethics and that we, theists and atheists alike, are able to apprehend certain moral truths with crystal clarity. Such a story could be and has been told with eminent reasonableness, showing that Antony's appeals to "intuitions" here are inadequate.

What Antony and Sinnott-Armstrong need to draw their ambitious conclusion is more ontology in their evidence, so to speak. So perhaps we could reformulate their argument along sturdier metaphysical lines as follows:

7. Rape is necessarily wrong.
8. If DCT is true, then rape is not necessarily wrong.
9. So, DCT is false. [(6)]

The argument, again, is obviously valid, and suppose we grant (7), which we're happy to do. Is it true that DCT implies that the wrongness of rape is a contingent matter? Again, Antony and Sinnott-Armstrong are assuming, for the sake of argument, that God never would or could command rape. So DCT, thus understood, would not render it possible that rape become right. But nonetheless, say the DCT detractors, in some conceptual space somewhere, if God did command rape, it would be right, according to DCT, and so DCT is wrong. And again, the idea, perhaps anyway, is that in the nearest impossible world in which God commands rape, rape would still be wrong even if God commanded it. What our confidence in the wrongness of rape would be deriving from, on this analysis, is that our moral sense is somehow privy to and tracking this necessary moral truth. In the closest impossible world in which God commands rape, rape would still be wrong. Otherwise the impossible world in question is doubly removed from actuality and possibility: it would be both that God commanded rape, presumed to be impossible in the first place, and that rape, of all things, or child torture, or some other despicable and reprehensible action would be rendered right by divine command. So this, we take it, is the sort of extended modal story that Antony might tell in order to capture what she really thinks is just an obvious intuition: not even divine command could make something so wrong to be right.

How should we respond to this argument? The issue, again, comes down to whether DCT somehow undermines the extended modal status of the wrongness of rape. By "extended modal status," we mean to refer to Antony's presumption that it's wrong necessarily, in all possible worlds, but also wrong in, if not all impossible worlds, at least the closest impossible world or worlds that we "examine" when trying to identify the truth value of the relevant ethical counteressentials.

What seems to be going on in the argument is that Antony and Sinnott-Armstrong are attempting to drive a subtle wedge between God and necessary truth. For Antony's "intuitions" imagine a scenario, a counterpossible she grants, in which God's commands stand completely at odds with necessary moral truth. One suspects, then, that she's implicitly assuming without argument that the necessary truth of morality, if such there be, is independent of God. But this is question begging and, though not an uncommon assumption, is open to dispute. To assume otherwise is to equate necessity and aseity, two rather different notions, an equation that philosophers from Morris to Plantinga to Craig have questioned. They have suggested, to the contrary, that theism best explains necessary truth. Robert Adams did the same in his 1980 piece in the *Journal of Philosophy*.[9] And in that same context he also suggested that divine dependence of the necessary truths could also make quite a bit of sense for our ability to apprehend such truths. So it's a story significant both ontologically and epistemically, and a story with an impressive history of Christian thought. It's no conclusive demonstration of anything, but it's one consideration among others in favor of a theistic account of both necessary truth and our epistemic access to it, so the substance of our point here is that tacit assumptions about the essential inconsistency of God and necessary truths should by no means go unchallenged or be accepted in sanguine fashion as obvious intuitions.

## EXPLANANS-DRIVEN CONSIDERATIONS

Explanans-driven considerations can also be used to subject Antony's argument to critical scrutiny, this time, though, by talking about operative conceptions of God among classical theists. Suppose that God and morality are both necessary, *and* that God exists in the Anselmian sense of being the bedrock of reality, the ground of all being, and the like. Must morality ontologically depend on God in this case?[10] We have excellent prima facie reason to think that in fact it would. An Anselmian God entails God's necessity, but God's necessity does not entail Anselmianism. Necessity is a necessary but not sufficient condition for the God of Anselm. Among additional qualities to Anselmianism, we are supposing, is that he is the ontological foundation of all that exists.[11]

With this in mind, let's inquire into a question concerning conditionals featuring God's nonexistence as the antecedent. Further, suppose again, to begin with, that God exists. For the consequent, let's use this proposition: "Moral facts obtain," and let's suppose that the truth value of the consequent is true and true necessarily, again in accord with this aspect of Platonism. The conditional in question, then, is this:

10. If God doesn't exist, then moral facts obtain,

and, again, recall we're assuming, for now, God's existence, which renders this conditional a counterfactual. The consequent is necessarily true, by supposition, which, according to the standard semantics of counterfactuals, has the same effect as a necessarily false antecedent, namely, that the conditional is trivially true.[12] Unless we affirm the trivial truth of (10), the natural question for us to consider is what's the right nonstandard semantic construal of the truth value of (10)? The answer seems to depend heavily on whether God exists, exists necessarily, and exists in the Anselmian sense. For consider these three variants of conditional (10):

10a. If (a merely contingent) God doesn't exist, then moral facts obtain.
10b. If a necessary God does not exist, then moral facts obtain.
10c. If an Anselmian God does not exist, then moral facts obtain.

(10a) would seem to be, again on the supposition that there are necessary moral facts, substantively true. Whether or not God exists, the moral facts would obtain. Even if that means that (10a) is just trivially true, it would show that a contingent God is largely irrelevant to moral truth. (10b) entertains the falsity of a necessarily existing God, which would entail the necessary falsehood of a necessary God and an Anselmian God, but would be consistent either with God's nonexistence or with the existence of a contingent God. In neither case would there be any reason to believe in a necessary connection, logically or metaphysically, between God and morality. So there would be no conceptual grounds (pertaining to inherent connections between the antecedent and consequent) for resisting what seems intuitively to be the nonvacuous truth of (10b). For whether a contingent God exists or atheism is true, either way the necessary moral facts we are presupposing would still obtain.

(10c), however, is different, because it asks us to envision a particularly problematic impossible world. We are asked to imagine a world where the being on whom all reality depends has been removed from the picture. If God exists contingently, or even if God exists as merely one necessary item among other equally necessary and independent realities, then we can make sense of treating God as potentially eliminable from the metaphysical equation without repercussions. Assuming his existence in these senses, counterfactuals and even counteressentials featuring antecedents denying God's existence arguably can often, rather persuasively, be treated as garden-variety counterfactuals or at most as glorified counterfactuals. If an Anselmian God exists, however, and if God is not only necessary but the ground of all being, then counterpossibles featuring antecedents denying such a God's existence are in a very different category. For all reality, including morality, would depend on this being. To remove the grounds for reality itself, and then to affirm that there could still exist reality without those grounds, seems incoherent. (10c) therefore seems nontrivially false.

So far we have been assuming that God exists, but let's suppose we ask about the truth value of (10) on the assumption of atheism. Recall (10): If God does not exist, then moral facts obtain. We can continue for present purposes to assume moral realism and thus the (necessary) truth of the consequent. On standard semantics, the necessary truth of the consequent renders all three versions of the conditional (trivially) true. Note that none of the conditionals are, if atheism is true, counterfactuals, much less counterpossibles. They are straightforward conditionals featuring, in each case, a true antecedent and a true consequent. An atheist's natural inclination, then, assuming she's a moral realist, is to affirm the truth of (10) in each of its variant readings, and probably in more than a trivial sense, understandably enough.

Note the large range of agreement that theists, even Anselmian theists, and atheists, assuming they're moral realists, can forge on the question of (10)'s truth value. (10a) and (10b), on the supposition of either theism or atheism, could be reasonably argued to be nonvacuously true. Theists are charitably playing along with the treatment of (10b) as a glorified counterfactual, and perhaps atheists might return the favor by admitting that they might be wrong and that God in fact may well exist and exist necessarily, yet still argue on principled grounds that (10a) and (10b) are nonvacuously true counterfactuals. And the theist could happily agree. So far the "worldview" distinction makes no practical difference in these assessments, which shows that none of this has yet gotten to the real bone of contention.

Up until now, atheists could imagine that God really does exist and inquire into the truth value of (10a) by treating it as a counterfactual, asking what its truth value would be in the "closest possible world," namely, a world almost or much like this one but in which a contingent God does not exist and objective morality obtains. (10a) would be true nontrivially, following this sort of counterpossible analysis. And even if God's existence is presumed by the atheist to be necessary, but not crucial to moral truth, the atheist can still, with some plausibility, extend the logic of counterfactuals to counterpossibles, inquiring, perhaps with some ambitiousness but not wholly implausibly, into the "closest impossible world," namely, a world without God but with morality. Since God is not, according to (10b), necessarily essential to morality, perhaps it makes sense to suggest treating (10b) much along the lines of (10a) by this sort of extended logic of counterfactuals. Again, theists can happily play along and agree that, on this construal, (10b) may well be nonvacuously true.

(10c), however, features a proverbial fork in the road. For here the supposition about God's existence or nonexistence makes a difference. If we think of (10c) as merely a conditional with a false antecedent and necessarily true consequent, as atheists (who are moral realists) naturally would, then its truth value would be at least trivially true and, more likely, in some sense substantively true. If, however, we think of (10c) as an Anselmian theist would—as a counterpossible featuring a strong conceptual and ontological connection between the antecedent and consequent—its truth value would be nontrivially false, and obviously so, whatever the ultimately right analysis of counterpossibles may turn out to be. Indeed, a good test of the right semantics of counterpossibles would be getting this truth value right! And (10c), we contend, is in the same boat as the scenario Antony envisions of an impossible world in which God commands rape, a world that, given the nature and status of the God of classical theism, couldn't be farther from the actual world since it features a rupture between God and necessary truths.

Now, what if the atheist were to entertain the possibility that an Anselmian God exists and that (10c) is actually a counterpossible? Would the atheist remain within his epistemic rights to construe this particularly formidable counteressential as a glorified counterfactual and one that's nonvacuously true? In light of the conceptual and ontological ties between the antecedent and consequent, we would argue that the atheist would assuredly *not* be thus rationally entitled. But suppose we were to grant him epistemic room to make this maneuver, however incoherent we consider it to be. At that point our epistemic charity would be exhausted. What would remain crystal clear and simply beyond negotiation is that the Anselmian theist would be, to put it most judiciously, under no constraint to follow suit. Rather, the most natural and rational course for the Anselmian would instead be to insist that (10c) is nontrivially false in virtue of the ineliminable metaphysical role that an Anselmian God plays. Treating God as merely one more garden-variety item in the inventory of reality is to abandon Anselmianism. Such a God simply can't be so cavalierly domesticated. We have offered two independent sets of reasons to think the prospects are dim that Antony and Sinnott-Armstrong will be able on principled grounds to undergird their intuitions with a non-standard semantics for counteressentials that would give them the truth values they want.[13]

Moreover, Antony and Sinnott-Armstrong may not even need such semantics, for in truth all that may really be going on here is that they are equivocating on "God." Let "G" represent "God commands rape," and "R" stand for "Rape is morally acceptable." Antony and Sinnott-Armstrong wish to affirm the following:

11.  $\sim\!\Diamond G \;\&\; (G \rightarrow R)$

But the God to whom they refer in the first conjunct is Anselmian, and the god in the second conjunct is arguably nonAnselmian, so they're potentially just equivocating. What they may really be saying is this:

12.  $\sim\!\Diamond G \;\&\; (g \rightarrow R),$

where "g" stands for a less-than-Anselmian god. The second conjunct has a non-vacuous truth value all right, namely, false, contra what Antony and Sinnott-Armstrong try to foist on the divine command theorist. For DCT doesn't work unless the operative conception of God is Anselmian (at least in the requisite respects). The bona fide import of their point would then simply be that DCT fails if God is less than Anselmian, a point with which Anselmian theists generally concur.

Supposing that one can entertain the proposition that "G → R" is akin to thinking that one can think deeply about and confidently describe a world in which twice two is five. That one can say some nontrivially true and false things about certain impossible worlds is the very reason that one can say that a world in which G → R is true is a nonsensical world.

The presumption that Antony and Sinnott-Armstrong manifest in their analysis is connected to the failure of (10c). It's not only impossible for an Anselmian God not to function at the center of reality or to issue an irremediably evil command. Those states of affairs obtain only in impossible worlds that could not be "farther" from the actual world. So a nonstandard semantics can't plausibly be used to casually suggest, as if it were somehow obvious, that such a world is even a remotely reasonable choice of the "closest impossible world" to consider. If some wish to insist on domesticating Anselmianism and ignoring and trivializing its implications, that's their prerogative, but their arguments constructed on this basis will be weak and unpersuasive. Standard arbitrariness objections to DCT are effective against Ockhamism, and Antony and Sinnott-Armstrong's extended arbitrariness objections are effective against non-Anselmian variants of DCT. But neither arbitrariness objection provides any evidence at all against non-Ockhamistic, Anselmian versions of DCT.

To the extent that claims about God's irrelevance to morality bring to a premature halt the needed discussion of the case for a dependence relation of morality on God, they are not just unprincipled, but an actual impediment to rational discourse. What is needed is an assessment of the case for a dependence relation of morality on God, not an a priori and unprincipled rejection of the very possibility before consideration of the relevant evidence. Antony's extended arbitrariness objection fails, and her promissory note of a nonstandard semantics that will give her the truth values she wants should not convince, especially in light of the two independent considerations provided against her argument and the real possibility that at the heart of her argument is a huge equivocation.


POSTSCRIPT

Subsequent to writing this analysis of the extended arbitrariness objection, we came across a recently published piece by Alexander R. Pruss, who himself had written a reply to this very arbitrariness objection, except, in his case, versions proffered by Wes Morriston and Erik Wielenberg.[14] Pruss offers his own effort at rebutting the arbitrariness charge, one consistent with our analysis, and Pruss does this while not himself embracing divine command theory. Pruss considers the following three-step dialectics: (13) Even if God (consistently) commanded torture of the innocent, it would still be wrong. Therefore Divine Command Meta-ethics (DCM) is false. (14) No: for it is impossible for God to command torture of the innocent. (15) Even if it is impossible, there is a nontrivially true *per impossibile* counterfactual that even if God (consistently) commanded torture of the innocent, it would still be wrong, and this counterfactual is incompatible with DCM. Pruss argues that the last step of this dialectics is flawed because it would rule out every substantive meta-ethical theory, consequentialist or nonconsequentialist.[15]

For example, consider meta-ethical Kantianism, according to which, roughly, something is obligatory provided that reason requires it and forbidden provided that it is contrary to reason. Now consider this proposition: (16) Even if it were categorically required by reason, torture of the innocent would still be wrong. As Pruss notes, (16) seems plausible for exactly the same reasons for which (13) is plausible, namely, the horribleness of torturing the innocent. Then Pruss reproduces the rest of the argument to demonstrate how a refutation of Kantianism results: (17) Claim (16) is nontrivially true as a *per impossibile* counterfactual; (18) if Kantianism is true then (16) is not nontrivially true. By parity of reasoning, the same argument could be deployed against other substantive meta-ethical theories, as well as to consequentialist accounts.[16] Pruss recognizes that someone might take this as evidence to think suspicious any and every substantive meta-ethical theory, but Pruss seems more inclined, as do we, to think the universal applicability of the argument undermines the force of the argument, because something seems to have gone wrong in the third step of the argument.

As to what has gone wrong, Pruss speculates, first, that we reason poorly about outlandish counterfactuals like (13) and its analogues, and very poorly about *per impossibile* counterfactuals. "The relevant problem seems to me to be," he writes, "that when we are very strongly sure that something is true and its truth is very important to us, we have a tendency to carry it over into counterfactual situations, even when doing so is inappropriate...."[17] He offers a down-to-earth analogue: "I am afraid of dogs, and I don't want to lose my fear of dogs, because were I to lose my fear of dogs, I would no longer avoid them."[18] Like we have done in this book, however, Pruss then reminds readers that classical theists offer good explanations of why we have such nonnegotiable moral intuitions, rendering their use against theistic ethics flawed. Second, Pruss recognizes that some might just question the idea of nontrivial truth of *per impossibile* counterfactuals altogether, despite the valiant efforts to make sense of them.[19] And thirdly, he suggests that what might allow (13) to have plausibility as a nontrivial counterfactual is our ignorance of the nature of God—rendering it equivalent in logical force to

(19): Were a diamond to have the molecular structure of $H_2O$, it still wouldn't be water,

which poses little challenge to the theory that water is $H_2O$.[20]

Pruss's excellent analysis provides further reason to think that the extended arbitrariness objection gives theological voluntarists little reason for concern, though it does provide another useful reminder of how vitally important is the question of not just God's existence, but his nature.

# Appendix B:

## Outrageous Evil and the Hope of Healing

In chapter eight, we assessed a series of arguments from the problem of evil, and argued that there are responses to those arguments that allow us to maintain rational belief in an Anselmian God in the face of the stiff challenge that critics pose on this score. This problem is far from a mere intellectual puzzle, however, and for many people it is an existential issue that tears at their heart in such a devastatingly personal way that it makes it difficult for them to believe there is a God of love. Here we wish to extend our discussion of the problem of evil in a more existential direction by probing the practical implications that flow out of our beliefs about the ultimate source and nature of morality. In particular, we will show that a theistic ethical vision of the type we have defended offers just the resources we need to take fully seriously our moral outrage in response to evil, but without succumbing to despair. Indeed, it equips us to maintain hope in the face of evil and suffering as well as our resolve to work for its defeat.

### MORAL OUTRAGE

One of the most distinctively human things about human beings is their sense of moral outrage. This sense is rooted in our awareness that there is a profound gap between the way things are and the way they ought to be. The sense of outrage we have in mind goes beyond the fact that we make moral judgments and evaluations. It is a deeply felt conviction that some things, such as the cruel mistreatment of innocent children, are so unspeakably bad that they deserve our severest condemnation. In its most extreme form it can make us feel that the gap between the way things are and the way they ought to be is so wide that reality itself must be indicted.

When moral outrage reaches these proportions, it can intensify the problem of evil to the boiling point, and make belief in a God of perfect power and goodness seem utterly implausible for the many who feel the pressure of this problem. If a God with such attributes had created our world, so it is argued, he would not have designed it in such a way that these sorts of outrages could occur. And if, despite all appearances, there is a God responsible for creating our world, our sense of outrage makes clear that our foremost moral obligation is to rebel against him.[1]

But often the reaction to horrendous evil goes beyond rebellion to the complete loss of faith. Elie Wiesel no doubt speaks for many who experienced the unspeakable atrocities of the Holocaust in his following memorable lines.

> Never shall I forget the little faces of the children, whose bodies I saw turned into
> wreaths of smoke beneath a silent blue sky. Never shall I forget those flames
> which consumed my faith forever. Never shall I forget that nocturnal silence
> which deprived me, for all eternity, of the desire to live. Never shall I forget those
> moments which murdered my God and my soul and turned my dreams to dust.[2]

Wiesel's description of how this experience destroyed his dreams illustrates what Marilyn Adams has recently called "horrendous evils." What makes such evils "so pernicious is their life-ruining potential, their power prima facie to degrade the individual by devouring the positive personal meaning in one swift gulp."[3]

Moral evil, particularly when it is so brutally heartless and performed at such an overwhelming magnitude as the Holocaust, is especially prone to evoke moral outrage. However, natural evil can also seem cruel to the point that it too elicits moral protests. The stunning devastation of the 2004 tsunami affected many people that way and provided skeptics with further confirmation of their conviction that our world cannot be the creation of a loving God.[4] Writing in the *New York Times*, David Brooks urged that events like this make it clear that we are mere "gnats" in an indifferent universe. "The earth shrugs and 140,000 gnats die, victims of forces far larger and more permanent than themselves."[5] Indeed, the tsunami may well become for this generation the symbol of natural evil that is the counterpart to the Holocaust as the symbol of moral evil, although the recent tragedies in Haiti and Chile make the earthquake another contender. The massive scale of these events magnifies the horror of evil and intensifies the outrage against a world where such things happen.

This intense sense that there is something radically wrong with our world, that so many things happen that ought not to happen, is a profound recognition that we and our world are in desperate need of deep healing if our lives are to be fully meaningful. In what follows, we want to begin by examining more closely the very moral outrage that signals our deep sense that things are askew. For now, we simply want to observe that the legitimacy of moral outrage is often taken for granted by those who deploy evil as a weapon to assault faith in God. That is, it is tacitly assumed that moral outrage has the same significance and meaning regardless of whether or not one believes in a good God, or even whether or not one believes in God at all.

We shall contend that this assumption is far from obvious, and requires careful scrutiny. To bring this claim into sharper focus, we shall briefly consider four starkly different options with respect to the nature of ultimate reality and then highlight the differences in how each of these accounts for our sense of moral outrage. To put it another way, we must examine the ontology of outrage in order to assess these matters honestly. To get at this ontology, we shall consider the view that there is no God, the view that God is supremely powerful but not good, the view that God is perfectly good but limited in power, and finally the classical view that God is both supremely good and powerful. We shall conclude with some reflections on the distinctive resources of Christian theology for addressing horrendous evil and renewing our deepest dreams.

What shall emerge is that the meaning and significance of moral outrage varies considerably, depending on our view of ultimate reality, and the practical implications do as well. We shall see that these beliefs determine not only how seriously we should take our sense of outrage but also what realistic hopes we have for healing the huge gash that separates the way things are from the way they ought to be. The practical implications we shall focus on have to do not only with how we should think about the victims of evil, but also with what realistic hope we have that our efforts to oppose and defeat evil might succeed. A healthy view of evil, we shall suggest, is one that is not only honest in the face of evil, but also allows us to retain hope. Denial and despair, by contrast, are unhealthy alternatives to an honest grappling with evil that maintains hope. The account of morality we have defended in this book underwrites honest hope.

## THE ONTOLOGY OF OUTRAGE

To get a preliminary idea of the argument, reflect on the following statement from C. S. Lewis's spiritual autobiography describing his mindset before his conversion. "I was at this time living, like so many Atheists and Antitheists in a whirl of contradictions. I maintained that God did not exist. I was also angry with God for not existing. I was equally angry with him for creating a world."[6] As this comment suggests, some reactions of anger are profoundly misguided. To be rationally warranted, moral outrage, at least as it is commonly expressed, requires certain beliefs—beliefs that may not in fact be accepted by the one expressing that outrage.To bring this claim into sharper focus, let us begin with the view that there is no God. The first point to highlight here is that, if this is true, then ultimate reality is amoral. If ultimate reality is matter, energy and natural laws, and if we along with our universe are the products of such impersonal causes, then our moral sentiments have the same origin. Our moral feelings and our tendency to make moral judgments have been produced by a reality that has no such feelings and makes no such judgments. In other words, our moral sensibilities, as well as our other mental and personal faculties, have risen above their source.

Given this shaky pedigree, it is highly doubtful that morality, including our sense of outrage, can have the same status and significance that it has in traditional thought. As we have seen in this book, naturalists themselves often admit that traditional ideas of moral obligation and objective right and wrong make little sense in a world whose ultimate constituents are matter and energy and whose resources for explanation are physical and biological. Consider for instance the comment of noted naturalist moral philosopher Peter Singer on the implications of explaining our moral principles in such terms: "Far from justifying principles that are shown to be 'natural,' a biological explanation can be a way of debunking what seemed to be eternal moral axioms. When a widely accepted moral principle is given a convincing biological explanation, we need to think again about whether we should accept the principle."[7]

What Singer acknowledges about particular moral judgments and principles applies more broadly to the notion of obligation itself. To whom or to what could we be obligated in a fully naturalistic world? Do we *owe* it to the natural order to behave in a certain way? Does it have the will or the power to hold us accountable if we choose to live selfishly, to deceive and to cheat, and moreover, if we have the savvy and resources to avoid getting caught?

Of course, naturalists will insistently remind us that they take morality quite seriously and can account for it in their own terms. We have already noted the view of Harvard biologist Edward O. Wilson, who believes that the "struggle for men's souls" in this century will be over precisely the issue of the origin of morality. Over against the traditional view that morality has a transcendent or supernatural source is the view that morality is a human creation. The essence of this latter view is that human beings have been genetically disposed over generations of biological evolution to make certain choices. Through the process of cultural evolution, some of these choices have hardened into laws and obligations. If the predisposition to so choose is strong enough, it is accompanied by the belief that the behavior in question is commanded by God, or in some other fashion required of us in an objective and absolute sense.

It would take us too far afield to pursue the details of this fascinating account of our moral feelings and judgments, but one point is worth emphasizing. According to this account, a crucial factor that gives morality its force over us is the influence of some beliefs that are objectively false, in particular, the belief that morality has behind it divine sanctions or some other such objective warrant. In an article written with Michael Ruse, Wilson put the point quite bluntly: "In an important sense, ethics as we know it is an illusion fobbed off on us by our genes to get us to cooperate."[8] In other words, evolution has wired us to believe morality is objectively binding on us, that we are categorically obligated to take it seriously and live by its dictates. In reality, there is no such obligation as we are inclined to believe, but the illusion is nevertheless a useful one for it moves us to cooperate and get along with each other.[9] Living by the rules of morality is a mutually beneficial thing, generally speaking, and obviously promotes survival, the one sacrosanct value of naturalistic evolution.

The same basic analysis goes for moral outrage for those who accept this account of morality. We have been wired to have this feeling about certain actions, and the disapproval this generates not only discourages such behavior but also moves us to punish it and to empathize with those who are the victims of it. This outrage, it must be emphasized, partakes in the illusory character of ethics that Wilson and Ruse identify. For the outrage stems from the deeply rooted conviction we feel that certain actions are violations in the most profound sense, and that such actions are utterly forbidden on pain of supernatural sanctions.

Next, let us consider the possibility that there is a God who is enormously powerful, powerful enough to create our world, but who is not morally good. Let us assume this

God is indifferent to our moral values and judgments, even our most basic ones. Let us assume he does not value our flourishing and happiness and that he is not committed to truth.

Given such a God, it is natural to ask why he would create us so that we have the moral sensibilities that we do. Here we could only guess. Perhaps he did so because he finds it amusing or takes a certain aesthetic pleasure in our moral expressions. Maybe he has even wired us to believe that he shares our deepest and best moral judgments. He wants us to believe he values what we call justice and that he is opposed to innocent suffering and that he can be counted on to support our own efforts in their behalf. But perhaps in reality, he is indifferent to our idea of justice and is entertained by human misery.

What this points out is that the idea of an amoral God creating us with the moral sentiments we have is deeply incoherent. A creator who designed us to have such strong feelings about justice and the like but did not share them himself would not be amoral, but rather, devious at best. If we were to discover that there actually were such a God, we would be deeply distressed. We would feel deeply deceived and the victims of a perverse delusion. So, given our strong moral valuations, if the one who created us to have them does not share them, the notion that he is morally indifferent is eliminated and we are left with an evil deity.[10]

Next, let us consider the idea that there is a God of limited power, but who is morally good. He may or may not have created our world, but he does not have sovereignty over it in anything like the traditional sense. Given this view, it is not altogether clear how to describe this God's relationship to the world. If he did not create the world, are God and the world mutually dependent? Did God somehow emerge from the physical world in something like the manner that naturalistic evolutionists believe human consciousness emerged?

Unlike the previous view, there are variations of this account of God that have been popular in contemporary theology. In some of these variations, God is a personal being, but in others it is less clear whether he is or not. Sometimes those who speak of God in these terms seem to think that our moral sensibilities and inclinations are themselves "God."

For the sake of discussion and in the interest of clarity, let us assume that this God is a personal being who is at least capable of communicating his will to rational creatures such as ourselves. Given this assumption, we could describe our moral sensibilities as a reflection of God's own moral nature. That is, our moral intuitions and judgments at their best are a response to what God has proposed to us with the intention of enhancing our lives and the overall beauty of the world. In this sense, we have God's support for our moral efforts and projects to improve the world.

Finally, let us consider the traditional view that there is a God of perfect power and goodness. On this view, ultimate reality is moral in the strongest sense possible. This world and all that exists were created and are sustained by a God of perfect love. We were created in his image, so our moral intuitions and judgments at their best are a reflection of God's very nature. Morality is neither a deceptive delusion wired into us by a devious deity, nor an illusion "fobbed off on us by our genes," but rather one of the best clues we have to understand ultimate reality and the meaning and purpose of our own lives. Morality is as deeply rooted as it could possibly be, because it is grounded in the nature of a being who not only desires that justice and goodness will prevail, but who also has the power and wisdom to ensure that it will. This is the account of morality we have defended at length in this book.

### THEODICY AT AUSCHWITZ?

The practical ramifications of these various views are perhaps already becoming apparent, so let us turn now to articulate these explicitly. As a preface to this discussion, we want to reflect for a moment on a couple of statements from an author who challenges the whole enterprise of theodicy. In contrast to the classical attempt to make rational sense of evil, Kenneth Surin urges a "practical theodicy" that seeks to take concrete action to relieve suffering and to do whatever is possible to eliminate it. In contrast to such practical measures, Surin alleges that traditional theodicy may even be immoral, for the attempt to explain how evil is compatible with the existence of God may subtly justify it in a way that makes it seem acceptable. In this sense, the project of theodicy is actually complicit with evil. To emphasize the contrast, Surin cites the view of J. B. Metz that "there can be prayer after Auschwitz because there was prayer in Auschwitz. But, and this is now the crucial question, was there 'theodicy' in Auschwitz? *Could* there have been 'theodicy' in Auschwitz?"[11] Prayer is seen as a practical attempt to cope with evil, whereas theodicy is a theoretical attempt to account for evil in rational terms. In the same vein, Surin quotes Irving Greenberg as follows: "No statement, theological or otherwise, should be made that would not be credible in the presence of the burning children."[12]

Despite Surin's intention, what we think these statements actually show is that it is profoundly misguided to set practical theodicy in opposition to theoretical theodicy. We can see this is in his suggestion that prayer is appropriate after Auschwitz, whereas theodicy is not, which simply begs a number of crucial questions. For a start, what must be assumed to make prayer a meaningful activity? Not only must God be a personal being, but he must also be a good being who cares for us. Moreover, he must have the power to help in some way. These are the very claims the traditional theodicist wants to affirm are compatible with the reality of evil in our world. To deny any of them is to make prayer a profoundly misguided activity, or at best an instinctive visceral utterance or primal cry with no rational content or intention whatever. To appeal to prayer while dismissing these claims as irrelevant is only a pious evasion posing as a higher form of sensitivity to the harsh reality of evil.

The hard reality is that all of us have to decide what we shall believe about God in light of the fact that terrible things happen in our world, not only due to horrendous choices of our fellow human beings but also due to natural forces that are utterly beyond our control. What we believe about this most fundamental of all questions, moreover, has enormous implications for the victims of such tragedies. In particular, what we believe about God determines what sort of hope there may be, if any, that the tragedy that befell them can be rectified. Furthermore, we have to decide what makes the effort to fight against evil worthwhile, and what, if anything, we should do to relieve the suffering of those whose lives have been devastated by tragedies.

What we think about these matters also has significant implications for our own psychological and emotional health. Psychologist Robert A. Emmons notes that there is a rapidly accumulating literature on "stress-induced growth" and that this literature places considerable emphasis on the notion of meaning as crucial for positive change in response to suffering. He notes the irony in the fact that many philosophers have cooled to the topic of the meaning of life while social scientists have been warming to it and investigating it with fruitful results.

> The scientific and clinical relevance of the personal meaning construct has been demonstrated in the personal well-being literature, in which indicators of meaningfulness predict psychological well-being, while indicators of meaninglessness are regularly associated with psychological distress and pathology.... The conclusions that a person reaches regarding matters of ultimate concern—the nature of life and death, and the meaning of suffering and pain—have profound implications for individual well-being.[13]

Emmons goes on to cite psychological studies that support the conclusion that a "religious or spiritual worldview provides an overall orientation to life that lends a framework for interpreting life's challenges and provides a rationale for accepting the challenges posed by suffering, death, tragedy and injustice."[14]

Keeping these points in mind, let us begin by thinking through some of the implications and practical consequences of the belief that there is no God. First, there is no rational ground to be angry at natural disasters, nor is there any rational target for our outrage. These are merely the product of a natural order that is not only blind but indifferent to the pain and suffering that it causes. Evil in this sense is hardly unexpected in a naturalistic universe, so it does not pose a problem in any sense analogous to the problem it poses for theists. The surprising thing in such a universe is not that there should be extreme pain and destruction, but that creatures should exist who have consciousness and make the sort of moral evaluations we do in response to it. In a naturalist universe there is nothing like God to hear our protests or to care about them. Quarks, gluons, and laws of nature cannot hear our cries of anguish or our expressions of outrage.

Moreover, the amoral nature of ultimate reality is underscored by the naturalistic account of how our universe will likely end. According to most atheistic cosmologists, our universe is destined to expand forever, losing energy and disintegrating as it does until all life is destroyed. Consciousness, love, and aesthetic and moral sensibility will be extinguished by the same natural order that accidentally produced them in the first place. The sober truth according to this view is that all the things that give our lives meaning are temporal, interim products of an order that did not intend them and has no awareness of them and will eventually obliterate them. In the long run, and in the big picture, our efforts on behalf of goodness and justice will vanish without a trace.

Moreover, our sense of moral outrage at horrendous actions by our fellow human beings is blunted by the claim that morality as it has traditionally been understood is an illusion. When Ruse speaks on these matters, he is often asked how morality can continue to have force if his account of it is true. Isn't it likely that people will see through the illusion, come to recognize their moral feelings as deceptive in some sense, and consequently feel less disposed to respect them and act on them? Ruse dismisses this suggestion as a groundless worry. He replies that our genes are working overtime to keep us in line, so we need not worry that there will be a widespread revolt against morality.

We are less sanguine than Ruse is about the ability of our genes to keep us in line if it comes to be widely accepted that the deeply ingrained human belief that morality is transcendent is merely an illusion genetically programmed into us by years of biological and cultural evolution. If the only obligation we have to avoid certain behavior is the demand of human law, and if we are not accountable for our choices to a moral source that has transcendent authority, then our whole sense of outrage at those who choose to flout our standards loses much of its edge.

It is an uncomfortable truth that the demands of morality are sometimes at odds with personal gain and even survival. If the dictates of morality are transient sentiments ultimately explained in terms of their survival value for the species, what good reason is there to choose morality over personal advantage for those not inclined to do so? This question is especially urgent in the case of those who gain the power and resources to disdain moral constraints that would protect innocent persons.

Naturalists may try to reason with those who burn children. They may, in their outrage, oppose them with force and may even prevail over them in the battle for survival. But what do they say in the presence of burning and drowning children? Or what do they say later, in the aftermath of such tragedies, to try to make sense of them and to maintain any sort of rational meaning? It is a well-known phenomenon that sometimes people give up their faith in God in response to such unspeakable tragedies, but eventually the implications of this choice need squarely to be faced. Not only have they given up the hope that such evils could ever be rectified to their own satisfaction, they have also consigned those very sufferers to oblivion. To conclude in the presence of a burning or drowning child that there is no God is to conclude that the child has gone up in smoke, or been swept away, never to be heard from again. It is to conclude that the child's death is a monument to the absurdity of life, an emblem of the eventual fate of all who breathe and love and grieve and rage. This conclusion is devastating for the goal of maintaining a positive view of meaning, not to mention the psychological health and well-being to which such meaning is integral.

In short, the practical upshot if there is no God is that moral outrage is in many ways a futile emotion, not only because ultimate reality is indifferent to it, but also because ultimate reality will eventually destroy everything we value most. It makes no sense to be mad at the blind workings of the natural order, and even our revulsion at treacherous human choices is a somewhat illusory product of a system that rewards survival above all.

Now let us consider the practical implications if there is a God of enormous power, who is perverse, if not outright evil. We have in mind here not the dualistic view that there is a good God as well as an evil one battling it out, but rather, the view that the only God is an evil one.[15] In this case, it would be altogether understandable to rebel against God, but a moment's reflection makes it clear that such rebellion would be utterly pointless. While we might experience catharsis or personal moral satisfaction from our expressions of rebellion and outrage, such a God would likely view them as amusing rants, the more eloquent and passionate, the better. Maybe he even manipulates our expressions of outrage and our efforts to achieve justice as dramatic fodder in what is for him a dark comedy. Burning and drowning children may be fortunate if a more horrific fate does not await them in future worlds. For, perhaps the suffering and injustice of this world is merely a warm up for the torment he has planned for us in future episodes. It is hard to imagine a view of life that could be more demoralizing and meaningless than this. If there is an evil deity who genuinely deserves our rebellion, our lives could not be more tragic and absurd. And our attempts to relieve suffering and promote justice could not be more futile.

Next, let us consider the practical implications of believing in a God who is morally good but limited in power to persuasion and suggestion. In this case, God empathizes with us in our expressions of outrage and supports us morally in our efforts to relieve suffering and promote justice. However, there is no reason to be confident that evil will finally be defeated, nor that the universe can ultimately avoid the fate predicted by naturalistic cosmologists. Victims of tragic evil may be remembered by God, but it is doubtful that there is personal conscious survival beyond the grave. While this view is not as demoralizing as the view that God is evil, it is severely limited in its resources to underwrite hope. This is not to deny that this view has its attractions, not the least of which is that it avoids implicating God in horrendous evil. Still, though, at the end of the day, it is not clear that this God offers us much more than an optimistic version of naturalism, with its confidence in human creativity and goodwill, can provide.

Finally, let us consider the practical implications of believing the traditional view of classical theism that there is a God who is perfect in power as well as goodness, the sort of God to whom we have argued in this book the moral argument points. In the first place, this view assures us that our outrage at evil resonates with the deepest reality, a God who loves us and desires our well-being. Moreover, we can oppose evil and work to relieve suffering and promote justice with the confidence, not only that God supports us in our present efforts, but also that he himself will complete the task of defeating evil conclusively and decisively in his coming kingdom. Such effort on our part is in no way vain or futile because evil and death are the temporal, transient realities and love and joy and goodness are the eternal realities that shall forever prevail when death and evil have been destroyed.

In addition to encouraging our moral efforts, this also has profound implications for how we should think about the victims of terrible tragedy. When children are burning at the hands of lawless dictators is the worst of all times to silence the claim that there is a God of perfect goodness and power, to whom we are all accountable, or to lose confidence in his love for us. Likewise, when children are swept away by the waves of a tsunami, it pays them no honor to conclude that the forces of nature are the ultimate reality, subject to no higher power. To trust that a God of supreme power and love hears the prayers of those who suffer unspeakable horror does, however, honor them. To trust in this fashion is neither to disrespect nor trivialize their suffering, nor is it in any way to justify the actions of their tormentors, but it is to insist on the continuing significance and dignity of their lives and the power of God to renew and heal them.

This is not to suggest that we know the details of why God allows such horrors to occur, and any theodicy that offers clean-cut answers is likely to seem incredible in the presence of burning or drowning children. In a very real sense, trust in God does not eliminate the problem of evil, but rather intensifies it. It is precisely because of faith in God's supreme power and goodness that evil seems so out of place in our world. The naturalist, as noted above, has no corresponding reason to find evil surprising or out of place in our universe, nor does anyone who could take seriously the idea of an evil deity. Ironically, however, not to have a problem of evil for these reasons is actually to have a far bigger problem, for evil on these scenarios is normal, if not ultimate in some sense. To a lesser, but still significant degree, the same is true for those who believe God is good, but rather limited in power. For those who believe in a God of perfect love and power, in poignant contrast, there is indeed something not only profoundly outrageous, but deeply abnormal, about evil and suffering.

The price of "normalizing" evil is a steep one that should be carefully considered. It is to give up the hope of deep healing for ourselves and our universe. Susan Neiman has pointed out this cost for those who come to view events previously understood as evils as merely natural events. "We no longer expect natural objects to be objects of moral judgment, or even to reflect or harmonize with them. For those who refuse to give up moral judgments, the demand that they stop seeking the unity of nature and morality means accepting a conflict in the heart of being that nothing will ever resolve."[16] To accept as irresolvable such a jagged conflict in the heart of being is a heavy cost indeed.

So, trust in a God who can never allow us to normalize evil is a two-edged sword. While it intensifies the problem in one sense, it also gives us the most powerful resources to maintain realistic hope in the face of it and to believe that the conflict Neiman identifies will be resolved. Such trust gives us reason to take moral outrage utterly seriously as an accurate gauge of the nature of ultimate reality and to believe that the difference between good and evil is profoundly real. We can fight against evil with the confidence that we are not fighting a losing battle against ultimate reality. We can be angry at evil while loving God and trusting in his goodness and love for us.

This fully honest and realistic appraisal of evil is actually a consideration in favor of taking seriously the Christian account of things. For an instance of this, consider William Abraham's autobiographical reflections on how this played a role in his conversion from atheism to Christianity.

> What I found carrying enormous weight was the extent to which Christianity
> absolutely refused to blunt the reality of evil by denying it, taming it, pushing
> it to the margins of existence, covering it up cleverly and the like. On the
> contrary, it took the reality of evil so seriously that evil showed up all over the
> place when one came to expound and explain its teachings and practices.[17]

Abraham's reference to the "teachings and practices" of Christianity that take seriously the reality of evil points us to the distinctive resources of Christian theism for dealing with this issue. At the heart of these teachings is the claim that Jesus of Nazareth was the incarnation of the Son of God whose death atoned for our sins. The climax of this story is a stark account of Jesus facing the forces of evil head on and defeating them at every turn, maintaining love in the face of hatred, and forgiveness in the face of treachery and injustice.[18] The brutal nature of Christ's death is an anchor of realism that forever demonstrates that God has encountered evil at its worst and can offer healing for the deepest scars it has inflicted.

Consider the story of Richard Hoard, whose father was a lawyer who was prosecuting a ring of bootleggers. When Hoard was a freshman in high school, he woke one morning to a loud blast that radically altered his life. The blast was from a bomb that had been planted in his father's car and instantly killed him when he turned the ignition. Hoard describes how the anger and bitterness from this tragedy contaminated his adolescence and infected all facets of his life. His fragile faith, moreover, was easily destroyed largely because he had a syrupy sweet picture of Jesus that seemed far removed from the horrors he had experienced. This picture was shattered one evening when he attended a meeting where someone had erected a rough wooden cross with the bark still intact, a vivid contrast to the sanitized brass crosses that often adorn churches. "'A hell of a way to die,' I thought, staring at the tree. 'Nailed up like that.' And suddenly a thought I had never before considered struck me clearly, like a sword piercing my heart: It was real. As real as my own father's murder."[19]

This insight was a crucial turning point for him. He came to see faith in Christ not as an evasion of the harsh reality of evil, but as an honest way to come to terms with the pain and sickness in his soul that had festered for years. After accepting forgiveness for his own sins he experienced further emotional and spiritual healing when he was able to forgive his father's murderer and release the anger and bitterness that had crushed his spirit and numbed his soul.[20]

All of this reminds us of the biblical doctrine that we live in a fallen world, a world in which we have significant freedom and where we often fall far short of God's intentions for us. The natural order is implicated in our disobedience and also falls short of what God ultimately intends for his children, when his will shall be done on earth as it is in heaven. In the meantime, as the apostle Paul wrote, the created order groans in anticipation as it awaits the final redemption of its human inhabitants.[21]

Paul's emphasis in this text on the redemption of our bodies points up the fact that the Christian hope goes beyond emotional and spiritual healing to embrace the entire cosmos. The ultimate ground of this grand vision of healing is, of course, the resurrection of Jesus.[22] For the Christian, that the man on the cross was the Son of God incarnate is a decisive demonstration not only of the depth of God's love for us, but also that he is intimately with us in our suffering. That he was raised from the dead gives us rational grounds to trust that the worst horrors of this life can be overcome by his creative power and that our hope that life has positive meaning will be fully satisfied. If Christ is raised, if the *resurrected one* is also the *crucified one* who knows firsthand the power of temptation, the agony of real nails, and the pain of betrayal, then indeed, we can understand evil in a way that is both *honest* and *hopeful*, and life is a comedy, not a tragedy. Nicholas Wolterstorff has made this point with passionate eloquence in a comment on the difference it makes in our outlook to believe that Christ was raised from the dead. His words carry a depth of personal conviction as they were written in the context of his own struggles with the problem of evil after the tragic death of his son in a mountain climbing accident.

> To believe in Christ's rising from the grave is to accept it as a sign of our own rising from our graves. If for each of us it was our destiny to be obliterated, and for all of us together it was our destiny to fade away without a trace, then not Christ's rising but my dear son's early dying would be the logo of our fate.[23]

To take Christ's rising as the logo of our fate is to believe that God has taken decisive action to show us the strength of love. It is to believe that it is there, not in the horrors of natural or human history, that we can best take measure of the reality that is larger and more permanent than ourselves. Wolterstorff continues:

> God is love. That is why he suffers. To love our suffering, sinful world is to suffer. God so suffered for the world that he gave his only Son to suffering. The one who does not see God's suffering does not see his love. God is suffering love.... So suffering is down at the center of things, deep down where the meaning is. Suffering is the meaning of our world. For Love is the meaning. And Love suffers. The tears of God are the meaning of history.[24]

Viewing things from this vantage point prevents faith in God's perfect power and love from degenerating into a desperate expedient in the face not only of history's worst horrors, but the worst tragedies in our own personal experience. We need not resort to hoping against hope that there is a God greater than evil, or holding onto faith in God because it is the only way to keep our sanity. More than sanity, indeed, psychological and emotional health is to be found in a view of reality definitively shaped by the view of morality we have defended, including its distinctively Christian resources, a view that allows us to face evil not only honestly but in hope that our healing will be complete when the work of redemption has run its full course.

# Notes

INTRODUCTION

1. Here is Whitlock's article: <http://www.wibw.com/nationalnews/headlines/50183042.html>.

2. Arthur Allen Leff, "Unspeakable Ethics, Unnatural Law," *Duke Law Journal* 6 (1979): 1229.

3. Ibid.

4. Ibid.

5. Ibid., p. 1230; elsewhere he calls it "the cosmic 'sez who'," p. 1232.

6. Ibid., p. 1249.

7. See his "The Biological Basis of Morality," *Atlantic Monthly* (April 1998), p. 70.

8. C. S. Lewis, "Is Theology Poetry?" in *The Weight of Glory and Other Addresses* (New York: Macmillan, 1965), p. 140.


CHAPTER I

1. C. S. Lewis, *Mere Christianity* (New York: Macmillan, 1943), p. 21.

2. William Lad Sessions attributes the decline of moral apologetics in the middle of the last century to four factors: the decline of the idealism with which such arguments were often presented; skepticism about speculative metaphysics; the rise of ethical noncognitivism; and general indifference to religious interests and the presumed primacy of science as the paradigm of rationally acceptable intellectual activity. W. L. Sessions, "A New Look at Moral Arguments for Theism," *International Journal for Philosophy of Religion* 18 (1985): 51–67.

3. By way of a short preview of coming attractions, allow us to point out just three contemporary philosophers who have offered reformulations of the

moral argument for God's existence: Linda Zagzebski, "Does Ethics Need God?" *Faith and Philosophy* 4 (1987): 294–303; John Hare, *The Moral Gap: Kantian Ethics, Human Limits and God's Assistance* (Oxford: Oxford University Press, 1996); and C. Stephen Layman, "A Moral Argument for the Existence of God," in *Is Goodness without God Good Enough?*, edited by Robert K. Garcia and Nathan L. King (Lanham, MD: Rowman & Littlefield, 2009), pp. 49–65.

4. William R. Sorley, *Moral Values and the Idea of God: The Gifford Lectures Delivered in the University of Aberdeen in 1914–1915*, 2nd ed. (New York: Macmillan, 1921), pp. 332–333; Hastings Rashdall, *Philosophy and Religion: Six Lectures Delivered at Cambridge* (Westport, CT: Greenwood Press, 1910; reprinted in 1970), Lecture III; John Henry Cardinal Newman, *A Grammar of Assent* (Notre Dame, IN: University of Notre Dame Press, 1979), chap. 5.

5. Karl Barth is a good representative of this approach.

6. For a memorable passage that captures some of the multiform texture of postmodernism, see Alvin Plantinga, *Warranted Christian Belief* (Oxford: Oxford University Press, 2000), p. 423.

7. Francis Bacon, *The Essays of Francis Bacon*, edited by Clark Sutherland Northup (Houghton, Mifflin, 1908), Essay 16: "Of Atheism," p. 51.

8. An interesting fictional portrayal of this line of thought can be found in the first chapter of Lewis's *Screwtape Letters.*

9. Bertrand Russell, *Mysticism and Logic* (New York: Barnes & Noble, 1917), pp. 47–48: "That Man is the product of causes which had no prevision of the end they were achieving; that his origin, his hopes and fears, his loves and his beliefs, are but the outcome of accidental collocations of atoms; that no fire, no heroism, no intensity of thought and feeling, can preserve an individual life beyond the grave; that all the labours of the ages, all the devotion, all the inspiration, all the noonday brightness of human genius, are destined to extinction in the vast death of the solar system, and that the whole temple of Man's achievement must inevitably be buried beneath the debris of a universe in ruins—all these things, if not quite beyond dispute, are yet so nearly certain, that no philosophy which rejects them can hope to stand. Only within the scaffolding of these truths, only on the firm foundation of unyielding despair, can the soul's habitation henceforth be safely built."

10. George Mavrodes, "Religion and the Queerness of Morality," in *Ethical Theory: Classical and Contemporary Readings*, 2nd ed., ed. Louis P. Pojman (New York: Wadsworth, 1995).

11. C. S. Lewis, *Mere Christianity* (New York: Macmillan, 1960), pp. 31–32.

12. Although we feel the force and in many ways resonate with Lewis here, perhaps he overstates the case in saying that God could only reveal himself in the moral order; if enough, say, irreducible complexity were able to be found in the natural world, we would consider it a rational inference that there's an intelligence behind it; or if a naturalistic cosmology is inadequate to account for the origins of the universe, an inference to a personal explanation would be warranted. But such arguments won't be pursued here.

13. For a solid synopsis of his approach, see Richard Boyd, "How to Be a Moral Realist," in Sayre-McCord, ed., *Essays on Moral Realism* (Ithaca, NY: Cornell University Press), pp. 181–228.

14. This critique of naturalism is consistent with affirming that, at least for many moral obligations, they may well and likely do supervene on natural facts. It's just a mistake to think that such supervenience provides so much as any evidence at all for a naturalistic worldview. In a piece forthcoming in *Faith and Philosophy* called "Naturalism, Theism, Obligation and Supervenience," Plantinga makes this point most rigorously, adding that one could "simply define supervenience as involving the subvening properties being more basic, fundamental, robustly explanatory, etc., than the supervening properties (or even that the supervening properties aren't anything 'over and above' the subvening properties); then 'supervenience' would express approximately the same property as Terence Horgan's 'superdupervenience.' ['From Supervenience to Superdupervenience: Meeting the Demands of a Material World,' *Mind*, 1993.] But then, of course, it is no longer at all obvious that moral properties super(duper)vene on descriptive or naturalistic properties."

15. See his *Essay in Aid of a Grammar of Assent* (Notre Dame, IN: University of Notre Dame Press, 1979).

16. W. G. Maclagan, *The Theological Frontier of Ethics* (New York: Macmillan, 1961), p. 80. William Sorley, in his 1914–1915 Gifford Lectures, had argued similarly that an authoritative Moral Law must be rooted in a mind, but since no mind of mere men will do, it must reside in the mind of God. Later published as *Moral Values and the Idea of God* (London: Cambridge University Press, 1935, especially chapter 13).

17. Lewis, *Mere Christianity*, p. 19.

18. We refrain from saying that egoism would render the moral argument altogether impotent, since if, as ethical egoism maintains, we have an objective moral obligation to pursue self-interest, then it is an objective moral obligation after all, and the existence of any kind of objective moral obligation is difficult, if not impossible, to reconcile with naturalism, or so we will argue. But objective ethical egoism would certainly not conduce, in other respects, to the sort of moral argument we will favor.

19. Plato, *The Republic*, Book II.

20. James Rachels, *The Elements of Moral Philosophy* (New York: McGraw-Hill, 1993). The eighteenth-century Anglican Bishop Butler gave an argument especially against the psychological egoism of philosopher Thomas Hobbes, who had argued in his *Leviathan*, first published in 1651, that a scientific account of human nature leaves no place for traditional ethics. Our behavior simply results from whatever desire or aversion is strongest in a person at any given time, and the notion, Hobbes thought, of anything like a special faculty of conscience lacks empirical foundation.

Butler was concerned to find an adequately testable understanding of human nature, but he asserted that as a reductivist, psychological theory, egoism fails to do justice to the complexity of reasons and motives that play a part in our decision-making as human beings. In his response to Hobbes, he attempted to show that a careful study of human nature reveals a far more complicated and subtle moral psychology than a reduction of all human actions to the motive of self-interest would allow. In addition to self-love, we also have a conscience, a principle of benevolence, and other particular impulses that are not reducible to self-love, benevolence, or to one another.

Perhaps the biggest problem for psychological egoism is that it's vulnerable to criticism for claiming to be a social scientific hypothesis. For such theories ought, in principle, to be able to be shown false. But no amount of seeming counterevidence dissuades the committed psychological egoist. The martyr, the hero, the saint, on the one hand, or the rapist, the terrorist, the pedophile, on the other, are all said to have the same moral motivation. Any appearance of genuine altruism is reducible to egoism, but this means that no evidence, in principle, seems enough to count against the theory, which raises the question of how seriously it deserves to be taken as a social scientific hypothesis.

Philosopher James Rachels gives the following sort of argument to show that the prescriptive theory of ethical egoism fails. Any moral doctrine that assigns greater importance to the interests of one group than to those of another is unacceptably arbitrary unless there is some difference between the members of the groups that justifies treating them differently. Ethical egoism, though, would have each person assign greater importance to his own interests than to the interests of others, even though there's no general difference between us by which to justify it. So ethical egoism is unacceptably arbitrary.

21. Henry Sidgwick, *The Methods of Ethics* (Chicago: University of Chicago Press, 1962).

22. Sidgwick, *Methods*, p. 405.

23. Mavrodes, "Queerness," p. 587.

24. Erick J. Wielenberg, *Value and Virtue in a Godless Universe* (New York: Cambridge University Press, 2005), p. 80.

25. J. L. Mackie, *The Miracle of Theism* (Oxford: Clarendon Press, 1982), p. 115.

26. Simon Blackburn, *Ruling Passions* (Oxford: Oxford University Press, 2001), p. 3.

27. See his *The God Delusion* (New York: Houghton Mifflin, 2006), p. 57. If Dawkins thinks that he has provided an effective argument against the religious foundations of ethics by means of this query, he's mistaken, as is Sam Harris, author of the fast-selling *Letter to a Christian Nation* (New York: Alfred A. Knopf, 2006, p. 49), when he writes that the reasoning of Christians is circular when we use our moral intuitions to authenticate the wisdom of the Bible and then use the Bible as confirmation of our intuitions. This isn't quite right, for true standards of morality, in principle, could be rooted in God but epistemically available to us apart from religious convictions, and we suspect, when it comes to certain clear moral intuitions, this is the case. The use of such inviolable intuitions to eliminate faulty theological paradigms (like versions of Calvinism that, in Lewis's words, sneak a bad god in through the back door) would not, in such a contingency, eliminate the theistic foundations of those intuitions. To think so is a mistake, in part produced by an equivocation on "our" when we speak of "our intuitions," as between intuitions we apprehend and intuitions being veridical independent of God. Shared ethical intuitions between theists and atheists, for the same reason, provide no evidence at

all to suggest that God doesn't function at the foundation of morality, contrary to the claim of Dawkins that "surely, if we get our morality from religion, [the moral intuitions of theists and atheists] should differ" (*God Delusion*, p. 225). Dawkins concludes that "we do not need God in order to be good." Again, God could be the foundation of ethics without the implication that atheists lack moral insight, that they think of the content of ethics in radically different ways from theists, or lack the capacity to behave morally. (Dawkins also equivocates on "get" in that line of his we just quoted, as between "know" and "ground ontologically." Thanks to Kyle Blanchette for this insight.)

28. Jean-Paul Sartre, "Existentialist Ethics," in *Classic Philosophical Questions*, ed. James Gould (New York: Macmillan, 1992), p. 180. Sartre later renounced this earlier essay and tried, we think unsuccessfully, to provide more objective grounds for ethics.

29. Mavrodes, "Queerness," p. 587.

30. John M. Rist, *Real Ethics: Rethinking the Foundations of Morality* (Cambridge: Cambridge University Press, 2002), p. 40.

31. Marc D. Hauser, *Moral Minds: How Nature Designed Our Universal Sense of Right and Wrong* (New York: HarperCollins, 2006), p. 420.

32. Steven Pinker, *The Blank Slate: The Modern Denial of Human Nature* (New York: Penguin Books, 2002), p. 177.

33. Pinker, *Blank Slate*, p. 177.

34. Pinker himself, a thoroughgoing naturalist, is open to a Platonic account of moral truth, which he thinks is consistent with a biological understanding of morality. He makes clear his openness to a Platonic account of moral truth in his chapter "Evolution and Ethics" in *Intelligent Thought: Science versus the Intelligent Design Movement* (New York: Vintage Books, 2006), edited by John Brockman. His game-theoretic considerations in favor of the possibility that morality has some external warrant in the nature of reality do nothing to provide any account of morality's *truth* or *normative force*, only its instrumental value or an account of our development of a moral sense. This point has its value, but those dissatisfied by its pretensions to provide insight into the real foundation of ethics seem altogether within their epistemic rights to insist on more.

35. In *Minds, Brains and Science* (Cambridge: Harvard University Press, 1984, especially chapter 6), Searle makes clear his view that compatibilist freedom is not enough to make sense of real ascriptions of moral responsibility, while also arguing that belief in free will invariably holds tenacity for us despite the scientific challenge posed by determinism. His reason for rejecting the adequacy of compatibilist accounts of free will is that they don't allow for our ever doing otherwise, antecedent conditions and the laws of the universe being what they are. But Searle attributes our refusal to let go of a commitment to freedom to the subjective sense of alternate possibilities that's built into the very nature of consciousness, rather than taking our sense of freedom as evidence for the inadequacy of a purely naturalistic account.

Other naturalists have echoed similar views. Thomas Nagel: "There is no room for agency in a world of neural impulses, chemical reactions, and bone and muscle movements." See his *The View from Nowhere* (New York: Oxford University

Press, 1986), p. 111. Nobel Prize–winning geneticist Francis Crick: "The Astonishing Hypothesis is that 'You,' your joys and sorrows, your memories and your ambitions, your sense of personal identity and free will, are in fact no more than the behavior of a vast assembly of nerve cells and their associated molecules.... This hypothesis is so alien to the ideas of most people today that it can truly be called 'astonishing.'" See his *The Astonishing Hypothesis: The Scientific Search for the Soul* (New York: Charles Scribner's Sons, 1994), p. 3. And philosopher Richard Rorty: "The idea that one species of organism is, unlike all the others, oriented not just toward its own increased prosperity but toward Truth, is as un-Darwinian as the idea that every human being has a built-in moral compass—a conscience that swings free of both social history and individual luck." See his "Untruth and Consequences," *The New Republic* (July 31, 1995): 32–36.

36. Derk Pereboom writes that "our best scientific theories indeed have the consequence that we are not morally responsible for our actions ...[we are] more like machines than we ordinarily suppose." *Living without Free Will* (Cambridge: Cambridge University Press, 2001), xiii–xiv.

37. Elliot Sober, *Core Questions in Philosophy: A Text with Readings*, 3rd ed. (Englewood Cliffs, NJ: Prentice Hall, 1995), p. 322. This is an introductory text in philosophy, not something Sober has published in a scholarly journal, but it's a good example of the standard line fed to countless introductory philosophy students.

38. Aristotle, *Nicomachean Ethics*, Book II, Sections 2 and 3.

39. *God Delusion*, p. 221.

40. Thanks to Mark Foreman for this reminder.

41. Francis Collins, director of the Human Genome Project and a committed evolutionist, rejects E. O. Wilson's attempts to explain altruism in terms of some indirect reproductive benefits to its practitioner. Collins considers altruism a major challenge for the evolutionist and "quite frankly a scandal to reductionist reasoning" as found in the likes of Dawkins. See his *The Language of God: A Scientist Presents Evidence for Belief* (New York, Free Press, 2006), pp. 27–28.

42. William James, "The Dilemma of Determinism," in *The Will to Believe and Other Essays in Popular Philosophy* (New York: Dover Publications, 1956), p. 147.

43. James, *Will to Believe*, pp. 160–61.

44. To the extent that Sartre *does* argue against determinism, he implicates himself in a contradiction. He writes that "there is no fixed human nature because there is no God to conceive it," so he seems to think that only God can make sense of a fixed nature that exists before we are thrust into existence. At the same time, however, he thinks that, if we *did* have a fixed nature, that would ground the conviction that determinism is true. On his view, it isn't an option to explain away our actions by reference to a fixed and given human nature, since there is no determinism on his analysis. Morality is possible because determinism isn't true. However, if God existed, Sartre claims, there *would* be this sort of fixed nature that would rule morality out. This claim stands in obvious tension with his claim that the loss of God resulted in the loss of an objective ethics prescribing how we behave. For if Sartre was right that God's existence and intentional creation of us would have given us a stable nature that would

have made us determined to behave the way we do, then God's existence would have militated *against* objective ethics. Being determined by this fixed nature, on his view, we would not have been able to do otherwise.

45. Wilson, a prominent contemporary thinker who holds the naturalistic worldview, says humanity's big problem is that some of its deepest desires are completely out of sync with reality. He puts it like this: "The essence of humanity's spiritual dilemma is that we evolved to accept one truth and discovered another." What he means is that as human beings evolved they came to believe in God, in life after death, and objective morality. But eventually, in modern times, they came to discover that God does not exist, that morality is something we created for our own purposes, that there is no meaning beyond this life. See his "The Biological Basis of Morality," *Atlantic Monthly* (April 1998), p. 70. Here's another quote from Wilson: "The Central Idea of the consilience worldview is that all tangible phenomena, from the birth of the stars to the workings of social institutions, are based on material processes that are ultimately reducible, however long and torturous the sequences, to the laws of physics." See his *Consilience: The Unity of Knowledge* (New York: Knopf, 1998), p. 266.

## CHAPTER 2

1. *Plato: Complete Works*, edited by John M. Cooper (Indianapolis: Hackett Publishing, 1997), p. 9.

2. Dan Brown, *The Da Vinci Code* (Doubleday: New York, 2003), pp. 267–268.

3. For a recent example of a discussion of the Euthyphro Dilemma, see John Milliken, "Euthyphro, the Good, and the Right," *Philosophia Christi* 11, no. 1 (2009): 145–155. For an excellent exegetical analysis of the Dilemma, see John E. Hare's *Plato's Euthyphro* (Bryn Mawr, PA: Bryn Mawr College, 1985). For other analyses of the *Euthyphro*, see Albert Anderson's "Socratic Reasoning in the *Euthyphro*," *Review of Metaphysics* 22 (1969): 461–481; William S. Cobb's "The Religious and the Just in Plato's *Euthyphro*," *Ancient Philosophy* 5 (1985): 41–46; S. Marc Cohen's "Socrates on the Definition of Piety: *Euthyphro* 10A–11B," *Journal of the History of Philosophy* 9 (1971): 1–13; and those are just a smattering of the references that could be adduced.

4. Louise Antony, "Atheist as Perfect Piety," in *Is Goodness without God Good Enough?: A Debate on Faith, Secularism, and Ethics*, edited by Robert K. Garcia and Nathan L. King (Lanham, MD: Rowman & Littlefield, 2009).

5. Ibid., p. 71.

6. The logical priority of what God *favors* rather than *commands* has led some theological voluntarists to be divine will theorists, though usually theorists of what's right rather than what's good. See, for example, Philip L. Quinn, "An Argument for Divine Command Ethics," in *Christian Theism and the Problems of Philosophy*, edited by Michael D. Beaty (Notre Dame, IN: University of Notre Dame Press, 1990), pp. 289–302.

7. Antony, p. 72.

8. Patrick Nowell-Smith, "Morality: Religious and Secular," in Baruch Brody's *Readings in the Philosophy of Religion: An Analytic Approach* (Englewood Cliffs, NJ: Prentice-Hall, 1974).

9. A. Janik and S. Toulmin, *Wittgenstein's Vienna* (New York: Simon & Schuster, 1973), p. 194.

10. Janine Idziak, ed. *Divine Command Morality: Historical and Contemporary Readings* (New York: Mellen Press, 1979).

11. Robert Adams, *The Virtue of Faith: And Other Essays in Philosophical Theology* (Oxford: Oxford University Press, 1987), chs. 7–9; Philip L. Quinn, *Divine Commands and Moral Requirements* (Oxford: Oxford University Press, 1978); Paul Rooney, *Divine Command Morality* (Brookfield, VT: Ashgate Publishing Company, 1996); Edward R. Wierenga, *The Nature of God: An Inquiry into Divine Attributes* (Ithaca, NY: Cornell University Press, 1989), chap. 8, and his "A Defensible Divine Command Theory," *Nous* 17: 387–407; et cetera.

12. The positive case that Philip Quinn builds for voluntarism is based on God's sovereignty, which he formulates in this fashion: "Necessarily, for all states of affairs p, if p obtains and p is wholly distinct from the state of affairs of God existing, then p is metaphysically dependent on being willed by God." Since this principle would not account for obeying God being obligatory, but this moderate principle avoids other troubling implications, Quinn is inclined to suggest that a voluntarist continue insisting that obeying God is obligatory and obligatory because God wills it, but that this is not a consequence of the doctrine of divine sovereignty. See Quinn, "An Argument for Divine Commands Ethics," in Beaty, ed., pp. 297, 299.

13. Ralph Cudworth, *A Treatise Concering Eternal and Immutuble Morality* (1731; rpt. New York: Garland, 1976), pp. 9–10.

14. This famous example was given by W. V. O. Quine.

15. Richard Mouw, "The Status of God's Moral Judgments," *Canadian Journal of Theology* 16 (1970): 61–66.

16. Robert Adams takes the import of Moore's question to be the need for a transcendent component to morality, an aspect of it that remains beyond our ability fully to articulate, carving out necessary room for a critical stance, something that a theistic explanation satisfies impeccably. See his *Finite and Infinite Goods: A Framework for Ethics* (Oxford: Oxford University Press, 2000), p. 78. For G. E. Moore's original argument, see his classic *Principia Ethica*, section 13.

17. Ecclesiastes 12:13.

18. Richard J. Mouw, *The God Who Commands: A Study in Divine Command Ethics* (Notre Dame, IN: University of Notre Dame Press, 1990).

19. Mouw, *God Who Commands*, p. 29.

20. Antony, p. 71. She seems to be using the notion of moral rightness in the same sense in which she uses moral goodness, since almost all of her analysis is in terms of moral goodness; we will point out the importance of this distinction momentarily. In the appendix to this book, we attempt to answer both Antony's arbitrariness and what we call her "extended arbitrariness" objection to divine command theory.

21. Ibid., pp. 71–72.

22. John Stuart Mill, *Utilitarianism, Liberty, and Representative Government*, with introduction by A. D. Lindsay (New York: E. P. Dutton, 1951), p. 26.

23. John Piper, *Desiring God: Meditations of a Christian Hedonist* (Sisters, OR: Multnomah Books, 2003; revised edition). A version of theistic rule utilitarianism was taken up and defended in earnest by William Paley. See his *Principles of Moral and Political Philosophy* (reprinted by St. Thomas Press; Houston, TX, 1977). Especially relevant is Book II, chs. 5–7, where he connects the divine wish for human happiness with utilitarianism rules.

24. Mouw, *God Who Commands*, p. 30.

25. Michael Levin, "Understanding the Euthyphro Problem," in the *International Journal of the Philosophy of Religion* 25: 90–91.

26. We insert the qualification "objectionable" here because even if moral truths are not "substances," it doesn't follow that they can't hold a place in one's ontology; if so, then they have ontological implications, but they just don't create problems for the ontology.

27. Ibid., p. 92.

28. For an analysis of such issues in James, see David Baggett, "On a Reductionist Analysis of William James's Philosophy of Religion," *Journal of Religious Ethics* 28, no. 3 (2000): 423–448.

29. Alvin Plantinga, *The Nature of Necessity* (Oxford: Clarendon Press, 1980), pp. 2–3.

30. M. Macbeath, "The Euthyphro Dilemma," *Mind* 91 (1982): 565–571.

CHAPTER 3

1. J. B. Phillips, *Your God is Too Small* (New York: Macmillan, 1979), p. 71.

2. Richard Dawkins, *The God Delusion* (New York: Houghton Mifflin, 2006), p. 51.

3. Philosophers of language tend to rigidly distinguish proper names from definite descriptions; a proper name is usually taken to be merely referential, contributing only its referent to the proposition expressed by sentences containing it, so if there's no referent, there's no proposition expressed by such sentences containing such a name. A definite description is analyzable according to Bertrand Russell in a way that it can still express meaning even if it doesn't refer uniquely to an existing referent. Names and descriptions are normally quite different. But plenty of atheists are willing to say "God doesn't exist" and assume their words are meaningful; if, though, "God" is a name contributing only its referent, and there is no referent, no proposition is expressed, so it would seem the sentence would lack meaning. What's a philosopher of language to do? We could treat "God" as a description or title, but that seems to leave behind the straightforward sense in which "God" is used as a name. One innovative solution, proposed by Mike McKinsey, is that "God" is among the small class of what he calls "descriptive names," by which he means it is a name, all right, but part of its (linguistic, not propositional) meaning derives from a limited number of salient descriptions that are publicly known. In God's case, qualities commonly and publicly attributed to Deity include omniscience, omnipotence, and the like. Descriptions used to fix the reference of a name may turn out to be wrong, as Saul Kripke noted in his argument that names aren't fixed by descriptions at all but rather by certain causal relations. McKinsey disagrees, replying that, even if some of the better-known descriptions by which the references of names get fixed are mistaken, there are other descriptions that would be

238    NOTES TO PAGES 51–58

accurate. For example, maybe Einstein didn't discover relativity after all, but instead stole the idea; but he'd still be accurately known as the fellow thought to have discovered it. McKinsey says the telltale sign of descriptive names, of which "God" is an example, is that the relatively few descriptions by which their referents are identified are such that they couldn't be mistaken. To say, for example, that "There's a being who is omniscient, omnipotent, and omnibenevolent, but isn't God," is nonsense. Of course it would be God. This is what makes "God" a descriptive name, McKinsey argues. See Michael McKinsey, "The Semantics of Belief Ascriptions," *Nous* 33, no. 4 (1999): 519–557.

4. A. C. Ewing, *Value and Reality: The Philosophical Case for Theism* (London: George Allen & Unwin, 1973), p. 199.

5. Kant thought that morality pointed to an Anselmian God. Morality, he argued, involves things that must happen and, as such, is connected to all other ends. It's God who functions to ensure the kingdom of ends, so this dimension of moral theology points us to God, not a finite god, but an infinite God whose supreme and unitary will serves to put all the moral laws into one. In aesthetic and teleological judgments, we can make suprasensible claims that are about more than appearances, and such judgments include oughts that go beyond what *is* to what *must be.*

6. In addition to such discursive considerations, we should also bear in mind this observation by Tom Morris: "The Anselmian's intuitions about God, or more broadly, all those intuitions which together yield the Anselmian conception of God, generate without intentional contrivance an overall belief-set in which it makes sense that there should be such intuitions and that they should be, at least a core of them, reliable. For if an Anselmian God exists, and creates rational beings whose end is to know him, it makes good sense that they should be able to come to know *something* of his existence and attributes without the need of highly technical arguments, accessible to only a few. It makes sense that there be reliable intuitions such as those which yield the Anselmian conception of God." Thomas V. Morris, *Anselmian Explorations: Essays in Philosophical Theology* (Notre Dame, IN: University of Notre Dame Press, 1987), p. 68.

7. "The Prescriptions against the Heretics," trans. S. L. Greenslade, in *Early Latin Theology*, vol. V in "The Library of Christian Classics" (Philadelphia: Westminster Press, 1956), pp. 31–32.

8. J. L. Tomkinson, "Divine Sempiternity and A-temporality," *Religious Studies* 18 (1982): 186–187.

9. Thomas V. Morris, *Anselmian Explorations*, p. 3.

10. Brian Davies, *The Reality of God and the Problem of Evil* (London: Continuum, 2006).

11. See Robert Adams, *Finite and Infinite Goods* (Oxford: Oxford University Press, 2000), p. 14.

12. Quoted in John Beversluis, *C. S. Lewis and the Search for Rational Religion* (Grand Rapids, MI: Eerdmans, 1975), p. 157.

13. Personal correspondence, November 2008.

14. See, for example, Bruce Reichenbach, *Evil and a Good God* (New York: Fordham University Press, 1982), chap. 7, and Stephen Davis, *Logic and the Nature of God* (London: Macmillan, 1983), chap. 6.

15. Nelson Pike, "Omnipotence and God's Ability to Sin," *American Philosophical Quarterly* 6 (1969): 208–216. Pavel Tichy, in "Existence and God," *Journal of Philosophy* 76 (1979): 410–411, similarly argues that "God" must be more a description than a name because it is otherwise a contingent matter whether God is omnibenevolent. For any individual, he writes, is "conceivably malicious." More recently, Timothy P. Jackson argues against impeccability for other reasons and in favor of God's moral goodness by other means in "Is God Just?" *Faith and Philosophy* 12 (1995): 393–408.

16. Thomas V. Morris, *Anselmian Explorations: Essays in Philosophical Theology* (Notre Dame, IN: University of Notre Dame Press, 1987), p. 47.

17. David Hume, *A Treatise of Human Nature*, 2nd ed., ed. L. A. Selby-Bigge, rev. P. H. Nidditch (Oxford: Clarendon, 1978), p. 32. Michael Hooker discusses the analysis of conceivability and its relation to possibility in "A Mistake Concerning Conception," in *Thomas Reid*, ed. Stephen Barker and Tom Beaucham (Philadelphia: Philosophical Monographs, 1977), pp. 86–93.

18. Rene Descartes, *The Philosophical Writings of Descartes*, 3 vols., trans. John Cottingham, Robert Stoothoff, Dugald Murdoch, and Anthony Kenny (Cambridge: Cambridge University Press, 1984–1991). See, for instance, "Principle 7" (1:194–195) and "Notes against a Program." Also see Descartes's second reply to the third set of "Objections" (2:121–137) and a letter to Gibieuf, January 19, 1642 (3:201–204).

19. See David J. Chalmers, *The Conscious Mind: In Search of a Fundamental Theory* (New York: Oxford University Press, 1996). A symposium discussion of this book held between Chalmers, Sydney Shoemaker, Christopher Hill, Brian McLaughlin, Stephen Yablo, and Brian Loar can be found in *Philosophy and Phenomenological Research* 59 (1999): 435–496.

20. Epistemic possibility was first discussed by G. E. Moore, "Certainty," in *Philosophical Papers* (New York: Collier, 1962), pp. 223–246, and later by Wildred Sellars, "Phenomenalism," in *Science, Perception, and Reality* (New York: Humanities Press, 1963), pp. 60–105, and Paul Teller, "Epistemic Possibility," *Philosophia* 2 (1972): 303–320. Also see R. S. Woolhouse, "From Conceivability to Possibility," *Ratio* 14 (1972): 144–154.

21. Michael Hooker, "Descartes's Denial of Mind-Body Identity," in *Descartes: Critical and Interpretive Essays*, ed. Michael Hooker (Baltimore, MD: Johns Hopkins Press, 1978), p. 178.

22. Ibid.

23. In *Anselmian Explorations*, Morris actually argues that all that is required to salvage impeccability is stable property exemplification, not even necessary existence. Chalmers, for one, admits that God's necessary existence would be a counterexample to his claim that there are no "strong necessities," but immediately claims that such a notion of a necessarily existing God is inconceivable. We do not doubt that Chalmers's conviction is that such a notion is inconceivable, but we have several reasons why we doubt whether such a notion indeed is inconceivable, some of which have been cogently presented by Robert M. Adams, "Divine Necessity," *Journal of Philosophy* 80 (1983): 741–752. At any rate, Morris's point, which seems persuasive, is that necessary

existence is not a prerequisite for the strong stability that a property like impeccability requires.

In his book and in the *Philosophy and Phenomenological Research* symposium, Chalmers expresses skepticism over the existence of any strong necessities that limit the range of metaphysically possible worlds to a set of worlds narrower than those circumscribed by logical possibility narrowly construed. In equating narrowly with broadly logically possible worlds he of course deviates from Plantinga's characterization of such distinctions in *The Nature of Necessity* (Oxford: Oxford University Press, 1974). Added to his allegiance to the conceivability principle, this leads Chalmers into views with which traditional theists will strongly disagree. For instance, he admits, "[o]f course a theist could take the second phrase ['ways the world really could have been'] literally, and perhaps call the resulting modality 'metaphysical modality'. This way we would use God to ground a modal dualism. Even so, it's not clear why God's powers should prevent him from creating any logically possible world...." This unrefined understanding of omnipotence and dubious "conceiving" (or lack thereof) on Chalmers's part underscores the potentially unreliable method of putting too much stock in finite and fallible cognizers' conceivings by entirely neglecting potential broadly logical internal constraints, such as moral ones, imposed on an Anselmian God's actions. Incidentally, Chalmers's basic sentiment here resonates closely with the argument against impeccability based in omnipotence. The theist's reply to Chalmers could follow the lead of Morris: "In a less than Cartesian sense, the God who is impeccable is the ground of all possibility. Our ability to describe situations which would involve God's contravening some duty should just remind us of the distinction between conceivability and possibility. They do not coincide. And omnipotence ranges over only what is possible." See Morris, "Impeccability," *Analysis* 43 (1983): 106–112, and his *Anselmian Explorations*. Also see Joshua Hoffman, "Can God Do Evil?" *Southern Journal of Philosophy* 17 (1979): 213–220, and Jerome Gellman, "Omnipotence and Immutability," *The New Scholasticism* 51 (1977): 21–37. For a considerably more nuanced conception of omnipotence than the one on which Chalmers bases his intuition, see Alfred J. Freddoso and Thomas P. Flint, "Maximal Power," in *The Existence and Nature of God*, ed. Alfred J. Freddoso (Notre Dame, IN: University of Notre Dame Press, 1983), pp. 81–113.

24. Cited in the aforementioned *Philosophy and Phenemological Research* symposium.

25. For instance, among such skeptics we have heard it suggested, no doubt due to Hume's continuing influence, that necessity has to remain a function of "what we mean by our terms." Like Alvin Plantinga, this leaves us baffled how *modus ponens* is made valid by anything that we as humans have done. In addition, since "God is our Creator" is an example of what we "mean" by our terms while being a presumably contingent matter, it is importantly different from the necessary analytic truth that "All bachelors are unmarried." Since both are cases of what we mean by our terms, something more is needed to explain the difference.

26. Arguments that God *can* sin come in about three main varieties, and are basically these: (1) God's sinning is conceivable, so possible; (2) God's freedom and praiseworthiness (for not sinning) require his ability to sin, so it's possible; and

(3) God's omnipotence requires that he be able to sin, so it's possible. The freedom and omnipotence arguments suffer a fate similar to the conceivability argument. The omnipotence argument can be dispatched most easily. If omnipotence is the ability to do anything metaphysically possible, then God's omnipotence isn't challenged by his inability to act contrary to his nature. For *his* doing so, given his nature, is metaphysically impossible. Does this make him less free, divinely determined by his own nature? It would seem that God *is* somewhat constrained, but not by anything external to himself. The notion of constraint and the surface grammar of sentences affirming impeccability are subtly misleading, because they make it sound like God's willings are stultified, that God is bucking up against his own limitations. But there's an important and privileged sense in which God is completely unconstrained if, as traditional theology would have it, there is perfect correspondence and consonance between God's nature and willings.

27. For a fuller version of the argument of this section, see "On Whether God Can Sin," *Philosophia Christi* 5, no. 1 (Fall 2003): 259–267.

CHAPTER 4

1. Lewis Carroll, *Alice's Adventures in Wonderland and Through the Looking Glass* (Madison, WI: Cricket House Books, 2010), p. 101.

2. Actually, there is evidence to suggest that Calvin himself rejected this doctrine of "limited atonement," but that historical question is not our present concern.

3. There are plenty of Arminians on both sides of the question of "once saved, always saved," a matter relatively peripheral in comparison to whether or not there are some with no hope for salvation by God's choice from the start.

4. Colossians 2:8.

5. "The Prescriptions against the Heretics," trans. S. L. Greenslade, in *Early Latin Theology*, vol. V in "The Library of Christian Classics" (Philadelphia: Westminster Press, 1956), pp. 31–32.

6. Hugh T. Kerr, ed., *A Compend of Luther's Theology* (Philadelphia: Westminster Press, 1956), p. 4.

7. See Jerry L. Walls, *The Problem of Pluralism: Recovering United Methodist Identity* (Wilmore, KY: Bristol Books, 1988), especially chap. 5.

8. Calvinists often like to characterize libertarian freedom as incoherent, yet if God had reasons to create the world as he did, reasons that he chose to act on without having to do so, then that's a paradigmatic example of libertarianism. Unless Satan or mankind's original sin could have been avoided, moreover, their sins seem ultimately attributable to God, making him the author of sin; so to preserve the holiness of God, again we have good reason to affirm the coherence of libertarian freedom.

9. Thanks to Kenneth Collins for this analysis.

10. Some sins might be culpable despite inability to do otherwise by the agent if they are the result of adequately free prior bad choices that resulted in a loss of freedom, such as a free rejection of salvation in Christ or an obstinate refusal to repent: choices which shape character in such a way that impedes freedom or even, finally, removes freedom altogether. An analogy is a drunkard who makes bad choices

that in his stupor he couldn't avoid, but his culpability resides in his freely having chosen that path of drunkenness in the first place.

11. Thanks to Tom Morris for helpful insights on this topic.

12. Perhaps here's another helpful way to look at it. Suppose there's a .5 probability that you will resist each sin you encounter in your lifetime. This would entail a .25 probability that you will resist the first two, a .125 probability you'll resist the first three, and so on. Imagine the probability of resisting every temptation over the course of a seventy-year life. It becomes a statistical unlikelihood so great that it defies description. Christians believe that only one man ever did it, or ever truly could, even if each sin is in principle such that it can be resisted by God's enabling grace. Thanks to David Lahm for this analysis.

13. There is a huge difference between theistic and secular compatibilists. Many theists might consider becoming compatibilists if they were atheists, for it's a view not without plausibility, despite the fact that it seems so immediately obvious that we are free in a stronger sense than compatibilism allows. Perhaps, as some argue, evolution has given us a strong, but false belief that we are free and it serves some evolutionary purpose. But the notion that God has given us an illusory sense of freedom and then, moreover, punishes us for acts he could have just as easily determined differently lacks any plausibility. None of the work that secular philosophers have done defending compatibilist freedom helps the (typical) Calvinist cause, unless the compatibilism in question can be shown sufficient to undergird not just ascriptions of genuine moral responsibility, but such responsibility sufficiently strong to undergird a doctrine of eternal hell understood retributively. We all await such a case; the import of the cumulative argument of this chapter is that no such account will be forthcoming.

14. As William Hasker writes, "All sorts of experiences and relationships acquire a special value because they involve love, trust, and affection that are freely bestowed. The love potions that appear in many fairy stories (and in the Harry Potter series) can become a trap; the one who has used the potion finds that he wants to be loved for his own sake and not because of the potion, yet fears the loss of the beloved's affection if the potion is no longer used." Hasker continues: "For that matter, individuals without free will would not, in the true sense, be human beings at all; at least this is the case if, as seems highly plausible, the capacity for free choice is an essential characteristic of human beings as such. If so, then to say that free will should not exist is to say that we humans should not exist. It may be possible to say that, and perhaps even to mean it, but the cost of doing so is very high." See William Hasker, *The Triumph of God over Evil: Theodicy for a World of Suffering* (Downers Grove, IL: InterVarsity Press, 2008), p. 156.

15. Arbitrariness problems and vacuity objections really go hand in hand, as a later chapter will explain in greater detail. So long as there are no constraints on God's will, and it's God's will that constitutes the standard for morality, then both of these implications follow: morality is whatever God says it is, no matter what, which introduces an arbitrariness problem; and God is good and right no matter what, which empties such terms of the determinate content they're thought to possess, rendering them vacuous in the sense that they are consistent with anything at all. Radical voluntarism produces both problems; the existence of the relevant constraints on

God's will enables us to avoid both problems, but radical voluntarism precludes any such constraints, even constraints internal to God's character.

16. Calvinists may deny universal possibilism and thus reject ontological Ockhamism; but in suggesting either that we're never in a position to identify a specific divine action precluded by God's goodness or that unconditional election qualifies as morally legitimate, they are epistemic Ockhamists, so the argument here designed to demonstrate their irrationality goes through. Their view might turn out to be right, of course, because our cognitive faculties and moral intuitions might really be just that warped; nonetheless, it's not rational to hold their view given the current evidence at our disposal. Our approach here echoes William Rowe's answer to Wykstra's cognitive limitation defense regarding the problem of evil.

17. Calvinists often demur at this point, insisting that it's only "hyper-Calvinism" that affirms the double predestination required to entail unconditional perdition. With John Wesley, we disagree with our Calvinist friends here; classical Calvinism entails that the non-elect have no hope for avoiding hell, so they are just as bound for hell as if they'd been specially elected just for that purpose. Theirs is a distinction that makes no difference.

18. Some Calvinists might wish to reply that they don't privilege God's will over his character, but instead are just as willing as anyone to assign primacy to God's nature, and that therefore they aren't voluntarists. Although that's technically right, their view is saddled with exactly the same problem Ockhamistic voluntarism has: morality is arbitrary. Voluntarism isn't exactly the problem. A rejection of voluntarism doesn't answer arbitrariness concerns unless the appeal to God's character assumes that God's character is recognizably good. Otherwise we can reject voluntarism and root morality in God's stable character yet end up with a morality just as arbitrary as the worst form of Ockhamism. Since the Calvinistic conception of God is lacking in recognizable goodness, evading the charge of voluntarism does nothing to avoid the force of the charge of moral arbitrariness and divine caprice.

19. John Calvin, *Institutes of the Christian Religion*, trans. Ford Lewis Battles, ed. John T. McNeill (Philadelphia: Westminster, 1961), 3.23.2.

20. Martin Luther, *Bondage of the Will*, trans. J. I. Packer and O. R. Johnston (Westwood, NJ: Revell, 1957), p. 217.

21. Luther, *Bondage*, p. 29. We clearly see here Luther's opting for the voluntarist horn of the Euthyphro Dilemma.

22. Four-point Calvinism, of course, is most often associated with an acceptance of all the traditional points of the TULIP except for limited atonement. That Calvinists can and often do reject limited atonement while still embracing unconditional election, the real culprit, demonstrates that limited atonement is not the root problem. Interestingly, a rejection of unconditional election is consistent with limited atonement; for suppose God, in his foreknowledge, knows who accepts Christ and who doesn't, then sends Jesus to die just for the elect. The offer of salvation could be a genuine offer to all, but it just so happens that God knows in advance who will freely accept it and who will not (though they could have done otherwise), and Jesus died for the former and not the latter. Although we don't accept this picture, it does effectively

demonstrate that the doctrines of limited atonement and unconditional election function independently of one another.

23. We will lay out this distinction more rigorously in a later chapter.

24. John Beversluis, *C. S. Lewis and the Search for Rational Religion* (Grand Rapids, MI: Eerdmans, 1985), p. 151. A revised version of this book was published in 2007.

25. See Gary R. Habermas's and Antony G. N. Flew's *Resurrected? An Atheist and Theist Dialogue* (New York: Rowman & Littlefield, 2005), p. 56.

26. One can't help but wonder if Lewis's aversion to extreme Calvinism is related to the hard thinking he did about damnation. Having deeply reflected about hell and written *The Great Divorce* to understand damnation morally, he was not one to swallow the doctrine unreflectively while harboring secret fears that it was utterly irreconcilable with his best moral intuitions. Perhaps those who *do* are more liable to fail to see the centrality of meaningful freedom in any rationally defensible construal of hell, and thereby more likely to think of Christianity as requiring the acceptance of morally hideous theology. The common misinterpretation of our argument in this chapter as an argument for universalism led us to this conjecture.

27. Some critics here might wish to suggest that Arminians face an equally big problem because God chose to instantiate this among other possible worlds, a world in which some would freely reject him, and God knew in another possible world they would have accepted him. To begin with, though, such a challenge requires something closer to middle knowledge rather than mere foreknowledge—as does the common challenge to Arminians of why God would create someone he knows will reject him and go to hell. Even supposing such an ambitious modal picture is accurate, it presumably involves people's genuinely free choices and their consequences. Just because God foreknows the content of our decisions doesn't mean he's responsible for determining that content, nor does it preclude the ability to do otherwise. It's a matter of some people responding positively (or at least not negatively through obstinate resistance to the end) to God's overtures, while others don't; but they all could have done otherwise. God happened to know how they'd respond, but that isn't his determining anything—or if it were, that would be compatibilism, which we have rejected. No, although there was *something* necessary, it wasn't a necessity that precluded the ability to do otherwise. The necessity was more de dicto than de re; necessarily one does X if one does X, that's all. But it wasn't the following kind of necessity: if one does X, then one *necessarily* does X. (By the way, it's been suggested by some Arminians and Molinists that hell is reserved for those who freely reject Christ in this and all possible worlds, an interesting conjecture that, if true, would entirely dispel doubts about God's goodness.)

28. See Richard Swinburne, *Responsibility and Atonement* (Oxford: Clarendon Press, 1989), p. 139.

29. We suggest reading Arminius rather than settling for dismissing vulgarized semi-Pelagian Arminianism as unworthy of serious consideration, bearing in mind that Arminius never saw himself as outside the Reformed tradition. An Arminian analysis of the relevant biblical texts has the further advantage of avoiding the individualist interpretation of election and predestination that, though a good fit with

the contemporary assignment of primacy to individualism, stands in tension with the much more communal mentality of first-century Jews.

30. British theologian Colin Gunton identifies key points at which he believes some central Christian doctrines got off track. One particularly interesting development is that in Western theology since Augustine, "the theme of love becomes subordinate to that of will"; that is, sovereignty, Calvinistically construed, trumps recognizable love. Part of the fundamental problem, he believes, is a deficient understanding of the Trinity, which above all shows that God necessarily exists in an eternal relationship of perfect love. Before there was ever a world over which to be sovereign, God was love; this makes the real question not how a God of sovereignty expresses his love, but how a God of perfect love expresses his sovereignty. See Colin E. Gunton, *The One, the Three and the Many* (Cambridge: Cambridge University Press, 1993), p. 120.

31. A full text of the Pope's speech is readily available in numerous places on the Internet. For example: <http://www.cwnews.com/news/viewstory.cfm?recnum=46474>.

32. Donald Miller, *Blue Like Jazz* (Nashville, TN: Nelson, 2003).

33. Here is a more formal articulation of our argument that we cannot rationally trust the teaching of Scripture unless we can trust our fundamental moral intuitions:

(1) If we're not justified to believe the Bible was inspired by a morally perfect God, then we're not justified to think it's reliable.

(2) If we're not justified to believe God is morally perfect, then we're not justified to believe the Bible was inspired by a morally perfect God.

(3) If God is not recognizably good, then we're not justified to believe God is morally perfect.

(4) If we're rational to believe that God damns those he could have saved without violating their free will, then God is not recognizably good.

(5) If it is rational to believe Calvinism, then we're rational to believe God damns those he could have saved without violating their free will. (analytic truth)

(6) If it is rational to believe Calvinism, then God is not recognizably good.

(7) If it is rational to believe Calvinism, then we're not justified to believe God is morally perfect.

(8) If it is rational to believe Calvinism, then we're not justified to believe the Bible was inspired by a morally perfect God.

(9) If it is rational to believe Calvinism, then we're not justified to think the Bible is reliable.

(10) We are justified to believe the Bible is reliable.

(11) Therefore, it is not rational to believe Calvinism.

(I: We are justified to believe the Bible was inspired by a morally perfect God; R: We are justified to think the Bible is reliable; M: We are justified to believe God is morally perfect; G: God is recognizably good; D: We're rational to believe that God damns those he could have saved without violating their free will; C: It is rational to believe Calvinism.)

246 NOTES TO PAGES 83–89

(1) ~I → ~R

(2) ~M → ~I

(3) ~G → ~M

(4) D → ~G

(5) C → D (analytic truth)

(6) C → ~G 4, 5, hypothetical syllogism

(7) C → ~M 3, 6, hypothetical syllogism

(8) C → ~I 2, 7, hypothetical syllogism

(9) C → ~R 1, 8, hypothetical syllogism

(10) R (axiom)

(11) ~C 9, 10, modus tollens, double negation

Unless the Calvinist can argue that some premise ought to be rejected, she has been shown to be irrational.


CHAPTER 5

1. Thomas Aquinas, *Summa Contra Gentiles*, Book I, chap. 40.

2. Richard Tarnas suggests a connection between the invariability and ontological independence of the truths of realism when he writes, "Despite the continuous flux of phenomena in both the outer world and inner experience, there could yet be distinguished specific immutable structures or essences, so definite and enduring they were believed to possess an independent reality of their own. It was upon this apparent immutability and independence that Plato based both his metaphysics and his theory of knowledge." See his *The Passion of the Western Mind: Understanding the Ideas That Have Shaped Our World View* (New York: Ballantine Books, 1991), p. 4.

3. As Cudworth writes, "That it is not possible that any thing [sic] should be without a nature, and the natures or essences of all things being immutable, therefore upon supposition that there is any thing [sic] really just or unjust, due or unlawful, there must of necessity be something so both naturally and immutably, which no law, decree, will nor custom can alter." See Janine Idziak, ed., *Divine Command Morality: Historical and Contemporary Readings* (New York: Mellen Press, 1979), p. 161.

4. Quoted in Alvin Plantinga, *Does God Have a Nature?* (Milwaukee: Marquette University Press, 1980), pp. 96, 101.

5. Quoted in Idziak, 1979, pp. 55–56.

6. Thomas V. Morris, *Anselmian Explorations: Essays in Philosophical Theology* (Notre Dame: University of Notre Dame Press, 1987), p. 168.

7. Plantinga, *Does God Have a Nature?*, p. 146.

8. For even if verification is tied to the deliverances of an ideally rational scientific community that had all the relevant evidence, the conditions under which a statement is verified depends on our having adopted a certain set of practices and modes of behavior.

9. Alvin Plantinga, "How to Be an Anti-Realist," *Proceedings and Addresses of the American Philosophical Association* 56, no. 1 (New York: State University of New York Press, 1982): 52.

10. Ibid., pp. 67–68.

11. Ibid., p. 68.

12. Whereas Plantinga tips his hat to the tradition of equating realism with mind-independence—or at least making the latter necessary for the former—we would rather revise the notion of realism to capture invariance and leave mind-independence out of it, since it's only there because it was mistakenly thought needed to avoid denying necessity.

13. Robert Adams, acknowledging his debt to Leibniz, echoes a similar sentiment. See Robert Adams, "Divine Necessity," *Journal of Philosophy* 80 (1983): 751. We quote the relevant passage at length in the appendix.

14. Alvin Plantinga, *Warranted Christian Belief* (Oxford: Oxford University Press, 2000), p. 280.

15. See Morris, *Anselmian Explorations*, pp. 171–172.

16. Norman Kretzmann and Eleonore Stump, "Being and Goodness," in *Divine and Human Action: Essays in the Metaphysics of Theism*, ed. Thomas V. Morris (Ithaca, NY: Cornell University Press, 1988), p. 284.

17. Ibid., p. 307.

18. Brian Leftow, in his fascinating article "Is God an Abstract Object,?" suggests that, though God is a person, he may nonetheless fulfill functions typically reserved for abstract objects. His effort to reconcile person and object bears a kind of resemblance to Tom Morris's effort to reconcile the humanity and divinity of Jesus in *The Logic of God Incarnate* (Ithaca, NY: Cornell University Press, 1986). See Leftow's "Is God an Abstract Object?" *Nous* 24 (1990): 581–598. Leftow also defends the doctrine of divine simplicity in this article by saying that either God creates his own nature or he doesn't, and since the former is implausible and theists wish to affirm God's aseity, God must be his own nature, as simplicity suggests. Notorious problems with simplicity, though, include that it's implausible to think that all of God's properties are identical, plus it seems to imply immutability that is hard to reconcile with God's active involvement in the world.

19. Following the direct reference theorists, Adams generalizes their insight about natural kinds to suggest a relation of natures to meanings, and hence about the relation of metaphysics to semantics. Whether or not the direct reference theorists are right about the way we use "water," for instance, he insists that we certainly could use a word in that way. And he proposes that we do use ethical discourse in an analogous way, which enables us to distinguish between the semantics of ethical discourse and what we may call the metaphysical part of ethical theory. Not that good, he insists, is a natural kind the way that Boyd suggests; but the meaning of the word "good" may be related to the nature of the good in something like the way that has been proposed for natural kinds. Adams writes, "As good is not a natural kind in the way that water is, the meaning of the word 'good' does not direct us to anything like a chemical structure. And we cannot assume that causal interactions with concrete samples will fix the reference of 'good' in the same way that the reference of 'water' is fixed. What is it, then, that connects the word 'good' with things that are good, or with the property that is goodness? It is possible, I think, to indicate a general pattern for the relation of

natures to meanings where the nature is not given by the meaning. What is given by
the meaning, or perhaps more broadly by the use of words, is a role that the nature is
to play. If there is a single candidate that best fills the role, that will be the nature of
the thing. In the case of a natural kind, arguably, the role its nature is assigned by our
language is that of accounting causally for the observable common properties of
identified samples. The role that the meaning of 'good' picks out for the nature of the
good will be rather different." See Robert Adams, *Finite and Infinite Goods* (Oxford:
Oxford University Press, 1999), p. 16.

20. We encourage readers to take a look at Gordon Pettitt's insightful "Moral
Objectivity, Simplicity, and the Identity View of God," *Philosophia Christi* 11, no. 1
(2009): 126–144. He stresses some of the limitations of simplicity in accounting for
an identity between God and the Good. Among his other insights is a good response
to Timothy Chappell's critique of Adams. The Good is clearly not a standard in
Chappell's sense: a method of measurement. Rather, the Good is a model by which
other entities may be compared, though never clearly and precisely due to our
fallibility in perceiving the standard. Not all standards need to be publicly identifiable
and serve as a practical utensil for measurement, as Chappell claims. The Good could
be a standard, even though measuring by that standard inevitably includes practical
and epistemological obstacles. Chappell's review of Adams's *Finite and Infinite Goods*
can be found here: *Faith and Philosophy* 19 (2002): 373–378.

21. C. Stephen Layman, "A Moral Argument for the Existence of God," in *Is
Goodness without God Good Enough? A Debate on Faith, Secularism, and Ethics*, ed.
Robert K. Garcia and Nathan L. King (New York: Rowman & Littlefield, 2009), p. 51.

22. Michael Martin, "A Response to Paul Copan's Critique of Atheistic Objective
Morality," *Philosophia Christi* 2 (2000): 84–85.

23. See John Milliken, "Euthyphro, the Good, and the Right," *Philosophia Christi*
11, no. 1 (2009): 145–155.

24. Ibid.

25. Alvin Plantinga, "How to Be an Anti-Realist," *Proceedings and Addresses of the
American Philosophical Association* 56, no. 1 (New York: State University of New York
Press, 1982). Robert Adams echoes a similar sentiment. At the end of one of his
articles, while discussing how to account for human knowledge of necessary truths,
finding other accounts lacking, and admitting a heavy indebtedness to Leibniz, he
writes in a way that parallels Plantinga. See Robert Adams, "Divine Necessity," *Journal
of Philosophy* 80 (1983): 751.

26. For several reasons to think that naturalism is inadequate to account not
just for morality, but for other important dimensions of human experience as well,
see J. P. Moreland's *The Recalcitrant Imago Dei: Human Persons and the Failure of
Naturalism* (London: SCM Press, 2009) and Stewart Goetz and Charles Taliaferro,
*Naturalism* (Grand Rapids, MI: Eerdmans, 2008).

27. John Rist observes that "Plato's account of the 'Forms' (including the Good) as
moral exemplars leaves them in metaphysical limbo. They would exist as essentially
intelligible ideas even if there were no mind, human or divine, to recognize them: as
objects of thought, not mere constructs or concepts. But, as Augustine learned, and as the

Greek Neoplatonists had asserted, the notion of an eternal object of thought (and thus for Plato a cause of thought) without a ceaseless thinking subject is unintelligible. Intelligible Forms, never proposed as mere concepts, cannot be proposed as Plato originally proposed them, as free-floating metaphysical items." John M. Rist, *Real Ethics: Rethinking the Foundations of Morality* (Cambridge: Cambridge University Press, 2002), p. 40.

28. Craig, "The Kurtz/Craig Debate: Is Goodness without God Good Enough?" in *Is Goodness without God Good Enough?*, pp. 25–46.

## CHAPTER 6

1. Immanuel Kant and Louis Infield, *Lectures on Ethics* (Indianapolis, IN: Hackett, 1980), p. 97.

2. *The Simpsons and Philosophy: The D'oh! of Homer* (Chicago: Open Court, 2001), pp. 54–55.

3. William P. Alston, in his now-classic "Some Suggestions for Divine Command Theorists," in *Christian Theism and the Problems of Philosophy*, ed. Michael D. Beaty (Notre Dame, IN: University of Notre Dame Press, 1990), pp. 303–326, encouraged this strategy of a more limited application of divine command theory to moral obligations.

4. For an excellent discussion of moral rightness, see Stephen Darwall, *The Second Person Standpoint* (Cambridge, MA: Harvard University Press, 2006).

5. Robert Merrihew Adams, *A Theory of Virtue: Excellence in Being for the Good* (Oxford: Oxford University Press, 2006), introduction.

6. As Robert Adams characterizes the work of analytic philosophers, "Their style of philosophy is called 'analytical' because it was long guided by the belief that the only way philosophy can make real progress in understanding is by analysis of the meanings of words or sentences. Philosophers were urged, accordingly, to shift from the 'material mode' to the 'formal mode'—from talking about the nature of things to talking about the meanings of words that signify them—for instance, from talking about the nature of the good to talking about the meaning of 'good'. The principal task of moral philosophy, on this view, was analysis of the meaning of the language of morals." See Adams, *Finite and Infinite Goods*, p. 15.

7. Alasdair MacIntyre, *A Short History of Ethics* (Notre Dame, IN: University of Notre Dame Press, 2007).

8. Elizabeth Anscombe, "Modern Moral Philosophy," *Philosophy* 33 (1958): 124.

9. MacIntyre, *Short History*, xviii.

10. Alasdair MacIntyre, *Whose Justice? Which Rationality?* (Notre Dame, IN: University of Notre Dame Press, 1998), and Lawrence S. Cunningham's *Intractable Disputes about the Natural Law: Alasdair MacIntyre and Critics* (Notre Dame, IN: University of Notre Dame, 2009).

11. "Which God Ought We to Obey and Why?" in *Faith and Philosophy* 3, no. 4 (1986): 359–371.

12. Later he recants this view and says the necessity in question is exhausted by the notion of physical necessity. Incidentally, on Putnam's earlier view of the relation

between the nature of water and the meaning of "water," which Adams finds plausible, the property of possessing the features of water described by competent users of the term (like its tastelessness) is not a property that belongs to water necessarily.

13. See Paul Helm, ed., *Divine Command and Morality* (Oxford: Oxford University Press, 1981), p. 113.

14. Adams, *Finite and Infinite Goods*, pp. 40–41.

15. Ibid., pp. 234–243.

16. In a paper, "From Adamsian Axiology to Theistic Natural Law Theory," Mark Murphy makes an interesting and insightful case that the excellence that Adams makes appeal to in his account of morality should lead Adams more in the direction of natural law than theological voluntarism. Although we are open to elements of natural law and think they may well in fact importantly supplement Adams's analysis, particularly an incorporation of aspects of the human condition necessary to ground normativity, we don't see a need for a wholesale departure from a divine command theory of moral oughtness. It's in God's image that we've been made, after all, so it's his nature that ultimately trumps when it comes to morality. If God's nature constrains God's commands, then DCT seems quite able to accommodate those salient features of human beings relevant to morality. Thomists' explication of moral oughts deriving from good "nondefectively" strikes us as, in certain respects, less effective than a voluntarist account, though in general our present concerns put a heavier emphasis on where such traditions agree than where they differ. Murphy's paper will appear in Mark C. Murphy, *God and Moral Law: On the Theistic Explanation of Morality* (Oxford University Press, forthcoming).

17. Craig, *Is Goodness without God Good Enough?*, p. 30.

18. Ibid., p. 73.

19. See Murphy's "Theism, Atheism, and the Explanation of Moral Value," p. 128.

20. Ibid., p. 177. If Craig is wrong to suggest that all moral obligations are necessary truths, and contra Craig some of them remain contingent after all, that would have the interesting result that not all moral obligations supervene on empirical properties after all, since two sets of relevantly similar empirical properties could potentially differ on the issue of whether a duty supervenes. Our resistance to the necessity of all moral obligations is related to our similar resistance to a Kantian insistence on moral universality.

21. Ibid., p. 128.

22. Ibid., p. 129.

23. Ibid.

24. The first section of William Wainwright's book on religion and morality features a portrait of the nineteenth-century philosophical landscape in which duty is seen as of paramount authority, even with the recession of confidence in theism and immortality. See his *Religion and Morality* (Aldershot and Burlington: Ashgate, 2005).

25. C. S. Lewis, *The Abolition of Man, or, Reflections on Education with Special Reference to the Teaching of English in the Upper Forms of Schools* (San Francisco, CA: HarperSanFrancisco, 2001).

26. C. S. Lewis, *Letters to Malcolm: Chiefly on Prayer: Reflections on the Intimate Dialogue between Man and God* (San Diego, CA: Harcourt, 1992), p. 120.

27. Mark C. Murphy, *An Essay on Divine Authority* (Ithaca, NY: Cornell University Press, 2002).

28. Even William Rowe, in *Can God Be Free?* (Oxford: Oxford University Press, 2004), seems to accept the propriety of worshipping and obeying God if the God of classical theism exists.

29. Thanks to Tom Morris for helping us think about this issue.

CHAPTER 7

1. John Stuart Mill, *The Autobiography of John Stuart Mill* (New York: Henry Holt, 1887), p. 40.

2. This issue is a timely one. Daniel Dennett calls the Old Testament God jealous and wrathful; Dawkins writes that God is an ethnic cleanser sanctioning bloodthirsty massacres with "xenophobic relish"; Christopher Hitchens casts God as furnishing "warrant for trafficking in humans" and slavery; and Samuel Harris claims that the consistent Bible believer should stone his daughter if she comes home from a yoga class a devotee of Krishna. See Daniel Dennett, *Breaking the Spell: Religion as a Natural Phenomenon* (New York: Viking, 2006), p. 265; Richard Dawkins, *The God Delusion* (Boston: Houghton Mifflin, 2006); Christopher Hitchens, *God Is Not Great: How Religion Poisons Everything* (New York: Twelve, 2007), pp. 101–102; Sam Harris, *Letter to a Christian Nation* (New York: Knopf, 2006).

3. See N. T. Wright's *Justification: God's Plan and Paul's Vision* (Downers Grove, IL: InterVarsity Press, 2009).

4. James 4:17

5. Paul Moser, *The Elusive God: Reorienting Religious Epistemology* (Cambridge: Cambridge University Press, 2008).

6. Walter Sinnott-Armstrong, "Why Traditional Theism Cannot Provide an Adequate Foundation for Morality," in *Is Goodness without God Good Enough?*, p. 106.

7. William Lane Craig, "This Most Gruesome of Guests," ibid., 172. We have devoted an appendix to spelling out in more thorough fashion a refutation of Sinnott-Armstrong's argument.

8. Deuteronomy 7:1–2.

9. References to Morriston, Rauser, and Copan in this discussion largely stem from a Symposium in a 2009 issue of *Philosophia Christi* (11, no. 1). Paul Copan's earlier article sparked the discussion; see his "Is Yahweh a Moral Monster? The New Atheists and Old Testament Ethics," *Philosophia Christi* 10 (2008): 7–37. In the Symposium itself, see Wesley Morriston, "Did God Command Genocide? A Challenge to the Biblical Inerrantist," *Philosophia Christi* 11 (2009): 7–26; Randal Rauser, "'Let Nothing That Breathes Remain Alive': On the Problem of Divinely Commanded Genocide": 27–41; and Paul Copan, "Yahweh Wars and the Canaanites: Divinely-Mandated Genocide or Corporate Capital Punishment?: Responses to Critics," 73–90. Joseph A. Buijs and Clay Jones also make very substantive contributions to this

Symposium. We refrain from reiterating many of the best points these writers make and confine our comments to ideas of our own and points of critique we offer, but we encourage readers to take a look at this fine Symposium for further reading on this important and difficult topic. Paul Copan hits the highlights of his work in his piece, "Are Old Testament Laws Evil?" in *God is Good, God is Great* (Downers Grove, IL: InterVarsity, 2009), pp. 134–154.

10. This is not to deny that the Canaanites truly were deeply corrupt; these weren't just *any* neighbors that God was asking the Israelites to wipe out. For a rhetorically effective statement of this point, see G. K. Chesterton's *The Everlasting Man*, the chapter: "War of Gods and Demons." In emphasizing the universality of the sinful condition, we are not denying the particular evils of any particular group of people; it's just not the primary way we are dealing with the moral issues that their destruction raised.

11. Such possibilities that we consider morally relevant in the overall assessment of this situation should not be read in isolation and interpreted along purely consequentialist lines. Driving God's intentions throughout salvation history, we suggest and argue, are a whole range of deontological constraints, including what his love for people entails, what intrinsic goods need to be preserved, and the like.

12. We find Aquinas's account of the apparent (but not actual) "sins of the fathers" (Canaanite genocide, Isaac's near-sacrifice, Hebrew midwives lying to Pharaoh, Israelites stealing Egyptian gold) helpful in delineating one important aspect of this discussion. He doesn't try to palliate what seems awful by trying to make out a case that the seeming atrocity, in this instance, just had to be done. Instead, he says that these acts, far from being a dispensation from Commandments like "Thou shalt not murder," just don't fall under that rubric; effectively, because God *owns us*, so he can dispose of us as he wills without the least taint of injustice. See the *Summa Theologica*, Prima Secundae, Q. 100, article 8, at: <http://www.newadvent.org/summa/2100.htm#article8>. This is one part of a big story that needs to be told here, to which we're just gesturing in this chapter since we don't have a whole book to devote to this topic.

13. N. T. Wright notes the "compassionate drift" in the law and Yahweh's character and saving action embedded within and surrounding Israel's legislation, including "protection for the weak, especially those who lacked the natural protection of family and land (namely, widows, orphans, Levites, immigrants, and resident aliens); justice for the poor; impartiality in the courts; generosity at harvest time and in general economic life; respect for persons and property, even of an enemy; sensitivity to the dignity even of the debtor; special care for strangers and immigrants; considerate treatment of the disabled; prompt payment of wages earned by hired labor; sensitivity over articles taken in pledge; consideration for people in early marriage, or in bereavement; even care for animals, domestic and wild, and for fruit trees." See his *Climax of the Covenant* (Minneapolis: Fortress, 1993), p. 181.

14. Nicholas Wolterstorff argued this in his paper "Reading Joshua," delivered at the "My Ways Are Not Your Ways: The Character of the God of the Hebrew Bible" conference held at Notre Dame, September 10–12, 2009. See also Lawson Stone,

"Ethical and Apologetic Tendencies in the Redaction of the Book of Joshua," *Catholic Biblical Quarterly* (1991): 53.

15. Robert Bretall, *A Kierkegaard Anthology* (Princeton: Princeton University press, 1973), p. 134.

16. Genesis 22:1. Since we know that it was not God's will to sacrifice Isaac, we think this story is perfectly consistent with the text from Jeremiah that Adams cites. That text condemns actual child sacrifice, which of course was not done in the case of Isaac, and indeed we concur that it never entered God's mind actually to desire such a sacrifice.

17. John 1:29

18. Hebrews 12:2.

19. Hebrews 11:17–19.

CHAPTER 8

1. David Hume and J. M. Bell, *Dialogues Concerning Natural Religion* (London: Penguin Books, 1990), pp. 108–109.

2. See Jerry L. Walls, "Hume on Divine Amorality," *Religious Studies* 26 (1990): 257–266 for an argument that Hume ignored a crucial and telling part of the created order, namely, our moral intuitions. When this is taken into account, the argument for amorality is undercut and we are led to believe that God is either truly good or he is perverse.

3. See his "Reflections on the Chapters by Draper, Russell, and Gale," in *The Evidential Argument from Evil*, ed. Daniel Howard-Snyder (Bloomington: Indiana University Press, 1996), pp. 234–235.

4. In this chapter, allowable sufferings, on Russell's view (roughly), will be those that satisfy this "counterbalancing criterion" of his, and sufferings that don't will be cast as gratuitous or excessive evils.

5. Russell's work can be found in various places: "The Persistent Problem of Evil," *Faith and Philosophy* 6 (1989): 121–139; with Stephen Wykstra, "The 'Inductive' Argument from Evil: A Dialogue," *Philosophical Topics* 16 (1988): 133–160; "Defenseless," in *The Evidential Argument from Evil*, pp. 193–205; and his latest, "The Problem of Evil: Why Is There So Much Suffering?" in *Introduction to Philosophy: Classical and Contemporary Issues* (3rd ed.), ed. Louis Pojman (New York: Oxford University Press, 2004), pp. 207–213.

6. The best explanation is *not* that there is not much more suffering of that sort than is needed, God exists and has his reasons for allowing it, but that we are ignorant of what the reasons are. So says Russell.

7. This premise will undergo an important revision later.

8. Russell, "Defenseless," p. 197.

9. "Infant-earthers" would reside in between those "young-earthers" who believe in an earth between six and ten thousand years old, based on a literalist biblical account, and "new-conception-earthers" who would take seriously Bertrand Russell's hypothetical that the earth is just five minutes old.

10. Intelligent theists insist this surely isn't the case. The theist usually argues that there are good reasons for belief in God, and that evils don't count decisively

against those previously formed beliefs. God is not some distant, wildly improbable hypothesis that we are betting everything we have on, and doing so foolishly. Theists are convinced by many different strains of reasoning that God is a reality who has a morally sufficient reason for the way he conducts the universe, even when we don't fully understand why. Russell's insistence that we set such evidence aside is just not realistic. Sure, if we consider the problem of evil in isolation, holding all things equal and inquiring whether God exists, we may not naturally gravitate to belief in God, but the problem of evil is not the only argument relevant to the case for or against God—it's not even the only argument in the arena of value theory, as this book's emphasis on moral apologetics has amply demonstrated. Moreover, without adequate foundation, much of Russell's case lacks credibility, and if the argument of this book is right, theism provides the much better foundation for our moral convictions than naturalism does. There is still the issue, of course, of the internal consistency of theism; but recall the way that Russell insists on delimiting the discussion just to the problem of evil. If a rich theistic picture is allowed, that will introduce new resources to answer the problem of evil.

11. The nonhuman created order is run by laws that reflect the inherent physical nature of things. This makes this world a doubly contingent universe with respect to human interests. Not only is free will a cause of suffering, it takes place within a physical context that allows free will to cause that suffering. What is more, the physical world, apart from human free will, runs, as it were, of its own accord, which causes horrible suffering. While the lawlike regular behavior of nonhuman created reality may from one perspective be rather determined, from a theological perspective God has also granted to the physical world a kind of freedom to develop and evolve, to act apart from constant intervention by God.

12. Indeed, it verges on a logical inconsistency to say both that God is wholly truthful (which is implied by the Anselmian conception) and that he has deliberately deceived his creatures as to the age of the earth.

13. C. S. Lewis suggested as much when he wrote, "Take your choice. The tortures occur. If they are unnecessary, then there is no God or a bad one. If there is a good God, then these tortures are necessary. For no even moderately good Being could possibly inflict or permit them if they weren't," in *A Grief Observed* (London: Bantam Books, 1976), p. 50. Mike Peterson offers an interesting take on this passage from Lewis in his chapter in *C. S. Lewis as Philosopher* (Downers Grove, IL: InterVarsity Press, 2008), ed. David Baggett, Gary Habermas, and Jerry L. Walls.

14. Peterson's work can be found in a variety of places, including *Evil and the Christian God* (Grand Rapids, MI: Baker, 1982) and "Evil as Evidence for the Existence of God," in *Kerygma and Praxis*, eds. W. Vanderhoof and D. Basinger (Rochester, NY: Roberts Wesleyan College Press, 1984): 115–131. See also William Hasker's "The Necessity of Gratuitous Evil," *Faith and Philosophy* 9, no. 1 (1992): 23–44; and "Must God Do His Best?" *International Journal for the Philosophy of Religion* 16 (1984): 213–223.

15. Although they conclude that philosophers can't yet responsibly claim that theism is inconsistent with gratuitous evil, Daniel and Frances Howard-Snyder accuse

Peterson of an idiosyncratic account of gratuitous evils, one different from William Rowe's conception, in their piece entitled "Is Theism Compatible with Gratuitous Evil?. See http://faculty.wwu.edu/howardd/istheismcompatible.pdf.

16. A. C. Ewing, *Value and Reality: The Philosophical Case for Theism* (London: George Allen & Unwin, 1973), pp. 212–213.

17. This murder took place on January 31, 2000.

18. Peterson's point that it's not evil, but its possibility, that free will and a stable natural order require goes to show what genuine openness to a deontological moral commitment looks like in this discussion. Russell, along with William Rowe, Eric Reitan argues (in "Does the Argument from Evil Assume a Consequentialist Morality?" in *Faith and Philosophy*, July 2000: 306–319), rather consistently couches the evidential argument in consequentialist terms. This has the effect of requiring God to produce (or us to produce for God) counterbalancing goods secured or worse evils avoided to justify each evil allowed, when instead all that's rationally required are countervailing goods or overriding deontological concerns that justify allowing the evils. Peterson, to our thinking, has effectively answered Peter Hare's and Edward Madden's case that a good God would not create the actual world. See the latter's *Evil and the Concept of God* (Springfield, IL: Charles C. Thomas, 1968).

19. To put it another way: God would not allow suffering unless allowing it were needed to prevent something even worse, on balance, or to promote something even better, on balance, unless that suffering were only slightly more than what is needed for one, or both, of those two ends. More recently Russell has preferred to express the premise this way: If God exists, he would not allow excessive and unnecessary suffering.

20. In a similar vein, it is worth pointing out that Roderick Chisholm has also distinguished *counterbalancing*, hooked up with a consequentialist notion, from *defeat*, hooked up with a deontological notion of how goods and evils, in combinations, can produce organic wholes or unities. The overall value of such unities may not necessarily be the sum of the value of their parts, and their goodness overall may be consistent and cohere with such deontological notions as justice and holiness. See Chisholm's "The Defeat of Good and Evil," *Proceedings and Addresses of the American Philosophical Association* 42 (1968–1969): 21–38.

21. These lines are from pp. 5–6 of his unpublished, "Unfriendly Atheism," which he has presented at a couple of places, including the 2008 meeting of the Central States Philosophical Association in Minneapolis, MN. In his 2000 review in *Philosophical Books* (pp. 222–224) of Swinburne's *Providence and the Problem of Evil* he wrote, "Good parents would not knowingly allow their teenage son to hit his baby brother with a hammer or set the neighbor's cat on fire," p. 223 in vol. 41 (no. 3), July 2000. Louise Antony echoes similar themes of God as a bad, indeed abusive parent in her presentation at the fall 2009 Notre Dame conference on the character of the God of the Old Testament, in a paper called "Does God Love Us?."

22. Bear this point in mind when in Chapter 9 we see Russell neglect this insight altogether.

23. Mark T. Nelson effectively makes this case in "Naturalistic Ethics and the Argument from Evil," in *Faith and Philosophy* (July 1991): 368–379.

CHAPTER 9

1. Mark Twain, *The Adventures of Huckleberry Finn* (New York, NY: Penguin Books, 2003), p. 100.

2. As MacIntyre puts it, we discover, "as our analogically and historically ordered concept of justice develops, that the standard by which we judged God is itself a work of God, and that the judgments which we made earlier were made in obedience to the divine commands, even though we did not and could not have recognized this at that earlier stage. God, it turns out, cannot be truly judged by something external to his Word, but that is because natural justice recognized by natural reason is itself divinely uttered and authorized." "Which God Ought We to Obey and Why?" in *Faith and Philosophy* 3, no. 4 (1986): 371.

3. John Milliken, "Euthyphro, the Good, and the Right," in *Philosophia Christi* 11, no. 1 (2009): 153–54.

4. James G. Hanink and Gary R. Mar, "What Euthyphro Couldn't Have Said," *Faith and Philosophy* (1987) 4: 254.

5. Arthur F. Holmes, *Ethics: Approaching Moral Decisions*, 2nd ed. (Downers Grove, IL: InterVarsity Press, 2007), p. 66.

6. Alasdair MacIntyre, "Which God Ought We to Obey and Why?" *Faith and Philosophy* 3, no. 4 (1986): 359–371.

7. In a slightly different respect, W. David Beck's version of the moral argument also emphasizes the social nature of morality. As evidence for his premise that naturalistic explanations of the objectivity of morality are inadequate, he writes that only "persons can be the source of values, yet no finite and socially conditioned person is in a position to determine authoritatively the values appropriate for other persons. So, if there really are objective values, there must be some 'ultimate' person who has the moral authority to set the standards of right and wrong." (By way of a critique, someone might suggest that the fact that no single person can set such values doesn't, in principle, preclude an aggregate of persons doing what no single person could; but Adams, recall, provides reasons to think that no purely human set of social relations can do the job.) See Beck's "God's Existence," in *In Defense of Miracles: A Comprehensive Case for God's Action in History*, edited by R. Douglas Geivett and Gary R. Habermas (Downers Grove, IL: InterVarsity Press, 1997), p. 160.

8. Accusations of anthropomorphism don't stick because the resonance between God's law and human nature is explained just as well by our having been made in God's image rather than vice versa.

9. Holmes, *Ethics*, p. 80. John Hare and Robert Adams both effectively refute J. B. Schneewind's characterization of Kantian autonomy. Pointing to passages in *Lectures on Ethics* that refer to God as deserving our reverence and his status as a holy lawgiver and, from the *Second Critique* and "Religion within the Limits of Reason Alone," references to recognizing our duties as God's commands, Hare argues that Kant's view on autonomy does not serve as evidence against divine command theory. Rather, God's commands, on Kant's view, are the source of our duties, and our task is to recapitulate God's will in ours. Hare resonates with Adams's notion of the "theonomous will": acting morally because we love God and also because we love what God loves. See John E. Hare, *God's Call* (Grand Rapids, MI: Eerdmans, 2001),

pp. 87–119, Hare's chapter on Kant in *God and Morality: A Philosophical History* (Oxford: Wiley Blackwell, 2009), and Robert Adams, "Autonomy and Theological Ethics," in *The Virtue of Faith* (Oxford: Oxford University Press, 1987), pp. 123–127.

10. Holmes, p. 81.

11. Although we have great appreciation of the work of Stanley Hauerwas (especially what he has to say about the ineliminable role of community in inculcating moral virtues), on whom MacIntyre has had a great deal of influence, we think that he tends to discount general revelation in his zeal to emphasize the distinctive aspects of Christian theology and the ineliminable role played by community in inculcating moral practices—which he likens with some legitimacy to language acquisition. When he writes, for example, that an "ethic claiming to be 'rational' and universally valid for all thinking people everywhere is incipiently demonic because it has no means of explaining why there are still people who disagree with its prescriptions of behavior except that these people must be 'irrational' and, therefore (since 'rationality' is said to be our most important human characteristic), subhuman," we think he's overstating a legitimate criticism of rationality-based attempts to construe ethics, not to mention leaving inadequate room for at least some clear deliverances of general revelation. See Stanley Hauerwas and William H. Willimon, *Resident Aliens* (Nashville, TN: Abingdon Press, 1989), p. 101. For an additional critique of rationality-based construals of moral objectivity and analysis of the role of community, see John Hare's *Why Bother Being Good?* (Downers Grove, IL: InterVarsity Press, 2002), chaps. 8 and 9.

12. C. S. Lewis, *A Grief Observed* (New York: Bantam, 1988), p. 74.

13. See Wesley's sermon "The Original, Nature, Properties, and Use of the Law," in *The Works of John Wesley*, ed. Albert C. Outler (Nashville, TN: Abingdon, 1985), 2: 4–19.

14. Cf. *The Works of John Wesley*, 2: 510.

15. Alvin Plantinga's epistemology is an intentional effort to put God right at its center, making full sense of why, on a Christian worldview, we are able to grasp truth. His is an effort, then, to make epistemic standards, too, a function of the divine mind. Christopher Menzel made a similar case for mathematical standards, and Menzel and Morris did the same with modal truths.

16. Victor Reppert, *C. S. Lewis's Dangerous Idea: In Defense of the Argument from Reason* (Downers Grove, IL: InterVarsity Press, 2003). Alvin Plantinga, *Warrant and Proper Function* (New York: Oxford University Press, 1993), pp. 216–237.

17. Bruce Russell, "Two Forms of Ethical Skepticism," in Louis Pojman, *Ethical Theory: Classical and Contemporary Readings* (New York: Wadsworth, 1998), p. 595.

18. C. Stephen Layman, "A Moral Argument for the Existence of God," in Garcia and King's *Is Goodness without God Good Enough?*, p. 52. He's referring to more than merely prima facie duties.

19. Ibid., p. 54.

20. Ibid., p. 55.

21. Ibid.

22. Ibid., p. 56.

23. Ibid., pp. 58–59.

24. Paul Moser, *The Elusive God: Reorienting Religious Epistemology* (Cambridge: Cambridge University Press, 2009).

25. Ibid., p. 111.

26. C. S. Lewis, "On Obstinacy of Belief," in *Philosophy of Religion: An Anthology*, ed. Louis Pojman (Belmont, CA: Wadsworth, 1987), p. 377.

27. A notable exception is Michael Polanyi's *Personal Knowledge: Towards a Post-Critical Philosophy* (Chicago: University of Chicago Press, 1974).

CHAPTER 10

1. Lennon, *Imagine*.

2. Blaise Pascal, *Pensees* (trans. Honor Levi) (Oxford: Oxford University Press, 1995), p. 143.

3. Readers are encouraged to read Alasdair MacIntyre's *Dependent Rational Animals: Why Human Beings Need the Virtues* (Chicago: Open Court, 2001) and Robert Adams, *A Theory of Virtue: Excellence in Being for the Good* (Oxford: Oxford University Press, 2006).

4. In her book on divine motivation theory, Linda Zagzebski offers a distinctively theistic account of the virtuous life. Her analysis, though departing from a standard divine command theory, is a thoroughgoing theistic one, providing a *divine motivation* theory of moral virtue. Hers is another example of the way that virtue theory and classical theism can dovetail in important ways. For an article-length treatment, see Linda Zagzebski, "The Virtues of God and the Foundations of Ethics," *Faith and Philosophy* 15 (1998): 538–553. Also see her *Divine Motivation Theory* (Cambridge: Cambridge University Press, 2004).

5. George Mavrodes, "Religion and the Queerness of Morality," in Louis Pojman, ed., *Ethical Theory: Classical and Contemporary Readings* (New York: Wadsworth, 1995), p. 588.

6. Immanuel Kant is an example of a philosopher who has expressed such a view.

7. Thomas V. Morris, *Anselmian Explorations* (Notre Dame, IN: University of Notre Dame Press, 1987).

8. See David Baggett and Gregory Bassham, "Resist Not Evil! Jesus and Nonviolence," in *The Passion of the Christ and Philosophy* (Chicago, IL: Open Court, 2004). Rights are an important topic that we have not undertaken to discuss in detail. One of us has done so elsewhere, however. See David Baggett and Mark Foreman, "*Amistad*: Human Rights and Human Nature," in *Steven Spielberg and Philosophy*, edited by Dean Kowalski (Lexington, KY: The University Press of Kentucky, 2008). We are firmly of the view that rights, too, depend on God's conferring them on us. They are best understood along the lines of justice, and more in terms of God's nature than human nature (accounting for the category of animal rights), and we are more drawn to Nicholas Wolterstorff's analysis of justice than that of John Rawls. See Wolterstorff's *Justice: Rights and Wrongs* (Princeton, NJ: Princeton University Press, 2007).

9. See Alasdair MacIntyre's "Intractable Moral Disagreements," in *Intractable Disputes about the Natural Law: Alasdair MacIntyre and Critics*, ed. Lawrence S. Cunningham (Notre Dame, IN: University of Notre Dame Press, 2009), p. 50.

10. Oliver O'Donovan, *Resurrection and Moral Order* (Grand Rapids, MI: Eerdmans, 1994).

11. "Through the Spirit, by faith, we wait for the hope of righteousness" (Romans 4:25), and "in [Jesus] we become the righteousness of God" (2 Cor. 5:21).

12. O'Donovan, *Resurrection*, p. 101.

13. Ibid., p. 246. "The true moral life of the Christian community is its love," O'Donovan writes, "and its love is unintelligible except as a participation in the life of the one who reveals himself to us as Love, except, that is, as the entry of mankind and of the restored creation upon its supernatural end." Gary Habermas, a leading expert on the historicity of the resurrection, adds: "A truly *Christian* ethic would of course need to be grounded in the teachings of Jesus Christ. Chief among those teachings is what we call the Gospel message—the Good News that Jesus Christ came to bring. And at the very center of that Good News is the resurrection of Jesus, which completes his work on the Cross and, in the New Testament, serves as the center for good apologetics, sound theology, as well as everyday ethical practice. So it is by no means a stretch to say that the resurrection of Jesus provides the grounding of Christian ethics." Personal correspondence, March 19, 2010.

14. The resurrection of Jesus is the best evidence for the truth of Christianity. To explore the evidential case for the resurrection and some of the philosophical questions such a case raises, see *Did the Resurrection Happen: A Conversation with Gary Habermas and Antony Flew*, ed. David Baggett (Downers Grove, IL: InterVarsity Press, 2009). Habermas has documented a historical account of the resurrection in several dozen publications, such as: *The Historical Jesus: Ancient Evidence for the Life of Christ* (Joplin, MO: College Press, 1996); *The Case for the Resurrection of Jesus* (Grand Rapids, MI: Kregel, 2004), with Michael R. Licona; and *The Risen Jesus and Future Hope* (Lanham, MD: Rowman and Littlefield, 2003).

15. Matthew 22:37–40.

16. This is a guiding motif in John Hare, *The Moral Gap: Kantian Ethics, Human Limits, and God's Assistance* (Oxford: Clarendon Press, 1996). Although we have not spent much time in this book dwelling on this issue, it's not because it isn't important; we just happened to be more interested here in spelling out the foundations of morality in an effort to construct a moral apologetic than delving into these important performative questions.

17. Thanks to Ben McCraw for this insight.

18. William James, *The Principles of Psychology* (New York, NY: H. Holt, 1890), p. 127.

19. See, for example, Lewis's *The Great Divorce*; a main thrust of the book is to accentuate the way the sufferings of hell are a function of sin and there being an intrinsic connection between sin and misery. Dante's symbolic depictions of hell and purgatory are perhaps best known of all along such lines.

20. Alasdair MacIntyre, *A Short History of Ethics* (New York: Macmillan, 1966), p. 144.

21. See Jerry L. Walls, *Hell: The Logic of Damnation* (Notre Dame, IN: Notre Dame Press, 1992), p. 155. John Duns Scotus's distinction is useful here between human affection for advantage and affection for justice. The former is an inclination or tendency toward one's own proper perfection or happiness; the latter is the inclination toward intrinsic goods for their own sake. By nature we put advantage over justice, which needs to be reversed. Submission to God involves primacy for the affection for

justice, leading us in principle to be able to say, like Job, though God slay us, yet we will trust in him. Or consider Moses's willingness to be blotted from God's book for the sake of the people (Exodus 32:32). Commitment to God's purposes should trump even healthy affections for personal advantage and natural love of self, but the beauty of Christianity is that, ultimately, these affections need not exist in irremediable tension.

22. George Mavrodes, in Pojman, p. 587.

23. For an extended defense of the moral significance of the doctrine of heaven, and its resources to resolve Sidgwick's dilemma, see Jerry L. Walls, *Heaven: The Logic of Eternal Joy* (New York: Oxford University Press, 2002), pp. 161–97.

24. William James, *The Varieties of Religious Experience: A Study in Human Nature* (Cambridge, MA: Harvard University Press, 1985 [1902]), pp. 41–42.

25. Donald Hubin, "Empty and Ultimately Meaningless Gestures?" in *Is Goodness without God Good Enough?*, p. 134.

26. Craig, ibid., p. 175.

27. Nicholas Wolterstorff, *Lament for a Son* (Grand Rapids, MI: Eerdmans, 1987).

28. For a nicely accessible work on the Stoics, see Tom Morris, *The Stoic Art of Living: Inner Resilience and Outer Results* (Chicago: Open Court, 2004).

29. Charles Taylor, *Sources of the Self* (Cambridge: Harvard University Press, 1989), 218–219.

30. See Isaiah 64:6.

31. Thanks to New Testament scholar David Bauer for this insight.

CONCLUSION

1. C. S. Lewis, "Is Theology Poetry?" in *The Weight of Glory and Other Addresses* (New York: Macmillan, 1965), p. 140.

2. The PhilPapers Survey was a survey of professional philosophers and others on their philosophical views, carried out in November 2009. The Survey was taken by 3226 respondents, including 1803 philosophy faculty members and/or PhDs and 829 philosophy graduate students. 72.8% accepted or leaned towards atheism, and just 14.6% accepted or leaned towards theism; while 56.3% continued to accept or lean towards moral realism. The results of the survey can be found here: http://philpapers.org/surveys/.

3. William James, *The Will to Believe*, sect. 9.

4. Ian S. Markham, *Against Atheism* (Oxford: Wiley Blackwell, 2010), ch. 2.

5. For a particularly insightful discussion of Nietzsche, readers are encouraged to read Alasdair MacIntyre's *Three Rival Versions of Moral Inquiry: Encyclopaedia, Genealogy, and Tradition* (Notre Dame: University of Notre Dame Press, 1990), ch. 2.

6. Gary Shapiro, "Friedrich Nietzsche," in Chad Meister and Paul Copan (eds.), *The Routledge Companion to Philosophy of Religion* (New York: Routledge, 2007), p. 171.

7. Many thanks to Albert Powers for reminding us of Lewis's writing on transposition, helping us see their relevance to the present discussion, and generously allowing us to avail ourselves of his inspiration.

8. C. S. Lewis, "Transposition," in *Transposition and Other Addresses* (London: Geoffrey Bles, 1949), p. 14. (See P. H. Brazier, "C. S. Lewis: A Doctrine of Transposition," *The Heythrop Journal* 1 (2009): 680.)

9. Ibid, p. 15.

10. C. S. Lewis, *The Chronicles of Narnia: The Silver Chair*, p. 632.

11. Ibid.

12. Ibid, p. 633.

13. Lewis, *The Weight of Glory*, p. 114.

14. Ibid.

## APPENDIX A

1. Philip Quinn preferred to express theological voluntarism in terms of God's will, rather than God's commands, since it's God's will that's prior to his commands. For present purposes we will use a command-theoretic model. The connection that DCT says obtains between the deontological status of actions (forbiddenness, obligatoriness, permittedness) and God's commands holds not merely accidentally, but with broadly logical necessity. See Philip L. Quinn, *Divine Commands and Moral Requirements* (Oxford: Oxford University Press, 1978), and Mark Murphy's "Divine Command, Divine Will, and Moral Obligation," 15: 3–27 and *An Essay on Divine Authority* (Ithaca, NY: Cornell University Press, 2002).

2. Walter Sinnott-Armstrong, "Why Traditional Theism Cannot Provide an Adequate Foundation for Morality," in *Is Goodness without God Good Enough?* (Lanham, MD: Rowman & Littlefield, 2009), p. 106.

3. Louise Antony, "Atheism as Perfect Piety," ibid., p. 71.

4. On standard accounts of counterfactuals like this, the necessary falsehood of the antecedent—God commands rape—would render the conditional at most trivially true. It would be on a nonsensical par with "If 2 + 2 = 5, then rape would be morally obligatory." We are reminded of the unwarranted certainty among certain thinkers who confidently presume to pontificate about features of an impossible world. We can only guess that it's the ubiquity of such cavalier pronouncements that imbues Sinnott-Armstrong with the courage to confidently proclaim what sounds like simple nonsense here. Craig, as we saw in an earlier chapter, puts his own reservations about Sinnott-Armstrong's (and Antony's) claim like this: "Even if we, with Antony, reject the usual semantics and allow that some counterfactuals with impossible antecedents may be nonvacuously true or false, how are we to assess the truth of a statement like this? It is like wondering whether, if there were a round square, its area would equal the square of one of its sides. And what would it matter how one answered, since what is imagined is logically incoherent? I do not see that the divine command theorist is committed to the nonvacuous truth of the counterfactual in question nor that anything of significance hangs on his thinking it to be nonvacuously true rather than false." See William Lane Craig, "This Most Gruesome of Guests," *Is Goodness without God Good Enough?*, p. 172.

5. As Trenton Merricks puts it, only the most dogmatic metaphysician refuses to consider what she takes to be counterpossibles; reflecting on them can give us the

chance to identify what's wrong with theories that may well be necessarily false. See his *Objects and Persons* (Oxford: Clarendon Press, 2001), p. 5.

6. For counterfactual and counteressential accounts, see David Lewis, *Counterfactuals* (Oxford: Blackwell Publishing, 2001); Linda Zagzebski, "What if the Impossible Had Been Actual?" in *Christian Theism and the Problems of Philosophy*, ed. Michael Beaty (Notre Dame, IN: Notre Dame University Press, 1990); Richard Brian Davis, *The Metaphysics of Theism and Modality* (New York: Peter Lang, 2001); Robert Stalnaker, "A Theory of Conditionals," in *Studies in Logical Theory, American Philosophical Quarterly* Monograph Series, No. 2, edited by Nicholas Rescher (Oxford: Blackwell, 1968), pp. 64–80; Brian Leftow, "A Leibnizian Cosmological Argument," *Philosophical Studies* 57 (1989): 135–155; Leftow, "God and Abstract Entitities," *Faith and Philosophy* 7 (1990): 193–217; Leftow, "Is God an Abstract Object?" *Nous* 24 (1990): 591–598; Leftow, "Impossible Worlds," *Religious Studies* 4 (2006): 393–402; the exchange between Richard Brian Davis and Brian Leftow in *Religious Studies* 42, pp. 371–402; Edward Wierenga, "A Defensible Divine Command Theory," *Nous* 17 (1983): 393–396; Wierenga's "Theism and Counterpossibles," *Philosophical Studies* 89 (1998): 87–103; and Wierenga's *The Nature of God* (Ithaca, NY: Cornell University Press), chap. 8.

7. One might object to the very idea of impossible worlds, but the idea is more palatable if one realizes that he need not be a modal realist. One can instead construe such worlds as maximal sets of propositions, or as misrepresentations of the actual world. Impossible worlds must fail to be governed by a classical logical system—i.e., each impossible world either fails to be classically closed or fails to be classically consistent. All impossible worlds fail to be classically consistent and all but the absurd world (the world at which all propositions are true) fail to be classically closed—that is, there is at least one proposition p such that p entails q and p but not q is true. Impossible worlds can be construed as ungoverned by any logical system, or they can be seen as governed by some nonclassical logical system (e.g., paraconsistent logic, relevance logic, as Antony suggested). This prevents the consequence relation from being "explosive," and prevents every impossible world from being the absurd world by preventing every proposition from being true at every impossible world.

8. For example, Murphy makes this distinction in his piece entitled "From Adamsian Axiology to Theistic Natural Law Theory," which he graciously allowed us to read. It will be part of his upcoming book *God and Moral Law: On the Theistic Explanation of Morality* (Oxford, forthcoming).

9. "Suppose that necessary truths do determine and explain facts about the real world. If God of his very nature knows the necessary truths, and if he has created us, he could have constructed us in such a way that we would at least commonly recognize necessary truths as necessary. In this way there would be a causal connection between what is necessarily true about real objects and our believing it to be necessarily true about them. It would not be an incredible accident or an inexplicable mystery that our beliefs agreed with the objects in this.

"This theory is not new. It is Augustinian, and something like it was widely accepted in the medieval and early modern periods. I think it provides the best explanation available to us for our knowledge of necessary truths. I also think that that fact constitutes an argument for the existence of God. Not a demonstration; it is a mistake to expect conclusive demonstrations in such matters. But it is a theoretical advantage of theistic belief that it provides attractive explanations of things otherwise hard to explain.

"It is worth noting that this is not the only point in the philosophy of logic at which Augustinian theism provides an attractive explanation. Another is the ontological status of the objects of logic and mathematics. To many of us both of the following views seem extremely plausible. (1) Possibilities and necessary truths are discovered, not made, by our thought. They would still be there if none of us humans ever thought of them. (2) Possibilities and necessary truths cannot be there except insofar as they, or the ideas involved in them, are thought by some mind. The first of these views seems to require Platonism; the second is a repudiation of it. Yet they can both be held together if we suppose that there is a nonhuman mind that eternally and necessarily exists and thinks all the possibilities and necessary truths. Such is the mind of God, according to Augustinian theism. I would not claim that such theism provides the only conceivable way of combining these two theses; but it does provide one way, and I think the most attractive." See Robert Adams, "Divine Necessity," *Journal of Philosophy* 80: 751. Plantinga of course argues similarly. See his "How to Be an Anti-Realist," *Proceedings and Addresses of the American Philosophical Association* 56, no. 1 (New York: State University of New York Press, 1982): 67–68.

10. Let's suppose there are necessary moral facts, facts that obtain in this and all possible worlds, a Platonic sort of idea. Might it be the case that morality, even if Platonism holds true, depends on God? Well, first, let's suppose that God does in fact exist. Is this enough to ensure that morality depends on God? Not necessarily, because suppose God's existence is contingent. This would mean that there are some moral truths that would obtain in worlds in which God does not. If the existence of such truths would show that morality does not depend on God, as seems reasonable, then morality in such a case would not depend on God. Unless, therefore, contingency is logically precluded from being one of God's attributes or necessity is logically precluded from being one of morality's attributes, then it's not a narrowly logically necessary truth that morality depends on God. A contingent God would also preclude a strong metaphysical dependence of morality on God. At most, God would play an epistemic or motivational role for morality in those worlds in which he does exist, but in terms of ontology, it would seem that God would depend on morality, not vice versa. Now continue to suppose that there are necessary moral facts, and that God exists necessarily as well. Might it be the case that morality depends on God ontologically then? Yes, on the assumption that necessary truths can exist in asymmetric relations of explanatory dependence. And this indeed seems reasonable to believe, for the necessary truth of God's existence would entail the necessary truth that "there is a personal being," for example. [William Lane Craig offers these nontheological examples of an asymmetric dependence relation of one necessary truth on another: "The axioms of Peano arithmetic are explanatorily prior to '2+2=4', as are the axioms of Zermelo-Fraenkel set theory to the theorems thereof." See his "This

Most Gruesome of Guests," p. 170, in *Is Goodness without God Good Enough?*. Explanatory asymmetric dependence likely points to a deeper metaphysical asymmetric dependence relation: supervenience, causal sufficiency, causal contribution, constitutive standard, analysis, or something of that ilk. Causal and supervenience theories seem not to penetrate to the necessary level of ontological dependence, but the challenges in explicating ontological dependence (modal, existential, essentialist, etc.), conjoined with possibilities of variations of ontological dependence, make it very hard to specify the precise nature of the dependence relation here.] *Must* it be the case, though, that morality depends on God if both morality and God are necessary? No, because necessary truths, presumably, can obtain independently of one another. That twice two is four and that all red objects are colored seem to be good examples. Even though there's no world in which one of these truths obtains and the other fails, the truth of one does not metaphysically cause the truth of the other. So the belief that God exists necessarily is not enough to show that morality depends on God. This shows a family resemblance to the claim that, if morality is necessary, God's contingency or nonexistence would indeed entail that morality does not depend on God. So far God's existence, contingent or necessary, has not entailed that morality depends on him.

    11. As Tom Morris writes, "Throughout the centuries, numerous philosophers have tried to construct a thoroughly theistic metaphysic—a general account of reality in which theism, the belief in an omnipotent, omniscient, maximally perfect being, functions not just as one more component in an overall metaphysical scheme, but rather as the central and regulative factor, at least partially determinative of other metaphysical commitments. This has been attempted by, for example, such great philosophers as Aquinas, Berkeley, and Leibniz, and has had in every case many results of quite general philosophical interest. At the heart of any metaphysic, and of any world-view, is its ontology. A thoroughly theistic ontology, one in keeping with the dominant theme of the Judeo-Christian tradition, will be one which places God at the center and views everything else as exemplifying a relation of creaturely dependence on him." See his *Anselmian Explorations: Essays in Philosophical Theology* (Notre Dame, IN: University of Notre Dame Press, 1987), pp. 161–162.

    12. Similarly, the conditional, "If God does exist, then moral facts obtain," would also be (trivially) true. For the necessarily true consequent would never allow for the possibility of a true antecedent implying a false consequent. On various occasions, however, there is an advantage to offering (or at least gesturing in the direction of) nonstandard semantics of counterfactuals, even counterpossibles, to enable us to identify some of them as nontrivially true or nontrivially false. One obvious example would be the following, since the existence of an Anselmian God is either necessary or impossible: "If (an Anselmian) God exists, then atheism is false." This seems nonvacuously true, substantively and not trivially, even if, indeed because, the locus of this truth is conceptual in nature. But on the supposition that an Anselmian God is impossible, note that the antecedent would be necessarily false, and the standard reading of the conditional trivially true. So a departure from standard semantics seems on occasion eminently justified. For those convinced instead that an Anselmian God

exists, then the same point can be made using the conditional, "If (an Anselmian) God doesn't exist, then this is not an Anselmian world," which seems to be nonvacuously true even if the antecedent is necessarily false.

13. Counterfactual analyses are of limited value in explicating the nature of the causal connection between morality and God. The limitation we see in the assignment of trivial truth by standard semantics to counterlogicals is likely just a specific instance of the broader limitation of counterfactual analyses in delineating the specifics of the asymmetric dependence relation of moral truth on God's sovereign sustaining work.

14. Wes Morriston, "What if God Commanded Something Terrible?" (paper presented at the University of Texas at San Antonio Philosophy Symposium, San Antonio, TX, 2008), <http://colfa.utsa.edu/ecpc/symposium_papers/what-if-God. pdf>. Erik Wielenberg, *Virtue and Value in a Godless Universe* (Cambridge: Cambridge University Press, 2005), pp. 41–43, 48–49.

15. Alexander R. Pruss, "Another Step in Divine Command Dialectics," *Faith and Philosophy* 26, no. 4 (October 2009): 432–439.

16. Including: applications of categorical imperatives, a Rawlsian veil of ignorance ensuring the original position, appeals to love, etc., for nonconsequentialist accounts and variants of utilitarianism for consequentialist ones.

17. Pruss, p. 438.

18. Ibid.

19. He cites Nicholas Rescher and Robert Brandom's *The Logic of Inconsistency* (Oxford: Blackwell, 1980).

20. Pruss, pp. 438–439.


APPENDIX B

An earlier version of this essay appeared as "Outrageous Evil and the Hope for Healing: Our Practical Options," *in Immersed in the Life of God: The Healing Resources of the Christian Faith*, edited by Paul L. Gavrilyuk, Douglas M. Koskela, and Jason E. Vickers, © 2008 Wm. B. Eerdmans Publishing Company, Grand Rapids, Michigan. Reprinted by permission of the publisher, all rights reserved.

1. Of course, we have in mind Dostoevsky's character Ivan Karamazov in *The Brothers Karamazov*, who focused his argument on the suffering of children. Nothing could justify such suffering, on his view, and he would sooner respectfully return God his ticket than be reconciled to so brutal a reality.

2. Elie Wiesel, *Night* (New York: Avon, 1969), p. 44.

3. Marilyn Adams, *Horrendous Evils and the Goodness of God* (Ithaca, NY: Cornell University Press, 1999), pp. 27–28.

4. Susan Neiman contends, however, that what marks modern consciousness is that the problem of "natural" evil such as the Lisbon earthquake is "utterly different" from moral evil such as the Holocaust. See her *Evil in Modern Thought* (Princeton, NJ: Princeton University Press, 2002), pp. 3, 39.

5. Cited in "The Tsunami: Asking the God Question," *The Week* 5 (January 14, 2005): 15

266 NOTES TO PAGES 219–227

6. C. S. Lewis, *Surprised by Joy* (New York: Harcourt, Brace & World, 1955), p. 115.

7. Peter Singer, "Ethics and Sociobiology," in *Religion and the Natural Sciences: The Range of Engagement*, ed. James E. Huchingson (Fort Worth, TX: Harcourt Brace Jovanovich, 1993), p. 321.

8. Michael Ruse and Edward O. Wilson, "The Evolution of Ethics," in *Religion and the Natural Sciences: The Range of Engagement*, ed. James E. Huchingson (Fort Worth, TX: Harcourt Brace Jovanovich, 1993), p. 310.

9. Of course, as we have seen, not all naturalists would agree that morality is an illusion. Platonists, for instance, and intuitionists would insist that morality is not only objective but self-evident. Utilitarianism is another instance of a naturalist account of objective morality. As Alasdair MacIntyre notes, however, intuitionism and utilitarianism declined into emotivism in the twentieth century. See *After Virtue*, 2nd ed. (Notre Dame, IN: University of Notre Dame Press, 1984), pp. 64ff.

10. It would take us too far afield to argue this in detail here, but one of us has done so; see Jerry L. Walls, "Hume on Divine Amorality," *Religious Studies* 26 (1990): 257–266. The notion of an evil deity has not often been put forth as a serious option, but one thinker who did so was Marquis de Sade. See Neiman, *Evil in Modern Thought*, pp. 170–196.

11. Kenneth Surin, "Taking Suffering Seriously," in *The Problem of Evil*, ed. Michael L. Peterson (Notre Dame, IN: University of Notre Dame Press, 1992), p. 342.

12. "Taking Suffering Seriously," p. 344.

13. Robert A. Emmons, *The Psychology of Ultimate Concerns* (New York: The Guilford Press, 1999), p. 145.

14. Emmons, *The Psychology of Ultimate Concerns*, p. 147.

15. C. S. Lewis discusses dualism in a few places, pointing out that if we mean that one of the two powers is actually wrong and the other actually right puts into the universe a third thing in addition to the two Powers: some law or standard or rule of good which one of the powers conforms to and the other fails to conform to. But since the two powers are judged by this standard, then this standard, or the Being who made this standard, is farther back and higher up than either of them, and will be the real God.

16. Neiman, *Evil in Modern Thought*, p. 268.

17. William J. Abraham, "Faraway Fields are Green," in *God and the Philosophers: The Reconciliation of Faith and Reason* (New York: Oxford University Press, 1994), p. 166.

18. Cf N. T. Wright, *Evil and the Justice of God* (Downers Grove, IL: Intervarsity Press, 2006), pp. 75–100.

19. G. Richard Hoard, *Alone among the Living* (Athens: University of Georgia Press, 1994), p. 207.

20. For Hoard's account of this, see *Alone among the Living*, pp. 196–215. We are reminded that the Stoics taught that death was of no account, not all that bad after all. Christian theology disagrees. Death is irremediably awful; it's ugly, it's tragic, it's unnatural. There's no sugarcoating or whitewashing it. Death grates against every ounce

of our being that yearns for eternity and for life. Death flies in the face of every such impulse, threatening to make a mockery of our every desire for immortality. Death tears at the fabric of our being, making us say early goodbyes, sometimes not giving us a chance to say goodbye at all, snatching our loved ones away at inopportune times and cutting short a plethora of potentials and possibilities, breaking our hearts. Only a supremely good and loving and all-powerful God can instill hope in the face of death.

21. Romans 8:18–25.

22. In our view, to make this claim requires taking seriously the historical evidence for the resurrection of Jesus as well as making the relevant philosophical arguments for the supernatural and the possibility of the miraculous. For examples of such argument, see William J. Abraham, *Divine Revelation and the Limits of Historical Criticism* (Oxford: Oxford University Press, 1982); N. T. Wright, *The Resurrection of the Son of God* (Minneapolis: Fortress Press, 2003); Paul Copan and Ronald K. Tacelli, eds., *Jesus' Resurrection: Fact or Figment? A Debate between William Lane Craig and Gerd Ludemann* (Downers Grove, IL: Intervarsity Press, 2000); Gary R. Habermas and Antony G. N. Flew, *Resurrected?: An Atheist and Theist Dialogue*, ed. John F. Ankerberg (Lanham, MD: Rowman & Littlefield, 2005); Richard Swinburne, *The Resurrection of God Incarnate* (Oxford: Clarendon Press, 2003); Michael R. Licona, *The Resurrection of Jesus: A New Historiographical Approach* (Downers Grove, IL: InterVarsity, 2010).

23. Nicholas Wolterstorff, *Lament for a Son* (Grand Rapids, MI: Eerdmans, 1987), p. 92.

24. Ibid., p. 90.

# Index

divine independence theory, Antony, 41–42
divine motivation theory, 258n4
divine necessity, God and goodness, 95–98
dogmatism, balance with fideism, 76–77
Dostoevsky, God and morality, 19
dualism
  modal, 240n23
  powers, 266n15
  of practical reason, 13–14, 18, 191
*Duke Law Journal*, postmodern morality, 2

earth age, infant-earthers, 147, 148–50, 253n9
Ecclesiastes, 41
Edwards, Jonathan, temporal parts theory, 87
egoism
  ethical and psychological, 12–13
  moral obligations, 231n18
  psychological, 231–32n20
Emmons, Robert A., suffering, 223
empiricist option, morality, 3–4
Enlightenment
  God and religion, 31–32
  morality without God, 202
  reality, 183
epistemic objection
  guided will theory, 38
  theistic ethics, 4, 34–35
epistemology/ontology distinction, 5, 48, 200
equivocation
  argument, 70, 215
  importance of avoiding, 65, 80
  radical, 34
  sovereignty as divine determinism, 78–79
equivocation/univocation distinction, 5, 48, 200
Erion, Gerald J., 103–4
eternity
  biblical faith and real freedom, 187–90
  death of death, 195–98
  ethics, 179–80
  hope of heaven, 195–98
  moral motivation, self-interest and sacrifice, 190–95

relational ethics, 185–87
  virtue, 180–85
ethical egoism, moral argument, 12–14, 231n18
ethical matters, labor exploitation, 10
ethics. *See also* theistic ethics
  range of, 105–6
  relational, 185–87
euphemism, objection to Calvinism, 72–73
Euthyphro Dilemma, 120
  distinctions answering objections, 4–5
  God's existence, 37–38
  guided will, 90
  objections to theistic ethics, 4, 32–33, 86
  seven distinctions, 46–48
  Socrates, 32
  struggle, 45–46, 57
evidentialist, commonsensical, 148
evil. *See also* problem of evil
  burning children, 222–26
  counterbalancing good and, 145–46, 150, 153, 154, 253n4, 255n18, 255n20
  free will, 255n18
  gratuitous, 254–55n15
  Holocaust, 218
  moral outrage, 217–19
  normalizing, 226
  ontology of outrage, 219–22
  problem of, 5, 143–45, 265n4
  reality of, 222–28
Ewing, A. C.
  goodness, 51
  human free will, 151
existentialism, Platonism and, 18–21
explanandum-driven considerations, divine command theory, 209–11
explanans-driven considerations, divine command theory, 209, 211–15

faith
  biblical, 76, 187–90, 197
  Christian, 79, 91, 195, 197–98
  evil, 218, 226
  freedom, 187–90
  Hoard, 227
  moral argument, 8
  and reason, 8–9, 79

resurrection
  Christian love, 184, 259n13
  Christian theology, 5, 53, 141–42, 157,
    180, 184, 194
  Christ's victory, 195, 197
  God's love, 227
  historical evidence, 267n22
  historicity, 259n13
  moral relevance, 201
  truth of Christianity, 259n14
retribution, 23, 71, 190
rewards, 14, 16, 39, 175, 190, 224
Rist, John, Platonic Good, 21, 95, 100,
    248–49n27
Rooney, Paul, divine command ethics, 36
Rorty, Richard, anti-realism, 88–89
Rowe, William, 145, 147
Ruse, Michael, moral outrage, 220,
    223–24
Russell, Bertrand
  atheism, 28
  evidence for God, 7
  man's achievement, 230n9
  moral obligations, 172
  "scaffolding of despair" litany, 10
Russell, Bruce
  argument from evil, 145–46
  factual premise, 150–53
  God and suffering, 144
  good parent analogy, 154–58, 170
  "infant-earther," 147, 148–50, 253n9
  interventions by God, 156–57
  moral skepticism, 168–71
  second thought experiment, 170
  sufferings, 153–54
  van Inwagen's Atlantis scenario, 144–45

sacrifice
  Christ, 142
  fatherhood, 2
  morality, 190–95
salvation
  earning, 3
  elect, 66
  God's intention, 252n11
  God's plan, 69–70, 72–73, 75, 76,
    186–87, 189, 198

Israel as God's chosen, 138–40, 141
  offer, 243–44n22
  "once saved, always saved," 241n3
  rejection, 241n10
  spreading message, 129
Sartre, Jean Paul, 183
  death of God, 29
  determinism, 234–35n44
  moral freedom, 26–27
  nonexistence of God, 19–20, 26
Satan, 94, 241n8
Savior, 37, 70, 195
scope distinction, 200
Scotus, Duns, 46
Scripture
  authority, 67
  Bible, 76
  binding of Isaac, 141
  Christian, 5, 53–54, 91
  interpretation, 137–38
  reliability, 68, 78
  teaching, 245n33
Searle, John, moral choices, 23–24,
    233–34n35
secular morality, 19–20
self-interest, morality, 190–95
semantics
  distinction, 200
  range of ethics, 105–6
Sessions, William Lad, 229n2
Shapiro, Gary, 203
Sidgwick, Henry, 7–8, 20
  dualism of practical reason, 191
  egoism, 12–14
  The Methods of Ethics, 13
  morality and happiness, 15, 18
  moral laws, 28
Siena, Catherine of, 41
simplicity
  doctrine of divine, 247n18
  God is the Good, 95, 248n20
The Simpsons, theistic ethics, 103–4
sin
  arguments that God can, 240–41n26
  culpability, 241–42n10
  probability in resisting, 242n12
Singer, Peter, moral principles, 219–20

CPSIA information can be obtained at www.ICGtesting.com
Printed in the USA
BVOW06s0958130916

461974BV00005B/12/P